BRITAIN AND THE SOVIET U

Also by Sir Curtis Keeble

THE SOVIET STATE: The Domestic Roots of Soviet Foreign Policy (*editor*)

Britain and the Soviet Union, 1917–89

Sir Curtis Keeble
H.M. Ambassador to the Soviet Union, 1978–82

St. Martin's Press   New York

First published in the United States of America in 1990

Printed in Hong Kong

ISBN 0-312-03616-7

Library of Congress Cataloging-in-Publication Data
Keeble, Curtis.
Britain and the Soviet Union, 1917–89/Sir Curtis Keeble.
p. cm.
ISBN 0-312-03616 7
1. Great Britain—Foreign relations—Soviet Union. 2. Soviet
Union—Foreign relations—Great Britain. I. Title.
DA47.65.K44 1990
327.41047—dc20   89—36456
                                                      CIP

To Margaret and all our colleagues in the Moscow
Embassy from 1978 to 1982

Contents

List of Maps

List of Illustrations

Preface

In the conduct of British foreign policy, the relationship with the Soviet Union has a unique quality and a unique potential for good or ill. It raises issues which have plagued the statesmen of the Western democracies for seven decades and which are still unresolved.

In the years between the two world wars, the new Russia was the unknown factor. Lloyd George did his best to draw her into the community of nations, but those who governed Britain throughout most of the 1920s and 1930s preferred not to deal with the Soviet Union. When, too late, they tried to deal, they found their prejudice confirmed by experience. Among the British people, some of us viewed her with hope, some with apprehension, some with detestation, some with scorn, most with perplexity and many with the sadness which comes at the sight of the corruption of brave ideals. Some few chose treason. All had their reasons, for the Soviet Union can show many faces. Might a more determined effort to establish a sound relationship with the Soviet Union in those years have lessened the suffering which Europe had to bear? The answer will never be certain. It is hard to accept that the effort should not have been made. It is harder to believe that it could have succeeded.

My first contact with the reality of Soviet power came as the wartime alliance was disintegrating into the post-war confrontation. Experience in the repatriation of British and Soviet prisoners of war revealed in stark clarity those qualities of the Russian character and the Soviet system which have, in peace and in war, made the conduct of relations such a frustrating task. I joined the Foreign Service in 1947, a year after Winston Churchill had made his 'iron curtain' speech at Fulton. My experience of the cold war and the beginning of detente was gained in West Berlin in the early 1950s and East Berlin twenty years later. When, in 1978, I was appointed to Moscow, it was possible to envisage in the aftermath of the Quadripartite Agreement on Berlin and the Helsinki Final Act the development of a better working relationship with the Soviet Union, and we had a promising base in the agreements signed between Harold Wilson and Leonid Brezhnev in 1975.

I was in fact to experience the full cycle of relations, as we moved from the false dawn of detente into the first chill of the Shcharansky and Orlov trials, the invasion of Afghanistan, the Western counter-measures and the Polish crisis. Throughout that period, as through the decades which preceded it, the West was confronted with essentially the same dilemma. The Soviet Union proclaimed a doctrine which required the eventual collapse of society as it was structured in the Western democracies and it implemented policies which in many respects were designed to achieve that result. Within its own borders it pursued practices which were abhorrent to Western standards of individual liberty. Outside them it demonstrated a readiness to use military force and political subversion to sustain and extend its imperial frontier. The 'evil empire' epithet evoked a certain resonance in the West and a Soviet response which, if less memorable, was no more amiable. Yet the realities of superpower weaponry required that both the Soviet Union and the Western powers should contain their conflict at a level which excluded the risk of armed conflict between them and the realities of national interest indicated a greater need for cooperation than for confrontation. Thus, while the 1970s ended with heightened tension between the West and the Soviet Union, they ended also with a recognition of the need for restraint in the deployment of national power and for the construction of a sounder and more stable relationship. What they did not bring was practical progress towards such a goal.

Today, with the Soviet Union a nuclear superpower and Britain's power much diminished, the elements of the bilateral relationship and the world within which it operates are very different from those which obtained in the first years after the Revolution. The confrontation of ideology and power, the uneasy relationship between the Soviet Union and its neighbours in Europe and Asia, the triangular relationship with Germany – all remain latent, if not active, sources of tension. The trading potential remains largely unrealised and the long-term objectives of Soviet policy are still unclear. Now, however, with a new Soviet leadership pursuing a new style diplomacy as it seeks to reshape both domestic and foreign policy, there is a new incentive, and possibly a new opportunity, to build the more constructive relationship which for so many years has proved unattainable.

While I have been working on this book, events have been moving fast. In his speech to the United Nations on 7 December 1988, President Gorbachev called for a new era of cooperation to replace the old ideological strife. Will the reality match the aspirations? Can the internal crisis of restructuring be surmounted? Can the external cycle of conflict be broken? In Moscow, when there was little basis for optimism, I was sometimes accused by my Soviet counterpart of being an optimist. Today, when the immensity of the task is plain and a healthy dose of realism will not come amiss, I still am. But, if hopes are to become reality, if the tensions are to be controlled, the burden of conflict to be eased and the potential benefits to be realised, optimism is not enough. There is no miracle recipe which can bring about the transformation. The imagination to perceive opportunities has to be matched by consistent, realistic and constructive states-manship to exploit them over a very long haul. Our policies may be the more effective and the more easy to sustain if they are based on an understanding of the course which we have travelled in our relationship with the Soviet Union in the years since 1917. The present work is therefore directed to the analysis of that relationship: to the British perception of the Soviet Union, the policies to which that perception has led and the relationship which has developed from them.

This is essentially a study of the evolution of British rather than Soviet policy, and it is undertaken from the personal standpoint of a practitioner rather than a historian. In tracing the development of relations, I have worked from the British documents, concentrating upon the inter-governmental aspect, as revealed in the diplomatic and other papers available in the Public Record Office, in the memoirs of those concerned, in the public statements of government policy and the contemporary press comment. Government policy is, of course, only one aspect of international relations. It is a characteristic of British–Soviet relations that this aspect should be dominant, but it is by no means the whole picture. It has, on the Soviet side, been accompanied by the largely unsuccessful attempt to sustain a distinct relationship through quasi-independent political channels. Alongside the governmental and party relationships is the complex network of commercial, cultural, personal and professional relations, in which governments have been more closely involved than is normal in the conduct of relations with non-socialist states. Beneath it all lies the whole area of covert intelligence activity. All are relevant, not only because of their intrinsic importance, but also because of the extent to which they may condition the climate within which governmental policy is formed. A detailed examination of them would, however, have taken this study beyond a reasonable compass. I am conscious, too, that there is an element of unreality in dealing with the British–Soviet relationship in bilateral terms. No one power, not even the United States, can conduct an effective policy towards the Soviet

Union on its own. British policy has, from the very beginning, been conducted in the context of alliance policies – the alliances of two world wars and of the post-war period. This will apply with equal or greater force in the future. But the alliance is composed of its individual members. Each country has unique problems, unique interests and unique experience. Each has the duty to formulate, within the alliance, its own national policy.

Lord Stockton recounts in *Winds of Change* the remark by Sir Winston Churchill, confronted by a shapeless dessert: 'Pray take away this pudding. It has no theme.' Marxist–Leninist theorists, skilled in rearranging international affairs to fit into the pattern of pre-ordained struggle and lead to the pre-ordained victory of socialism, established the theme of confrontation. Their task today is more complex. So is my theme. I write from the standpoint of one who has been concerned with the frequently untidy and equivocal profession of diplomacy. My theme is the oscillating Anglo-Soviet relationship, each swing reflecting a change in the balance between the search for a basis of mutual interest, be it only the basic interest of self-preservation, and the profound conflict of ideology and power. Its course runs through many of the critical episodes of twentieth-century European history, episodes where it was identifiable and relevant, but only occasionally dominant. In following it, I have had to sketch the background in crude terms, treating major events with scant justice as well as simplifying and omitting much interesting and significant detail. My theme is illustrative, not dogmatic. Neither its course nor its conclusion is pre-ordained.

Tomorrow's circumstances will be different. Tomorrow's actors will be different. The decisions of the day must be determined by the political realities of the day. But the theme which has run through the Anglo-Soviet relationship for these seventy years will remain recognisable. It is well that we should learn not merely to recognise it and to control it, but to move forward from it. There are periods in history when the pressures of interest, ideology, precedent and power shape a mould which no effort of political will can break. The moments of flux, when new patterns may emerge, are brief. The ability to perceive and to exploit them is the test of statesmanship. I believe that in the relationship with the Soviet Union we are now at such a point and that, in shaping the response to the positive challenge of Soviet reform, the British Government can play as important a part as it did in shaping the response to the negative challenge of Soviet power. My hope is that this book may assist in that process.

London, July 1989 CURTIS KEEBLE

Acknowledgements

In its origin, this book owes much to the stimulus which I received from the late David Watt and Hugh Seton-Watson. The analysis of the official records would not have been possible without the work of earlier scholars, whose detailed studies of various periods are referred to, with grateful acknowledgement, in the Notes. The staff of the Public Record Office have been unfailingly helpful in the tracing of individual documents. Within the Foreign and Commonwealth Office I have had much help from my former colleagues in the Soviet and Research Departments as well as from Miss Barnes and the staff of the Library. For the maps I am indebted to the FCO cartographers and also to Jonathan Eyal of the Royal United Service Institute. Crown Copyright material is reproduced with the permission of the Controller of Her Majesty's Stationery Office.

I am particularly grateful to Sir Frank Roberts for giving me the benefit of his unrivalled personal experience in the conduct of British–Soviet relations from the 1930s onwards; to Lord Callaghan for his comments on Chapter 10; to Robin Edmonds on Chapters 6 and 7; and above all to Sir Michael Howard and Dr Stephen White for their many helpful suggestions. I have also been fortunate in enjoying the support of Alex Pravda, his colleagues in the Royal Institute of International Affairs and in particular the Library staff who met with a cheerful and helpful response each tedious request. A special debt of gratitude is owed to Keith Povey for the combination of great speed and meticulous care in his editorial work. For the errors and inadequacies the responsibility is mine.

C. K.

Introduction: Britain and Imperial Russia

7 NOVEMBER 1917

In the heart of Leningrad, on the Palace Embankment of the River Neva, stands a substantial classical building, formerly the Embassy of His Britannic Majesty's Ambassador to the Emperor Nicholas II of Russia. A few hundred yards along the river bank the tourists queue to view the treasures of the Imperial Winter Palace and on the opposite bank they file across the deck of the cruiser *Aurora*, whose gun signalled the attack on the Palace in November 1917. Today, a symbol of the Revolution, she lies at her mooring not far from the simple log house where Peter the Great lived while supervising the first stages of the building of his new capital city. As the name of Russia's capital, St Petersburg had too Germanic a flavour for the mood of 1914 and, shortly after the outbreak of war, Peter's city was rechristened Petrograd.

On the afternoon of 7 November 1917, the British Ambassador at Petrograd, Sir George Buchanan, stepped out of the Embassy for his usual breath of fresh air. At 64 he was at the peak of his diplomatic career. Tall and distinguished in appearance, an excellent linguist, but not a Russian speaker, he combined courtesy and firmness in a measure which commanded respect both in Petrograd and in London, as he strove to promote British interests in Russia, while seeking to understand and to interpret to London the travail through which that country was passing. He had gained experience of the problems of Central and Eastern Europe during service in Vienna and Sofia, but had then been sent to The Hague and had remarked to King Edward VII that he was afraid he might sleep away the remaining years of his career as a kind of diplomatic Rip Van Winkle. 'Something is sure to turn up', said the King, and in July 1910 Sir George had received the invitation from Sir Edward Grey to fill the post at St Petersburg. 'The place', wrote the Foreign Secretary, 'is one of great importance, as, though our relations with the Russian Government

1

are happily cordial, there are questions which present difficulties for both Governments, which require constant tact and skill on the part of the Ambassador at St Petersburg.'[1]

Now, after seven years in Russia, the Ambassador had heard that the troops of the Petrograd garrison had gone over to the Bolsheviks, that the city was virtually in their hands and that the *Aurora* had arrived from Kronstadt to join them. The decision to form a Bolshevik Government had been proclaimed and Kerensky had left the capital in an attempt to muster support among the army. Sir George's afternoon stroll was uneventful and he noted only a few soldiers visible near the bridges. He returned to the Embassy and shortly afterwards heard the *Aurora*'s gun signal the attack on the Winter Palace, where Kerensky's ministers, guarded only by some cadets and a company of the women's battalion, were awaiting the end. It came that night. The attack on the Palace was soon over. The garrison surrendered and the ministers were marched off to imprisonment. The Ambassador was not surprised. He had already reported that Kerensky might have to make way for a Bolshevik Government. Even if this happened, however, he did not think that things could be much worse than they were at present. In any case, 'such a Government would not be of long duration and before long would provoke counter-revolution'. Now it had happened. He sent his telegram reporting the events of the day. 'Order prevails', he concluded, 'at present all quiet.'[2]

THE HISTORICAL BACKGROUND

A new era in international relations had begun. In diplomacy, however, one cannot start with a clean sheet. There is always a legacy of half-remembered history, political prejudice, personal friendships and antipathies, commercial and financial interests and domestic pressures. If we are to understand how the British Government reacted to the news of the Bolshevik Revolution, we need to see it in the context of the relationship between Britain and Russia as it had developed prior to the Revolution. A Soviet official, anxious to persuade me of the longstanding links between our two countries, once pointed to the fact that King Harold's family had sought refuge in Russia after the Norman invasion of Britain and that in 1079 his daughter had married the Russian prince, Vladimir Monomakh. The story was one of limited contemporary relevance, but some of the other episodes which, over the centuries, have lodged in the crevices of history, may with greater justice be recalled today. London merchants formed the Muscovy Company in 1551 and two years later, when Richard Chancellor arrived in Moscow after the failure of his attempt to find a route to the Far East through the northern oceans, he began a process which was to bring the first commercial agreement between Ivan IV and Elizabeth I. Elizabeth was not interested in a wider-ranging alliance. Trade was to remain for several centuries the core of the relationship and it is not wholly fanciful to see a thread running from the Elizabethan adventurers to Lloyd George's trade agreement of 1921, by which Britain became the first among the wartime Allies to open relations with Soviet Russia. Or, for that matter, from Peter the Great's study of Dutch and British shipbuilding techniques in 1697–8 to the current Soviet interest in the acquisition of Western technology. From the time of Peter the Great's drive to open Russia's window to the West, his country was a factor in the shifting pattern of European alliances and, for Britain, a potential counter to French preponderance.

Yet, in truth, the relationship between Britain and Imperial Russia may best be seen as one of only brief periods of common interest throughout the centuries, separated by much longer periods of mutual irrelevance and indifference, with occasional friction as the two nations developed and as they built up their empires, the one by sea from the Western border of Europe, the other by land to the East. The menace of the control of the main land-mass of continental Europe by a hostile and expansionist power could drive the two countries alternately into conflict and then into alliance against Napoleon, but the natural coincidence of interest was temporary. By the late nineteenth century, as Britain was consolidating and extending a democratic, constitutional form of government, there was a growing antipathy among British opinion towards the politically primitive Russian autocracy. In foreign policy, too, the southward thrust of the Russian Empire had brought friction in the Balkans, and Russian pressure on Persia and Afghanistan seemed to threaten the British rule in India. Half a century after the Crimean War, the Russian press could still quote Asquith's description of the two countries as being 'catalogued as nations which are natural foes'.[3]

THE MOOD OF 1900

The early years of the twentieth century saw an important change in the relationship. The revolution of 1905 brought concessions which suggested that the Russian political system might move, if painfully, towards a greater recognition of the rights of the individual and make that country a more acceptable partner to Britain. On the international scene too, the signature of the Anglo-Russian Treaty of 1907 did much to alleviate the friction resulting from rival imperial ambitions in Central Asia. With the improving political relationship, the British set out to rediscover a strange and fascinating country. Between 1900 and 1914 there was quite a flow of books on Russia, translations of Chekhov and Tolstoy, little descriptive volumes oddly reminiscent of the sixteenth-century works of Chancellor and his contemporaries, and a new edition of Mackenzie Wallace's massive *Russia*, first published in 1877.[4] Typical of the period was a book by R. J. Barrett, the editor of *The Financier and Bullionist*, who made his own voyage of discovery in 1907 and published the results in *Russia's New Era*. 'The mists of prejudice are clearing off' he wrote, 'and old estrangement seems an evil dream'. He found a country, in its growing pains, but one which was 'bound to be a world's wonder'. A year or so later, Stephen Graham wrote of Russia awaiting the British 'with all the freshness and allurement of newly discovered country'. The mood of the Russophiles was well summed up by the *Russian Year Book* published in London in 1911:

> There are no two powers in the world and there have been no other two in history more distinct in character, less conflicting in interest, or more naturally adapted for mutual agreement and support than are Britain and Russia. Of these vast sovereignties, one is essentially a maritime empire and the other a continental dominion. The former is commercial and rich in capital, the latter is agricultural, with immense potential resources still undeveloped. Whether regarded from the political or the economic standpoint, these powers are not competitive, but complementary; and experience shows that as the two empires, by their fundamental conditions, are marked out for friendship and not for antagonism, the two races in their private relations, so far from finding difficulty in getting on well with each other, are as sympathetic in tendency as they are contrasted in temperament.

Sir George Buchanan must have felt something of this new

enthusiasm when he arrived in Russia, but it was tempered by the caution of the experienced professional. In British political circles, the resentment at Russian pressure on Persia was still combined with abhorrence of Tsarist repression and recollections of the repeated and vicious anti-Jewish pogroms. In one of Buchanan's first despatches he wrote of the two countries as 'friends over whom still hung the shadow of past differences and misunderstandings' and who 'had not yet cast aside the mutual suspicions with which they had for more than half a century regarded the trend of each other's policy'.[5] The friction over Persia continued during the early years of Sir George Buchanan's time and was not wholly allayed by a visit which M. Sazonov, the Tsar's Foreign Minister, paid to Balmoral. In 1912, when an impressive British delegation representing Parliament, the Church, the Army, the Navy and the press, visited St Petersburg, it evoked the comment from the Russian side that 'for the first time the two great powers stand side by side on a footing of political equality'.[6] Nevertheless, in a generally complimentary leader on the tercentary of the Romanovs, *The Times* of 6 March 1913 could still speculate on whether the European sense of order or the 'wild Asiatic instinct for the spasmodic and monstrous' would prevail in Russia, and when, in early 1914, Tsar Nicholas spoke of his desire for 'a closer bond of union between England and Russia, such as an alliance of a purely defensive character',[7] there was no response. Buchanan summed up the issue succinctly in his memoirs: 'What really barred the way to an Anglo-Russian alliance was the fact that it would not have been sanctioned by public opinion in England'.[8]

THE COMMERCIAL RELATIONSHIP

In its commercial relationship with Russia at the beginning of the twentieth century, Britain was struggling against the growing power of the German traders. Prior to Buchanan's appointment, the British share of Russia's trade had been declining. There had been an influx of British capital into Russia in the years after the Crimean War and British mercantile interests had for a time predominated over German, but by 1913 Russian imports from Britain, at 170 million roubles (£17 million), were not much more than a quarter of the value of imports from Germany. There was a resident British community of some 7000 in Russia, about a third of them in St Petersburg. Many were engaged as technical experts running the textile mills owned by firms such as Coates in the region around Petrograd and Moscow. Others were in the grain and flax trade, the metallurgical and mining industry, some were in banking, and a doughty regiment of British nannies, governesses and tutors was engaged in the upbringing of the Russian nobility. The fine street fronting the Neva close to the Imperial Palace, where the British merchants had traditionally resided, was known as the English Embankment and names of British manufacturers of farming equipment such as Howard and Ransome were household words in Russian agriculture. For the most part, however, the British commercial community seem to have lost the dynamism of their predecessors and to have become a somewhat conservative and unenterprising group, losing ground to more thrusting German competitors. By 1913 the British flag still covered 35 per cent of all shipping entering Russian ports, but here too the British share was declining. The total British capital investment in Russia was estimated in 1910 at £38 million,[9] only just over 1 per cent of total British overseas investment. About a quarter of this was in state bonds and the remainder in trade and industry. It was, however, increasingly rapidly. The new oil industry was causing considerable interest and it was said that the naphtha area of Maikop had attracted 200 million roubles (£20 million) from Britain in the two years 1909 and 1910.[10] An estimate of £60 million or so for the value of private British investment in Russia at the time of the Revolution may therefore be not far from the mark.

THE RUSSIAN ÉMIGRÉS IN LONDON

In the early years of the century there was a Russian community of some 4000 or 5000 in London, among them a group of political exiles whose main point of contact was the Herzen Circle which had a room in the Communist Club at 107 Charlotte Street. In 1912, on his way to join them, a young man, Ivan Maisky, stepped off the boat at Dover. He recounts[11] how, travelling third class, he was required to produce the sum of £5 in order to satisfy His Majesty's Government that he would not be a burden upon British resources. Sadly, his total resources amounted to £3 15s. He was threatened with immediate deportation, but succeeded in securing entry as a political refugee. Maisky settled in London and became a leading member of a group which included Maxim Maximovich Litvinov, already settled for some years in London and married to an English girl. On the outbreak of war in 1914, they were joined by a member of a Russian aristocratic family, of Italian origin, Georgii Vasilievich Chicherin, who had thrown up his post in the Tsarist Foreign Ministry in order to join the revolutionary socialist movement and had lived since 1905 in Germany and France. The Russian émigrés were on good terms with the leaders of the British Labour and trade union movement, although, as Maisky was later to write, 'their peace of mind, their complete indifference to theory and their profound belief in evolutionary progress through the medium of parliament' made them totally different from the Russian socialists.

Litvinov, Chicherin and Maisky were to play an important role in British–Soviet relations during the whole period of the inter-war years. Litvinov became Lenin's first representative in London immediately after the Revolution and then Deputy to Chicherin as Commissar for Foreign Affairs, succeeding him in 1930 and holding the office until May 1939. Maisky, the refugee of 1912, was to return as a diplomat and to be expelled in 1927, before finally being conveyed by State Coach to Buckingham Palace to present his credentials to King George V as Soviet Ambassador in London. Thus, throughout these early, crucial years, Soviet policy was in the hands of men who knew England well, spoke the language and even, despite the fact that both Litvinov and Chicherin had experienced periods in British gaols, had a certain respect for this country, if little sympathy with its political leaders. In one respect only was the relationship reciprocal. The British security authorities were, by the time of the Revolution, only too aware of the linkage between the new rulers of Russia and the network of conspiratorial activity which, although less significant in Britain than elsewhere in Europe, contributed to the unease which was sweeping away the comfortable certainties of Edwardian England.

ALLIANCE IN THE WAR WITH GERMANY

In the summer of 1914, with the improving Anglo-Russian relationship still in its early stages, there was much to be done in terms of the political and the commercial relationship, but Sir George Buchanan could look back with some satisfaction at the progress made during the first few years of his stewardship. Then, having rejected the suggestion of an Anglo-Russian alliance, the British Government nevertheless found itself, as a consequence of the existing Franco-

Russian alliance, committed alongside Imperial Russia in the war against Germany, a commitment which was formalised in 1915 by the Treaty of London, precluding either party from negotiating a separate peace. Four years later, Imperial Russia had been swept away and British forces were engaged in operations on Russian soil in an undeclared war against the successor government of their former ally. The origins of the Bolshevik Revolution and the extent to which it was precipitated by the strains of the war with Germany have been exhaustively treated elsewhere and do not belong in this volume. What is relevant, however, is the way in which the existence of the wartime alliance and the dominant influence of military considerations upon British foreign policy determined the British reaction to the Revolution and conditioned British policy towards the Soviet Government in its early years.

As the war in the West dragged on, it had become increasingly apparent to the British Government that the prospect of ultimate victory depended to a significant extent upon the maintenance of an Eastern front which would continue to tie down substantial enemy forces. Some 80 German and Austrian divisions were engaged on that front in a war in which it was estimated that Russia had lost three and a half million in dead and wounded and two million prisoners. Had it been open to the Germans to deploy even half these forces in the West at an early stage in the war, it is questionable whether the Allied front in France would have held. As it was, defeated at Tannenberg, the Russian army continued the struggle into 1917 at a level which prevented the bulk of the German forces from being withdrawn. In an attempt to shore up the Russian forces the British Government gave substantial support in the form of supplies and finance. British wartime loans to the Russian Government amounted to £562 million,[12] of which some £74 million was in respect of supplies from the United States. But things were going badly. There was growing concern in London about the demoralisation of the Russian forces and the growth of German influence in Russia. In October 1916 Sir George Buchanan had reported to the Foreign Office: 'Never since the war began have I felt so depressed about the situation here, more especially with regard to the future of Anglo-Russian relations.'[13] The whole country was in mourning and Britain was blamed for the colossal losses which Russia was sustaining in a war from which it seemed she had nothing to gain. The situation went from bad to worse and in January 1917 the Ambassador had a memorable final interview with the Tsar.

After warning him bluntly of the incompetence and worse of his ministers and of the revolutionary talk in Petrograd, he concluded: 'You have, Sir, come to the parting of the ways, and you have now to choose between two paths. The one will lead you to victory and a glorious peace – the other to revolution and disaster.'[14] The warning was not heeded. It was, in any case, already too late to save the Tsar.

It might not, however, be too late to save the Russian army. In Britain, David Lloyd George had for some time been deeply concerned that the Russian front might collapse because of the desperate shortage of ammunition, and when he became Prime Minister one of his first acts was to despatch Lord Milner to Petrograd in February 1917 for an inter-Allied conference designed to improve the supply of munitions to the Russian forces as well as the efficiency of the forces themselves. In consequence, upwards of two million tons of military stores had been delivered through Murmansk, Archangel and Vladivostok.[15] The Allied supply bases and the military links associated with their establishment were to become a major factor in the intervention in 1918. As yet, however, although revolution was foreseen, its nature and its consequences were not.

THE REVOLUTION OF MARCH 1917

A month after Buchanan's warning, revolution had come and the Tsar had abdicated. There were those at the time who held Buchanan responsible for having played a part in instigating the Revolution. He had seen and indeed warned the Tsar of the need for change, but it should, in his view, be change by evolution, not by revolution. What is of interest is not so much Buchanan's personal role, but rather this illustration of the authority which, in Petrograd of 1917, attached to the opinions of the British Ambassador concerning the internal development of Russia. It reflected in part the personality of Buchanan, but in greater measure the power which he represented and against which the Bolshevik leaders were before long to be engaged.[16]

The British Government wasted no time in coming to terms with the situation created by the March (old style February) Revolution. It was more than ever necessary to try to instil into the new Russian Government the will to continue the war, and at its meeting on 21

March the War Cabinet approved a draft by the Prime Minister of a resolution to be passed by the House of Commons:

> That this House sends the Duma its fraternal greetings and tenders to the Russian people its heartfelt congratulations on the establishment among them of free institutions, in full confidence that they will lead not only to the rapid and happy progress of the Russian nation, but to the prosecution in close alliance with the constitutional governments of Western Europe and with renewed steadfastness and vigour of the war against the stronghold of autocratic militarism which threatens the liberty of Europe.'[17]

The Ambassador was instructed that he had authority to recognise the Provisional Government, but must obtain guarantees that they would carry out the engagements of their predecessor. It was a swift and sound response, inspired by the hope that a constitutional Government in Russia might, with British support, prove a stronger ally than the crumbling, inefficient autocracy of the hesitant Nicholas and his German-born Tsarina. As for the Tsar, despite the affection which King George V had for his cousin, both the King and his Ministers were in some doubt as to whether it was expedient for the Imperial family to take up residence in Britain, even if the Bolsheviks would permit this.[18] The reluctant offer of asylum subsequently – and fruitlessly – conveyed by Buchanan indicated that if they were to come to Britain the Russian Government must be responsible for their maintenance.

In British left-wing circles the new regime in Russia was welcomed with particular enthusiasm. A great rally was held in the Albert Hall and, helped by a Committee with Maisky as its Chairman, Litvinov as Secretary and Chicherin as a member, the émigrés began a return to Russia. By the time Litvinov's turn came, events had moved on and he was forced to unpack his trunks. In June a United Socialist Council, including MacDonald and Snowdon, called for the setting up in Britain of councils of workers and soldiers in order 'to do for this country what the Revolution had accomplished in Russia'. By contrast, between March and November, the references to Russia in the minutes of the War Cabinet were few, brief and gloomy. By May the Chief of the Imperial General Staff was already putting forward a paper on the 'possible effect of Russia's secession from the war'.[19] Ministers considered 'that the success or failure of the Allies in this war depends to a great extent on what Russia is going to do'.[20] They wondered whether they should replace Buchanan by someone whose standing would not be affected by a previous close relationship to the Imperial Government. It was thought that Mr Arthur Henderson, the Labour leader, might command the respect of Kerensky's Government, but having paid a long visit to Petrograd, Henderson advised that Buchanan should be left at his post. The right-wing press, in particular the *Morning Post*, waged a bitter campaign against the Provisional Government. The Prime Minister offered words of encouragement and another 58 000 tons of shipping for supplies to Russia. In Petrograd, it seemed to Buchanan for a moment that the Government might have regained its grip by the decision to put down the Bolsheviks in July. Buchanan's daughter records[21] how one of Kerensky's officers came to the Embassy on July 18, to be received by the Ambassador, clad in a greatcoat over his pyjamas, and to warn him that the Embassy would be in the direct line of fire as the troops ejected the Bolsheviks from the Peter and Paul fortress. With the Siamese cat packed safely into its travelling basket, the Ambassador and his family watched the successful attack from the drawing room window. But the moment of success was brief. Kerensky took over the leadership from Prince Lvov, but as summer moved into autumn, there could be little doubt that his hold was slipping away. The abortive Kornilov *coup d'état*, ending in the arrest by Kerensky of his Commander-in-Chief, accelerated the disintegration, but did nothing to weaken the subsequent determination of the British Military Attaché in Petrograd, General Knox, to support the anti-Bolshevik military leaders. Knox was to play a not insignificant role in the later conduct of British policy.

For Lloyd George, 1917 had been a bad year. As Kerensky came to power, the U-boats had savaged British shipping to such effect that disaster seemed imminent. The introduction of the convoy system had made a dramatic improvement, but a British Prime Minister could spare little time for the internal politics of Russia as 400 000 British and Canadian soldiers were being killed or wounded, floundering through the mud of Passchendaele in an ill-conceived offensive. By October, the British forces under Allenby were moving into Palestine, but the Italian front was in danger of collapse. One thing only mattered so far as Russia was concerned – that by some means she should be kept in the war, if only until the weight of American men and equipment could begin to turn the scales in the West.

This was the situation in which, on the evening of 7 November 1917, Sir George Buchanan despatched his telegram reporting the Bolshevik seizure of power.

1 Response to Revolution

THE PROBLEM FACING THE WAR CABINET

Britain was approaching the fourth dreary winter of an apparently interminable war when, on 9 November 1917, the news of the Bolshevik Revolution broke in the morning newspapers. Under the heading 'Anarchy in Petrograd', *The Times* carried a full report of the proclamation by the Revolutionary Military Committee announcing the fall of the Government and the transfer of power to the Soviets. In a leading article, headed 'Russia's critical hour', it remarked that the latest events would hardly surprise those who had watched events in Petrograd: 'Russia, free for an instant, has found herself bound afresh.'

In the Prime Minister's absence, the Conservative Bonar Law, Chancellor of the Exchequer, was in the chair at the meeting of the War Cabinet that morning. The main item on the agenda was the progress of the German offensive in Italy, which was causing considerable concern. Arthur Balfour, the Foreign Secretary, had, however, received Sir George Buchanan's telegrams reporting the Revolution. The Cabinet minutes record only that he read them to his colleagues.[1] They moved to the next item of the agenda. The process of adjusting British foreign policy to the Bolshevik Revolution had now to begin.

The next four years were to see a remarkable, but in retrospect understandable, sequence of conflicting policies as Britain struggled to make up its mind whether it wanted to try to work with the Bolsheviks or to break their power. Two great figures of British twentieth-century politics, David Lloyd George and Winston Churchill, were to contest the issue, and the political, military and economic realities were to decide it in Lloyd George's favour. In these early years, as the Bolshevik power was established in the old Imperial Russia and as its first external impact was felt, many of the problems which were to recur throughout the twentieth century were encountered and the seeds of subsequent disputes were sown. They were years crowded with events, years not only of strategic policy but also

12

of extraordinary incident, years in which at one point British motor torpedo boats sank a large part of the Russian Baltic fleet, at another gas was used against the Bolshevik forces, and at yet another a British commander, without reference to London, established a Government for North-West Russia. They saw the creation of legends, which still live, about British complicity in the murder of the Baku commissars and the Lockhart plot against the Soviet Government. Although the history of the period has been much researched and documented, it tends for most of us to fall into that historical limbo, beyond the range of personal recollection but not yet into that of familiar history. It cannot be retold here in all its complexity. This and the succeeding chapter will, however, trace the main steps by which the British Government, acting sometimes independently, sometimes in concert with and sometimes in opposition to their wartime Allies, sought first to establish an unofficial relationship with the Bolsheviks while simultaneously supporting the anti-Bolshevik forces in Russia; were led into an escalating but never wholehearted military intervention designed initially to further the conduct of the war against Germany and later to overthrow Bolshevik power; deployed tiny British forces thousands of miles apart, from Archangel and Murmansk in the North, to Vladivostok in the East and the Caucasus/Caspian in the South; withdrew them as the White forces crumbled; strove to reshape their policy as the Poles advanced to Kiev and the Russians to the gates of Warsaw; and finally became the first of the wartime Allies to give de facto recognition to the Soviet Government.

In his memoirs Lloyd George wrote: 'The problem with which the British Government and indeed the Allies as a whole were faced, was a purely military one. We were not concerned with the internal political troubles of Russia as such.'[2] Was the description wholly honest? The evidence of the Cabinet minutes is clear that at the outset the pursuit of the war against Germany was indeed the one issue which mattered. It was in terms of relevance to the war that the Government determined policy towards Russia. So far as Russian internal policy was concerned, it would be naive to suggest that the Government could have been indifferent as to the nature of the new regime. The fall of the Tsar had caused little regret and the Provisional Government had, as we have seen, commanded a wide measure of sympathy from all but the extreme right of the British political spectrum. The sympathy had waned as Kerensky's inability to control the march of events became apparent, but the Bolsheviks seemed to have nothing to recommend them. Their political philosophy was a challenge to the whole social and economic structure represented by the British Government and their methods were an affront to all constitutional democrats, whether of the right or the left. Marxist doctrine had its echoes in Britain, but Lenin's Government was regarded as no more than a disagreeable and probably transient stage in the political evolution of Russia. There can scarcely have been one of those gathered around the Cabinet table on the morning of 9 November who did not wish to see the Bolsheviks fall. Nevertheless, irrespective of their personal opinions on the nature of a Bolshevik Government, most of the members of the War Cabinet did not see it as their business to interfere. What they had first to do was to form a judgment on two aspects of the problem:

a) Would the Bolsheviks be able to retain their hold on power and establish themselves as the Government of the whole of the former Imperial Russia?

b) What would be the effect of a Bolshevik Government in Russia on the prosecution of the war against Germany?

According to their judgment on these questions, Ministers had to decide whether there was any action which the British Government and its Allies could take in order to redress the potential damage to their collective military effort against Germany.

On the first point, there was no good reason for Ministers to dissent from Buchanan's advice that Lenin's Government would not be of long duration. For the moment, they controlled the central civil power and probably the principal military power of the state, but their grasp appeared localised and tenuous. The quality and strength of the opposition to them was unproven, but its existence was beyond doubt. The Bolsheviks might in time consolidate their authority, but to predict that they would do so would at this stage have required a remarkable prescience. With no substantial case, on the facts available, for immediate recognition either of the Bolsheviks or of any other group, there was everything to be said for waiting to see how matters would develop and meanwhile keeping all options open.

THE MILITARY IMPLICATIONS OF THE REVOLUTION

On the military effect of the Revolution, there was less room for doubt. The disintegration of the Russian army was already far gone and it was doubtful whether Kerensky's Government would have been capable of continuing the war for very much longer. Nevertheless, a million or more German and Austrian troops were still engaged on the Eastern front. Many of these were substandard, but General Haig's estimate[3] was that there were perhaps 32 divisions which were fit to take part in severe fighting on the Western front, where both sides, pausing after the bloody struggle of October 1917, were preparing for the coming year. In the West, the scales, for the moment, seemed evenly balanced. The German submarines had been checked and with America now in the war, the Allies could hope that the flow of men and material across the Atlantic would build up to a point which might make victory possible in 1919. They would need to conduct a spring offensive in 1918, but it seemed premature to hope for victory in that year. For Germany, on the other hand, 1918 offered possibly the last chance of a decisive offensive which would defeat the Allied forces in France and win the war before the combined pressure of the Allied blockade and the American reinforcements turned the tide. The one factor which might assure the success of such an offensive would be the victorious conclusion of the war in the East, permitting not only the transfer to the West of the German forces engaged there, but also the addition of Russian grain and raw materials as a blockade-free reinforcement to the economic resources of the Central Powers. It was very much a matter of time. Could the Eastern front be held open for another twelve months?

The Allies had done and were still doing all they could to sustain the Russian forces by supplying arms and other military supplies as well as raw materials. These supplies would, however, be of no avail unless the men in the field, their commanders and their Government had the will to continue the fight. By the time the Revolution took place, the army was already disintegrating fast and the prospects were thoroughly bad. Immediately upon assuming power, Lenin read a proclamation to the peoples and governments of all the nations at war. He proposed immediate peace without annexations and without indemnities, with a three month armistice as a first step, and called upon the workers of England, France and Germany to join the struggle for peace and the liberation of the exploited working masses. To the British Government, it seemed that, if the Bolshevik Government were firmly established, the prospect of keeping a Russian army in the field against Germany was slender indeed. Without that army, defeat in the West seemed not inconceivable and stalemate quite probable.

For a time, Lloyd George and his ministers clung to the hope that perhaps Buchanan might be right and the Bolsheviks would be overthrown. By 12 November *The Times* was reporting that Kerensky had gathered forces to retake the capital and its leader writer opined that Lenin's reign was apparently drawing to a close. Soon, however, it was clear – and confirmed by a telegram from the Military Attaché in Petrograd – that there was no prospect of Kerensky regaining power. Moreover, the Bolsheviks were quickly extending their control over the country and, within a week, held not only Petrograd and Moscow, but many provincial centres. It was clear, too, that they were resolved to end the war against Germany.

As the Bolshevik power grew, so the issues with which the British Government was confronted were sharpened. Buchanan received an 'insolent communication' from Trotsky threatening to negotiate a separate peace and, in default of recognition, to appeal to the peoples as against their Governments. The Ambassador recommended that Russia should be freed from her obligation under the Treaty of London and left to take her own decisions on continuing the war or negotiating for peace. He was authorised to issue a lengthy statement to the effect that 'the Allies . . . are ready as soon as a stable government has been constituted that is recognised by the Russian people as a whole, to examine with that Government the aims of the war and the possible conditions of a just and durable peace'.[4] It was, however, soon clear in London that there was no realistic prospect of preventing separate Russo-German peace negotiations. But if the Bolsheviks were determined to make peace, could the terms be influenced in such a way as to minimise the loss to the Allied cause? If the Bolshevik grip were still not total, could those Russian commanders who were known to be hostile to the Bolsheviks be induced, by the grant of money and supplies, to continue the fight? These were the questions which were in the minds of British Ministers as they sought to work out policy in a series of Cabinet Meetings and Allied Conferences during November and December of 1917.

THE POLICY OF DELIBERATE DRIFT

It is necessary to set the decisions which British ministers reached in regard to Russia against the background of contemporary British opinion. In Parliament, Lloyd George commanded a substantial majority, but it was a Coalition majority, in which the Conservatives were by the far the largest element. The Coalition existed for the pursuit of the war against Germany and in Parliament as in the country the war dominated all other issues. To the great body of Conservative backbenchers, dealings with Bolsheviks who were about to betray their Allies were tantamount to treason. On the left, the first warnings of Labour and Trade Union troubles were perceptible, but there was little sympathy for the Bolsheviks. They were denounced in the *Herald* for their terrorism, fanaticism and violence as well as for being false to their own internationalist creed in contemplating a separate peace without explicit assurances for Belgium, Serbia and Romania.[5] Nowhere was there a significant body of opinion which would have welcomed early recognition of Lenin's Government.

Against this background, ministers confronted the basic choice which was to remain for many years, in one way or another, before Western Governments. It was set out in Minute 13 of War Cabinet 294 on 7 December:

> It was suggested that the many questions arising out of the state of affairs in Russia would be easier of settlement if the policy of the Allies was more clearly defined. It was open to the Allies:
>
> a) to recognize the Bolsheviks and make the best arrangements possible with them
>
> or b) to refuse to recognize them and to take open and energetic steps against them.

It was easy enough to phrase the choice in these terms, but another matter to make the decision. Arthur Balfour, the Foreign Secretary, was certainly not the man to rush into a hasty decision. Describing a later stage of the debate over Russian policy, Lloyd George was to say of him that he 'as usual saw very clearly the arguments on both sides and felt that whichever way we decided there would be a strong case. He was therefore on the whole indifferent and prepared to support either course, but with a natural disinclination for energetic action on either side.'[6] After discussion with Lloyd George, Balfour put to the War Cabinet a memorandum recommending a 'wait and see' policy.[7] The British Government, he argued, had not concerned itself with the composition of the Russian Government during the Tsar's reign and it need not do so now. The Bolsheviks were fanatics, 'dangerous dreamers . . . who would genuinely like to put into practice the wild theories that have been germinating so long in the shadow of the Russian autocracy'. But their aspirations – and, for that matter, those of other political parties – were a matter of concern only so far as they bore on the conflict with the Central Powers. For the remainder of the war, the Bolsheviks were going to fight neither Germany nor anyone else, but even if Russian could not fight, she would not be easily overrun. If she could not be kept in the war, then the purpose of policy should be to ensure that she was as helpful to Britain and as harmful to the enemy as possible. No policy would be more certainly fatal than to give the Russians a motive for welcoming German officials and German soldiers as friends and deliverers. Balfour did not call for recognition, but expressed his entire dissent from the view of those who had suggested that the Bolsheviks could only be regarded as avowed enemies. 'I am clearly of opinion', he wrote, 'that it is to our advantage to avoid as long as possible an open breach with this crazy system. If this be drifting, then I am a drifter by deliberate policy.'

SUPPORT FOR THE COSSACKS AND UKRAINIANS

In opposition to the policy of Balfour and Lloyd George were those who were not only convinced of the essential hostility of the Bolsheviks, but also saw in the anti-Bolshevik forces a means of holding open the Eastern front. If the result of supporting these forces were the overthrow of the Bolsheviks, so much the better. But the primary objective was the pursuit of the war against Germany. At this stage, Winston Churchill played little part in the debate. His energies were fully occupied with his responsibilities as Minister of Munitions. Oddly enough, it seems to have been Lord Robert Cecil who provided something of a focus for the interventionist group. Cecil, who is remembered today as the father of the League of Nations, combined the responsibilities of Minister for the Blockade with those of Under Secretary in the Foreign Office and, in Balfour's absence, he was frequently able to nudge policy in the direction of intervention. Political decisions might be deferred, but the war had to be fought. So, with military considerations paramount, the essential policy choice was gradually preempted and the first steps were taken which were to lead inexorably to armed intervention by Britain and her Allies. Even before the members of the War Cabinet considered Balfour's memorandum, they had decided, in the absence of the Prime Minister and the Foreign Secretary, that Buchanan should be told that the policy of the British Government was to support 'any responsible body in Russia that would actively oppose the maximalist movement and at the same time to give money freely and within reason to such bodies as were prepared to help the Allied cause'.[8] At that stage, the most promising anti-Bolshevik leader seemed to be Kaledin, the leader of the Cossacks. Buchanan understood the situation and warned that the Cossack and Ukrainian movements were concerned with the internal political situation, not with the continuation of the war against Germany. He was, however, authorised to make available 'to Cossacks or Ukrainians any funds necessary by any means you think desirable'.[9]

ANGLO-FRENCH COORDINATION

The interventionists in the British Government derived further support from the need to coordinate policy with Britain's allies. In practice, at the end of 1917, Allied policy was Anglo-French policy and Clemenceau was in no mood for such nonsense as recognition of a Bolshevik Government. On the British side, the task of working out a joint policy was entrusted to Lord Robert Cecil, Lord Milner, Secretary of State for War, and General Macdonogh, Director of Military Intelligence. The group visited Paris and it would have been scarcely surprising if their visit had produced a clearly interventionist policy. It did, indeed result in the conclusion on 23 December 1917 of an Anglo-French Convention,[10] dividing southern Russia into British and French 'zones of influence' for the purpose of support to the anti-Bolshevik forces. But the policy document which emerged,[11] in the form of a British draft approved by Clemenceau, very fairly represented the division of view in the War Cabinet and left the British Government with the option of backing either side, both sides or neither. Each country would 'get into relations' with the Bolsheviks through unofficial agents. It would be made clear 'that any idea that we favour a counter-revolution is a profound mistake', but at the same time the two Governments would 'keep in touch as far as we can with the Ukraine, the Cossacks, Finland, Siberia and the Caucasus etc'.

AN UNOFFICIAL LINK WITH THE BOLSHEVIKS

While Lloyd George and his colleagues were struggling to define policy, events in Russia were taking their course. Buchanan, with no valid accreditation to the new regime, was trying to maintain the Embassy, but his health was failing and in November he had already been forced to ask for permission to return home. As it happened – and rather to the relief of the Foreign Secretary – he was able to stay on for a little longer, but, with no prospect of early recognition of the Bolshevik Government, his position was becoming increasingly anomalous. It is risky, but not impossible and sometimes very useful, for an Embassy to maintain some form of contact with various warring factions in a country torn by civil war, but Buchanan could not himself have conducted relations between the British Government and the Bolsheviks without breaching the agreed policy of non-recognition. Consequently, implementing the decision to establish unofficial contacts, the Prime Minister appointed a young British consular officer, Robert Bruce Lockhart, to carry out this task.

Few of Her Majesty's Ambassadors to the Soviet Union have enjoyed the opportunity to establish such a close relationship with a member of the Soviet leadership as was open to Lockhart with Trotsky during the first half of 1918. The son of a Scottish schoolmaster, boasting proudly that there was no drop of English blood in his veins, Lockhart was a remarkable mixture of strength and insecurity, best summed up in his own autobiography, in which he speaks of his ineradicable romanticism and says that 'the strongest impulse of the moment has governed all my actions'.[12] In 1912, at the age of 24, after a brief and disastrous attempt to become a rubber planter in Malaya, Lockhart had joined the Consular Service and had been appointed Vice-Consul in Moscow. He remained there until September 1917, by which time, enjoying to the full all that Russian society had to offer, he had acquired a deep feeling for the country and its people. His qualities matched those of many Russians and his circle of friends was as wide as it was varied. At the beginning of 1917, he met Milner in Petrograd and then took responsibility for Milner during his visit to Moscow. It is clear that they got on well and when, in 1917, Lockhart was abruptly removed from Moscow after an over-public attachment to a Russian lady, Milner did not forget him. It was Milner to whom, three months later, in London, he repeated his arguments about the need to establish contact with the Bolsheviks, it was Milner who introduced him to Lloyd George and it was Milner who briefed him before his departure to the very new Russia of January 1918. In many respects he was uniquely well qualified for the appointment, but the qualities which fitted him for it did little to help him to secure respect for his views in Whitehall. He certainly felt that this lack of understanding between the man at the centre and the man on the spot, a common lament of diplomatists, was a significant contributory factor in the eventual failure of his mission. In truth, however, it was a mission doomed from the beginning.

Lockhart's brief, received orally from Milner, was to do as much harm to the Germans as possible, to put a spoke in the wheels of the separate peace negotiations, to stiffen by whatever means he could the Bolshevik resistance to German demands and to gather all the information he could as to the real nature and strength of the Bolshevik movement.[13] He travelled to Bergen by the cruiser which was to bring the Ambassador home and eventually reached Petrograd on 29 January, bearing with him a letter from Maxim Litvinov to Trotsky commending Lockhart as 'a thoroughly honest man who understands our position and sympathises with us'.[14]

Almost simultaneously with Bruce Lockhart's appointment, Trotsky had appointed Litvinov as the Bolsheviks' unofficial representative in London. Working for a time under the pseudonym of Maxim Harrison and married to an English girl, Ivy Low, Litvinov had already acted as representative of the Bolshevik party in the International Socialist Bureau, in which capacity he had come to the attention of the British security authorities. Through the intermediary of a Foreign Office official, Rex (later Sir Reginald) Leeper, Litvinov and Lockhart had met in London shortly before Lockhart's departure and the introduction to Trotsky was written out in the Lyons Tea Shop where they met. In the same letter, Litvinov mentioned that the question of his own recognition was not yet settled, but that he was making the acquaintance of the representatives of the Labour movement and had issued an 'appeal to the English working-men in all the Socialist papers'.

Thus, by the end of 1917, the pressure of events was bringing the first period of 'wait and see' to an end and the elements which were to determine the early years of the Anglo-Soviet relationship were falling into place. On 31 December the War Cabinet decided[15] that 'executive action with regard to South Russia', in other words the organisation of support for the anti-Bolshevik forces, should be concerted by a Committee sitting in the Foreign Office under Cecil's chairmanship and with War Office and Treasury representation. The flow of British military supplies had been cut off, but there were still large dumps at Vladivostok and smaller ones at Archangel. A naval force, comprising the battleship *Glory* and eight trawler-minesweepers under Admiral Kemp still lay at Murmansk.[16] The links with the Russian army, forged during the wartime alliance, were still maintained by British officers and served as a basis for relations with the anti-Bolshevik forces. Meanwhile, the Bolsheviks were pressing ahead with negotiations for a separate peace and on the same day that the Russia Committee was established in the Foreign Office the German negotiators arrived in Petrograd. In all but name, the war between Russia and Germany was over and it seemed that unless the anti-Bolshevik forces could be turned against the Germans, the German High Command would be able, by the spring, to concentrate the whole of its forces for the final offensive in the West. To make matters worse, the Bolsheviks were maintaining a propaganda of world revolution and in London Litvinov was already active enough to alarm a significant part of the British establishment, if not to make much impact on the Labour movement.

2 Intervention

THE NEED TO CHOOSE

The contradictions inherent in the situation at the end of 1917 had now to work themselves out.[1]

I have pointed out to the Foreign Office that we shall have to choose between coming to some working arrangement with the Bolsheviks or breaking with them altogether. . . . He [Trotsky] and Lenin are out to overthrow all the so-called imperialistic governments, but it is against Great Britain rather than against Germany that their main offensive will be directed. The situation is quite hopeless, as the Bolsheviks have monopolized all the energies and organizing power of the nation.[2]

This entry in Buchanan's diary was written just before his final departure for London, early in the New Year of 1918. The mission which had started with such promise was ending in failure and the Ambassador had good reason to be in a gloomy mood. A young British officer who stayed behind in Petrograd was equally gloomy. He summed up the scene in a blunt letter to London:

Attitude to British bad. We are considered quitters and weak kneed. This is because the English out here, chiefly business men, have chucked up the sponge and bolted, while the Germans have been trying hard to get what the English have left. Other Englishmen, not only civilians, have lost their tempers, cursed Russia and departed. The attitude of the British Government in recognising no one, helping no one, wishing to help no one is only making us unpopular with everyone. The silly perpetual attacks on the Bolsheviks in the English press – Lenin is a German agent etc etc – mislead people at home and infuriate the Bolsheviks here. It's too childish. The French are worse. But the Yanks are playing more astutely.[3]

When Buchanan returned to London, he was accompanied by his

Military Attaché, General Knox, who was subsequently to figure prominently as an advocate of British intervention and as British military representative in Siberia. The Counsellor of the Embassy, Francis Lindley, was left as Chargé d'Affaires in Petrograd, with the task of maintaining the rump of an Embassy accredited to a vanished regime, and matters were complicated when, at the end of January, Lockhart arrived to take up his unofficial mission to the Bolsheviks. Balfour's policy of deliberate drifting was achieving little and there were many pressures on the British Government to come off the fence and commit itself for or against the Bolsheviks. For the time being, however, Lloyd George and his colleagues had no option but to pursue a policy based on the realities of political power in Russia as they saw them. Unfortunately, not only was reliable information hard to come by, but the politico-military map was changing day by day as the various parties staked out their positions. Poland, Finland, Estonia, Latvia and the Ukraine – all formerly within the Russian Empire or subordinate to it – had declared their independence. Armenia, Georgia, Azerbaidjan and Daghestan had proclaimed a Federal Republic of Transcaucasia and Bessarabia had formed an independent Moldavian Republic. The Bolshevik forces had already launched their offensive against the Ukraine, only to be forced to withdraw by the Germans, and there was bloody fighting against the Cossacks. In the East, all was confusion. Stranded in the apparently disintegrating Russian Empire was a body of Czechoslovak troops, variously estimated at between 45 000 and 70 000, whom the Czechoslovak National Council, with the strong support of the French Government, was seeking to evacuate to the West as an organised military body. The only substantial organised military force in the country was that of Germany, and Lenin had not yet made peace with them. It was by no means clear that the Bolsheviks would survive, but there was no other single body which offered a convincing alternative central government. The British Government's policy was therefore to try, without recognising the Bolsheviks, to establish some kind of working relationship with them, while, at the same time continuing to support any groups which seemed to have the potential to act as a focus for resistance to the German army.

On 19 January, the Bolsheviks took a step which went far towards disillusioning their supporters abroad and reinforcing the hatred of their enemies. Faced with a newly elected Constituent Assembly in which they held only 175 out of the 707 seats, they had to choose between observance of the normal standards of constitutional

democracy and the maintenance of their hold on power. The choice
was easy. The Assembly was forcibly dissolved. If there had been
hesitations on the part of the British Government about the kind of
men they were dealing with, this might have removed them. Certainly
it helped to turn Buchanan into an ardent supporter of intervention,
a course which he advocated in a series of speeches in Britain during
1918.

In Petrograd, Lindley, with no illusions about the Bolsheviks,
nevertheless recommended recognition, on the ground that 'It will
be necessary for us to humour them by getting into closer touch if
we desire to remain here'.[4] This produced from Balfour a lengthy
reply, explaining that 'Wherever any de facto administration is set
up, we have the right to establish informal relations with it, without
prejudice to the informal relations we may choose to cultivate with
organisations beyond its effective jurisdiction.' In other words, the
British Government would deal with anyone who held power in a
particular area. As for the Bolsheviks, although they neither could
nor would fight the Germans, this was apparently true of every party
in Russia. So, the Foreign Secretary concluded, very much as he had
done consistently since the Revolution: 'Delay seems desirable, if
only because it will give time for the situation to develop in South
Russia and elsewhere.'[5]

LOCKHART AND TROTSKY

It was on this equivocal basis that Lockhart had to begin the task of
establishing a relationship with the Bolshevik leaders. He found
Trotsky bitter against the English, yet he was able to report to
Balfour that some cooperation might be possible. The price would,
however, be the abandonment of support for the anti-Bolshevik
forces. It was the classic price demanded by revolutionaries throughout the ages, as soon as they begin to grasp power. It placed the
British Government in the classic dilemma. Should they abandon
traditionally more friendly groups in favour of those whose aims were
in many respects hostile to their own and whose hold on power was,
as yet, far from being established throughout the country they
purported to rule? Balfour was not a man to gamble and he was
certainly not going to 'abandon our friends and allies in those parts
of Russia where Bolshevism cannot be regarded as the de facto
government'.[6] When Lockhart next saw Trotsky on 23 February,

Trotsky's mood was worse: 'While you are here trying to throw dust in my eyes, your countrymen and the French have been intriguing against us with the Ukrainians, who have already sold themselves to the Germans. Your Government is working for Japanese intervention in Siberia.'[7]

There was much substance to Trotsky's complaint. The British Government had placed high hopes on the Ukraine. As early as the beginning of January they had informed the French Government that they considered official recognition of the Ukrainian Government desirable, but there is a certain irony in the fact that, two weeks before Lockhart's second interview with Trotsky, the Prime Minister had commented in Cabinet that 'It had turned out that the Ukrainians whom we had regarded as our friends had failed us'.[8] A project to stimulate Japanese intervention in Siberia had been under discussion since the previous December, when the Allied Military Representatives at Versailles had submitted Joint Note No. 5 recommending the opening of a direct line of communications to friendly groups in Russia through Vladivostok and the trans-Siberian railway. It was in fact only two days after the interview with Trotsky that the War Cabinet decided to seek the concurrence of the United States Government in such a project.[9] By the time it came to fruition the war with Germany was virtually over. At the beginning of 1918, however, the Allies were desperate to find any means they could of preventing Germany from exploiting her victory over the Russian armies.

GERMANY DRIVES HOME HER VICTORY

In the chaos which was Russia, only the German army, it seemed, had the ability and the will to achieve dominance. It was poised to resume the offensive against an enemy, its view of whom is illustrated by the note by General Hoffman on 17 February: 'The whole of Russia is no more than a vast heap of maggots – a squalid, swarming mass.'[10] Yet, although the Germans had the military power available inside Russia, it was by no means easy for them to determine how best to deploy it. They were stretched to the limit. Their top priority was the conduct of the war in the West and the maximum reinforcements were needed from the Russian front in order to mount a major land offensive in France in March 1918. Both sides knew that this attack had to come and both were preparing for it. The

Germans had already withdrawn 35 divisions for this purpose during the winter of 1917–18.[11] At the same time, there was a desperate need for both Germany and Austria to obtain Russian supplies, if they were to break the economic strangulation of the Allied blockade. Lloyd George in his memoirs quotes evidence given before the German Reichstag Committee after the war by General von Kuhl, who cited a report to Ludendorff in December 1917, stating 'the state of our food supplies of breadstuffs and provisions makes it a matter of extreme urgency to give first place to the possibility of bringing corn from Russia'.[12] The Austrian situation was even more desperate. Corn from the Ukraine was essential if collapse and revolution were to be averted. It would suit Germany to acquire her supplies by agreement with Russia, if this were possible, but, if it were not, then she would have to press on and take them. In any case, a resumed offensive would stand a good chance of inducing an unstable Bolshevik Government, struggling to avoid its own total collapse, to concede all Germany needed. Not surprisingly, the Germans decided to use negotiation and force in combination. They needed a final decision within a matter of weeks in order that their full force might be concentrated against the Allies in France. Otherwise they faced the prospect of defeat.

BREST-LITOVSK

On 10 February Trotsky, faced at Brest-Litovsk with German demands which he saw as unacceptable, attempted the ingenious manoeuvre of 'no war – no peace': 'We are going out of the war, but we feel ourselves compelled to refuse to sign the peace treaty'.[13] Against a desperate German High Command it produced the predictable result. The German advance was resumed and it appeared that Petrograd itself would shortly fall. So, after a historic debate in the Central Committee at which Lenin, with a threat of resignation, secured approval for immediate acceptance of still harsher German peace terms, the Treaty of Brest-Litovsk was signed on 3 March. The leader of the Bolshevik negotiators in the final stages, Grigori Sokolnikov, was later to become the first Soviet Ambassador to the Court of St James. By the Treaty, Russia surrendered territory containing about a third of her population and a third of her industrial potential. The margin of time was slim. The German offensive in France opened on 21 March.

28

FROM BREST-LITOVSK TO STALINGRAD

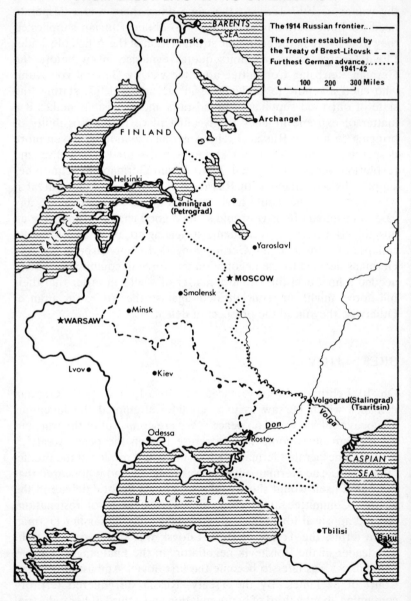

The 1914 Russian frontier... ———
The frontier established by
the Treaty of Brest-Litovsk _ _ _
Furthest German advance.......
1941-42
0   100   200   300 Miles

BARENTS
SEA

Murmansk

Archangel

FINLAND

Helsinki

Leningrad
(Petrograd)

Yaroslavl

★MOSCOW

Smolensk

★WARSAW   Minsk

Lvov   Kiev

Odessa   Don   Rostov

Volgograd(Stalingrad)
(Tsaritsin)

Volga

CASPIAN
SEA

BLACK SEA

Tbilisi   Baku

German policy in relation to the Western and Eastern fronts had been well coordinated, both militarily and economically. With the first-line fighting divisions concentrated on the Western front, the Treaty of Brest-Litovsk eliminated the Russian front and at the same time provided the potential for a substantial increase in economic resources, vital for the prosecution of the war and of major importance for the subsequent enhancement of Germany's power, whether the war ended in victory or stalemate. In fact, the military gain was not enough to secure victory in the March offensive and Germany and Austria lacked the strength to continue the fight long enough to realise the potential economic gain. This, however, was not apparent to the Allied Governments at the time. What they could see was a possible major alteration of the strategic balance and they reacted accordingly, trying, by any means they could devise, to prevent Germany from reaping the gains of Brest-Litovsk.

THE PLAN FOR ALLIED INTERVENTION

In these circumstances, some form of military intervention by the Allies began to seem both important and urgent. This was in fact the point at which the war was about to swing decisively in their favour, but in the context of British–Soviet relations, it was the point at which Balfour's policy of drift was effectively, although not explicitly abandoned and at which the British Government, still uncertain of both its objectives and its methods, set out with its Allies on the course of direct military operations in Russia. We have seen how, as early as December 1917, the plan for a Japanese landing at Vladivostok had been recommended by the Allied Military Representatives. At an Allied Diplomatic Conference held in London on 16 March it was decided to send to the United States Government a despatch prepared by Balfour asking for active American support for Japanese intervention through Siberia. 'What Germany desires', he wrote, 'is that Russia should be impotent during the War, subservient after it, and in the meanwhile should supply food and raw material to the Central Powers.' Russia could not help herself, so she must be helped by her friends. Only Japan had the necessary manpower and Siberia was for her the most accessible route. Lloyd George claims that he was dubious as to the wisdom of this step, but gave way under strong pressure by France for immediate Japanese intervention.[14] At the same time, however, he left Lockhart to continue the search for a basis of cooperation with Trotsky's new armies.

The German offensive in France demanded the complete attention of the War Cabinet and for a week Russia disappeared from the agenda. By the end of the month, however, it was back again, with attention focused by a paper by Lord Curzon.[15] What worried Curzon was the fact that, faced with conflicting advice, the Government seemed to be courting disaster by continuing with the pursuit of mutually incompatible policies, seeking simultaneously to deal with the Bolsheviks and to fight them. 'While great events are happening in France,' he wrote, 'we seem to be in some danger of losing sight of what is going to happen in Russia.' On the one hand he saw Lockhart as 'acting in the closest collaboration with Trotsky and repeating to us daily with increasing passion the Trotsky formulas: Creation of a new Russian revolutionary army; Allied assistance in this undertaking; no Allied or Japanese intervention in Vladivostok; no Allied or British intervention at Murmansk or Archangel'. As against this, there was, he said, no Russian army and 'the majority of our advisers tell us that the hope to create a new state or a new army out of the shattered debris of Bolshevism is a fantastic dream'. General Poole was advising occupation of Murmansk and Archangel and opinion even among Russians was veering in the direction of Japanese intervention in Siberia. 'Ought not we to decide between the two policies?', he concluded. 'To believe in one while we pursue the other or to believe in neither but to pursue both seems equally to lead to destruction.'

Cecil came in quickly in support, arguing[16] that 'on the whole, since the outbreak of the Bolshevik Revolution, almost every step taken by the Bolshevik Government has been precisely that which would have been desired by the German General Staff'. He did not recommend actually obstructing the construction of Trotsky's army, but 'we should take all other steps we can to secure Russia from German penetration, quite irrespective of anything Trotsky may be doing or saying that he is doing'.

So it was that the War Cabinet moved to a policy of armed intervention in Russia, with the principal effort to be made by the Japanese moving westwards along the trans-Siberian railway in order to link up with the Czech forces in Central Siberia. British, American and Japanese naval vessels had for some time been lying off Vladivostok and concern over the safety of the supply dumps was growing. The town itself was not controlled by the Bolsheviks, but their influence was growing and early in April small detachments of Japanese and British marines were landed to maintain order and protect the supply dumps. On their withdrawal, the Bolsheviks took over, only to be ejected two months later. Various factions were fighting for local control in Siberia at this time and the pattern of conflict was further complicated by Japanese support for a peculiarly unsavoury ex-Cossack adventurer, Semenov, who had indeed, for a time, enjoyed British support.

In April, when the Czech forces were far to the West on the trans-Siberian railway, the British Government still hoped that large-scale intervention might take place without the opposition of the Bolshevik Government, and Lockhart was instructed that his main task was to secure their concurrence. The scheme, as he was to put it to Trotsky, was set out in a telegram from Balfour dated 13 April.[17] The Bolshevik administration should try to raise an efficient national army, organise guerrilla warfare against the Germans and prevent supplies from reaching them; they should invite Allied military and naval assistance at Murmansk if the railway was threatened and, in any case, through Vladivostok; the Allies should bind themselves to evacuate all Russian territory at the end of the war and, while in Russia, should take no part in political or economic controversy. The whole Allied object would be to free Russian soil from the enemy and to restore Russia's independence. 'There was', said Balfour, 'little use in making the attempt to persuade the Japanese to accept the plan if Trotsky refused to play his part'; but in that event Japan might intervene on her own, with all the disadvantages and few of the advantages, so far as Russia was concerned, of the British plan. This was indeed a risk, since Japan's interest in establishing herself on Russia's Pacific Coast could be met without in any way serving the British interest in relation to the war against Germany.

A stream of diplomatic communications passed between London, Washington and Tokyo as the British Government sought American support for the planned Siberian operation. It became increasingly clear that President Wilson profoundly disliked the proposed scheme and the British Government, losing patience, took the first step towards intervention with action at Murmansk and then at Archangel. At Murmansk, there was a certain coincidence of interest between the British, who needed to prevent the port falling under German control, and the local Soviet, who faced a Finnish threat. For a brief initial period their cooperation even had the blessing of Trotsky. At Archangel, the situation was rather different. In April, an armed icebreaker and two supply ships were sent, followed quickly by a cruiser, and it was decided that, although the captain should not prevent by force the removal of the Allied stores, he should be given wide discretionary powers to deal with any situation without reference back to the Admiralty. At the beginning of May, a Committee of Milner, General Smuts, the First Sea Lord and the Chief of the Imperial General Staff (CIGS) met to consider action 'to organise military resistance to the enemy in Russia while correspondence with America and Japan is proceeding'. It was recommended that General Poole should take charge of military affairs in Russia, with his initial base in Murmansk and a small office in London 'to assist him in organising the Czechoslovaks and other forces of intervention from Archangel and Murmansk'. The Committee expressed the opinion that 'undue weight had been placed in our recent correspondence on the desirability of an invitation for intervention from the Bolshevik Government'.[18] The War Cabinet approved the report and also decided to send a reinforcement of 350 Royal Marines to Murmansk. Thus, by a series of separate decisions, the British Government had moved close to the point at which British forces were to be committed to military operations in Russia in opposition to the Bolshevik Government.

SUPPORT FOR THE ANTI-BOLSHEVIK FORCES

In following the gradual development of British policy during this period, it must be remembered that, from the earliest stage after the Revolution, the British Government, like the French, had been trying by various means to prop up the assorted groups within Russia which were opposed to the Bolsheviks and which, it was hoped, might hold open the front against Germany. The tale of intrigue is too long and too complex to recite here. Not much of it appears in the minutes of the War Cabinet and this is in itself significant. The experience of more recent times has shown how hard it is for those who interfere in other countries' revolutions to understand the objectives of the various factions and how much harder still to determine the use to which arms and money will be put once they are in local hands. It was inevitable that, once broad ministerial approval for support to the anti-Bolshevik forces had been given and funding authorised, the Cabinet would lose effective control, with operational decisions falling to assorted agents on the spot and their controlling Departments in

London. It was precisely in the operational detail that the potential for disaster lay. Support for the anti-Bolshevik groups was, both before direct military intervention and subsequently, the means by which the British Government's agents, including Lockhart, were implementing a major part of the Government's policy. It was this activity, more than the formal statements of the Government's desire not to interfere in the Russian political scene, which constituted the effective policy and which impressed itself upon the Bolshevik leadership. It was this activity, too, which created implicit obligations to continue support to the White forces after the end of the war with Germany, thus involving the Allies in the prolongation of the Russian Civil War and converting the intervention from an operation directed at the defeat of Germany to one directed at the defeat of the Bolsheviks. Although the support to the anti-Bolshevik groups was, in part, covert, much had to be done openly. Throughout Russia, British and Allied representatives were being besieged by all those who saw in the defeat of the Bolsheviks their only hope for the future of themselves and their country. In London a running battle was waged between the Foreign Office and the Treasury over the supply of funds for a variety of ill-fated schemes advanced by plausible claimants upon British beneficence; and it was with remarkably innocent faith that the British Government's representatives were authorised to advance significant sums in sterling to those who claimed to be able to provide roubles to the anti-Bolshevik forces. It may suffice to quote a minute by the Russian Department of the Foreign Office in reply to a letter from the Treasury dated 11 November 1918, seeking the recovery of funds advanced for the purpose of obtaining water-marked currency paper and printing ink for notes to be printed in Tiflis for the Trans-Caucasus Confederacy: 'As far as we can discover, neither the paper nor the Government for which it was supplied is still in existence.' Not all those who were dependent upon British support disappeared so quickly and the disentangling of the British Government's inherited obligations was to prove a major element in later policy.

THE CONFLICT OF PROFESSIONAL ADVICE

During the critical period leading to armed intervention in Russia without the consent of the Bolshevik Government and without the full support of the United States Government, the British Government was handicapped by sharply conflicting assessments from its professional advisers. The whole problem was considered primarily in military terms and it was natural that the views of the Government's military advisers should carry special weight. Prominent among the advocates of intervention was the former Military Attaché in Petrograd, General Knox.[19] Knox's views were supported by the CIGS and counted for much in the consideration of the question by the War Cabinet, but their bias was probably recognised, at least by Balfour, who said of him on a later occasion that he was 'not a reactionary as the term was understood by members of the Cabinet', but 'there was no doubt that he was anti-Bolshevik, while a man of his strength of character, knowledge and ability was bound sooner or later to play a political part'.[20] Knox was bitterly hostile to Lockhart and so, too was the Director of Military Intelligence, General MacDonogh, who argued at one point that General Poole, as the military representative in Russia, should be given authority for all questions, whether political, military or financial, and that Lockhart, if he were to be retained at all, should have only a consultative function. Balfour, however, minuted that he saw 'great objection to a military mission controlling our whole policy, even in Russia'.[21] He seems to have had some sympathy with Lockhart, but others in the Foreign Office certainly did not. Lockhart's telegrams sorely tried their patience and drove the Under-Secretary, Sir R. Graham, to minute, 'With every desire to make allowances for Mr Lockhart, the tone of his telegrams can only be described as intolerable'. The conflict of professional advice must have aggravated the problems of the War Cabinet. A glimpse of the conflict emerges from the remark by the CIGS in the War Cabinet that General Poole was just leaving for Russia and was 'quite sanguine as to raising a large army' to which the Prime Minister replied that Mr Lindley was also going and apparently had no belief that anything could be done at all in Russia. The response to the Milner report suggests, however, that by May the divergence of views among ministers had been reduced. Even the Prime Minister was arguing that Britain should if necessary proceed without the United States and Japan, on the ground that the Germans were withdrawing troops from the Russian front, the British army was bearing the brunt of the fighting in France and no material American contribution had yet arrived.[22]

It was at this point, two months after Brest-Litovsk, that a new note of urgency was introduced by the appointment of a German Ambassador, von Mirbach, in Moscow. The situation was promptly assessed by Lockhart, who had accompanied the Bolshevik leadership when they moved from Petrograd to Moscow. On 23 May he reported that there had been a marked change in the situation in Russia so far as Germany was concerned. The Germans had announced that their military operations had been completed; that they had no intention of occupying Petrograd or Moscow and that they were anxious to cooperate economically with the Russian Government. Lockhart went on to argue that the changed situation in Russia left the British Government with two alternative courses: to recognise the Bolsheviks and conclude an economic treaty with them, accompanied by a provision that they would accept Allied intervention in the event of any further German aggression; or to undertake large-scale Allied intervention, preferably with Bolshevik consent, but, failing that, without it.[23] He came down in favour of the latter, but warned that no substantial assistance could be expected from pro-Allied forces in the early stage. A few days later, he telegraphed again, urging that, with Bolshevik power decreasing, the Allies could expect neither an invitation, nor consent to intervention, but that they would never have a more favourable moment for it. From the Consul in Petrograd, came a recommendation that nothing but armed force could protect British interests and that Archangel and Murmansk should be occupied with a division at each.

Lockhart had for some time harangued London with a series of telegrams and it was noted with irritation in the Foreign Office that he had now recognised what others had seen two months earlier. His ever-changing recommendations brought a telegram from Balfour which bears traces of having been personally drafted and which testifies to the problems the Government faced in dealing with the differing counsels of their advisers and the differing interests of their Allies.[24] Having assured Lockhart that his work was not unappreciated and that he had not in any way lost the Government's confidence, Balfour continued:

Your telegrams during the last five months have faithfully reflected the variation in opinion produced and no doubt justified by the constantly changing aspects of the present transitional period of Russian history. You have at different times advised against Allied intervention in any form; against it by the Japanese alone; against it with Japanese assistance; against it at Vladivostok; in favour of it at Murmansk; in favour of it with an invitation; in favour of it without an invitation since it was really desired by the Bolsheviks;

in favour of it without an invitation, whether the Bolsheviks desired it or not.

Balfour then set out, with a patience which in the circumstances was remarkable, the problems of the alliance, the contradictory reports and the differing conclusions, with Britain, France and Italy thinking the dangers of intervention less than its advantages, America taking the contrary view and Japan unwilling to do anything on a great scale without an invitation. 'The only thing on which everybody agrees is that without the active participation of America nothing effective can be accomplished through Siberia and active participation of America has so far been refused.' The Bolshevists were behaving as the tools, willing or unwilling, of the Central Powers and no other party seemed able to do anything against them. So, Balfour concluded, 'We can do no more than press our views on the Administration at Washington and hope that by the time the necessity of intervention is universally admitted and common action becomes . . . possible it may not prove too late.'

It is not difficult to see how, at this point in mid-1918, six months after the Revolution, there should have been a broad measure of agreement in Britain among the members of the War Cabinet and their professional advisers on the need for some means of preventing Germany from securing the full fruits of her military victory over Russia. The Bolshevik power was by no means assured and it was not wholly impossible that Germany might have secured a degree of control over Russia's economic resources, which, if it could not have brought victory in the West, might at least have brought a stalemate from which Germany could have withdrawn to renew her strength. What is more remarkable – and for this a measure of responsibility must rest with the government's military and political advisers – is the faith which was placed in the ability of the Allies to prevent such an outcome by means of an operation which, to have had any chance of success, would have required the deployment of forces far in excess of anything which could realistically have been expected. What was envisaged was in effect an attempt to reconstitute Russian national resistance to the German forces by means of landings of relatively small Allied contingents at three points separated by several thousand miles of exceptionally difficult terrain. As a scheme, it bordered on the fantastic. The case for it could only be sustained by the political judgment that, once Allied landings in force had taken place, the Russian people would rise in welcome and overthrow the Bolsheviks.

Exactly this point had been made when the idea was mooted in January. At that time Balfour, commenting on the proposal for intervention put up by the Interdepartmental Russia Committee, declined to offer any opinion on its practicability, commenting only that it had been devised by important members of the War Office and the Foreign Office and deserved careful consideration by the War Cabinet. General Macdonogh, the Director of Military Intelligence, was asked for his assessment and wrote a most cautious letter to Balfour on 27 January, pointing out that a statement of the feasibility of the scheme from the military point of view would be a purely theoretical exercise, since 'the question is entirely dependent on the attitude of the Russians which is a political rather than a military matter'.[25]

Five months of discussion and the absence of any alternative plan had left Ministers so wedded to the scheme that by June they were prepared to close their eyes to its inherent impracticability and to abandon all reserve. Cecil was arguing in Cabinet that without intervention in Siberia there was no prospect of a successful conclusion to the war. His view was embodied in a formal memorandum in which it was stated that unless Allied intervention in Siberia was undertaken forthwith 'we have no chance of being ultimately victorious and shall incur serious risk of defeat in the meantime'. British and French reserves would have been exhausted by June 1919 and the Germans might then obtain a decision in their favour in the West. In any case, 'No military decision in the Allies' favour can ever be expected as a result of operations on the Western front alone'. Only by immediate Allied intervention would it be possible to prevent the complete absorption of Russia by the Central Powers which would imply world domination by Germany'.[26]

CONCERN ABOUT TRADE PROSPECTS

Although, by the summer of 1918, the British Government was concerned primarily with the preparation for armed intervention in Russia, it did not wholly ignore the need for some more constructive longer-term policy. The British financial interest in Russia was substantial, in respect not only of the direct financial assistance given for the pursuit of the war, but also of British industrial and mining investments which it was hoped to recover. These issues were, for many years, to play a dominant part in the British–Soviet relationship and they were first considered in June 1918, when the War Cabinet took a joint memorandum[27] by the Foreign Office and the Department of Overseas Trade on the question of future economic relations with Russia. It was decided to send a mission of officials and businessmen to explore the situation and recommend how best to develop trade. The mission left, with no very high expectations, on the same ship which was taking Lindley back to Russia as British Commissioner with the intervention forces in the North. By the time they reached Moscow the Allied landings were only a few days off. It was, as Lockhart said, a Gilbertian situation, and it illustrated very clearly the way in which up to the last moment the British Government sought to hedge its bets. But it was the last such attempt for a long time.

THE DECISION TO INTERVENE

The final stage of the preparation for intervention began on 28 June, when the Imperial War Cabinet approved a formal resolution: 'The British Imperial War Cabinet . . . having carefully considered the military situation and prospects of the Allies in all theatres of war have come to the conclusion that immediate Allied armed intervention and armed assistance to Russia is imperatively necessary.' The Government appealed to President Wilson to accept this policy, but the American reply was firm. The proposed military intervention 'would add to the present sad confusion in Russia rather than cure it, injure her rather than help her and would be of no advantage in prosecution of our main design, to win the war against Germany'. The United States therefore could not take part in such intervention or sanction it in principle. What the United States Government would do was to assist in the consolidation of the Czechoslovak forces and in the guarding of military stores. The President also made clear, however, that he was not seeking to set limits to action by America's associates.

ALLIED LANDINGS AT VLADIVOSTOK

This statement, unsatisfactory as it was from the British point of view, left the Allies free to go ahead – and they did so. Not surprisingly, each envisaged a substantially different operation. Britain still cherished the objective of establishing an independent Government in Siberia, linking up with the force moving south from Archangel and providing a base for support of anti-Bolshevik forces in southern Russia. Japan wanted to establish its own power in Russia's Pacific provinces. France, having been consistently the most hostile of the Allies towards the Bolsheviks, sought to control the Siberian operation, but made little material contribution to it and wanted mainly to secure the transfer of the Czech forces to the Western front. The United States, instinctively disliking the whole operation, was determined not to move beyond the limited initial objective of facilitating the evacuation of the Czechs. Such were the circumstances in which on 3 August 1918, with the war against Germany almost won, a battalion of the Middlesex Regiment landed in Vladivostok, to be followed by 70 000 Japanese, 8000 Americans and contingents from France, Canada and Italy, as well as a second British battalion.

– AND AT ARCHANGEL

While urging on President Wilson the case for intervention in Siberia, the British Government had to decide whether to exploit its toehold at Murmansk and mount a major operation from Archangel. When the War Cabinet considered this aspect of the Russian problem in June[28] the CIGS said that the occupation of the two towns would require two and a half divisions of infantry alone. He was inclined to abandon the Murman coast unless the operation there were backed up by intervention through Siberia. The Prime Minister, however, argued that, even if the Siberian operation could not be implemented, Archangel and Murmansk would be invaluable as inlets to Russia and it was essential to maintain the British position 'if such could be achieved without the expenditure of large forces'. So the build-up of forces went ahead and, with Lindley as his political adviser, Poole took the Anglo-French landing party into Archangel on 2 August, a day before the first British battalion landed in Vladivostok.

– AND IN THE CAUCASUS

The principal point of friction prior to the Revolution had been the southward thrust of the Russians in Afghanistan and Persia, the border zone between the Russian and Indian Empires. In 1918 the old friction was revived in two new forms. On the one hand, Bolshevik propaganda directed at the Moslem world carried the threat of insurrection against British rule. On the other, the collapse of Russian resistance to the German armies raised the risk that German–Turkish imperialism might replace Russian imperialism in Central Asia. German–Turkish domination of the Caucasus might lead in the short term to control of the Baku oil fields and possibly, in the longer term, to a threat to the border areas of the Indian Empire. In these circumstances, it seemed to the strategists in London that control of the Caucasus should be an important element in British policy and in January 1918 Major-General Dunsterville was appointed as British Representative at Tiflis in Georgia, where he sought to mobilise opposition to Turkish and German encroachment. After considerable hesitation in London, he was eventually given permission to take a force of two battalions to Baku and was invited by the local anti-Bolshevik authorities to help in the defence of the city. The first battalion arrived on 4 August. The timing owed much to chance and little to plan. It is, however, of interest to note that these three operations, Archangel, Vladivostok and Baku, began effectively on 2 August, 3 August and 4 August.

The full irony of the timing is best illustrated by the passage in Lloyd George's *War Memoirs* in which he notes how on 8 August the Anglo-French offensive on the Western front had convinced both General Ludendorff and the Kaiser that the war had been lost. 'We are at the limits of our endurance. The War must be brought to an end', the Kaiser had written.[29] Had the operations in Russia been in fact rather than in theory part of a concerted drive from East and West to break the power of Germany, they might have had a certain logic. They were, however, conceived against a different and earlier strategic assessment and implemented with no clear or agreed purpose. The sector of the Eastern front which was to prove important in precipitating the final collapse of the Austrian and German forces was the southern, Salonika sector, not the Russian and certainly not the Siberian. So it was that by August 1918, just three months before the end of the war with Germany, Britain embarked on operations in Russia which had minimal relevance to the outcome of the war,

but which were to dominate the Anglo-Soviet relationship in its
immediate post-war phase.

'WE ARE COMING AS FRIENDS'

On 9 August 1918, with the commencement of the phase of active
intervention, the British representatives in Murmansk, Archangel
and Vladivostok were instructed to issue a 'Declaration by the British
Government to the Peoples of Russia':

> We are coming as friends to help you to save yourselves from
> dismemberment and destruction at the hands of Germany. . . .
> We wish solemnly to assure you that while our troops are entering
> Russia to assist you in your struggle against Germany we shall not
> retain one foot of your territory. . . . Our one desire is to see
> Russia strong and free and then to retire and watch the Russian
> people work out its destinies in accordance with the freely expressed
> wishes of the people.[30]

The declaration, of a type which is not unfamiliar in situations of
'liberation', may well have been issued in good faith, but it would
have required a remarkable degree of trust on the part of the
Bolshevik leadership to accept it at face value. The British
Government were now committed to a policy, the logic of which was
that the claim by the Bolsheviks to constitute the central Government
of Russia was not merely unrecognised, but was directly challenged.
Either the Bolshevik power had to be broken, or the intervention
had to fail. This was the dilemma which the War Cabinet had long
perceived and long sought to avoid. Although the breaking of
Bolshevik power would have been by no means unwelcome to the
majority of the Cabinet, it had not been the direct objective of their
policy. Even in August not all members of the Government would
have accepted that it was a necessary implication and there was no
clear concept as to the preferred alternative to Bolshevik power. The
question whether a state of war existed between Britain and Russia
was one which did not particularly trouble the British Government
so long as the operations in Russia were seen as part of the war
against Germany. After the end of the German war the problem was
to become rather more acute, especially in relation to the continuation
of the blockade. The conclusion then was that although, in practice,

war was being waged, it could not be declared as such against a body, the Bolsheviks, who were not recognised as the Government of Russia.

So far as the Bolsheviks themselves were concerned, there was some uncertainty as to whether a state of war existed, but little doubt as to Allied intentions. Lockhart reported[31] that immediately after the first landings Lenin had emphatically declared at an official and public meeting of the Soviet that a state of war existed between the Allied powers and the Russian Republic. However, in the face of a *démarche* by the Allied representatives, Chicherin replied that it was a 'state of defence rather than one of war' and that his Government wished 'to continue relations with the Allied powers as they had done with Germany under analogous circumstances'. In its official history of Soviet Foreign Policy, the Soviet Government presents the August intervention as a step in the implementation of a policy of armed invasion and civil war which had already been decided on by the end of 1917.[32] With the availability of contemporary official documents, the absence of a serious Soviet attempt to analyse these complex developments is regrettable. It is, however, scarcely surprising that the Soviet Union should have sought to depict the Allied intervention in the blackest light. In August 1918 it would have been hard for a Bolshevik Government, itself born of conspiracy and skilled in the arbitrary and violent use of power, to avoid the interpretation, incorrect though it was, that Allied policy since the Revolution had been directed continuously, by whatever means were available, to the overthrow of Bolshevik power.

In the period prior to August, the attempt by the Allies to organise anti-Bolshevik forces into an effective opposition to German domination of Russia had been relatively ineffective. The threat to the Bolshevik hold on the country was, however, under constant threat from various sources, some financed by one or other of the Allies, others quite independent of any Allied support and all pursuing their own ambitions. The summer of 1918 was a period of particular tension. On 4 July came the open denunciation of Lenin by the Socialist Revolutionary Spiridinova at the Fifth All-Russian Congress, followed on 6 July by the murder of the German Ambassador von Mirbach and the seizure by Socialist Revolutionaries under Boris Savinkov of Yaroslavl, only 125 miles from Moscow. Savinkov had links with French agents but was also probably receiving finance from the British agent Sidney Reilly. The Czech forces which were to be the main element in the Siberian intervention were gaining the upper hand well before the main Allied landings and on 16 July, as they outflanked the city of Ekaterinburg, the Czar and his family were murdered.

Then, on 30 August, a Socialist Revolutionary shot and killed Uritsky, the head of the Petrograd branch of the CHEKA. This predecessor of the OGPU and KGB, its acronym standing for the All-Russian Extraordinary Commission for Fighting Counter-Revolution and Sabotage, had at its head the Polish Communist Dzerzhinski and its central office in Lubyanka Street in Moscow. Throughout the succeeding decades it was to symbolise for Soviet citizens and for foreign observers the processes of espionage, repression and terror by which the Soviet leadership sought to sustain their personal power and the revolutionary purity of the Soviet state.

On the day of Uritsky's murder Lenin was severely injured by two bullets fired by Fanny Kaplan in Moscow. Lenin himself called this the most critical period of the Revolution and it must have seemed equally possible both to him and to the Allied Governments that the Bolshevik experiment was on the point of failure. The effect of these events was significant in both the short and long term, not only for the development of Soviet Russia, but for the British–Russian relationship.

THE 'LOCKHART PLOT'

The landings at Archangel and Vladivostok effectively meant the end of Lockhart's mission. The immediate Bolshevik response was the arrest of British and French residents of Moscow, including members of the Consular staff. Although most were quickly released, they were not permitted to leave the country. On 9 August, the British Consul-General, Oliver Wardrop, handed over the responsibility for the care of the British community to the Netherlands Embassy. Negotiations for permission for the British to leave Russia in exchange for permission for Litvinov and his staff to leave London were continuing, when the murder of Uritsky was followed by the storming of the former British Embassy by agents of the Cheka and the murder of the Naval Attaché, Captain Cromie, who shot two of the intruders before himself being killed. In Moscow, Lockhart was arrested immediately after the attack on Lenin, and although briefly released, was re-arrested on 4 September. The official Soviet legend was created that 'the most dangerous of the anti-Soviet conspiracies was the Lockhart plot'[33] aimed at physically exterminating leaders of the party and the Soviet Government, first and foremost Lenin.

With British forces operating on Russian soil and the British Government, with Lockhart as their agent, actively supporting military operations by groups in various parts of Russia, the allegation is not entirely surprising. Lockhart was certainly in contact with various anti-Bolshevik groups and was providing finance for the forces which Alexeyev, the former Commander-in-Chief, was gathering in southern Russia. The British intelligence authorities were operating through agents such as Paul Dukes, Sidney Reilly and George Hill in a mixture of operations, some directed against the Germans and others against the Bolsheviks. Cromie's activities against the Germans had, according to Lindley, brought him 'more or less into cooperation' with anti-Bolsheviks. Reilly was closely involved with Savinkov and was attempting to suborn the Kremlin guards in preparation for a coup d'état against Lenin's Government. The overthrow of that Government was certainly not the direct objective of British policy and, with the archives closed, there is no evidence of the extent to which Reilly's activities, although doubtless known to Lockhart, had been approved by Balfour. Nor is there a known link between Fanny Kaplan and the British agents. A telegram from Balfour indicating his concern that Lockhart should not be placed in a compromising position may be interpreted either way. In the absence of any convincing evidence, it may well be that Lockhart's personal complicity in the plots to overthrow Lenin and his Government was minimal, but the personal accounts of Hill and others[34] indicate the varied operations of the British intelligence services in Russia at that time.

THE END OF UNOFFICIAL RELATIONS

The negotiations for an exchange of Lockhart and other British subjects against Russians in Britain had been in train for some time when the news of Cromie's death was received. In an attempt to secure some extra leverage, the War Cabinet decided to arrest Litvinov and instructed the Foreign Secretary to threaten reprisals against Lenin, Trotsky and other Bolshevik leaders if the lives of British subjects were not safeguarded.[35] Balfour's message stated that the members of the Soviet Government would be held individually responsible for any further acts of violence and that the Government would 'make every endeavour to secure that they shall be treated as outlaws by the Governments of all civilized nations and that no place of refuge shall be left to them'. After difficult negotiations, agreement was reached and Lockhart arrived back in London on 19 October. On his return, he wrote a report on his mission.[36] The Bolsheviks, he wrote, had been in power for exactly a year, their power was stronger and more consolidated than at any previous period and they possessed one fundamental attribute of any real Government, the physical power to enforce their decrees. He saw Bolshevism as such a danger that it had to be crushed. It was no use relying on anti-Bolshevik forces in Russia to do this. What was needed was Allied intervention on 'a proper scale', with an Allied force of 50 000 driving north from the Black Sea to Moscow and at least as many moving through Siberia. 'Very interesting, but I fear the conclusion is impracticable', minuted Lord Robert Cecil. Lockhart went off to Scotland on half pay. Having abandoned a reluctant and half-hearted attempt to establish some kind of relationship with the Bolsheviks, the British Government was now committed to an equally reluctant and half-hearted military intervention.

Among the British public, the murder of the Tsar did not of itself cause a great public reaction, but the murder of Cromie, the campaign of terror which followed the attack on Lenin and the accumulating reports of Bolshevik atrocities did much to harden opinion. On the other side of the political divide, the bulk of the British Labour movement had no love for the Bolsheviks, but throughout the spring and summer, as talk of the impending Allied operations grew, opposition to intervention had begun to build up. Litvinov had been doing his best to encourage pro-Bolshevik sentiment among the British workers and had been under close observation by the security authorities, who provided the Cabinet with regular reports on subversive activities. As early as 9 March 1918 the *Herald* was writing of the 'peril from the East' and saying to 'our comrades' in Russia: 'We share your shame and your indignation. The blow struck at your heart strikes at our heart too'. Cecil was described as 'the most reckless militarist now in office in Europe' and when the main landings took place the *Herald* registered its protest: 'Great Britain and her allies are at war with the Bolshevik Government of Russia . . . British Labour dare not stand by without protest'. Douglas Young, the Consul in Archangel, who had long realised the inconsistency of his Government's policy, returned to Britain in the autumn of 1918 and wrote an article 'Britain and Russia' for the *Herald*, expressing his hatred of Bolshevism, but his anger that 'the British Government played a dirty and double game with the Soviet Government in Russia'.[37] At this stage, with the war against Germany still the dominant factor in public opinion, the Government had little need for concern, but, with its ending, the political background to British policy was to undergo a significant change.

INTERVENTION – THE FANTASY AND THE REALITY

The first news of the Allied military operations was encouraging. The CIGS put a paper to the Cabinet in September[38] reporting that control of the trans-Siberian railway from Vladivostok to the Volga had been secured, that the Czech forces ought to be able to link up with Poole's forces driving south from Archangel and together they could then join the anti-Bolshevik forces under General Alexeyev between the Don and Volga, thus opening up by the spring of 1919 a new Eastern front against Germany. For generals who had deployed men by the million to gain ground by the yard in France, it must have been exhilarating to plan on their maps these grand designs across thousands of miles of Russia. It was far from certain that the Bolsheviks would be able to consolidate their power and there were moments in the early autumn of 1918 and again in the autumn of 1919 when it looked as though the fantasy had a chance of realisation. Fantasy it was, both political and military fantasy, but it was to be another year and a half before the Bolshevik power was finally established. Politically, the Japanese Government wanted only to hold the Pacific Coast and they made it clear that they had no desire to move east of Lake Baikal, at which point they were still some 2000 miles from the Volga. Politically, the American objective of helping the Czechs was realised by the opening of the railway which would make possible their evacuation through Vladivostok, and President Wilson had never proposed to become involved in a campaign to control Russia. Politically, the anti-Bolshevik forces lacked the will to create a system which might have commanded the mass of popular support. Militarily, the British would soon have to dig in for the Arctic winter on the Archangel front, the Czechs had all they could do to sustain their existing positions and the Allied lines of communication within Russia would have become increasingly vulnerable to guerrilla attack. So long as the war in France continued, Britain could not find the forces or the transport for major operations in Russia and, with the ending of the war, it would be a political impossibility to embark on another major campaign. Perhaps most important of all, the various Russian groups supported by the Allies were continuing in pursuit of their separate and sometimes conflicting objectives, for the most part unable to comprehend the change in the mood of Russia and unable to capture that popular enthusiasm which alone might have justified and secured their victory. Lloyd George consistently took the line that the anti-Bolshevik forces deserved the chance to show whether they could win that support, but that if they could not, no Allied support would save them. He soon had to recognise that the latter was the case.

It was not long before the War Cabinet began to doubt whether the Volga line could be held. They still hoped that the Americans might yet be persuaded of the need to do so: 'If we were now to ask the Czechs to withdraw to the East of the Urals, that would be to cut off from Alexeyev and those with him their last hope of Allied assistance.'[39] Meanwhile, the political attempt to consolidate an anti-Bolshevik Government in Siberia and to raise a Russian force was pursued. The Government appointed Sir Charles Eliot, Vice-Chancellor of Hong Kong University, as High Commissioner for Siberia. A Siberian Provisional Government was functioning at Omsk and it was thought that, if the link with Alexeyev in the South could be made, there might be a possibility of developing a provisional Russian Government under military leadership.

It was at this point, just two months after the commitment to intervention, that, with a rapidity which took the Allies wholly by surprise, the war with Germany ended and Britain faced the prospect that she would be left with forces on Russian soil in pursuit of an unsustainable and irrelevant policy. The forces committed to the intervention were by then approximately as follows:[40]

Siberia: 70 000 Japanese; 8000 Americans; 4000 Canadians; 2000 British; 1500 Italian; 1000 French, in addition to a Czech force estimated at between 45 000 and 70 000.
Murmansk and Archangel: A total of 13 000, mainly British, but also including contingents from France, Italy, Canada and the United States.
The Caspian: 5000 British.

For the most part, the British forces had not at this time been involved in major actions against the Bolsheviks. In Murmansk, they were able to establish a satisfactory relationship with the local Bolshevik administration, but at the price of a breach between the latter and Moscow. At Archangel, where the local Soviet was loyal to Moscow, Poole had to organise a coup and dispose of the existing administration before establishing one favourable to the Allied occupation. Having done so, his attitude to the inhabitants was that of a commander holding conquered territory.[41] Probing southwards from the two ports, the British forces had been engaged in minor but sharp operations designed to hold off the Bolsheviks and extend the bridgehead. In Vladivostok, by the time the main landing was made, the town was held by an administration which was not subject to orders from Moscow. The British troops moved westwards down the railway to Omsk, but, with the remarkable exception of a naval gun team, made little contact with the Bolsheviks. In the South, Dunsterville was working in cooperation with the Socialist Revolutionary administration which had replaced the Bolsheviks in Baku and was forced to withdraw after a bitter engagement not with the Bolsheviks but with the Turks. On the other side of the Caspian at Ashkhabad, Major-General Malleson was also cooperating with a Socialist Revolutionary and Menshevik administration. His small British–Indian force fought off the Bolsheviks and established a small flotilla on the Caspian. It was Malleson's Socialist Revolutionary allies who gave rise to one of the legends of the intervention when, without his concurrence, they shot the 26 Bolshevik Commissars who had left Baku after the Socialist Revolutionary takeover.

The British officers, operating with minuscule forces in a vast and war-torn country, had little option but to make such arrangements as they could with the factions controlling the areas in which they operated. The commitments they made were in line with the general tenor of British policy and, indeed, necessary if the intervention were to succeed. With a political direction from London which could, at best, be described as fitful, the consequence was, however, a casual accretion of formal and informal obligations, lacking either political or military coherence and, in sum, constituting a significant complicating factor in subsequent British policy.

POST-WAR POLICY

The ending of the war with Germany compelled the Cabinet to rethink its whole military policy in Russia. Cecil saw the dilemma. He made it plain in Cabinet that 'he hated the idea of abandoning to Bolshevik fury all those who had helped us, but he quite saw that it might end badly if we tried to destroy Bolshevism by means of military interference'.[42]

Not for the first nor for the last time, ministers succeeded in diagnosing the problem correctly, before embarking on the wrong course. The War Cabinet met on 14 November to consider recommendations of a meeting in the Foreign Office at which the Foreign Secretary, Cecil and Milner, together with Foreign Office officials and the Directors of Military and Naval Intelligence and Operations considered the whole field of policy in Russia. The British Government could not, said the Foreign Secretary, 'embark on an anti-Bolshevik crusade in Russia' despite the contrary advice from advisers on the spot who were 'obsessed with the external and visible violence of Bolshevism'. Cecil agreed. So did the Prime Minister, but everyone then agreed with Milner that East of the Don and the Volga, where anti-Bolshevik Governments were in existence, they should be supported. Specifically, the War Cabinet approved the recommendations[43] that the 'border states of Western Russia from the Baltic to the Black Sea' should be recognised; British forces should remain in occupation of Murmansk and Archangel; the Omsk Directorate in Siberia should be recognised as a *de facto* Government; the Siberian expedition should be maintained; the Baku–Batum railway should be held; Denikin, who had taken command in southern Russia after the death of Alexeyev, should be given all possible assistance in military material; so, also, should the Baltic states when they had Governments ready to receive and utilise it; the British sphere of 'influence' defined in the Anglo-French agreement of 1917 should be extended to cover the country between the Don and the Volga; and consideration should be given to taking over Krasnovodsk on the eastern shore of the Caspian. At the same meeting the Prime Minister for the first time expressed his concern about the need to ensure that the 'great inflammable industrial population' of Britain understood what Bolshevism meant in practice and measures to this end were put in hand. So, in the moment of victory, the members of the War Cabinet reaffirmed, with no apparent dissent, a policy which, originally conceived as part of the war with Germany, was now in practice a policy for the internal reconstruction of Russia.

It was a policy which would have to be carried through against a very different background. With the ending of the war, the victorious Allies were to gather in Paris at the beginning of 1919 for the Peace Conference and were to concern themselves effectively with the post-war structure of Europe. What was to be the position of Russia, their ally for most of the war? There was no longer an Allied Russian Government to sit with them at the table. The Allies were not formally at war with Russia, but their armed forces were engaged in conflict with the Bolsheviks and there was no other group which could claim effectively to control the territory of Russia. The boundaries of post-war Europe could not be settled without any settlement of the boundary of Russia. Independent, quasi-independent and would-be independent states had been carved or were in the process of being carved out of the territory of Imperial Russia. The Treaty of Brest-Litovsk was denounced on 13 November and all was in flux. It might fairly be said that the future of Russia was the business of the Russians. But what was Russia? Who were the Russians? How were they to decide their future?

LLOYD GEORGE AND CHURCHILL

By the time the Peace Conference assembled, Lloyd George's power had been substantially enhanced by the overwhelming Coalition victory in the December election. With the formation of the post-war Government, Winston Churchill was to move from his post of Minister of Munitions to become Secretary of State for War, an appointment which Lloyd George had seen as concerned with the readjustment of the army to the peace. As Churchill described it, he, having been responsible for no commitment in relation to Russia – and, indeed he had not – 'became an heir to the pledges and tragedies' of the situation.[44] His policy was 'Contract your commitments; select your obligations; and make a success of those to which you are able to adhere'. In practice, however, Churchill was to become the principal advocate of policies designed to secure the military otherthrow of the 'nameless beast' of Bolshevik Government. Time and again he was to urge upon the War Cabinet the need for a clear policy, which he believed should be a policy of active intervention, in relation to Russia. Lloyd George recognised clearly the force of opinion against Bolshevism. In *The Truth about the Peace Treaties* he describes how there was 'throughout the Allied countries, especially amongst the propertied classes, an implacable hatred, born of real fear, of Bolshevism'. There could, he said be no doubt 'that the great majority of the inhabitants of Western Europe and America would have liked to see Bolshevism crushed, but no one was prepared to undertake the task'. He recognised, too, the inherent contradictions of the existing policy, but whereas Churchill drew the conclusion that a concerted effort was needed to overthrow the Bolsheviks, Lloyd

George sought, not always consistently, to end the intervention and bring Russia back into the community of nations. 'We could', he wrote, 'prolong the Civil War, perhaps for years until Russia had become a continent of desolation stretching from Central Europe to the Eastern shores of Asia, but we could not achieve any solution by force and certainly not a final or satisfactory solution.'[45]

The great debate began at the meeting of the Imperial War Cabinet on the last day of 1918,[46] when Churchill sought to swing his colleagues in favour of decisive collective intervention, while Lloyd George made it clear that he was opposed to intervention in any shape and argued that the one sure way of establishing the power of Bolshevism in Russia was to attempt to suppress it with foreign troops. In accepting Lloyd George's arguments, the Cabinet nevertheless registered provisos about the need to continue material help to the anti-Bolshevik forces and to support, without military intervention, those who might be threatened by external Bolshevik aggression. The continuing debate can be traced through the Cabinet minutes and documents of 1919 and 1920. Lloyd George commented[47] that Churchill 'threw the whole of his dynamic energy and genius into organising an armed intervention against Russia'. It is legitimate to wonder whether, had it not been for the pressure of Churchill, Lloyd George's policy might have prevailed more quickly and a constructive relationship with Russia been established much earlier. It is equally legitimate to wonder whether, had Churchill's advice been followed, the actions which at various times brought Kolchak from Vladivostok to the Volga, Denikin to within 250 miles of Moscow, Yudenich to the gates of Petrograd and the Poles to Kiev might have brought about the fall of the Soviet Government. The truth is, however, that the great debate was of more symbolic than practical significance and was largely irrelevant to what actually happened in Russia.

British policy continued to be inspired in the peace very much as it had been in the war – and indeed very much as it has been in the decades which have followed – by an attempt to grapple with the practical day-to-day realities rather than by the adoption of one or another grand design. Policy had to be developed within the limits imposed by the physical impossibility of immediate withdrawal of the forces in Russia and the practical difficulty of any significant reinforcement; the war weariness of the British people; the financial burden of continued intervention; the balance of political opinion, with the strident anti-Bolshevism of Lord Northcliffe and the main body of the Conservative party confronting the growing force of left-wing sentiment; the discord among the former Allies; and the failure of the anti-Bolshevik forces in Russia to recognise the new mood of the Russian people. The war in Russia was politically and militarily unwinnable with the forces which could be committed to it. Yet simply to walk away from the problem was an option which no member of the Government would have advocated. So Russia worked out her own future while Britain, moving by fits and starts over a period of eighteen months, gradually withdrew first her own forces and then her support for the anti-Bolshevik forces, having sought first to break and then to come to terms with the reality of the power of the first Soviet Government.

BOLSHEVIK PEACE OVERTURES

The first practical trial of strength between those who were more inclined to fight the Bolsheviks and those who were inclined to do a deal with them came when feelers were put out by the Bolsheviks for an armistice between the Russian and British forces and the opening of peace discussions. Chicherin himself spoke of 'buying ourselves out as we did in Brest'[48] and it is reasonable to conclude that the initiative was serious, although any agreement might well have proved as ephemeral as the Brest treaty. What is important for the assessment of British policy is that the War Cabinet decided[49] to follow up the first approach. President Wilson approved. The French Government were then consulted and in the face of their strong opposition no action was taken.

PRINKIPO

With the opening of the Peace Conference, the policy making process was further complicated by the need for the Prime Minister and Balfour to spend much time in Paris, leaving Curzon in temporary charge of the Foreign Office until he finally took it over in 1919. Neither in London nor in Paris could effective British policy be made. In the Conference Lloyd George tried to secure agreement that the Allies should deal with the Soviet Government as well as with the various anti-Bolshevik authorities located in Paris. Once again, in the face of French refusal 'to make any pact with this criminal regime' he failed, but it was possible to secure agreement to a proposal that the various parties in Russia should cease military action and meet the Allies on Prinkipo Island in the Sea of Marmora. To the considerable satisfaction of the French Government, the initiative failed because the Bolshevik acceptance, although embodying substantial concessions, was qualified by a refusal to cease military operations and was met by a flat rejection by the other parties.

At Churchill's request the War Cabinet considered policy once again.[50] The Bolsheviks, he said, were getting stronger every day. If we were going to withdraw it should be at once. If we were going to intervene we should send larger forces. He foresaw the menace of an eventual alliance between Germany, Japan and a Bolshevik Russia and was for intervention. 'A million men?' queried the Prime Minister. The Cabinet decided to commission a paper on the various options. Two days later Churchill went in Lloyd George's place to the Peace Conference, argued the case for disposing of the Prinkipo proposal if the Bolsheviks would not agree to cease military operations, and put forward a 'Proposal for a Committee of the Associated Powers to examine the possibilities of Allied Military Intervention in Russia'. Lloyd George, concerned that Churchill was 'planning a war against the Bolsheviks', telegraphed, agreeing to the disposal of Prinkipo, but begging Churchill 'not to commit this country to what would be a purely mad enterprise out of hatred of Bolshevik principles'.[51] So, both the plan for discussions and the plan for concerted intervention were abandoned, the Russian Civil War took its course and the Western frontier of Russia remained to be settled. An Anglo-Russian bilateral agreement would probably not have been attainable in the current state of British opinion and the Prinkipo initiative could scarcely have resulted in agreement between the Bolsheviks and their opponents within Russia. That struggle could only be resolved by force. What Prinkipo might have done was, however, to have facilitated the process of withdrawal from intervention. As it was, with the movement towards a more stable relationship, whether on a bilateral or a multilateral basis, frustrated, the British Government was left with its policy of half-hearted intervention, exhorted to belligerence by France and to withdrawal by the United States, while Japan pursued her own interests in Siberia, and Germany was, for a brief period, in no position to undertake any independent action.

WITHDRAWAL OF BRITISH TROOPS

So far as the direct involvement of British fighting units was concerned, the decisions of principle were taken quickly by the British Government. On 4 March 1919 the War Cabinet decided to withdraw from North Russia[52] and on 6 March the decision was taken to withdraw from the Caucasus and the Caspian.[53] The withdrawal from the North was not accomplished before a volunteer relief brigade had been recruited and, the better to cover the evacuation, had carried out a substantial drive southwards from Archangel. In the South, an attempt to transfer responsibility for the Caucasus to Italy ended in a fiasco, but, with the withdrawal of the two battalions from Siberia, the only British fighting unit left in Russia by the autumn of 1919 was a battalion which remained at Batum until the Turkish peace settlement in 1920. Thus, the decision to withdraw the limited British ground forces which had been deployed in Russia between the summer of 1918 and the autumn of 1919 was taken without their having been engaged in substantial hostilities against the Bolsheviks and without their direct operations having had any significant effect upon the outcome of the Civil War. Before the withdrawal could become effective, however, the fortunes of the anti-Bolshevik forces were to change dramatically.

CONTINUED SUPPORT FOR THE WHITE FORCES

Far from implying the end of the British involvement in the Civil War, the decision to withdraw marked the beginning of a more serious phase. There was some force in the argument which the British Government had espoused shortly after the Revolution, that the Russian state had disintegrated and that, in the absence of an effective central Government, other powers were fully entitled to deal with such autonomous bodies as had established themselves in parts of it. Where, as in the case of Poland and Finland, the Bolsheviks themselves accepted the creation of new independent states, the doctrine was unexceptionable, even if the application of it was anything but simple. Beyond this, however, the complexities escalated with the differing situation of the Baltic States, whose independence would in due course be recognised; the Caucasian states of Georgia, Armenia and Azerbaidjan which had a good case but could not sustain it against the Bolshevik armies; and regions such as Siberia, the Ukraine and White Russia which could not have been severed from the control of Moscow without reducing Russia to something like the principality which confronted the Tartars in the fifteenth century. Moreover, among the anti-Bolshevik commanders were some who sought primarily local objectives and others whose aim was to establish a new Imperial Russia within its pre-Revolutionary borders. Thus it was that, ignoring President Wilson's advice not to meddle in other people's revolutions, the British Government was led into a post-war stage of intervention in which its political and financial commitment was substantial and its power to control events minimal. Confronted by the need to determine whether British interests would be better served by the further disintegration of Imperial Russia or by the establishment of a strong non-Bolshevik central Government, the British Government was divided, but the pressure of anti-Bolshevik opinion in Britain had its effect in prolonging and extending the moral and material support which was given to the forces of Kolchak in Siberia, Alexeyev, Denikin and Wrangel in succession in the South and Yudenich in the North. Their story is the story of the Russian Civil War and this is not the place to retell it. What we must note here is the tangle into which the British Government was led by the decision not to abandon those whom it had regarded as its friends in Russia. The support to the anti-Bolshevik forces was continued not only out of a sense of loyalty, but in response to the widespread hope in Parliament and in a substantial sector of public opinion that those forces would prevail and that in consequence the Government of Russia would pass into the hands of men who would not seek to overthrow the whole structure of European society.

Lloyd George was faced in April 1919 with a Parliamentary revolt occasioned primarily by concern about reparations, but also by worries among the Conservatives about his apparently over-accommodating attitude to the Bolsheviks. In a statement clearly designed to appease right-wing criticism, he took the opportunity to repudiate not only the idea of recognition of the Bolsheviks, but even the enquiries which the American diplomat William Bullitt had made, after discussions with British officials, as to possible terms for the ending of hostilities in Russia and the establishment of normal relations and which had elicited a specific and not unpromising Soviet response. The Prime Minister described military intervention as 'the greatest act of stupidity that any Government could possibly commit', but at the same time justified continued material support for the anti-Bolshevik forces on the ground that it would have been thoroughly unworthy to say to those who had tried to reconstruct the Eastern front, 'Thank you; we are exceedingly obliged to you. You have served our purpose. We need you no longer. Now let the Bolshevists cut your throats.'[54] Describing his handling of the debate Lloyd George wrote subsequently:[55] 'To the majority of British citizens Bolshevism was a hideous and a terrifying monster. The action of the British Government in attempting to deal with it was represented as tendering a friendly hand to murder whilst it was reeking with the blood of its victims.'

It was against this background that the British assistance to the anti-Bolshevik forces was maintained and indeed increased. It took the form not only of supplies of equipment, but also of military and political missions, whose task was to maintain political liaison with the Russian generals and their embryo Governments, to administer the supply of equipment and to assist in the training of those who were to use it. During the spring and summer of 1919 Major General Ironside and later General Rawlinson were in North Russia, with Foreign Office political advisers; Major-General Knox, the former Military Attaché in Petrograd, was with Kolchak in Siberia where Sir Charles Eliot was High Commissioner; Major-General Holman was in the South with Denikin; Major-General Thomson commanded the two British divisions which had not yet been withdrawn from the Caucasus; and Lieutenant-General Gough with a civilian British Commissioner was with Yudenich in the Baltic provinces.

It was with no great enthusiasm that Lloyd George agreed to the continuation of supplies to the anti-Bolshevik generals, but suddenly, in May 1919, it seemed that they were on the verge of success and that, with the German war over, the fantasy of the previous year was about to be realised. Kolchak and the Czechs advanced west of the Urals, almost to the Volga, and a junction with Ironside's forces moving south from Archangel did not seem out of the question. In the South, Denikin had begun the advance which was to carry him to within 250 miles of Moscow. In Paris and London Ministers began to think of the nature of the Government which, after the victory, would succeed the Bolsheviks. A note to Kolchak was despatched on 27 May over the signatures of the French, British, Italian, American and Japanese heads of Government, specifying conditions for the establishment of a democratic Russia with independence for Finland and Poland and autonomy for Estonia, Latvia, Lithuania, and the Caucasian and Trans-Caspian territories. If Kolchak and his associates gave satisfactory guarantees on these points, they would be assisted with 'munitions, supplies and food to establish themselves as the Government of all Russia'. A satisfactory reply was received and on 12 June the heads of Government confirmed their willingness to extend to Kolchak and his associates the promised support. As Churchill commented,[56] 'The moment chosen by the Supreme Council for their declaration was almost exactly the moment when that declaration was certainly too late.'

THE BLOCKADE OF RUSSIA

The summer of 1919, when the British Government had already decided to withdraw its operational forces from Russia and to continue only with the supply of material, proved to be the high point of the intervention. It was a high point in the advances made by the anti-Bolshevik forces; in the degree of political recognition accorded to them; and in the direct involvement of British forces in their operations. It was at this stage that the British Government was forced to consider whether it was now at war with the Bolsheviks. The issue was precipitated not by the operations on land, but by the attempt of the Allied heads of Government to agree upon a policy for the continuation, after the signature of the peace treaty with Germany, of the blockade of Russia. The blockade was administered by units of the British fleet in the Baltic. President Wilson was adamant that, if there was no state of war with Russia, there was no legal justification for a blockade of Russia. The British Cabinet decided on 4 July[57] that 'a state of war did exist between Britain and Bolshevik Russia' and in consequence British naval forces were authorised to engage the enemy. The blockade, although enforced by the British navy, was, however, a matter for collective decision by the Allies. It was Balfour who drafted the telegram for the other heads of Government to send to President Wilson on the justification for the blockade. In true Balfourian style, it neatly evaded the question:

> Russia during this period of transition is not a state, but a collection of *de facto* governments at war with each other . . . . The Allied and Associated powers are not in a state of belligerency with Russia, but it is quite true to say that they are involved in military operations with one of these *de facto* governments and are supplying

arms and ammunition to the others. . . . It may not be right to describe this condition of things as war, but it cannot be right to consider it as peace.[58]

It was not until the autumn that a compromise was agreed upon among the Allies and the German Government and the neutrals were asked to operate an embargo on commercial and financial transactions with Russia.

CHANGING FORTUNES IN THE CIVIL WAR

On land, events had moved with remarkable swiftness and the Cabinet was left struggling to adapt its policies to the changing fortunes of the various parties in the Civil War. The proclaimed decision of the Allied Governments to assist Kolchak to establish a Government for the whole of Russia stimulated a Bolshevik offensive which met with such success that within two months Curzon had written Kolchak off as a lost cause.[59] At the beginning of July, as Kolchak was retreating, Denikin launched his major offensive from the South, sweeping towards Moscow on a front of 1000 miles. Abandoning Kolchak, the Cabinet decided[60] to concentrate British assistance on the southern theatre, bringing home the two battalions from Siberia and giving all the available resources to Denikin. Among the equipment supplied to him had been tanks and aircraft. It made sense that the British mission should contain officers and men capable of instructing the Russians in the use of this equipment, but the Cabinet can scarcely have envisaged that these instructors should themselves take the British tanks and aircraft into action against the Bolsheviks. As it was, their operations played a significant part in Denikin's swift advance. Orel, 250 miles from Moscow, was reached early in October. Moscow itself seemed within his grasp and it was necessary for the War Office to intervene to prevent the bombing of the capital by British aircraft.

Even before Denikin began his advance from the South, Yudenich was gathering an army in the Baltic provinces and seeking Finnish support for an attack on Petrograd. The British Government and the Allies collectively, while indicating their readiness to concur in a Finnish attack, refused to take responsibility for it. Consequently, the Finns held back and there ensued a ludicrous incident in which General Gough's assistant, Brigadier-General Marsh, acting on

Gough's instructions, with the support of Pirie-Gordon, the Acting British High Commissioner and of French and American representatives, but in the absence of both Gough and Yudenich, virtually ordered the members of Yudenich's Political Council to constitute themselves as the North West Russian Government for the Provinces of Pskov, Novgorod and Petrograd. Not until it was all done were the War Office and the Foreign Office informed. A bewildered Balfour was left to report belatedly to the Supreme Allied Council in Paris on 20 August, with the comment that the representatives of the three countries 'seemed to have been engaged in fostering a coup d'état without consulting their own Governments'.[61] Gough was reprimanded and recalled, but the attack on Petrograd was launched without Finnish assistance. On 18 August British motor torpedo boats, supported by British aircraft, sank two Russian battleships, a destroyer and a submarine depot ship. Yudenich penetrated into the suburbs of Petrograd, but his victories were ephemeral and by November his army and his Government had ceased to exist. In the Archangel sector, where the British Government had decided in March to withdraw its forces, the summer of 1919 saw some of the fiercest fighting as the two relief brigades, enlisted to support the evacuation, were used for offensive operations against the Bolsheviks in the course of which the British forces used gas, albeit without any great effect,[62] before their final withdrawal in the autumn. The autumn also saw the withdrawal of the British forces from the Caucasus.

The last, flickering hopes that the Bolsheviks might be displaced as the Government of Russia came in the autumn, when, at the height of Denikin's success, Kolchak launched a counter-offensive in Siberia and there came renewed pressure for formal recognition. The British Government had reason to be grateful for Curzon's scepticism, when he minuted on 19 October:[63] 'We seem to be swinging round rather rapidly.' A fortnight earlier he had been reading the predictions by the head of the Russian Department, J. D. Gregory, of the failure of Kolchak and the impending collapse of Denikin. Now, he found Gregory 'advocating . . . the hasty despatch of Commissioners right and left so as to catch the rays of the rising sun'. Gregory, in reply, argued the need to adapt to any change in the situation 'with no matter what rapidity it upsets previous calculations', but Curzon fortunately saved the British Government from yet another humiliating muddle by deciding to wait. He did not need to wait long. By the beginning of 1920 the British Government was considering how to organise the evacuation to the Crimea of the remnants of Denikin's forces; on 6 February 1920 Kolchak was executed by the Bolsheviks in Irkutsk; in March the post of High Commissioner in Siberia was abolished. The Caucasus was closer to Curzon's heart and as the Bolshevik forces moved southwards and eastwards in the wake of Denikin's retreating army, Oliver Wardrop, formerly Consul-General in Moscow and now British High Commissioner for Transcaucasia, urged the need for support. On 10 January 1920, at Curzon's recommendation, the Allied Foreign Ministers decided upon immediate *de facto* recognition of Georgia and Azerbaidjan, leaving Armenia's future for consideration in the context of the peace treaty with Turkey. Fortunately Curzon was dissuaded from the idea of reintroducing the two British divisions which had just been withdrawn and thus the creation of a new area of British military involvement against the Bolsheviks was avoided.

The British Government, which had been eager to introduce Japanese forces into Siberia, showed rather more caution in responding to suggestions that Finnish forces should be used in order to capture Petrograd and rejecting the use of Bulgarian forces to prop up Denikin. Plans for the use of various foreign forces had been a feature of the Civil War and had originated, above all, in France. Lloyd George recounts how, early in 1919, Marshal Foch 'outlined a scheme for a vast attack on the Soviet Union by Finns, Esthonians, Letts, Lithuanians, Poles, Czechs, Russians – in fact all the peoples that lie along the fringe of Russia – all under Allied direction' with Poland as its base and Polish forces as its spearhead.[64] Later, when Yudenich's offensive against Petrograd was hanging in the balance, serious consideration was given to the use of German troops in his support. In a speech in April,[65] Churchill had aired the idea, much to Lloyd George's alarm, that Germany might find 'a way of atonement' through the fight against Bolshevism and he gave more specific expression to this idea in a Cabinet memorandum written in September[66] in which, while pointing to the potential danger of a future German–Russian combination, he was inclined at least to use the German forces in the Baltic states to sustain Yudenich, if not to join him in the attack of Petrograd. The Foreign Office view was clear: 'It would be better that Petrograd should not be captured at all than that it should be captured by the Germans', and nothing came of the idea. More serious however, was the resurrection, in that autumn of 1919, of Foch's scheme for an assault based on Poland. Preoccupied with fighting on three fronts, against Kolchak in Siberia,

Yudenich in the Baltic and Denikin in the South, the Bolsheviks
were at that time in no position to wage war against Poland. The
new Polish Government took advantage of the situation to establish
a hold on territory well to the East of that to which they had a clear
ethnographical claim and on 14 September the Allied Council
considered a proposal by Paderewski, the Polish premier, to provide
half a million men to march on Moscow at a cost to the Allied
Governments of £600 000 a day. The minutes record that, 'In response
to an enquiry by M. Paderewski, M. Clemenceau explained that the
Council did not desire that the Poles should march on Moscow'.[67]
The British Government did, however, seek, without success, Polish
cooperation with Denikin's forces. The Polish–Soviet War was to
break with full fury in the following year, and to become a significant
factor in Anglo-Soviet relations. Before that, however, the British
Government, reluctantly accepting the failure of the intervention,
had begun, under Lloyd George's personal stimulus, the reversal of
policy which was to make Britain, hitherto the most active, albeit
not the most vehement, participant in the policy of intervention, the
leader in the movement to establish relations with the Soviet Union.
It was the first of those major oscillations which were to characterise
the relationship throughout the next seventy years.

3 Facing the Facts[1]

A NEW RELATIONSHIP – THE FIRST MOVE

The Lord Mayor's Banquet provides the traditional occasion for a major speech by the Prime Minister. On Saturday 8 November 1919, for the first time since the end of the war, the dignitaries of the City of London, the Ambassadors to the Court of St James, the judges, the clergy and members of the Government, gathered in the full splendour of the victorious citadel of free enterprise to listen to David Lloyd George. *The Times*, reporting the speech on the Monday, said 'Few utterances more serious in effect or involving issues wider than their bearing upon the welfare of the Empire have ever been made by a British Prime Minister in the historic Guildhall'. What the Prime Minister had done was to give the first indication of a change of policy in relation to Russia. His words were carefully chosen: Britain could not afford to continue the intervention and he was glad that the troops were out of the Russian quicksand. He hoped that the time was not distant when the Prinkipo attempt might be renewed and 'when the winter gives time for all sections there to reflect and to reconsider the situation, an opportunity may offer itself for the Great Powers of the world to promote peace and concord in that great country'.[2]

Cautious though the Prime Minister's language was, his intentions were far-reaching. Intervention had failed. If the power of the Bolsheviks could not be broken, then its reality must be accepted. The time had come to turn back to the path first hesitantly trodden with the Lockhart mission, the Prinkipo proposal and the attempt to respond to Chicherin's peace overtures. A stable relationship had to be established with the new Russia, but now the route to it was to lie through the resumption of trade. The responsibilities of international statesmanship and the requirements of British interest coincided.

The steps by which, in the course of just over a year, Lloyd George secured the conclusion of the Anglo-Soviet Trade Agreement of 1921 and thus made Britain the first of the wartime Allies to accord *de facto* recognition to the Soviet Government are one of the more fascinating episodes of diplomatic history.[3] The British Government had simultaneously to construct a totally new relationship with the Soviet leadership; to liquidate the remains of the intervention policy by jettisoning those anti-Bolshevik forces which it had hitherto supported; and, with the outbreak of a bitter Polish–Soviet war, to grapple with one of the perennial problems of Russia's relationship with the West. Discussions which had been presented as a limited negotiation with representatives of the Russian cooperatives on a possible exchange of goods rapidly became the first attempt by a Western government to confront the central issue of the relationship with Soviet Russia: Was the Soviet Government determined to establish itself as the driving force behind a process of doctrinally-determined revolutionary change throughout the world or was it prepared to renounce this role and establish relations on a basis of mutual interest? The issue was to be confronted in these terms. It was to be put bluntly to the Soviet leadership. But it was not to be resolved.

The Prime Minister had never been happy with the policy of intervention. By the autumn of 1919, the disastrous effect of the war on Britain's finances had not yet fully impressed itself on the public and it was to be nearly another two years before the 'Geddes axe' was to fall on government expenditure. Already, however it was abundantly clear that the demobilisation of the wartime army, the war-weariness of those who were still serving, the burden of debt and the growing financial stringency left neither the military nor the financial resources for continued intervention. The mounting pressure of the Labour party and the trade unions for a change of course was shifting the balance in the direction Lloyd George wanted, but politically, both in Britain itself and in relation to France, his room for manoeuvre was limited. In the summer of 1919, in protest at the offensive operations being undertaken by the British relief brigade in Archangel, the Labour party at its annual conference had passed a resolution denouncing intervention and instructing the National Executive to consult the Parliamentary Committee of the Trades Union Congress 'with the view to effective action being taken to enforce these demands by the unreserved use of their political and industrial power'.[4] The threat of strike action was not implemented, but the mood of the left was clear and the Government recognised it when taking the final decision on British withdrawal.[5] On the right, however, there was still no disposition to have dealings with the Bolsheviks and Lloyd George's Guildhall speech was met with fury.

The CIGS commented in a private letter, 'Our PM seems to have thrown a Prinkipo fly into the turtle soup with the result that the City Fathers vomited up the whole dish'.[6] *The Times* quoted a French press reference to 'capitulation to the Bolsheviks', demanded no 'bartering with Bolshevism' and, denouncing the Prime Minister's 'irresponsible improvisations', sought to reassure its French friends that 'fortunately his voice is not the voice of Britain'. In reply to a barrage of Parliamentary questions, Bonar Law explained that what the Prime Minister had expressed was 'simply a hope that there may be some method of arranging peace in Russia'. The Prime Minister himself made a statement two days later, pointing out that in the past twelve months some £100 million had been spent or sanctioned in support of the anti-Bolshevik forces. New obligations could not be contemplated. A settlement of the Russian problem was essential, but it would have to be discussed by the Allied and Associated powers and there would be no new British policy without full discussion in the House.

Then, quietly and deviously, Lloyd George went ahead. His Foreign Secretary, Curzon, was at this time preoccupied with the fate of the Caucasus. In the lower reaches of the Foreign Office Lloyd George would certainly have found support. Mr Harvey, later as Sir Oliver Harvey to serve as Ambassador in Paris, had written a paper[7] some months earlier, arguing the case for an early negotiation on the ground that the bulk of the Russian people accepted the Bolshevik Government and that Lenin's Government might as well be left to justify itself in the light of its works. The sooner Britain negotiated, the better the terms would be. At that time the Cabinet had, however, committed itself to further support for Denikin. Harvey's paper never reached Curzon. So, when the time for a change of course came, Lloyd George relied upon his own staff, Hankey and Kerr, and in particular E. F. Wise, an official of the Ministry of Food and principal British representative on the Supreme Economic Council, who was later to become a Labour MP and economic adviser to the Soviet cooperative trading organisation. It was Wise who proposed that this organisation, Tsentrosoyuz, should be used to provide a non-governmental cover for the resumption of trade.[8]

THE ALLIES ARE CONSULTED

Lloyd George's Guildhall speech had been badly received in Washington, but Clemenceau was by this time weary of the muddle of intervention, concerned about Germany and anxious simply to put a barbed wire fence around Russia. He made little difficulty over the idea of some non-political commercial exchanges and thus, after a brief discussion on 16 January 1920, the Supreme Council put out an announcement that it would 'permit the exchange of goods on the basis of reciprocity between the Russian people and the Allied and neutral countries'. Clemenceau, on behalf of the Supreme Council, informed the American Government, explaining that the attempt to overthrow the Bolshevik regime by anti-Bolshevik forces supported by the Allies had failed; Russian food was needed in the West and the reorganisation of trade would be the best means of destroying the 'extremist forms of Bolshevism' in Russia; it was not proposed to recognise the Bolsheviks or permit their representatives to enter Allied countries; there would be a policy of non-intervention within Russia, but support for neighbouring states, including Georgia, Azerbaidjan and Armenia, if their independence were threatened.[9]

At a subsequent conference in London, Lloyd George secured Allied agreement on the broad lines of his new policy and the Allied Governments made a formal statement[10] to the effect that:

i) They would not advise 'the communities which border on the frontiers of Soviet Russia and whose independence or *de facto* autonomy they have recognized . . . to continue a war which may be injurious to their own interests'. If, however, Soviet Russia were to attack them inside their own legitimate frontiers, the Allies would give them every possible support;

ii) They would not enter into diplomatic relations with the Soviet Government 'until the Bolshevist horrors have come to an end and the Government of Moscow is ready to conform its methods and diplomatic conduct to those of all civilised governments';

iii) Subject to this, commerce between Russia and Europe would be 'encouraged to the utmost degree possible'.

iv) The Council of the League of Nations should be invited to send a fact-finding mission to Russia.

So there began, at British initiative, the process of establishing relations with Soviet Russia, but for the present, in deference to right-wing opinion, it could not be described as such. The great debate was not over. Nor, in Russia, was the fighting. There can be a peculiar viciousness to civil war and the reports coming out of Russia lost nothing in the telling. There was terror on both sides and, with the collapse of administration, its direct effects were aggravated by malnutrition and disease. Returning British residents like the Reverend F. W. North, the Anglican Chaplain from Moscow, argued that trade would merely prolong Russia's agony. Against them a group of the Government's former military and civilian advisers in Russia addressed a memorial to the Prime Minister arguing for peace, pointing out the risk of growing German influence in Russia and claiming that the non-Bolshevik Governments in Siberia and the South had not proved superior in humanity to the Bolsheviks, while in energy, union and resource they were inferior. Their view of the ability of the Bolsheviks was shared by the CIGS who, in a letter of September 1919, had noted that with the single exception of Denikin, there was no doubt that Lenin and Trotsky and those around them were far the abler men.[11]

In the public campaign against any accommodation with the Bolsheviks, Churchill spoke of 'the ghost of the Russian bear padding across the immense field of snow', sitting outside the Peace Conference in silent reproach, disturbing Afghanistan, distracting Persia and creating agitation and unrest in India. On the day after the decision to re-open trade had been taken, he debated with his colleagues Curzon's proposal to send troops to the defence of Georgia and Azerbaidjan. His own policy, said Churchill, was what it had been throughout 1919: 'Have a definite policy of making war on the Bolsheviks with every available resource and by every possible means.' But, if this could not be done,

> 'then do not let us blind ourselves to the facts which we have to face; and do not let us, in a pitiful effort to conceal those facts from our own minds or from the public at large for a few months longer, fling a few handfuls of British soldiers and sailors into positions from which it may be impossible to extricate them and where their poor lives will only be another unavailing sacrifice to the prolonged indecision of the Allies'.[12]

By this time, there was no will among British ministers to embark upon another half-hearted military campaign in Russia, and although the CIGS hated Lloyd George's politics he was determined to avoid the strain of new commitments on Britain's overstretched forces. Curzon's proposal stood no real chance and it was only a few months before the Caucasian states, whose governments had so recently been recognised by the Allies – *de jure* in the case of Georgia – were forcefully taken over by the Bolsheviks. It took but a little time before the whole thrust of British policy was turned towards the liquidation of the British commitment in South Russia in order to reach an accommodation with the Bolsheviks.

THE POLISH–SOVIET WAR

The first effective negotiations between the British and Soviet Governments had begun in the autumn of 1919 when, after an exchange of radio messages between Curzon and Chicherin, the Labour MP James O'Grady was appointed to negotiate with Litvinov on neutral ground in Copenhagen, for an agreement on the exchange of prisoners. The agreement,[13] which was concluded on 12 February 1920, was less than watertight in its drafting and was to give rise to substantial difficulties in implementation.

Concurrently with the signature of this agreement, preliminary discussions on trade were begun. Before they could be developed into substantive negotiations, the British Government were to encounter major problems in relation to Poland and to the White forces in South Russia, where Wrangel had taken over the command from Denikin. The new Polish Government, purporting to liberate a quasi-independent Ukraine, sought to take advantage of the chaos of Russia and push forward its own eastern frontier. In January 1920, Lloyd George had made it clear to the Polish Foreign Minister that the British Government was not prepared to encourage Poland to make war on the Bolsheviks and would not support Poland against a Soviet attempt to regain areas which were indisputably Russian. Britain would, however, assist Poland if a sincere attempt to make peace on fair terms were rejected and Poland were attacked.

While Polish–Soviet negotiations dragged on through the spring of 1920, Lloyd George was busy, setting up the arrangements for trade talks. Then, in April 1920, the Polish forces launched a major offensive which, by 7 May, was to bring the capture of Kiev. Curzon had already decided upon a policy of non-intervention,[14] but a minor domestic crisis erupted when British dockers, having consulted Ernest Bevin, refused to load guns and ammunition consigned to Poland. Bonar Law put the Government's case in Parliament, stating that neither the British Government nor the British people had the will

to throw British forces into the dispute and the Poles should be left
to work as they thought best. With Poland on the offensive, non-
intervention looked an easy option, but within a few months, Soviet
forces were to be at the gates of Warsaw and there was to be talk of
a new European war in defence of Poland. That, however, was for
the future. For the present, Curzon's preoccupation was with the
attempt to arrange terms for the honourable surrender of the remnants
of the anti-Bolshevik forces under Wrangel and thus to eliminate
without discredit to the British Government the last remnant of
the intervention. Lloyd George's was to push on with the trade
negotiations.

THE TRADE NEGOTIATIONS BEGIN

The prize of a trade agreement with Britain, the world's leading
financial and commercial power and the main supporter of the
intervention, meant a great deal to the Soviet Government. They
quickly brushed aside the existing, non-Bolshevik, London representatives of the cooperatives and nominated a delegation led by
Litvinov, with Leonid Krasin as his deputy. Krasin, an electrical
engineer and previously manager of the Siemens plant in Russia, had
been responsible for the supply of equipment for the new Red Army
and was now Commissar for Foreign Trade. The negotiations were
quite clearly now to become formal and inter-Governmental. In
order to sustain something of the appearance of conducting purely
discussions about commercial exchanges, with no political recognition, Lloyd George refused to permit Litvinov to enter Britain and,
with the agreement of the Allies, the delegation led by Krasin were
received for the discussion of 'general questions arising out of the
resumption of trade', while Litvinov, still nominally their leader,
remained in Copenhagen.

Rather than prejudice the opening of discussions, the Soviet
Government accepted not only the exclusion of Litvinov from Britain,
but also a requirement that the members of the Delegation should
give a formal undertaking, orally from Krasin and in writing from
the others, not to interfere in British politics or internal affairs and
not to speak to the press without the approval of the British
Government. They knew that, whatever the British Prime Minister
might say in order to appease his critics in Britain and in France,
they now had the opportunity to achieve both the substance and the

form of recognition. Curzon, too, had his political objectives. He set them out in a paper for the Cabinet.[15] He wanted, and his Cabinet colleagues agreed, to deal with those cases 'in which the Bolsheviks are either openly at war with peoples or States in whom we are concerned, or are engaged in propaganda, plots and alliances directed against British interests or the British Empire in the East'. He was particularly concerned about Soviet pressure on Afghanistan. He also wanted to secure the effective implementation of the February agreement on the exchange of prisoners. The Cabinet decided to seek a 'comprehensive agreement' on these matters, including the curbing of Communist propaganda in Britain and, if possible, some understanding on debts to British creditors. Soviet 'propaganda' was for many years to be a source of concern to British Governments and some misunderstanding may have been caused by the tendency to use the term to cover the whole apparatus of Soviet ideological penetration and subversion. The foundation of the Comintern (the Third International) in 1919 as the vehicle through which the Russian Communists would stimulate and control the further worldwide spread of revolution symbolised this threat. The Comintern's relative ineffectiveness, stemming largely from Lenin's insistence upon rigid adherence to Moscow doctrine, did little to lessen the concern of the British Government at the steady flow of reports of its aims and activities, if not successes. The search for formal safeguards was a feature of British–Soviet relations in the 1920s, culminating in the Arcos raid and the breach of relations. So far as trade was concerned, it was hoped that there might be an exchange of British goods for Russian gold, but a major objective was to secure a resumption of Russian supplies of food and raw materials to Europe. In view of the wide-ranging British objectives, the French Government were invited to join the talks, but refused.

The first meeting of the British and Soviet negotiators in 10 Downing Street on 31 May 1920 marked, in a very real sense, the beginning of the attempt to establish an effective and durable working relationship between the Soviet Union and the Western democracies, a task still unaccomplished today. *The Times* did not mince its words about the reception of Krasin, 'this representative of a blood-stained despot', or about Lloyd George's policies, which had been 'kept from the public eye when he has been afraid that in their nakedness they would revolt the public conscience'.[16] The two sides set out the obstacles which they saw to the conclusion of a trade agreement. These, in effect, were their political objectives. For the Soviet side they were the ending of the state of *de facto* hostilities and, in particular, the Polish war, the formal lifting of the blockade, the legal protection of Soviet assets and the exchange of trade representatives with certain diplomatic privileges. For the British side, they were the problems of the comprehensive agreement on Bolshevik penetration which the Cabinet had agreed to seek.

The White forces in Russia were now jettisoned. On receiving the news of a new offensive by Wrangel on 6 June, Curzon decided that in good faith towards the Soviet Government the British mission to Wrangel must be withdrawn and all assistance terminated. That position was firmly held. An attempt to negotiate on behalf of Wrangel was abandoned and when, some five months later, the Soviet forces broke through into the Crimea, the British Government, despite an appeal from King George V on behalf of the women and children, refused any help, even with the evacuation.

Progress in the trade negotiations was, in some respects, by today's standards, surprisingly quick. Chicherin, the Soviet Foreign Minister, was prepared to contemplate a deal under which his Government would give far-reaching guarantees as to its foreign policy, including undertakings as to its participation in 'hostile activities'. Such guarantees could, however, only be given in the context of a broader settlement, preferably a general peace conference, in which similar guarantees would have to be given by the powers which had made war on Russia. As for the question of debts, these could only be considered on the basis of an agreement recognising the Soviet claims arising from the intervention. This, however, went beyond anything which Lloyd George could accept. He needed his guarantees as the price for a trade agreement and he needed an assurance on debt repayment without qualification. When Krasin held firm, he suspended the negotiations with a memorandum dated 30 June 1919, asking for 'categorical replies, yes or no' to the statement of conditions on which the British Government was willing to enter into a trade agreement. Abrupt in form, the memorandum nevertheless made a concession to the Soviet objective by proposing 'what is tantamount to a general armistice, as the condition of the resumption of trade relations, in the hope that this armistice may lead ere long to a general peace'.[17]

THE POLISH-SOVIET FRONTIER

A NEW THREAT OF WAR

There was in fact at this point incentive enough for the Soviet side to conclude a deal, but before that could happen the Polish–Soviet war was to take an alarming turn. With the capture of Kiev, the Polish forces had badly overstretched themselves. A Soviet counter-attack met with swift and dramatic success and it seemed possible that Poland might be overrun.

Lloyd George was meeting the French and Italian Prime Ministers at Spa in July of 1920 in order to discuss the growing problems of the application of the Treaty of Versailles to Germany. While he was there, the Polish crisis erupted and he was faced with the task of reconciling three elements of the Russian problem: a telegram from

Chicherin accepting the principles of the British memorandum on the trade agreement; an appeal by Poland for assistance in the war against Russia; and a perceived growing threat in terms of the German–Soviet relationship. Here were critical elements which were to recur throughout the years, as the British–Soviet relationship developed. In 1920 it was Britain which was in a position to exert a dominant influence over the outcome and it was Lloyd George who effectively controlled not only British, but also Allied policy. He could not, however, afford to quarrel too openly with France – despite his strong inclination to do so – and France was vehement, if not always practical, in support of Poland. A wireless message was therefore sent to the Soviet Government on 11 July with the Allied proposals. Poland was to sign an immediate armistice and withdraw to the line which the Supreme Council had fixed on 8 December 1919 and which became known as the Curzon line. (See map, p. 71.) The Soviet forces should stand 50 kilometres to the east of this line and there should then be a conference in London to make peace between Russia and the states on her Western borders. The British Government would neither assist Poland 'for any purpose hostile to Russia' or itself take any action hostile to Russia, but if the Russians were to refuse an armistice and take action against Poland on Polish territory, the British Government and its Allies would 'feel bound to assist the Polish nation to defend its existence with all the means at their disposal'.[18] Qualified though the commitment to Poland was, the CIGS was later to note in his diary: 'He [Lloyd George] is thinking of declaring war on the Bolsheviks, having thrown away every card in the pack.'[19] Britain might indeed have been drawn into the defence of Polish independence against Russia in 1920 and, as in 1939, would have had no means of giving direct and effective aid.

By the time Poland was ready to sue for an armistice, the Red Army had swept beyond the Curzon line in an advance which by mid-August was to bring it to the suburbs of Warsaw. Lloyd George was trapped. He had told Parliament[20] that 'if the Russian army still marches on, we shall have to give such assistance as is in our power to the Polish Government', but he knew, and the Cabinet was unanimous, that there was no question of committing British troops to the fight. He needed direct discussions with Russia. The Soviet Government rejected the London proposal for a conference in the form in which Lloyd George had put it forward, but agreed that a Soviet delegation should come to London 'not merely to conclude the trade agreement between Russia and the Allied Governments[*sic*] but also to discuss preliminary arrangements for the proposed peace conference'.[21] Krasin thus returned to London, accompanied by a member of the Politburo, Kamenev, with credentials 'to enter into negotiations with the British Government and also with the Governments of its Allies for the complete restoration of peaceful relations between the above mentioned countries and to sign to this effect a peace treaty as well as any other political and economic agreement'.

There was probably at this point more community of interest between Lloyd George and the Russians than may have appeared. For Lenin and his colleagues, a comprehensive settlement, recognising *de jure* Soviet Russia, ending foreign support for the remnants of the White armies and establishing Russia's western border was a prize worth gaining. If, at the same time, the Red Army could force a Communist Government upon Poland, so much the better. The Soviet tactic was therefore simultaneously to negotiate in London and fight in Poland. For Lloyd George, Poland was an embarrassment which he could not wholly shake off, but he was determined not to see British troops committed to another operation against Russia. In Russia itself, he wanted to avoid any new obligation to support the remnants of the White forces under Wrangel. Above all, he wanted to come to terms with the effective new rulers of Russia. Soviet and British interests might be reconciled, but the Soviet ideological offensive, backed by the Red Army, came close to frustrating Lloyd George's efforts.

In the summer of 1920, with its internal power nearly established and its armies pouring westwards, the Soviet leadership was inspired by the dream of carrying the revolution southwards into Moslem Central Asia, westwards into Poland and Germany and ultimately into Britain and France. Curzon had to watch, impotent, as the Caucasian republics fell to the Red Army. Pushing into Persia, a small Soviet force ejected the British garrison from Enzeli on the Caspian and with the withdrawal from Batum on the Black Sea, Curzon's first line of defence had gone. His anxiety to prevent the incursion of Soviet power into Afghanistan was the greater. But it was in Europe that the crisis broke. As the Soviet negotiators returned to Downing Street and the Soviet leadership proclaimed its respect for Polish independence, a Provisional Revolutionary Soviet was formed in occupied Poland and armistice terms were drafted, requiring the drastic reduction of the Polish army and the arming of Polish workers under the supervision of Russian, Polish and

Norwegian trade unions. Recognising that British opinion would not have tolerated a settlement designed so blatantly to force a Communist Government upon Poland, Kamenev put to Lloyd George terms for a Polish armistice which, while referring to a Citizens' Militia, obscured the reference to the arming of the Polish workers. The British authorities were able to break the Soviet Delegation's cypher and consequently had available the text of most of the messages exchanged between the Delegation in London and Chicherin in Moscow.[22] Deciphering took some time, however, and although the British Government were doubtful about the accuracy of the terms communicated to them by Kamenev, they decided on 10 August to send them to the Poles, commenting that if these terms were offered and if Poland refused them the British Government could not assume the responsibility of taking hostile action against Russia. In the event, Kamenev's manoeuvre was pointless, since the terms actually offered contained the requirement he had concealed and were seen by an angry French Prime Minister as leaving Poland 'entirely at the mercy of the Bolsheviks'. Lloyd George had warned that if Russia was 'out to challenge the institutions upon which the liberties of Europe and civilisation depend, we shall meet in the gate'.[23] He made clear that no Allied troops would be sent to Poland, but plans for a resumption of the blockade of Russia and other naval measures in the Baltic and Black Sea were prepared. *The Times* was calling for the 'same unanimity and same courage with which we faced the crisis of 1914', and there was widespread public alarm at the prospect of war with Russia.

THE LABOUR PARTY AND RUSSIA

The threat of conflict with Russia over Poland brought a political crisis in Britain. In 1920, interest began to develop as to the nature of the society which the Bolsheviks were creating. One of the first of the pilgrims to Moscow was George Lansbury, editor of the *Herald* who, on his return, wrote of the Bolsheviks 'striving to build a new Jerusalem'. Shortly after Lansbury came a Joint Labour party/TUC Delegation whose report, a relatively sober and balanced piece of work, praised the achievements of the Bolsheviks, but was sharply critical of their methods. At the same time Bertrand Russell was making his own visit, which was to result in the publication of *Bolshevism: Practice and Theory*, a work in which, with a sharper eye than he was sometimes to use in his later years, he wrote of the 'elaborate dogmas and inspired scriptures' of this movement inspired by violence and conflict and drew an analogy between Bolshevik power in Russia and the British Raj in India.

While the British Labour movement was trying to understand Russia and prevent British intervention, Lenin and his colleagues were doing their best to exploit industrial unrest and direct the course of revolutionary Communism in Britain. Their efforts resulted in almost complete failure at the hands of the great mass of the British Labour movement. With the founding on 1 August 1920 of the British National Communist Party and its explicit subservience to the doctrinal control of Lenin, exercised both direct and through the Moscow-based Third International, there was no room for compromise with the Labour Party. The Communist attempt to secure affiliation was rebuffed under the influence of men like Shinwell who spoke of the 'rigid cast-iron discipline imposed by Moscow', the miners' leader Hodges, who denounced the 'intellectual slaves of Moscow' and Ramsay MacDonald who warned against those who came holding out their right hand while concealing in their left the dagger which they would stick in the Labour Party's back. The struggle for the body and the soul of the British Labour movement was a not insignificant element in the tangled history of international Communism and, when the Communists lost, the International Labour Office was to write, 'London and Moscow are henceforth two antagonistic forces struggling for the supremacy over the working masses: the two poles round which the Socialist forces will crystallise.'[24] The early struggle was to have its significance not only at the time, but later, when Labour in power was to show itself fully alive to the reality of Soviet power and the techniques used in its deployment.

Conscious though the Labour Party was of the Bolshevik threat to its own independence, it was in no mood to tolerate military action against Russia in a war with Poland for which Poland was by no means blameless. The Report of the Labour Party/TUC Delegation coincided with the high point of anti-interventionist fervour during the Soviet–Polish war. A Council of Action was formed by the Labour Party and the Trades Union Council with the objective of deploying 'the whole industrial power of the organized workers' to prevent war with Russia, and Ernest Bevin led a delegation to speak to the Prime Minister. The anti-interventionist mood of the main mass of British Labour certainly had its effect on the Government. Ramsay MacDonald exaggerated when he wrote later of Labour's action saving Britain from war over Poland, but the Cabinet minutes of the period contain repeated references to the strength of public feeling against intervention and in a conference with the French Prime Minister at Lympne on 8-9 August, Lloyd George justified his caution by making the point that the working classes were frankly hostile to intervention. Certainly the Labour Party's position must have strengthened Lloyd George's resolve to press on with the task of constructing an inter-governmental relationship with Soviet Russia.

THE EXPULSION OF KAMENEV

Warsaw was saved by a successful Polish counter-offensive, but at this point Lloyd George's search for an agreement was almost frustrated by the determination of the Soviet leadership to use Kamenev and Krasin to promote the Bolshevik cause in Britain. As a condition of the opening of the trade negotiation, the Soviet delegation had undertaken not to interfere in the British political scene. It became apparent to British ministers, as a result of their interception of Soviet communications, that the delegation were ignoring this undertaking. Not only had Kamenev deceived the British Government over the terms offered to Poland, but the delegation were in close contact with the Council of Action in an effort to influence government policy over Poland and were also providing finance to the *Herald*. Litvinov, in a telegram sent from Copenhagen to Chicherin in Moscow, commented that 'In Russian matters it acts as if it were our organ'.[25] The Cabinet considered the evidence[26] and concluded that the conduct of Kamenev and Krasin was 'not compatible with the conditions under which their mission had been permitted to proceed to England'. Action was deferred until the situation in Poland was clearer, but as the Poles advanced eastwards, ministers received an intercepted telegram from Lenin telling Kamenev that, with an early Soviet victory over the Poles unlikely, the delegation should regard as its 'chief task' the spread of agitation among the British masses.[27] A Conference of Ministers chaired by Bonar Law on 2 September agreed that the delegation had been engaged in 'propaganda aimed at undermining the present economic organisation of society' and that they should be asked to leave.[28] This was possibly the make-or-break point in the negotiations. Those who were urging the expulsion of the delegation saw the possibility of frustrating a line of policy by Lloyd George which they believed to be fundamentally against the national interest. Lloyd George, for his part, was determined that his whole strategy of establishing relations with Soviet Russia through the medium of a trade agreement should not be jeopardised. Fortunately, Kamenev had already come to the conclusion that there was little point in his remaining in London. It was therefore possible for Lloyd George to make the gesture of accusing Kamenev of a 'gross breach of faith' and requiring him to leave, but continuing the negotiations with Krasin. In dealing with Kamenev, Lloyd George spoke in terms which can have left little doubt that his telegrams had been intercepted. A valuable source of intelligence may thus have been compromised, although subsequent intercepts continued to play a part in the determination of British policy. Such was the Soviet Government's interest in securing the trade agreement that Krasin was left to complete the negotiations.

CONCLUSION OF THE TRADE AGREEMENT

With the success of the Polish counter-offensive and the conclusion of a Polish–Soviet agreement under which the Polish frontier was established well to the east of the Curzon line, a major source of Anglo-Soviet tension was, for the moment, removed. Three other major problems remained:

i) The release of British prisoners, some of whom, despite the O'Grady–Litvinov agreement, were still held.
ii) The need for an assurance about recognition of outstanding Russian debts.
iii) The requirement for an ending of Soviet activity directed against British interests and, in particular, against the British position in India.

On 1 November, after the Government had restrained the Admiral commanding the British Mediterranean fleet from bombarding Odessa by sea and air, agreement was reached on the release of the remaining prisoners. This left the two remaining British points of principle to be argued out in a hard-fought Cabinet meeting on 17–18 November.[29] Lloyd George made it plain that he was no longer prepared to defer to the feelings of his more intransigent colleagues, above all Curzon, who argued against giving up the trump card of the trade agreement while British interests and the British Empire were 'exposed without mitigation to the ceaseless and deadly assaults on the part of the Bolshevik Government and its agents'.[30] This group demanded an end to hostile activity before conclusion of an agreement. Lloyd George knew he could not get this. He could require the inclusion of guarantees of this type – for what they might be worth – in an agreement, but to require that they should be honoured in advance was, he knew, unrealistic and, as Curzon knew equally well, tantamount to saying that there would be no agreement. Meanwhile the depression would grow deeper and unemployment would mount. Lloyd George won,[31] but against the votes of Austen Chamberlain, Chancellor of the Exchequer, Curzon, Foreign Secretary, Churchill, Secretary of State for War, and of the Colonial Secretary and the First Lord of the Admiralty. Significantly, Montagu, who held the responsibility for India, was not among those who dissented. Thus the decision to conclude the trade agreement was taken. The remaining negotiations lasted until 16 March 1921. On that date Krasin and Horne, President of the Board of Trade, concluded the formal agreement under which 'pending the conclusion of a formal general peace treaty', the two countries agreed broadly to most-favoured nation treatment of trade and shipping, together with consequential arrangements including the appointment of 'official agents'. The two parties were to refrain from 'hostile action or undertakings' and 'official propaganda against each other's institutions'. The Soviet Government undertook to refrain from hostile action against British interests, especially in India and Afghanistan and the British Government gave a similar undertaking in respect of 'countries which formed part of the former Russian Empire, and which have now become independent'. A separate joint declaration left the claims of both parties and their nationals to be dealt with in the context of a general Peace Treaty and in a side letter Horne spelt out in detail the British complaints about Soviet actions designed 'to secure facilities for attacks through Afghanistan against the peace of India'.[32]

It had taken Lloyd George about a year and a half from the Guildhall speech to signature of the agreement. The attempt to break Soviet power had ended in what Ramsay MacDonald described as 'nothing but absolute, nothing but complete, nothing but unmitigated failure'.[33] Was it realistic to suppose that it could now be tamed? Certainly, the road was now open to move from a limited trade agreement to a comprehensive settlement. Defending the agreement in Parliament,[34] Lloyd George spoke of the 'gentlemanly process of instruction' of the Soviet leaders, a process which would result in their conversion and would put an end to their 'wild schemes'. But to hope for such an evolution was to ignore the political realities in both countries. The signature of the agreement helped to establish Soviet power, but it did nothing to moderate Soviet ideology. Nor did it end the political debate in Britain. The divisions ran deep – divisions within the Cabinet, in Parliament and in the country. *The Times* reminded Curzon of his warning that *de facto* recognition would be used by the Soviet Government 'to spread the tentacles of their poisonous influence throughout the world'.[35] The distrust of Soviet intentions was profound. It was to dominate the course of relations during the two critical decades which saw the destruction of the Europe of Versailles.

4 Working Relations

With the signature of the Trade Agreement, the British Government recognised that the Bolsheviks were in control of Russia. The attempt to break their power, never pursued with conviction or determination, was over. It remained to be seen whether cooperation was possible.

Symbolically, the change of course was dramatic. The problems, however, remained largely unchanged. The two Governments had recognised 'in principle' their liability to compensate private individuals in respect of goods or services supplied and had declared that their own claims and those of their nationals should be 'equitably dealt with' in a general peace treaty. They had agreed to refrain from hostile action or propaganda against one another. Whether these mutual assurances would have any effect would be determined as the practical working relationship developed. With no basis of mutual confidence, the debts were to remain largely unpaid and the hostility unassuaged. Yet, after twenty years, mutual interest was briefly to override ideology and when British and Soviet forces were next to encounter one another it was as allies, not as enemies.

In presenting the Trade Agreement to Parliament[1] the Prime Minister was at pains to point out that it was 'purely a trading agreement', not a treaty of peace and that all claims against the Soviet Government were reserved for settlement in the context of an eventual general agreement. Meanwhile, 'you cannot rule out half Europe and a vast territory in Asia by ringing down the fire curtain and saying that until it has burnt itself out you will never send another commercial traveller there.' Clearly, however, he was much impressed by the New Economic Policy under which Lenin was permitting the resumption of some private commercial activity in Russia. 'We are simply converting them', he said. The Soviet leaders were men of great ability and they would realise that to achieve prosperity they would have to 'put an end to their wild schemes'.

Here, in its most optimistic form, was enunciated a line of thought which has characterised one side of the debate about policy towards Soviet Russia throughout the whole period since the Revolution:

maximise the practical day-to-day contacts and gradually the objec-
tionable features of Communist doctrine will be abandoned. The
history of the British–Soviet relationship in the 1920s and 1930s is
the history of a tussle between those who accepted this and those
who held the contrary thesis: that the price of acceptance into
the international community must be the acceptance of British
commercial principles and the abandonment of policies contrary to
British interests; that the principles and the practice of a Communist
Soviet Union were manifestly incompatible with this; that it was
indeed essentially hostile to British interests and that there should
therefore be no dealing with it. There was, of course, a broad
spectrum of opinion ranging from the uncompromising hostility of
the 'diehards' at one extreme to the unquestioning support for Soviet
policy of the British Communists at the other. In the middle, in all
parties, were those who, though their estimates of the nature of the
Soviet regime differed widely, recognised the need to accept it as a
fact of international life and to come to the best terms possible with
it.

In the years since 1945, British policy has for the most part been
based in the middle ground. In the 1920s and 1930s, it tended to
oscillate between the extremes, the oscillations coinciding broadly,
but by no means precisely, with the ascendancy of the Labour and
Conservative parties respectively. It was not that in the pre-war years
the bulk of the Labour party were violently pro-Soviet and the bulk
of the Conservative party violently anti-Soviet. Even *The Times*, at
the height of the outcry over the Zinoviev letter, pointed out that
Ramsay MacDonald and his ministers hated the Communists and
had excluded them from the party. Within the Conservative party
the 'diehards' were a vocal and powerful minority, but still a minority.
The oscillations in fact resulted from the triggering effect of changes
in the political balance which enabled the stronger elements of
opinion on either side of the divide to acquire a temporary ascendancy.
Thus the pursuit of a consistent policy was totally frustrated and
successive British Governments gradually frittered away the leading
position which in 1921 Britain enjoyed in the formation of Western
policy towards the Soviet Union. This chapter will trace the course,
the causes and the consequences of these oscillations of policy in the
years between 1921 and 1930.

THE OFFICIAL BRITISH AGENT IN MOSCOW

With his Russian policy established, Lloyd George found his attention required by more pressing developments at home. Unemployment was rising, a miners' strike threatened public disorder and the situation in Ireland was critical. For a time, Russia disappeared from the Cabinet agenda. It was now for the officials and the traders to turn the provisions of the Trade Agreement into reality. Trade prospects were poor, but nevertheless British industry was taking up the threads. There were plans for the supply of railway equipment, the oil companies had their eyes on the Russian fields and those who had invested in Tsarist Russia were looking for compensation or for the return of physical assets. Early in August 1921 Mr R. M. (later Sir Robert) Hodgson arrived in Moscow as Official British Agent. He found the country already beginning to suffer from famine, the city in a sorry state and the officials more ready to promise assistance than to provide it. It was, he reported, as yet too early to decide how far his treatment was dictated by an intention to obstruct and how far by ineptitude and incompetence.[2]

Hodgson was not left to concentrate on commercial matters for very long. Within weeks of his arrival, he was confronted with the unresolved problem of Russian political activity against British interests. Curzon was not one to give up easily. He had wanted to require evidence of Soviet good intentions before conclusion of the Trade Agreement. Having failed to carry the Cabinet with him in requiring this, he was determined to ensure that the undertakings embodied in the agreement would be put into effect. Information was carefully collected from various sources, including intercepted communications and intelligence reports. No hard evidence of subversive activity in Britain itself could be obtained, but there were clear signs of continued pressure against British interests in Central Asia. An Interdepartmental Committee on 'The Bolshevik menace to the British Empire' was established. On the basis of its labours and of a detailed indictment prepared by the Government of India, Hodgson was instructed to hand to Chicherin a note setting out the evidence and complaining in strong terms about Soviet breaches of the assurance embodied in the Trade Agreement.[3] Soviet policy was illustrated by a report made by Stalin from the Eastern Secretariat of the Third International, setting out a 'general guiding purpose' of 'exerting pressure upon the capitalist powers of Western Europe through their colonies' and arguing that 'the problems connected with the class struggle in the West will be incomparably easier of solution if the external power of France and England can be undermined'. Lenin was quoted as telling the Congress of the Third International that they should 'carefully prepare the revolution in capitalist states'. These policy statements were then supported by specific allegations relating in particular to India, Persia, Turkey and Afghanistan.

The Soviet response, while protesting a desire to 'promote friendly and sincere relations' with the British Government, was to describe the allegations as a 'mass of forgeries and inventions' and to prefer counter-charges against the British Government in respect of assistance to the remnants of the White armies. Curzon had the source of his information carefully checked, found most of it proven to be accurate, noted on the file that, although he did not feel completely satisfied, the report was 'on the whole reassuring', flatly rejected the Soviet denial, but left matters at that and brought the exchange to an end. Some of Curzon's evidence had been obtained by the theft of documents from the office of the Chief of the Political Section of the Soviet Mission in Berlin. One immediate result of its production – and apparent confirmation of its authenticity – was the despatch of a circular to all Soviet missions about the need to tighten security and the dismissal of fifteen members of the Berlin staff.[4] Whether the exchange had any effect on Soviet policy is more difficult to say. It does, however, seem that there may have been some modification, for the time being, of the Soviet drive for power and influence in Central Asia. Soviet Russia at that time had few friends. France remained bitterly hostile and, although the Soviet leadership saw Britain too as seeking the eventual downfall of their regime, they believed and commented publicly that it was with Britain that they could best make progress.[5] It was in their nature then, as it has been subsequently, to reject any accusation of breach of an agreement as a total fabrication, but it may be that, knowing that Curzon's charges were not unfounded, fearing cancellation of the trade agreement, and suffering in any case from a desperate shortage of funds, they concluded that some temporary change of emphasis would be prudent. The incident, in itself, was insignificant, but as a foretaste of Soviet policy, not uninteresting. There has subsequently been considerable room for the Soviet leadership to adjust the scale of activity in the third world in accordance with the requirements of the superpower relationship and the availability of finance. The security of the Soviet state has always been an absolute, but the expansionist ideological drive, was then, as indeed later, variable in its application.

FAMINE IN RUSSIA

Concern with Soviet penetration into Central Asia remained a dominant influence on Curzon's policy, but for a time it had to give way to the considerations of economic policy. Three years after the end of the war, Europe was already in a bad way. France was pressing for drastic action to secure payment of German reparations, but it was plain that Germany was near to the end of her resources. In Britain, the economy was depressed and unemployment was mounting. Russia was stricken by drought and by a famine which, disastrous even by Russian standards, was aggravated by the effect of the Civil War and the Bolshevik requisitioning of food reserves. It is not easy for a Western observer to understand the scale of suffering in Russia at that time. The bald figure of five million famine deaths reflected a reality of misery, pillage, murder and, it was said, even cannibalism, against which the formal processes of intergovernmental diplomacy had an almost grotesque unreality. An international relief effort was mounted, but the British Government was not alone in refusing to finance the purchase of grain unless the Soviet Government would recognise its liability for existing debts and provide security for any new credit. The burden of relief was therefore taken up by voluntary agencies and, on a massive scale, by the United States.

In Western Europe, the unenforceability of the Treaty of Versailles was becoming ever more apparent. Tension between France and Germany was rising and, as it did, the Franco-British relationship came under increasing strain. It was in such a situation that Lloyd George conjured up the vision of an international economic conference in which Russia might be restored as a full member of the world community at the price of acknowledging at least a scaled-down debt obligation. He saw the re-opening of full relations with Russia as offering a stimulus to economic revival and affording commercial opportunities to foreign traders and investors which might enable Germany to procure the resources to service her reparation debt. Thus, in turn, some of the tension might be taken out of the Anglo-French relationship and, at a stroke, the political and economic scene in Europe could be transformed. To it all Russia was to be the key.

THE GENOA AND HAGUE CONFERENCES

It was at a meeting with M. Briand at the beginning of January 1922 that Lloyd George, having discussed the problems of German reparations and European security, proposed that Britain and France should march together for the economic and financial reconstruction of Europe. He proposed the summoning of an economic conference including all the countries of Europe. 'Russia?', asked Briand. 'Yes, Russia', replied Lloyd George.[6] So it came about that on 10 April 1922, at the Palazzo San Giorgio in Genoa, the Soviet representatives, Chicherin, Litvinov, Krasin and Joffe took their seats at, in Lloyd George's words, 'the greatest gathering of European nations which has ever assembled in this continent'. Right-wing opinion in Britain shared none of Lloyd George's dream. In the words of *The Times*:[7]

> The Bolshevists . . . whose aim is the destruction of the present social order, who in subterranean conclaves have for years thought out their plans and methods and elaborated their scheme of action – are now, by the fatuous condescension of the leaders of Europe, placed in a position where they can display their consummate conspiratorial abilities to the full.

The basis of the Conference had been set out in a resolution proposed by Lloyd George, adopted by the Supreme Allied Council at Cannes[8] and sent with a letter of invitation to the Soviet Government. The terms of the resolution covered political guarantees such as refraining from aggression against neighbours and from 'propaganda subversive of order and the established political system', as well as commercial and financial guarantees on matters such as recognition of debts and compensation for confiscated property. They were clearly directed at Russia and designed, as Lloyd George put it, to 'make it quite clear to Russia that we can only trade with her if she recognises the honourable obligations which every civilised country imposes upon itself'. It was indicated that acceptance of the resolution would be a prerequisite for recognition of the Soviet Government. At the opening of the Conference, Lloyd George said that the participants met on terms of equality, but only on acceptance of the equal conditions defined in the invitation. Chicherin, in reply, remarked that, while accepting the Cannes principles, the Russian delegation reserved the right to put forward supplementary articles and amendments. He then proposed that the conference should deal not only with economic reconstruction, but also with disarmament and that it should lead to a universal congress at which workers' organisations should also be represented. Thus, at the very outset, was raised another of the perennial themes of East–West relations. As Lloyd George replied: 'Before you get disarmament, you must have understanding . . . when you have got the understanding and the goodwill, when Russia and all the other powers have understood each other and go home in a spirit of friendship, then disarmament comes.'

RAPALLO

The Genoa Conference totally failed to achieve Lloyd George's grand design.[9] The Cannes resolution had been over-ambitious in seeking to secure Soviet recognition of the inherited debt liability and comprehensive safeguards for Western European private interests in Russia. The formal proceedings were consequently concerned very largely with the questions of debt and compensation. The war credits advanced by the British Government to the Russian Government in the period from the outbreak of war to the October Revolution were now estimated at about £650 million. Private claims amounted to between £300 and £350 million, of which about £30 million was accounted for by investment in industry and manufacturing and about £180 million in respect of mining and oil investment. The latter figure was believed by the Foreign Office to be 'considerably inflated' and is not easy to reconcile with the pre-war figures of British investment.[10] The Government had little expectation of being able to recover any of the war credits, but found difficulty in compromising over private debt, the more so as the French Government, whose citizens had more substantial private investments in Russia, was intransigent. So, no agreement was reached.

In reality, the seeds of failure were planted deeper than this. Lloyd George had gone as far as he could in the prevailing political climate to reach an accommodation. Not only French intransigence, but also his own Parliamentary position, made it essential for him to insist upon guarantees going beyond anything which Russia was likely to accept. Between Germany and Russia there was what he later called 'a community of misfortune, a community of debasement'. The equality of the participants was no more than nominal. Lenin might have expressed himself rather differently from the leader writer of *The Times*, but he shared the latter's view of the opening for Soviet manoeuvre and had instructed the Soviet delegation to play on the disunity in the 'bourgeois countries'.[11] He scarcely needed to do so. Less than a week after the opening of the Conference, the German Government, concerned that the former wartime Allies might come to an arrangement which would disadvantage them, slipped out to the Soviet Delegation's headquarters in a hotel close to Rapallo and signed a treaty, the terms of which had been negotiated by German and Soviet Delegations in Berlin, prior to the conference, but to which at that point the German Government had hesitated to commit themselves. Now, to the contemptuous satisfaction of the Soviet delegates they did so, agreeing to a mutual waiver of claims, most-favoured treatment for trade and full diplomatic representation. It was a major political success for Soviet Russia. For Germany, it was a first step towards regaining that primacy in the Russian market which she had enjoyed before 1914 and which she still largely enjoys today. It was, said Lloyd George 'an act of base treachery and perfidy'. By any standards it was a remarkable act. The fear of German exploitation of Russia's resources had long haunted British Governments. It had taken shape with the signature of the Treaty of Brest-Litovsk and had been a major factor behind the policy of military intervention. With Brest-Litovsk swept away by the defeat of Germany, it had taken less than four years for the old fear to be realised again in a new form. The shadow cast forward to the Nazi-Soviet Agreement of 1939 was already discernible. Lloyd George saw it. Warning Parliament of the grave potential if nations such as these, treated as pariahs, were driven to despair, he argued that some arrangement with Russia was necessary in the interest of the peace of the world. But while Rapallo demonstrated the validity of Lloyd George's policy towards Russia, it left little of his grand design for Genoa.

The Conference toiled on after Rapallo. The Soviet Delegation still had an incentive to secure full recognition from the remainder of Europe, but the price was too high. The Allied request for acknowledgement of debts was met with a Soviet demand for £5000 million compensation in respect of losses sustained during the intervention and, although concessions were made by both sides, the gap was unbridgeable. The end result was agreement to establish separate non-Russian and Russian Commissions to meet at The Hague with the object of settling the questions of debts, private property and credits. A 'pact of peace' between the Russian Government, plus its allies, and the other participants provided that, in order to restore confidence, all parties should abstain from aggression and subversive propaganda for a period of four months. On his return to London, Lloyd George defended his policy 'that abhorrence of the principles and conduct of a Government should not preclude relations with it which would enable you to deal with the people under its sway'. His defence of the ideal which inspired Genoa was firm. Whether the process would ultimately succeed, he would not say.[12]

The Conference at The Hague was very different in character from that at Genoa. Three non-Russian Commissions, dealing respectively with debts, private property and credits met separately to prepare their own positions and then met the Russian Delegation at intervals over a period of three weeks in June and July of 1922. Some information was exchanged, but the Allies would not commit themselves to new credits without Russian acknowledgement of existing debts and either return of nationalised property or compensation. On this crucial nexus neither side would move. Litvinov made a last minute offer to refer to his Government a formula under which debts would be acknowledged and the right to effective compensation for nationalised property admitted, with the amount left for agreement between the Russian Government and the individuals concerned. There was, however, no reason to expect that even this qualified formula would be accepted in Moscow and the Conference broke up with no more than an Allied comment that such a declaration would 'help to create a favourable atmosphere for any further negotiations' and, if loyally carried out, would 'contribute to the restoration of confidence'.

The end of the Conference at The Hague may be seen as marking the end of the initiative begun by Lloyd George, with his Mansion House speech of 1919, to bring Soviet Russia back into the community of nations. Although, in its broadest sense, the initiative had been frustrated, it had not been wholly fruitless. Much had changed over the three years. Soviet Russia was still not recognised *de jure* by any of the Western powers other than Germany, but the British trade agreement had set a precedent which others were following and none could pretend that power over most of what had once been Imperial Russia did not now lie with the Bolsheviks. Without foreign credits, Russia would have to make her way by her own efforts, but Lenin, now close to death, could be well pleased. He was to make one final, personal intervention in the course of Anglo-Soviet relations.

THE URQUHART AGREEMENT

The Litvinov formula had envisaged negotiation between the Soviet Government and the former owners of nationalised property. For some time, negotiations had been conducted with Leslie Urquhart, Chairman of Russo-Asiatic Consolidated Limited and President of the Committee for British Industrial Interests in Russia. After the breakdown of the Hague Conference, these negotiations had been continued and agreement had been reached in respect of a claim by Russo-Asiatic for £56 million, representing about a quarter of the total British claims in respect of nationalised property. Although acting privately, Urquhart was seen by the Russians as a representative of the British Government and there can be little doubt that the agreement with him was a political gesture, designed to influence Britain to move further towards full diplomatic recognition. Immediately after signature, however, the British Government sought to exclude Russia from participation in the Lausanne Conference dealing with Near Eastern questions and, in particular, the question of access to the Black Sea through the Dardanelles and Bosphorus. It was a foolish move, reflecting Curzon's intense distaste for any dealing with the Russians, and it could not be sustained. The French Government was at this time beginning to realise that Lloyd George's more flexible policy had begun to give Britain an advantage in the Russian market. M. Herriot, as Mayor of Lyons, visited Russia to promote French commercial interests and with some skill and subtlety French policy moved in the direction of reconciliation with Russia at precisely the moment when British policy was being turned by Curzon in the opposite direction. As a result of French and Italian pressure, Russia was invited to Lausanne, but, meanwhile, Curzon's gesture of ill-will had been enough to induce Lenin to intervene personally and prevent ratification of an agreement with Urquhart which he described as 'bondage and plunder'. Formally the rejection was based on the 'absence of friendly, stable and settled relations' and Litvinov explained that it was a response to the 'new and negative' British policy towards Russia. He may have been merely scoring a point in respect of an agreement which, in any case, he saw as going too far in conceding the return of property to pre-war foreign owners. It is, however, very probable that it was Lenin's political assessment which turned the scale.

A NEW AND NEGATIVE POLICY

By the autumn of 1922, the Welsh wizard's spell was broken. A wartime Liberal Prime Minister remaining in office in the peacetime years by courtesy of a Conservative Parliamentary majority was bound to be vulnerable. Lloyd George held on too long, pursuing an ill-advised and nearly disastrous policy of support to Greece in the Greco-Turkish war. The failure of Genoa was only a minor factor in his inevitable fall. In October he gave up the office of Prime Minister to Bonar Law and British policy towards Russia entered a new cycle of development. Now was the time for Curzon to take the handling of relations with Russia out of the hands of Downing Street, move it across the road to the Foreign Office and set in train the dismantlement of Lloyd George's policy. Within a matter of months, British policy was to swing between the two extremes which were long to characterise it. From the Genoa policy of bringing Russia into the world community and gradually influencing her development, it had turned through 180 degrees to the policy of excluding her until she demonstrated acceptance of Western standards.

The Lausanne Conference itself was marked by a continuation of the bitter clash between Curzon and the Soviet representatives, primarily as a result of Curzon's determination to keep the Straits open to passage by warships and the Soviet determination to close the Black Sea to all but littoral states. The change of tone in British policy could scarcely be mistaken in Moscow. Chicherin commented to Curzon that the new British Government seemed much more hostile to Russia than its predecessor had been. He asked about British intentions. Curzon, replying with total frankness, went over the long list of complaints about Soviet action against British interests in Asia, which had formed the substance of the note communicated by Hodgson the previous year. He recognised that 'permanent estrangement was an international loss', but 'until there was an absolute desistence from this pestilent activity, there could be no real reconciliation'.

The mood of the Foreign Office at the time is well illustrated by a memorandum prepared by O'Malley for Curzon to circulate to his colleagues in April 1923 on 'The Policy of the Russian Soviet Government, March 1921 – December 1922'.[13] It argued that, had matters been left in the hands of the Foreign Office, the Russian Government 'uncourted and isolated at Moscow . . . might have been induced gradually to commit itself to a further step on the road to a saner policy'. As it was, the invitation to Genoa has merely 'ministered to the unfounded belief that Russia was at least as necessary to Europe as Europe was to Russia'. There was no intrinsic value in a 'paper agreement' with the Soviet Government, the Pact of Peace was 'a verbal undertaking without any kind of sanction to refrain from hostilities which no power had ever contemplated' and the firmness which led to the failure of the negotiations at The Hague would contribute more to the re-establishment of relations with Russia than any agreement at Genoa could have done. Turning to the future, O'Malley pointed out that 'armed intervention, direct and indirect, was tried and failed and considerations of public opinion and finance obviously render reversion to it impracticable'. The only practical choices were to renew Lloyd George's advances to the Russians, to break off relations, or to 'adhere to the cautious and negative policy which has been pursued during the last five months'. The last course was favoured: 'Where, as in Russia, there are so many imponderable factors, inaction is desirable for its own sake.' There should be 'so much intercourse with Russia as is necessary to dissipate the impression of a "blockade", but no more'. Curzon was at first inclined to endorse O'Malley's paper, but by the time it had been printed for circulation, his opinion had hardened still further.

THE CURZON ULTIMATUM

Under a new constitution, enacted at the end of 1922, Soviet Russia had become the Union of Soviet Socialist Republics, a change which the Foreign Office refused for some time to acknowledge. Concurrently with the later stages of Lausanne, Curzon returned to the attack with the newly renamed state on the theme of bilateral British–Soviet relations. Tension had been rising in connection with three matters:

(i) British opinion was much exercised over the treatment of the churches by the Soviet authorities and matters had come to a head over the execution of a priest. A sharp exchange of notes took place, in which the Soviet Government denounced attempts to interfere in the internal affairs of their country and pointed to the action taken to sustain British rule in Ireland, India and Egypt.

(ii) A dispute over the extent of Russian territorial waters, which antedated the October Revolution, had flared up again and British trawlers had now been arrested.

(iii) A British subject, Mr Davison, had been executed and another, Mrs Harding, imprisoned on charges of espionage during the Civil War.

In addition, Curzon was pursuing his allegations of hostile Soviet action in Persia, Afghanistan and India. In May 1923, sharpening O'Malley's policy recommendations, he brought all these matters together in a step which is still recollected with some bitterness in Moscow. Hodgson was instructed to deliver a note requiring an undertaking by the Soviet Government to comply fully and unconditionally with British requests for the withdrawal of their notes regarding the trial of priests; the release of trawlers and crews, compensation and an assurance of non-interference in future outside the three-mile limit; compensation in the case of Mr Davison and Mrs Harding; and the 'disowning and recall' of the Soviet representatives in Persia, Afghanistan and India. In respect of Soviet activities in Central Asia, the note was founded on intercepted communications, but it was agreed by ministers that this source should not be disclosed to Parliament. Hodgson was instructed to state that in the absence of full and unconditional compliance within ten days, the British Government would recognise that the Soviet Government 'do not wish the existing relations between the two Governments to be maintained' and that, albeit with much regret, the 'experiment' would be terminated and the British Government would consider itself free from the obligations of the Trade Agreement.

At the time the ultimatum was issued, Bonar Law was ill and Curzon presided over the Cabinet. As the storm of left-wing protest rose, Bonar Law died. Curzon had confidently expected to succeed him and the choice of Stanley Baldwin, in his place, was a profound blow to this brilliant, sick and embittered Foreign Secretary. There could scarcely have been a greater contrast in political motivation between his intellectual pursuit of an old-style imperialism and Baldwin's pragmatic pursuit of commercial and industrial interest. The problem of relations with the Soviet Union was dealt with as a matter of urgency at a meeting of ministers held even before Baldwin had formally assumed office. It was agreed that full satisfaction should be required and Curzon was fortunate in that it was obtained. The offending Soviet notes were withdrawn, compensation in the Davison and Harding cases was promised, a convention permitting fishing in the area outside the three-mile limit was offered, together with compensation for the arrest of the trawlers. Only in respect of the withdrawal of its representatives in Central Asia did the Soviet Government demur, proposing instead a detailed bilateral discussion. The representative in Kabul was, however, replaced. *The Times* was able on 14 June to congratulate Curzon on the 'refreshing vigour' of his handling of a 'tyranny more bloodthirsty than that of any Tsar' and the Cabinet was able to record a 'highly successful issue' to the dispute.[14] The Soviet reaction had demonstrated the key position which Britain held in the conduct of relations with a Soviet Government which was still ostracised by the great body of inter-national opinion.

With the withdrawal of the ultimatum there was a certain revival of interest in the possibility of trade with Russia, and a delegation of businessmen, led by Mr F. L. Baldwin, a cousin of the Prime Minister, visited Russia. On his return, Baldwin said he was 'infinitely more hopeful'. The Delegation had found a Soviet Government tackling its financial problems with 'extraordinary ability' and a people who, although shabby, did not seem poverty stricken. *The Times* might denounce the travellers for their 'rosy views, not to say illusions', but Lenin's New Economic Policy, permitting a limited return to free enterprise, had made a certain impression on British opinion. The need for markets for British industry was desperate and, even if prospects in Russia were limited, the mood of the country was turning towards a more positive policy.

FULL RECOGNITION

Stanley Baldwin's first tenure of office as Prime Minister was brief. The election of December 1923 brought Labour to power for the first time, with Ramsay MacDonald as Prime Minister, dependent upon Liberal support. The Labour and Liberal parties were both committed to the principle of full recognition of the Soviet Union and there was strong pressure from the left wing of the Labour Party and the trade unions for the pledge to be swiftly implemented. MacDonald himself had little time for revolutionaries. There was no bond of sympathy between him and the Bolsheviks, whom he saw as historical curiosities, 'socialists in crinolines', impediments on the road to a practical modern socialism, based on parliamentary democracy. However, the pressure from his own party was made the greater by the imminence of an agreement on the establishment of relations between the Soviet

Union and Italy and, a mere ten days after taking office, MacDonald
instructed Hodgson in Moscow to inform the Soviet Government
that they were recognised 'as the *de jure* rulers of those territories of
the old Russian Empire which accept their authority'. (With this
phrase the British Government tacitly disposed of its *de jure* recognition of the independence of Georgia.) There was, however, a
warning that 'genuinely friendly relations cannot be said to be
completely established so long as either party has reason to suspect
the other of carrying on propaganda against its interests and directed
to the overthrow of its institutions'. Negotiations were proposed on
all outstanding issues. King George V was not disposed to forget or
forgive the fact that his cousin Nicholas, with his wife and children,
had been murdered, their bodies chopped up and burned by the
Bolsheviks. In deference to his unwillingness to receive a Soviet
Ambassador, Hodgson was given the diplomatic rank of Chargé
d'Affaires and it was stated that a Soviet Chargé d'Affaires would
be welcome in London. As Hodgson reported,[15] Soviet opinion was
not unanimous in welcoming an event which brought Russia once
more into the ambit of Western civilisation, but the Soviet Union
had now emerged from the struggle as a world power and the party
had every reason to be satisfied. Ominously, he added: 'The more
recalcitrant may find consolation in Zinoviev's assurances [at the 13th
Party Congress] that the Labour Government in England is after all
ephemeral and marks but a milestone on the road which leads to the
inevitable world revolution.' So the Soviet Government notified its
formal acceptance and Rakovsky, who – after the unique experience
of being accepted, rejected and then again accepted by the British
Government – had succeeded Krasin as Soviet Agent in London,
was given diplomatic status.

THE DRAFT TREATIES OF 1924

The Anglo-Soviet Conference began on 14 April 1924. Progress in
the negotiation of a comprehensive bilateral treaty relationship was
swift, but the difficulties were substantial. The political balance of
Parliament might have changed, but the problems had not. The
Soviet Union, having attained at no cost the objective of recognition,
wanted to follow it by securing a commitment to a substantial British
credit without a parallel commitment to the full satisfaction of British
claims. Nevertheless, by August of 1924 agreement had been reached

on the text of a General Treaty and a Treaty of Commerce and Navigation. Both were signed as drafts by a less than wholly enthusiastic Ramsay MacDonald and were to become effective only upon ratification. The Commercial Treaty established mutual most-favoured-nation treatment. The General Treaty dealt with formal matters concerning earlier treaties, established fishing rights on a satisfactory basis, provided that claims in respect of debts and nationalised property should be assessed by a Commission of three persons from each side and established that, when this commission had completed its work, a third treaty should set the amount of compensation, finalise the settlement of property claims and determine the amount and conditions of a loan to be guaranteed by the British Government. Governmental claims and counter-claims were effectively put into cold storage and the Treaty, lacking a definitive commitment on the extent of compensation or the amount of a loan, was in essence little more than an agreement to agree. Its supporters could claim that it committed the Soviet Government to the principle of compensation and that it secured useful fishing rights; and that the grant of full recognition was inevitable. Its critics could argue that the British Government had sacrificed its principles, undertaken to finance its avowed enemy, and gained nothing of substance in return. The Conservative press and politicians were vociferous in their denunciation and even Lloyd George, who had worked so passionately to establish relations, thought it 'a thoroughly unbusinesslike agreement, a thoroughly grotesque agreement'.[16]

THE ZINOVIEV LETTER

Without Liberal support, Ramsay MacDonald could not have secured ratification of the treaties and failure would probably have brought the fall of the Labour Government, when Parliament reassembled after the summer recess. As it happened, however, the election of October 1924 was precipitated by a different issue, an allegation that MacDonald, under pressure from the left wing, had persuaded the Attorney-General to drop proceedings under the Incitement to Mutiny Act against J. R. Campbell, the editor of the *Workers' Weekly*. From this point on, the question of Communist subversion was on the election agenda. It was, however, to take a more dramatic form with the publication of the 'Zinoviev Letter'.

While the treaty negotiations were in train, the Foreign Office had received from the Home Office copies of two letters allegedly sent by Zinoviev as President of the Comintern to the British Communist Party, urging direct action in support of the Soviet Delegation. MacDonald decided that until there was evidence of some action, no steps could usefully be taken on the letters. Then, in the last week of the election campaign, the Foreign Office received from the Intelligence Service a copy of a third letter from Zinoviev dealing with the treaty and also instructing the party on the formation of cells in the army which might be 'in the event of an outbreak of actual strife, the brain of the military organisation of the Party'. This last and most dramatic document was copied also to the *Daily Mail* and it is difficult to resist the clear implication that this action was taken – whether by an émigré organisation or by a Conservative party supporter – with electoral considerations in view. Prior to publication by the *Daily Mail*, MacDonald had agreed that, provided he could be sure the document was authentic, a formal complaint should be made to the Soviet Chargé d'Affaires. He asked for a draft to be prepared 'to see how it looks'. A draft complaining of Soviet 'violation of specific and solemn undertakings' was sent to him while he was out of London. He amended it, but did not specifically authorise its despatch and that most meticulous of public servants, Sir Eyre Crowe, having been confined to bed for two days, failed to notice that the letter had not been initialled. It was therefore sent. Crowe's oversight may not have made much difference to the Government's fortunes, since had no action been taken, the Government would doubtless have been attacked for attempting to conceal the document. Despatch of the note did, however, mean that the authenticity of the letter was apparently accepted by the Government. Crowe subsequently minuted that it had been obtained from an absolutely trustworthy agent in Russia and its receipt confirmed by an independent source in Britain. He admitted, however: 'We have no photograph of the document and, as it is only a copy of the original, it would be useless if we had.'[17]

The whole incident was the subject of detailed investigation.[18] The Soviet Government maintained that the letter was a forgery and it may well have been. A Committee of Inquiry constituted by MacDonald before he left Downing Street found it 'impossible on the evidence before them to come to a positive conclusion' as to the letter's authenticity. It was well known that forged Soviet documents were being circulated by various White Russian sources. The frustration of the British–Soviet treaties must have been a major objective for the émigrés and the timing was singularly appropriate for their purpose. The letter itself shows features, some technical and others substantive, which make it seem improbable that it did in fact emanate from Zinoviev. Against this, it must be said that, whether or not the letter was genuine, the Comintern's objective was to spread the revolution and Britain was a major target. The Soviet Government had consistently sought to dissociate itself from the Comintern and to argue that it could not be held responsible for the 'private' activities of those leading personalities who linked the three elements in the control of Soviet foreign policy: the Politburo, as the central organ of party control of the Soviet state; the Government – and in particular the People's Commissar for Foreign Affairs – who were responsible for the conduct of relations with foreign Governments; and the Comintern, through which the party sought to promote the world revolutionary process. The disclaimers had a hollow ring. The letter itself was well enough in harmony with a speech by Zinoviev at the Thirteenth Party Congress. The willingness of the Soviet Government to use its resources for the destabilisation of capitalist society and the destruction of British imperial power could not be effectively gainsaid. Thus, behind all the synthetic furore of the election, was a real and continuing issue of British policy. Was it right to establish closer relations with a state under the total control of a party whose objective was the worldwide triumph of an alien and hostile ideology?

The 1924 election had already been polarised in gross caricatures of this substantial issue. Labour was portrayed as the friend of revolutionaries. One Conservative election poster showed a brigand-like figure grasping a pile of coins, with the caption, 'It's your money he wants'. Another, 'You cannot trust him or his rag. Put your trust in Britain's flag.'

The political significance of the Zinoviev letter, inserted into this campaign, was obvious. The fact that a protest had been sent to the Soviet Chargé d'Affaires implied that the Government accepted its genuineness. If the treaties had not been dead before, they certainly were now. On polling day, four days later, Labour still managed to increase its share of the vote, but lost 40 of its 191 seats. The Liberals were extinguished as a major party, falling from 159 to 40 and the new Parliament was dominated by a massive Conservative majority. One can only speculate whether, had it not been for the letter, the result would have been substantially different. Certainly it would be reasonable to assume that the rightward drift would have been smaller, but it may well be that MacDonald was doomed from the time he went to the polls. Whatever its effect on the outcome of the election, the Zinoviev Letter must have contributed to the polarisation of British opinion and thus have influenced substantially for the worse the chance of securing a stable and rational policy towards the Soviet Union. Those who believed the letter to be genuine were reinforced in their hatred of Bolshevist international conspiracy. Those who believed it to be a forgery were reinforced in their conviction that the enemies of Soviet Russia would go to any lengths to frustrate an accord. For the next phase of the relationship, it was the former who were to regain the ascendancy.

5 Relations Broken and Resumed

AUSTEN CHAMBERLAIN: 'AS DISTANT AS POSSIBLE'

Stanley Baldwin's tenure of office in 1923 had been brief. So, too, was his absence from it. In November 1924 he returned to Downing Street, fortified by a majority of more than 200 over the combined strength of Labour and the Liberals. Curzon, with only a few months to live, accepted the office of Lord President of the Council and the Foreign Office went to Austen Chamberlain. Chamberlain was to execute the policies which again brought Britain's policy towards Russia full circle. Within a period of a little more than three years, the relationship which had so recently been formalised was to be severed. The years between the autumn of 1924 and the winter of 1926 were the last period in which Britain still held a clear priority over any other power in her ability to set the pattern of relations with Russia. They were years in which the Diehards of the Conservative Party were to gain the ascendancy and in which the Government, by the progressive reduction of British–Soviet contacts, was to sap its own ability to influence the course of events. Austen Chamberlain was no 'drifter' in the mould of Balfour, but it is perhaps legitimate to see a certain parallel between the way in which each, under the pressure of intractable circumstances, allowed the effective control of events to pass to the proponents of a more actively anti-Bolshevik policy. As Balfour's drift led to the policy of intervention, so did Chamberlain's policy of 'wait and watch' end with the severance of relations.

The circumstances of the 1924 election had been such that policy towards Russia was bound to take priority on the agenda of the new Cabinet. A Committee of Enquiry under the Chairmanship of the Foreign Secretary reached the unanimous conclusion that the Zinoviev Letter was genuine[1] and it took the Government little time to decide not to recommend MacDonald's two Treaties to Parliament. Austen Chamberlain told the House that there was 'not a shadow of doubt as to the authenticity of the document' and that normal diplomatic relations were not appropriate without respect for the 'courtesies and conventions of international life', but for the time being, policy should be to 'wait and watch'.[2] Hodgson in Moscow was instructed – much as I was in the different circumstances of 1980 – that he should not be more than 'correct' in his relations with the Soviet authorities.[3] A Soviet overture for the resumption of negotiations was rebuffed, the Diehards, led by Joynson-Hicks, the Home Secretary, Birkenhead, Secretary of State for India and Churchill, stumped the country on the theme of the 'Red menace', and in one of those inter-departmental tussles which can do much to shape the course of governmental policy, Joynson-Hicks established the supremacy of the Home Office over the Foreign Office in the handling of matters concerned with Bolshevik 'propaganda'.

The first substantial foreign policy issue concerning Russia arose when the Diehards made allegations of Bolshevik instigation of disorders in Peking the basis of a call for more resolute policies to prevent the erosion of British influence in the Far East. Austen Chamberlain resisted the pressure for a breach of relations. His philosophy was set out in a memorandum written after a discussion in Geneva, where he was attending the Council of the League of Nations:[4]

> It would be very inexpedient to provoke a controversy with the Soviet Government if it can be avoided. . . . The less attention we pay to them the more anxious they will be to come to terms with us. If we make them the subject of our denunciations, they feel that we are afraid of them and they are pleased, but when we ignore them entirely they are afraid because it shows that we have no need of them and nothing to fear from them and that we can afford to leave them out of account.

This was the policy which he then enunciated in Cabinet, concluding that:

> The proper course was to keep a watchful eye on their proceedings, to reserve liberty to take any action that might be deemed necessary when sufficient evidence of their misdeeds was forthcoming; to keep the formal relations as distant as possible; but in the meantime not to yield to the demand in some quarters for an early breaking off of relations.[5]

Commenting on Chamberlain's policy, Chicherin remarked that the

Foreign Secretary was wrong in thinking that if he looked the other way long enough the Soviet Union would come asking to be looked at and talked to.

LOCARNO

Although policy towards the Soviet Union had been a central element in the election campaign and had preoccupied the new Cabinet for a short time, it quickly fell back to the periphery of ministerial concern. The year 1925 was one when the Dawes scheme seemed at last to have removed the problem of German reparations and when Austen Chamberlain secured his triumph with the Treaty of Locarno. Britain, France, Germany, the Netherlands and Belgium were united around a package of agreements, central to which were guarantees of the Franco-German and Belgo-German frontiers. At last, it seemed, there might be a basis for peace and prosperity in Western Europe. Franco-Polish and Franco-Czech treaties formed part of the package, but there was no place for the Soviet Union in the Locarno scheme of things. All that the British Government desired was that it should not be a disruptive influence. Excluded, the Soviet leadership saw more potential menace than reassurance in Locarno and Chicherin spoke of Britain as playing the chief part in the effort to form a united front against the Soviet Union.[6] The suspicion that Britain and France would arrange relations with Germany at the Soviet Union's expense was to poison the British–Soviet relationship throughout much of the inter-war period.

Stalin could still speak of the growth of a revolutionary movement in Britain 'under the banner of friendship in Russia',[7] but with no prospect of a positive development in the British Government's policy the Soviet Union began to concentrate its diplomatic efforts upon Germany and France. In April 1926 a Soviet–German Treaty of Neutrality and Friendship was concluded, bringing the potential threat of Rapallo a step closer to realisation. At the same time, it seemed to the Foreign Office that, despite his public position, Stalin might be moving away from ideological communism to a more pragmatic concern with Russian national interest. If this were so, the threat of revolutionary infection in Britain would be reduced and the classical threat of German–Russian rapprochement enhanced. There was therefore a case for questioning whether a more active British–Soviet relationship might not prove more profitable. Even a group of Conservative MPs who visited Russia in April 1926 were favourably impressed and there was a suggestion that Chicherin was ready to resume negotiations. Hodgson, his views reinforced by five years experience of post-revolution Moscow,[8] argued the case for a resumption, and preliminary work on a new treaty was put in hand by Chamberlain. It was at this point that domestic policy gained the upper hand. The General Strike broke out and work on the new treaty was soon abandoned.

THE GENERAL STRIKE

Zinoviev had for some time been actively pursuing his attempt to link the British and Soviet trade unions and to exploit this linkage as a basis for eventual revolutionary action. An Anglo-Soviet Conference of trade unionists was held and a Joint Advisory Council formed, but the victory of the moderates, among them Ernest Bevin, in the 1925 election to the General Council of the Trades Union Congress was a severe setback to Soviet hopes. At the Home Office, Joynson-Hicks was pursuing his campaign against Communist subversion and in the autumn of 1925 the whole leadership of the British Communist Party was arrested. Neither the Comintern, nor, even less, the Soviet Government, could reasonably have been held to have any direct responsibility for instigating the strike and when it was announced on 1 May 1926, the structure for the exercise of Soviet influence over its course was in poor shape.[9] Financial aid, by way of 'fraternal assistance' from the Russian trade unions was immediately offered, but a first instalment of £26 427 was returned by the General Council of the TUC, who recognised only too clearly how they would be compromised by acceptance. A second instalment of £100 000 was blocked by emergency regulations introduced by the Government. The damage was, however, done. It took the Diehards another year to secure the severance of relations, but from the time of the General Strike they had the upper hand.

THE 'DIEHARD' CAMPAIGN

Joynson-Hicks launched his major attack at a Cabinet meeting on 16 June 1926, at which the minutes record complete unanimity that in view of the 'malignant hostility to the British Empire in the Soviet

Government repeatedly announced by its leaders and acted upon in all parts of the world and on every opportunity', a breach of relations would be fully justified. Nevertheless, a majority still believed that the immediate political advantage might be outweighed by the practical disadvantages and that 'the moment was not opportune for a rupture.'[10] From Moscow, Hodgson had for some time been pointing to the 'eternal contradictions which mark Soviet policy' – on the one hand a 'revolutionary dogmatism demands that every interest be subordinated to the one object of world revolution'; on the other the 'practical exigencies, the waning of revolutionary ardour, indifference to outside things as material prosperity within the country increases and inevitable erosion of the party monolith'.[11] His views were reflected in a Foreign Office memorandum[12] which may have substantially influenced the majority view. It set out the argument for maintaining relations in terms which have recurred throughout the course of British–Soviet relations. Distinguishing the Soviet Government's interest in satisfying the practical needs of the Russian people from the interest of 'the pure revolutionary and disturber of the order and welfare of other countries', it argued for the 'ultimate power of sanity'. Contact with the outside world, it claimed, would bring home to the rulers of Russia 'the obstacles which the revolutionary side of their work puts in the way of their practical efforts to improve the welfare of their country'. Moreover, the Foreign Office argued, Russia was almost as invulnerable economically as she was militarily. She could support with ease a rupture of trade relations, which would not only damage British trading interests, but would also lead to an increase of antagonism and an intensification of propaganda. For the time being, the Foreign Office prevailed and the Cabinet's policy was endorsed by Parliament. The House of Commons accepted the Foreign Secretary's argument that to break relations would be to introduce a 'new and disturbing issue' into both domestic and European politics.[13] The Government had, however, published a Blue Book[14] containing documents seized when the communist leaders were arrested and this, in the words of *The Times*, showed a 'constant and systematic promotion by institutions in Moscow of a movement directed to the ruin of British trade, the overthrow of the British Constitution and the destruction of the British Empire'. The Diehards then stepped up their campaign in the country. Hicks spoke of conduct 'such as no civilized nation in the world would have been guilty of'; Churchill, speaking as Chancellor of the Exchequer at a dinner given by the Lord Mayor, castigated the 'representatives of a hateful and subhuman barbarism'[15] and on 15 July a mass meeting on the theme of 'Clear out the Reds' was held in the Albert Hall.

Krasin returned to London as Chargé d'Affaires and began the task of restoring relations, but the current of opinion was against him and when, on 24 November 1926, he died, the Cabinet decided to oppose the appointment of a successor. The Diehards succeeded in bringing the issue back to Cabinet in February 1927[16] and by this time, with further trouble in China, the opposition to them was crumbling. The minutes record: 'The view generally accepted by the Cabinet after considerable discussion was that, given the state of public opinion in this country, if the present policy of the Russian Soviet Government was continued, a breach of relations within the next few months was almost inevitable.' Again, however, Austen Chamberlain was able, with Baldwin's support, to avoid the immediate breach.

Gregory, in charge of the Russian Department, had circulated a memorandum on the case for and against a breach of relations. 'The ejection of the Bolsheviks from this country', he wrote, 'would be a thoroughly pleasurable proceeding, but it would be rather the satisfaction of an emotion than an act of useful diplomacy.' British Ambassadors in the European capitals were consulted and showed no great enthusiasm for a breach. Sir Ronald Lindsay in Berlin, for instance, argued that 'we are at a new kind of war with Russia and . . . within the limitations that its peculiar character imposes on us we must wage it so as to injure Russia wherever we can', but to expel the Soviet Mission would be to 'blind ourselves' and would represent 'a very long step indeed towards converting the present peculiar struggle into an armed conflict of the old fashioned sort'.[17] The argument which carried the day was probably that British–Soviet relations could not be considered in isolation. Despite Locarno, Europe was in an uneasy state, with tension over the continued Allied occupation of the Rhineland and doubt over the durability of the Franco-German understanding. In such a situation, Austen Chamberlain might not be disposed to seek an improved relationship with the Soviet Union, but was concerned that a formal breach might prove an additional cause of instability.

Taking account of his concern, ministers agreed to confine immediate action to the despatch of a Note demanding that the Soviet Government should refrain from interference with purely British concerns and should abstain from hostile action or propaganda against

British subjects. The Note, delivered to the Soviet Chargé d'Affaires in London on 23 February 1927 complained of 'grievous outrages and injuries to British interests' and stated that the continuation of such acts would sooner or later render inevitable abrogation of the Trade Agreement 'and even the severance of ordinary diplomatic relations'. It was supported by quotations from Soviet speeches and articles, some referring to 'English imperialism egging on its faithful hirelings' against the Soviet Union, others urging support for the English miners and the Chinese revolutionaries as sectors of major importance in the world revolutionary process. It complained of a 'grossly insulting and mendacious cartoon' in *Izvestia* of 29 December 1926, showing Chamberlain applauding the execution of Lithuanian Communists, but while clearly demonstrating Soviet hostility, it cited no hard evidence of improper Soviet activities in Britain.[18] It was therefore scarcely surprising that the Soviet reply should expose the lack of hard evidence; draw attention to speeches by Birkenhead about the 'band of murderers and robbers' in Moscow and by Winston Churchill about the 'dark conspirators of the Moscow Kremlin'; profess the Soviet Government's desire to establish competely normal relations; and stress that a breach would be on the full responsibility of the British Government.

The whole issue of relations with the Soviet Union was debated in the House of Commons on 3 March 1927.[19] The tenor may be judged by the speech of Sir Robert Horne, the signatory of the 1921 Trade Agreement who confessed 'that everything I hoped for has failed to materialise and everything in which I believed has proved a failure'. Still, however, the Foreign Secretary said that the Government would give the Soviet Government 'one more opportunity to conform . . . to the ordinary comity of nations and abstain from the effort to promote world revolution and from all interference in our internal affairs'.

THE ARCOS RAID AND THE BREACH OF RELATIONS

The Diehards must have realised that it would now take only one piece of evidence to push Austen Chamberlain over the edge. In May Joynson-Hicks mounted his final and successful blow for the severance of relations. The occasion for it was a report that a confidential War Office document, a training pamphlet, had been seen by a British employee in the office of Arcos, the organisation of Soviet Cooperatives which had been the first vehicle for Lloyd George's trade negotiations and which shared offices with the Soviet Trade Delegation. Among the advisers to Arcos was E. F. Wise, Lloyd George's principal adviser on relations with the Soviet Union during the critical period from 1919, through the Genoa Conference and up to the conclusion of the Trade Agreement. Arcos enjoyed no diplomatic immunity. Chamberlain could scarcely have refused – and did not refuse – Joynson-Hicks's request for his concurrence in a police raid on its office. The Trade Delegation as such also had no immunity, but the Head of the Delegation, in his capacity as Official Agent, had. In executing the raid, the Police made no distinction between the offices of Arcos and those of the Delegation, except that the safes of the Head of the Delegation were marked 'To be preserved for decision'. It seems probable that Chamberlain did not at first realise that the search would cover an office which was arguably immune from search and Joynson-Hicks, determined to push the search to the maximum, may have been less than frank about its precise extent. In the event, the Government decided to rest on the claim that it was difficult, with two offices in the one building, to say where one began and the other ended and that, in any case, the raid was justified by the abuse of privileges by the Russians themselves, in conducting activities contrary to the terms of the 1921 Agreement.

The documents seized were in fact barely adequate to sustain such a charge. The mood of the Cabinet had, however, passed a point of no return and on 23 May 1927,[20] with Chamberlain now favouring a breach, the Cabinet decided that the Agreement should be terminated, the Soviet diplomatic mission expelled and the British diplomatic mission withdrawn from Moscow. The Arcos staff, except for those who had been engaged in 'illicit interference in internal affairs' would be allowed to remain and trade would continue as it did in the case of countries such as the United States which had no formal agreement with the Soviet Union.

In putting the Government's case to Parliament, Joynson-Hicks relied largely on evidence, including intercepted communications, from sources other than the Arcos raid and spoke of 'one of the most complete and one of the most nefarious spy systems that it has ever been my lot to meet'.[21] Accordingly, on 26 May 1926, the Soviet Government were informed that because the police examination had 'conclusively proved that both military espionage and subversive activities against the British Empire were directed and carried out from 49, Moorgate', the British Government regarded themselves as free from the obligations of the 1921 Trade Agreement and the existing relations between the two Governments were suspended. The German Government took over the protection of Soviet interests in Britain and the Norwegian Government that of British interests in the Soviet Union. As Winston Churchill put it: 'We have proclaimed them [the Soviet representatives] treacherous, incorrigible and unfit for civilised intercourse.'[22]

It was widely believed at the time that the British Government's action was the prelude to a more active offensive against the Soviet Union and possibly to war. In the Soviet Union, the whole country was said to be 'plunged into a state of nervous tension', with moderates regretting the break and blaming party zealots for it, the subterranean organisations 'peeping like rabbits from their holes' and the security authorities setting out to 'exterminate the agents and spies of the British Government'.[23] Russians who had been employed by the British Mission were arrested on charges of espionage and sentenced to exile. A number of other people were shot as a result of unfounded allegations of espionage on behalf of Sir Robert Hodgson.[24] There was considerable concern in Germany, where the suspension of relations was seen as an inevitable stage in the age-long struggle, not between Communism and capitalism, but between Russia and England. Stalin wrote on 28 July: 'The English Government has entered firmly and decisively on the road of organising war against the USSR'[25] and Austen Chamberlain found it necessary to reassure Stresemann that no further action by Britain against Russia was contemplated. In doing so, he also expressed the view that there was no real danger of Communism in England and that while the Soviet leadership regarded Conservatives as their natural enemies they looked upon the more moderate Labour leaders as traitors. Nor, in his view, was there any likelihood of a new revolution in Russia. Thus, over a period of six years a full cycle in the development of Anglo-Soviet relations had been run. For the moment, British policy was at a dead point, with neither the means nor the will to develop it in either a positive or a negative direction. So it was to remain for the two years which were left of Baldwin's second premiership.

From the summer of 1927 to the summer of 1929 there was no movement in relations, but, despite the absence of official contact, there was a moving incident when in August 1928 the Soviet navy handed over with full naval honours the coffins of sailors drowned when the British submarine L55 had been sunk while taking part in operations against the Bolsheviks in June 1919.[26] The British Government professed its intention to encourage the development of a normal trading relationship, but, in the absence of any formal links, the volume of British exports to the Soviet Union fell from over £11 million in 1927 to less than £5 million in 1928 and it was made clear to a group of British industrialists who visited Moscow that there could be no significant expansion without a resumption of diplomatic relations. Concern about the economic situation was undermining the political base of Baldwin's Government and in June 1929 the end came with a disastrous defeat at the polls. A Low cartoon portrayed Baldwin and his ministers waiting in vain for the arrival of another Zinoviev Letter to save them, but on this occasion the Russian issue was not a substantial factor in the election. It was on domestic policy that the Government was defeated.[27]

THE RESUMPTION OF RELATIONS

A Foreign Office memorandum written in 1931 pointed out that one of the unfortunate legacies of the war was that Anglo-Soviet relations had become a subject of the most acute political controversy in Britain: 'From being a pre-war enigma, Russia has become a post-war obsession. So long as one section of opinion, even if a small one, hitches its wagon to the Soviet star, and another longs for nothing so much as the star's eclipse, the task of reducing Anglo-Soviet relations to normal remains hopeless.'[28] When the second Labour Government took office under Ramsay MacDonald, nothing in the realities which underlay the British–Soviet relationship had changed since 1927, but the mood was swinging in favour of a resumption of relations and industry was adding its voice. The party was, in any event, committed to resumption and as soon as the Government took office the process was begun. In place of Austen Chamberlain as Foreign Secretary was Arthur Henderson, who, as a member of Lloyd George's wartime coalition, had been considered as a replacement for Buchanan as Ambassador in Petrograd in the immediate aftermath of the February Revolution and had seen at first hand the conditions there. MacDonald and Henderson were not by temperament disposed to rush matters but there was pressure from the left of the Labour party for early action. Henderson's negotiating position was correspondingly weakened and the Soviet Government, no doubt sensing this, made it plain that they would not accept the prior negotiation of guarantees as a prerequisite for the resumption of relations. The first step, in 1921, had been the exchange of Trade Representatives and the second in 1924 had raised the representation to the diplomatic level with the appointment of Chargés d'Affaires. Now it was agreed that, subject to Parliamentary approval, Ambassadors should be exchanged and that, immediately thereafter, negotiations should be instituted on the following questions:

1) Definition of the attitude of both Governments towards the treaties of 1924.
2) Commercial treaty and allied questions.
3) Claims and counter-claims, intergovernmental and private; debts, claims arising out of intervention and otherwise, and financial questions connected with such claims and counter-claims.
4) Fisheries.
5) The application of previous treaties and conventions.[29]

The House of Commons approved the resumption on this basis, but there was no bipartisan support. The Conservatives voted solidly against the resumption and in the House of Lords they succeeded in obtaining a resolution that diplomatic recognition of the Soviet Government was at the moment undesirable. It was thus against a background of continuing British political controversy that Sir Esmond Ovey presented his credentials on 21 December 1929 as the first British Ambassador to the Soviet Union. He was a career diplomat who had joined the Service in 1903, by 1925 had risen to be HM Representative in Mexico City and was about to leave for Rio de Janeiro when he was told to proceed instead to Moscow. There he found, despite the 'distinct impression of a lack of paint', a clean hotel and a 'state of dilapidation not greater than that which distinguishes many of the smaller towns and outskirts of larger towns in North America'. Simultaneously Grigorii Yakovlevich Brilliant, now known as Grigorii Sokolnikov, a commander of Bolshevik armies during the Civil War, presented his credentials to the Prince of Wales on appointment as Ambassador to the Court of St James. As their first official act, the Ambassadors confirmed the entry into force of the mutual pledge with regard to propaganda which had been in the unratified General Treaty of 1924. That pledge merits quotation in full even today. The parties affirmed:

their desire and intention to live in peace and amity with each other, scrupulously to respect the undoubted right of a State to order its own life within its own jurisdiction in its own way, to refrain and restrain all persons and organisations under their direct or indirect control, including organisations in receipt of financial assistance from them, from any act, overt or covert liable in any way whatsoever to endanger the tranquillity or prosperity of any part of the territory of the British Empire or the Union of Soviet Socialist Republics, or intended to embitter the relations of the British Empire or the Union with their neighbours or any other countries.

Against the background of this renewed pledge, the negotiation of the substantive agreements was taken up between the Foreign Secretary and the Soviet Ambassador. Some progress was made. A temporary commercial agreement of April 1930 provided broadly for mutual most-favoured nation treatment, together with certain special features such as the grant of national treatment to British vessels in Soviet ports. A protocol to the agreement provided for the elimination of political discrimination, with particular reference to legislative or administrative action on commercial matters. The British Government saw this as a means of preventing political discrimination by Soviet purchasing agencies and the Soviet Government saw it as a means of preventing British political discrimination in the grant of export credit guarantees. The Soviet Trade Representative and his two deputies were accorded diplomatic privileges and immunities and the immunity attached also to the Delegation's offices. The Trade Agreement was followed by a temporary fisheries agreement concluded in May 1930 which gave British fishermen the right to fish up to the three-mile limit of Soviet waters.

In respect of the two long-standing issues of claims and propaganda no progress was made. The British Government put forward once again a claim in respect of intergovernmental debt (now amounting to £902 million) which it had no real hope of recovering, plus a somewhat exaggerated figure of £262 million for private debt. In earlier negotiations the Soviet Union had had some incentive to reach a settlement, in that the grant of export credits was made conditional upon it. Now, however, they had secured the credits without making any concession on claims and could afford to prolong the negotiations indefinitely. On propaganda, it soon became apparent that the reiteration of the 1924 pledge was unlikely to have any practical significance. On January 1930 the *Daily Worker* came into existence, featuring in its first issue a message from the Executive Committee of the Communist International hailing it as the champion of the proletariat in the class struggle against the Labour Government. Growing concern over the activities of Soviet agents caused the Government to set up a special committee in the summer of 1930. On five occasions representations were made to the Soviet Ambassador, until eventually the Foreign Office concluded that this course was not only useless, but progressively more undignified.

DENUNCIATION OF THE 1930 TRADE AGREEMENT

The years of Ramsay MacDonald's second Government were years of economic crisis in which unemployment in Britain rose from just over one million to nearly three million. In such a situation foreign trade was vitally important and, as the crisis deepened, there was disappointment in the Government at the relatively slow growth in exports to the Soviet Union. At the same time, from the Conservatives, came growing agitation, supported by the press, on the dumping of Soviet wheat and timber, the use of forced labour for export production, and religious persecution. A leading part was taken by Joynson-Hicks, Home Secretary at the time of the Arcos raid and now, as Lord Brentford, Chairman of the Trade Defence League, designed to bring home to the people of Britain and of other nations the threat that the Soviet Union would use economic policy as a road to world revolution and to urge the need for a united front against the common enemy, Communism. Stanley Baldwin took up the cry and called for tariff protection, if necessary at the price of once more denouncing the trade agreement with Russia. The pressure had its effect. In early 1931 the Foreign Secretary reminded the Soviet Ambassador that the volume of trade was not yet back to the level of 1925–7 and that, in such a situation, 'the main argument in support of normal Anglo-Russian relations lost most of its value'.[30] The economic crisis brought the collapse of the Labour Government and when the National Government, formed in August 1931, was returned later that year with a massive, Conservative-dominated majority, the relationship with the Soviet Union came under threat once again.

With Ramsay MacDonald as Prime Minister, power was nevertheless very much in the hands of Stanley Baldwin as Lord President of the Council and leader of the Conservative party, but it was the Liberal lawyer, Sir John Simon, who, as Foreign Secretary, was to preside over the next critical stage in relations. In February 1932 he warned the Soviet Chargé d'Affaires that the adverse balance of trade was such that the British Government 'could not continue to acquiesce indefinitely' and would be forced to consider steps – which he did not define – to remedy the situation. That action was not long delayed and it initiated a new period of tension. The immediate cause for action was the introduction of Imperial Preference as a result of the Ottawa Conference in the summer of 1932. On 1 October 1932, in accordance with commitments entered into at Ottawa, and in order to leave itself free to take such action as might be deemed necessary against Soviet goods, the British Government gave formal six-months notice of termination of the 1930 temporary trade agreement with the Soviet Union. It was in these inauspicious circumstances that Ivan Maisky, the penniless refugee of the pre-Revolutionary era, arrived, proclaiming a policy of 'common sense', to succeed Sokolnikov as Soviet Ambassador in London.

The termination of the 1930 agreement was not, in itself, a matter of great moment. It was seen by the Government as a necessary consequence of Ottawa rather than as a major move in British-Soviet relations. The depth of the economic crisis was such that almost any measure to improve matters could have been justified. It mattered little that Soviet exports were largely irrelevant to the troubles of the West. The trade agreement with the Soviet Union had been a disappointment in its direct results. There had been no satisfaction of the British financial claims and the resumption of diplomatic relations had done nothing to reduce the continuing aggravation of the ideological offensive of the Comintern. The United States, France, Canada and other countries had all introduced discriminatory measures against Soviet exports and there was Canadian pressure for protection against Soviet exports of grain and timber. The British Government gave the required period of notice and in the House of Commons Mr Baldwin indicated the Government's readiness to negotiate a new agreement if they could secure a better proportion of Soviet orders and also the right to stop imports damaging to domestic industry.[31] The Soviet reaction was one more of sorrow than of anger. Litvinov, who had succeeded Chicherin as Foreign Minister in 1930, was pessimistic about the prospect for future negotiations, but his experience of the course of British policy since 1917 could scarcely leave much room for optimism. An anti-British campaign was briefly worked up in the Soviet press, but surprisingly a sharp complaint by Sir Robert Vansittart brought an apology from the editor of *Izvestiya* which was duly communicated by Maisky and accepted by Sir John Simon and the Prime Minister. Negotiations for a new commercial treaty were opened on 15 December 1932. The British Government might well have congratulated themselves that the process of terminating the agreement had been satisfactorily concluded and it is interesting that Gromyko and Ponomarev, in their history of Soviet Foreign Policy, made no mention of it. By an odd chain of circumstances, however, this may have marked a turning point in Britain's ability to influence Soviet policy.

This was the point at which the policies of the major powers were beginning once again to turn upon a German hinge and at which a certain reassessment of the pattern of Soviet foreign relations was perceptible. In July 1931 Litvinov spoke to the British Ambassador of his concern about the possible emergence of 'some form of Fascist Government' in Germany. The Japanese invasion of Manchuria in September 1931 revived all the old Russian fears of the threat from the East and gave added force to the Soviet Union's search for security. On 25 July 1932 a Soviet non-aggression treaty with Poland opened the way for conclusion of a similar treaty with France in November of that year. The major tests of the will to resist Japanese, Italian and German aggression lay in the future, but already the pattern of diplomatic relationships which was to condition the response of the other powers was beginning to form. It may be that the search for collective security could never have succeeded, but it was unfortunate that, at the very time of Hitler's accession to power, Britain faced a new crisis in her relationship with the Soviet Union.

THE METROPOLITAN-VICKERS TRIAL

In January 1933 Adolf Hitler became Chancellor of Germany and Europe began the swiftly accelerating course to war. In the spring and summer of 1933, it was not, however, the menace of Hitler which dominated the British–Soviet relationship, but the show trial in Moscow of six British engineers employed by the Metropolitan-Vickers company. The company had a long tradition of business with Russia, particularly in respect of heavy electrical generating plant and related equipment. They were responsible not only for supply, but also for installation and servicing of equipment and they consequently maintained, under the direction of a small team of British engineers, a group of British and Russian technicians dealing with plant in various parts of the Soviet Union. On 12 March 1933 Soviet security police raided the company's premises near Moscow. Six British and twenty Russian staff were arrested on varying charges of military and economic espionage, bribery and wrecking of plant.

It is probably the case, as Lord Strang has suggested,[32] that the trials were not conceived primarily as an act of foreign policy. More probably, they derived from the difficulties in the capital equipment programme under the five-year plan. On the very day the British engineers were arrested, it had been announced that thirty-five officials had been shot for counter-revolutionary activity and sabotage affecting agricultural production. It must have been tempting to seek at least one foreign scapegoat, easy to proceed from the failure of imported plant to the allegation of sabotage by the installer and easy to proceed from the normal collection of information to the allegation of espionage. Metropolitan-Vickers were vulnerable because of the scale of their activities, the close association between British and Russian staff and, finally, because of the bad state of British–Soviet relations after the cancellation of the commercial treaty.

British ministers were satisfied that the charges were effectively without foundation and the stage was set for a trial of strength between the two Governments.[33] Baldwin stated in Parliament on 15 March that the Government was convinced that there could be 'no justification for the charge on which the arrests were made' and warned of 'unfortunate consequences to Anglo-Soviet relations'.[34] Vansittart saw Maisky who, after a year as Soviet Ambassador, must have been finding London somewhat chillier than he had found it as a refugee some twenty years earlier. Maisky was told that unless the prisoners were released, there would be a 'rooted and growing disinclination to proceed with commercial negotiations'. The public Soviet response, not surprisingly, was a statement that no pressure and no threats would induce the Soviet Government to suspend or mitigate its laws with regard to British subjects. On 20 March[35] the British Government announced that negotiations for a commercial treaty were being suspended and in Moscow Sir Esmond Ovey informed Litvinov that a reference to the possible prohibition of Soviet imports was omitted only in view of indications that immediate release was still possible. On the advice of Vansittart, the Cabinet decided against threatening a second breach of diplomatic relations, but when it became clear that the trial would take place, a Bill was introduced giving the Government power to prohibit imports from the Soviet Union and after a bitter exchange with Litvinov, Ovey was instructed on 29 March to return for consultation, leaving Strang as Chargé d'Affaires. In view of the indictment of both espionage and sabotage, Sir John Simon made a further formal Parliamentary statement to the effect that none of the accused had ever been employed directly or indirectly in connection with any branch of the Intelligence Service and that neither they nor the company had ever supplied any information to any such branch. After a trial marked by the classic features of Soviet show trials, five of the accused were convicted, two being sentenced to terms of imprisonment and the others to expulsion. (The two principal accused, Thornton and MacDonald, subsequently described at a meeting with Foreign Office officials the methods which had been employed to secure a confession by the former and a guilty plea by the latter. No physical violence had been employed or threatened, but, by exploiting the feeling of helplessness on the part of the accused and by accumulating scraps of information, in themselves innocent enough, the interrogators had brought Gregory to the point at which 'he would have signed his own death warrant'. MacDonald's guilty plea was secured by the threat that if he persisted in pleading not guilty his Russian housekeeper would be made to give evidence and that this would 'make things much worse' for all concerned.) The embargo on Soviet imports was proclaimed on 19 April, to take effect from 26 April. On 20 April the Soviet Government responded with an embargo on British goods and measures against British shipping to remain in force for the whole period of the British embargo.

The crisis in relations was resolved almost as swiftly as it had erupted. It quickly became clear that the Soviet Government, having insisted upon their sovereign right to bring the Metro-Vickers employees to trial, were anxious to conclude the incident. In June, Litvinov visited London for the abortive World Economic Conference and in the course of two private meetings with Simon, it was agreed that there should be simultaneous release of the prisoners, cancellation of the embargoes and announcement of the resumption of negotiations for a new trade agreement.

More interesting than the fact of the Metro-Vickers settlement was the political assessment which made it possible. Ramsay MacDonald subsequently complained that Vansittart had pushed him into a wrong decision in applying the embargo and, indeed, it may well have been an over-reaction. Yet, in practice, the over-reaction may have served to make the Soviet Government realise the danger which it ran in needlessly antagonising British opinion at the very time when the constant threat from Japan to the Eastern frontier was being matched by the growing threat from Germany to the West. From Moscow, Strang reported that Stalin had expressed to a colleague his annoyance at having been brought to sanction the arrest and trial 'without having been warned by those whose duty it was to know of the risk of serious repercussions on world opinion and on Anglo-Soviet relations'. The report could not be confirmed, but it seems inherently likely that in a potentially dangerous situation, the Soviet leadership was disinclined to aggravate still further an essentially hostile Britain. This certainly was the tenor of comment made to Strang in Moscow after the affair was over.[36] In an analysis of Soviet foreign policy[37] he argued that the imperialist policy of Japan and the seizure of power by Hitler had played a decisive part in reorienting Soviet foreign policy. Britain, which, in Soviet eyes, had now replaced France as the instigator of anti-Soviet movements in Europe, was seen as a less open, but not less dangerous enemy than Germany and Japan, seeking to turn German interest to the East and to cripple the Soviet economy. In this situation, Strang saw Soviet policy as essentially defensive, playing upon imperialist antagonisms, seeking equally to avoid a reconciliation which would permit the imperialists to join forces against the Soviet Union and a general war which might involve the Soviet Union and jeopardise the revolution. Litvinov's 'policy of peace' was, in his view, at that time, genuine. A temporary sacrifice of prestige or interests could be accepted by a state 'whose governors are, it seems, confident that its area, its population, its natural resources, its system of government and its programme of planned economic development will in the long run render it all-powerful and that the principles upon which it is founded are fated to capture the world'.

The analysis was perceptive in terms both of the immediate future and of the policies leading to the outbreak of war six years later. The German and Japanese threat provided a motive for a Soviet–British rapprochement and there could be a coincidence of interest, but the deeper contradictions remained. The long-term revolutionary objectives of the Soviet Union might not be a direct threat to British society, but they did little for mutual confidence, while on the Soviet side the suspicion persisted that an inherently hostile, capitalist Britain would seek to protect her own security by turning German expansion eastwards. Neither concern was wholly justified, but neither was without foundation. The story of the next six years is the story of the triumph of mutual mistrust.

6 The Approach to War

In the preceding chapters we have followed the development of the political relationship between Britain and the Soviet Union from the ending of military intervention by Lloyd George in 1919; through the negotiation of the 1921 Trade Agreement and the failure of the attempt to work out a multilateral settlement at Genoa and The Hague; Curzon's ultimatum of 1923; the establishment of diplomatic relations by Ramsay MacDonald and the signature by him of the two Anglo-Soviet Treaties in 1924; the rejection of the 1924 Treaties by Baldwin in the same year; the abrogation of the 1921 Trade Agreement and the breach of relations by Baldwin in 1927; the re-establishment of full relations, with the appointment of Ambassadors and the negotiation of a new Trade Agreement by MacDonald in 1929–30; and finally the notice of termination of the 1930 Agreement by Baldwin in 1932, followed by the Metro-Vickers crisis. Two years of confused politico-military action against the Bolsheviks were followed by fourteen years in which successive British Governments oscillated between attempts to establish a practical working relationship with the new Soviet state and attempts to banish it from the international community. Neither course could be said to have been marked by any significant measure of success. Now, as the potential of a rearmed and aggressive Germany began to be perceived, the stage was being set afresh. Would the script be rewritten? Before we trace the stages through which, over a period of eight years, successive Conservative or Conservative-dominated Governments moved from ostracism of the Soviet Union, close to open conflict and then to full military alliance, it may be helpful to stand back from the day-to-day unfolding of policy in order to look at the political and social climate within which it was being formulated.

THE MOOD OF THE 1930s

It was in the 1930s that the great schism in British attitudes towards

117

the Soviet Union was at its most evident. The thinness of the official documentation contrasts vividly with the outpouring of comment from other sources. In 1932 a young Conservative politician, Harold Macmillan, spent several weeks travelling with a friend in the Soviet Union. Later, in *Winds of Change*, he was to write of the impulse behind that visit:

> While the capitalist world seemed, to many observers, in decay if not in mortal agony, the Bolsheviks had apparently consolidated their power and stability. In the early years of my political life, Bolshevism was regarded in Britain with feelings ranging between contempt and fear. But by 1932 many British people were beginning to wonder whether, after all, the regime which had imposed itself over a vast part of the world's territory might not be worth careful and, if possible objective, study.[1]

Macmillan must have typified many of his generation. Born at the zenith of Victorian Britain's imperial power, he had served in the Grenadier Guards throughout the 1914–18 war, had seen the promise won by the suffering of those years squandered in the political bickering and economic bankruptcy of the 1920s. Now, with economic depression at home and the rising menace of the dictators abroad, he needed to assess where he stood and take new bearings. In his book, he reprinted many of the letters which he wrote home to his mother from Russia. It was 'a kind of looking-glass world, where everything was the opposite of what one would expect'. Like many who were to make a similar journey then – or indeed later – he found a proud and kindly people in the grip of a rigid political system whose practice bore little comparison with the grandiloquent proclamation of its ideals. Like many, he breathed more freely as he crossed the Soviet border on his way home. A quarter of a century later, he was to be the first British Prime Minister to visit the Soviet Union in peacetime.

Macmillan represented a broad cross-section of opinion – lying between the zealots of right and left – prepared to examine seriously and impartially the great Russian experiment, on the whole more saddened than encouraged by what they saw, but certainly not disposed to ignore the new Soviet state as a factor in the march of European politics. To his right the impulse of protection against the contamination of Communist ideology and the competition of Russian imports motivated a significant sector of the Conservative party. Little that they had heard of the first decade of Soviet Communism had modified their abhorrence at its practical consequences and, as the 1920s ended, the world heard the first reports of the great forced collectivisation, the deportations, the cattle slaughtered by the peasants and peasants by the militia, as the country dwellers of Russia were hammered into the Stalinist mould. On the left, Sidney and Beatrice Webb were producing the second edition of their great work, *Soviet Communism. A new Civilisation?*, and, unworried by the Stalinist excesses, removing the question mark. The Society for Cultural Relations with the USSR, with J. M. Keynes and H. G. Wells as its first two Vice-Presidents, was serving as a focus for the support of men like the 'Red Dean' of Canterbury, Hewlett Johnson, who was to describe Soviet Communism as 'majestic in range, practical in detail, scientific in form, Christian in spirit . . . a programme which thinks not in terms of a privileged class, but in terms of each individual soul' and whose book, *The Socialist Sixth of The World*, was to go through twenty one impressions between 1939 and 1945. The 1930s have, with some justice, been called the Pink Decade. So they were for an important and influential body of intellectual and political opinion. So, too, they were for a young man, Donald Maclean, at 19 in his second year at Cambridge when Macmillan went on his Russian tour. Many in that decade trod the path to Moscow. The governmental relationship was, however, another matter altogether.

When Macmillan first visited Moscow, no minister in any British Government since the Revolution had set foot in the Soviet Union. Ramsay MacDonald was still Prime Minister, but now, as nominal head of a National Government, a broken politician and a spent man. In his two brief periods of effective power in 1924 and 1929–30 he had committed the country to the establishment of a full relationship with the Soviet Union, but had lacked the political power to carry the relationship into effect. Although still respected by Baldwin for his grasp of foreign policy, there is little sign that, after 1931, he sought to exercise any great influence on the handling of relations with Russia. In all but name, Stanley Baldwin was in charge of His Majesty's Government and he was only too happy to leave matters to the Foreign Secretary, Sir John Simon.

Baldwin was not as negligent of foreign policy as he has sometimes been presented, but it was never of consuming interest to him and, in the realm of foreign policy nothing was more alien to him than the Soviet Union and its political system. It was alien to his roots in the kindly landscape of Worcestershire, to his instinct for a capitalism based upon responsible industrial partnership between the employer and his men, individually and collectively and, above all, to his concept of a democracy based on respect for the individual citizen. 'The Christian state', Baldwin once said, at an Empire Rally of Youth, 'proclaims human personality to be supreme. The servile state denies this. Every compromise with the infinite value of the human soul leads straight back to savagery and the jungle.'[2] Baldwin's experience of dealing with the Russians was lengthy, but never very close. He had been President of the Board of Trade immediately after the signature of the 1921 Trade Agreement and played his part in the preparation for Genoa, where he is recorded as siding with Churchill. Coming into office after the Zinoviev Letter, he had presided over the demolition of the relationship in the years from 1924 to 1929 and was scarcely likely now to rekindle it with much fervour.

There was not in his Russian policy the cold hostility of Curzon, the crusading spirit of Churchill or the bludgeon of Joynson-Hicks, but rather an antipathetic indifference, perhaps best summed up by his comment, as the Nazi menace developed: 'If there is any fighting in Europe to be done. I should like to see the Bolsheviks and the Nazis doing it. . . . If he [Hitler] moves East, I shall not break my heart.'[3] In Simon, Baldwin had a Foreign Secretary who was seen by some as an avowed hater of the Soviet Union and all its works. The record scarcely bears this out. The picture which emerges is much more that of a shy, aloof man, a good legal brain confronting dispassionately the problems of the British–Soviet relationship when they forced themselves upon him, but with little political impulse to shape the course of events.

Thus it was that for several critical years the conduct of British policy towards the Soviet Union lacked any positive ministerial lead. Eden, with a stronger personal involvement and a greater sense of the political relevance of the Soviet Union, might have had a substantial impact on the course of policy, but with the accession of Neville Chamberlain, the control of foreign policy moved back across Downing Street into the hands of the Prime Minister. The indifference of Baldwin was gone and the antipathy towards the Soviet Union was heightened.

At the time of Macmillan's visit, the Ambassador in Moscow was still Sir Esmond Ovey. The Counsellor was William Strang. Strang, the son of a Scottish farmer, brought up in Essex, educated at the local village school, followed by grammar school and a scholarship to London University, entered the Diplomatic Service from the Army through the special examination held in 1919. He first comes into the story of British–Soviet relations when, as a junior member of the Northern Department of the Foreign Office, he was the only one to notice that MacDonald had not initialled the celebrated note on the Zinoviev Letter. His service in Moscow was marked by the trial of the Metropolitan-Vickers engineers. As Counsellor, he was left in charge of the Embassy when Ovey was recalled and the experience convinced him of the need to deal firmly with the Soviet Government. He wrote critically of the subjectivity of those like the Webbs 'who would not see what was plain' before their eyes, and remarked upon the way in which foreign opinion in Moscow had welcomed the British embargo as evidence that 'some government had at last taken resolute and decisive action against the arbitrary tyranny of the OGPU and that foreigners in the Soviet Union had acquired additional security thereby'.[4] In a despatch to the Foreign Office, sent during the trial, he warned against the trap of Soviet peace proposals and the continued goal of world revolution: 'The present Soviet policy of the "breathing-space", of the peaceful co-existence of the two systems, should not blind us to the ultimate and still living revolutionary purpose of the first proletarian state.'[5] Strang, himself, was, however, no doctrinaire Bolshevik-hater, but rather one of the many who, looking impartially at the performance of the Soviet Government, could not ignore the menace either of its ideology or of its policies. A few years later it was he who was sent back from the Foreign Office to join the Ambassador for the abortive negotiations for a British–French–Soviet agreement in the summer of 1939.

At the time of the Metro-Vickers trial Strang's superior as Permanent Under Secretary in the Foreign Office was Robert Vansittart. Vansittart, who was more conscious of the German threat than most of his generation, may for that reason have been more charitably disposed to the Soviet Union. Certainly, in a memorandum to Sir John Simon he described his own views as 'consistently less drastic' than Strang's,[6] although the Secretary of State professed himself unable to find the difference. Vansittart himself was to figure significantly in the course of dealings with the Soviet Union only in his initiation of a series of lengthy conversations with the Soviet Ambassador, Maisky, in the summer of 1934. Maisky recalls the 'highly constructive spirit' of those discussions.[7] For Vansittart himself,[8] it was a matter of regret that 'Russia and Britain were alike exposed to German designs and could never get together', but he had little doubt where the blame lay. 'The mental confusion of the Communists was as deep as their duplicity. Collaboration was basically impossible with people who would not willingly achieve their ends in peace.' Recalling an accusation by Winston Churchill of having a rigid mind, he commented that in respect of Communism, Deutschtum and homosexuality he was ready to be called illiberal. Maisky claims that Vansittart turned against the Soviet Union after the war through alarm at the growth of Soviet power. There is little reason to doubt that his natural antagonism was deeply rooted, but as a good public servant he did what he could to create with the Soviet Union in the mid-1930s the kind of relationship which might have formed the basis of collective security against Hitler.

In Moscow, from 1930 until he was succeeded by Molotov in May 1939, the People's Commissar for Foreign Affairs was Maxim Litvinov. Having lived in London since the early years of the century, married to an Englishwoman and responsible for Soviet foreign policy under Chicherin in the 1920s, he was as well equipped as any member of the Soviet leadership to formulate a constructive policy towards Great Britain if, in the judgment of the Soviet leadership, the interest of the Soviet state and its Communist party should point in this direction. His tenure of office was to be marked by a significant reorientation of Soviet foreign policy, the establishment of relations with the United States, membership of the League of Nations and, above all, the search for collective security. As People's Commissar for Foreign Affairs, Litvinov's power base was slender. With success, he might have enhanced it, though it must be questionable whether he would ever have enjoyed the full confidence of Stalin. But speculation is irrelevant. He was to fail and in the summer of 1939 his policies were to be jettisoned with their architect.

AN ENCOURAGING START

The closing months of 1933 saw the realignment of Soviet foreign policy beginning to take shape. At the end of October Lord Chilston arrived as HM Ambassador in Moscow, some six months after the recall of his predecessor. Litvinov had just returned in triumph from Washington, having secured American recognition of the Soviet Government and Chilston was much impressed with Soviet success in asserting itself as 'one of the greatest factors of world politics'. He saw a country setting out to make itself the most powerful state in the world, but thoughts of world revolution had given place to 'complete consolidation of communistic rule in this Empire'. Above all the Soviet Union needed peace and security: 'Peace is sought and will be ensured at all costs except in the event of an attack from outside.'[9] In Ankara, Sir Percy Loraine was explaining patiently to the Turkish Foreign Minister that 'a very large proportion of opinion in England held the view that the whole political system and creed of Soviet Russia was the work of Satan'. He nevertheless suggested gently that it might on the whole be better 'to give the Russians a seat at the dining-table, rather than have them poisoning the soup in the kitchen'. Simon was not greatly impressed by the potential for relations with the Soviet Union. But then it was not in Simon's nature to be greatly impressed by anything. He saw advantage in the Soviet desire at the moment to maintain the status quo, and noted their undoubted desire for better relations with Britain, but he was not convinced of the permanence of their sentiments and he was disinclined to hurry on a rapprochement. The Soviet Government could be left to make the running but it was 'all to the good that they and we should work, if not together as yet, at least on parallel lines'.[10]

The next few months saw a significant development in relations, with the signature on 16 February 1934 of a new Temporary Commercial Agreement establishing the principle of mutual most-favoured nation treatment between the two countries, an agreement which, despite its temporary character, was to govern the trading relationship for the next forty years. Although largely overtaken as a result of the Common Commercial Policy of the European Community, it still remains valid. On the Soviet side, the hope was expressed that the commercial agreement might serve as the starting point for the improvement of Anglo-Soviet relations as a whole.

THE BEGINNING OF COLLECTIVE SECURITY

Soviet foreign policy was in fact at a turning point. With growing awareness of the menace of Germany and Japan, the Soviet leadership was seeking a less confrontational relationship with Britain and France. The leading role, for a time, was to fall to France rather than to Britain. The signal was the visit of M. Herriot to Moscow in August 1933, when it is probable that the first mention was made by the Russians of a possible Franco-Soviet alliance. This went too far for the French and instead they mooted a collective mutual assistance pact between Russia, Poland, Czechoslovakia and Germany, backed by a French guarantee to the Soviet Union and by a Soviet commitment to underwrite the Locarno structure. At Soviet insistence, the concept was enlarged to include the Baltic states. The French, for their part, made it plain that Soviet membership of the League of Nations was a prerequisite. So the concept of an Eastern Pact for the Guarantee of Mutual Security, the 'Eastern Locarno', was born. On Christmas Day 1933 Stalin indicated in a press interview that membership of the League of Nations might become possible and early in 1934 soundings were taken to this effect. After some hesitation, the British Government decided not merely to acquiesce in Soviet membership, but to join France in lobbying for it and also, after a Franco-British ministerial conference, to support the Eastern Locarno, on the clear understanding that Britain herself would not enter into any new regional commitment. In the foreign affairs debate in Parliament on 13 July 1934, the Foreign Secretary stated that the Government would 'welcome Russia warmly' to the League. He welcomed also the proposal for an 'Eastern Locarno' and, although Britain would not join in the pact, it undertook to commend it to the other Governments concerned. Here, in the words of Winston Churchill, was 'the reassociation of Soviet Russia with the Western European system . . . an historic event'.[11]

British–Soviet relations at this point were interestingly poised. On 3, 12 and 18 July, concurrently with the Parliamentary debate, Vansittart and Maisky had a series of private discussions[12] after which Vansittart wrote to Chilston in Moscow, instructing him to put the basic issue of the British–Soviet relationship to Litvinov.[13] The Soviet press, Vansittart said, used about Britain language which they would never use about the French, the Italians or the Americans. (In this, he had some justification. The Soviet press had spoken of Britain taking the 'leading role for the preparation of war against the USSR'.)[14] He continued: 'The Soviet Government cannot have it both ways and they must now choose between a policy of real friendship with us in all respects and the policy they have been pursuing hitherto, for they must realise that the public here is not yet convinced of their friendly intentions.'

For a time, relations did indeed improve. The attempt to organise an Eastern Locarno made little progress, but on 18 September 1934 the Soviet Union was duly elected to membership of the League of Nations, with a permanent seat on the Council and Litvinov commented that he was 'particularly gratified' at the improvement in British–

Soviet relations.[15] He wasted little time in putting his concern about the Hitler regime bluntly to Eden: 'So long as the Hitler regime existed in Germany, there could be no real security for Europe.'[16] His proposals for the future of the League and the Disarmament Conference roused little interest in the West and it is reasonable to doubt whether, at this point, his doctrine of collective security commanded significant support among the leadership in Moscow. Nevertheless, the Soviet Union was now beginning to be seen as a factor in the European political scene. Policy had moved a long way since the abrogation of the trade agreement and the crisis over the Metro-Vickers trial. It was summed up by Sir Robert Vansittart in a memorandum of 21 February 1935.[17] The Soviet Government, he said, considered that they had only two enemies of real political importance, Japan and Germany, and, rightly or wrongly, they feared an attack by either or both. Consequently, they had become supporters of the status quo, had concluded pacts of non-aggression with all their European neighbours, had worked for *rapprochement* with France and Britain and had joined the League of Nations. 'It can hardly be maintained', he continued, 'that the attitude of the Soviet Government is not of great importance to us. We have gained much, both directly and indirectly, from the recent change in that attitude; and we stand to lose heavily if it is changed in the reverse direction.' The direct gains were increased trade, the cessation of Soviet pressure on Afghanistan, some consideration for British interests elsewhere in Asia and a diminution in anti-British propaganda. Indirectly Britain had gained by the general realisation in Europe that the Soviet Union was seeking the friendship of powers opposed to a change in the status quo.

So far as the Soviet Union was concerned, the immediate test of Western readiness for a new relationship was the Eastern Locarno. A pact of this nature, bolstered if possible by a direct Franco-Soviet alliance – and indirectly by the Franco-British link – was for them the key to British and French readiness to oppose a possible German move eastwards. Without it, they saw any increase in Western European security and, in particular, any easing of the British–French relationship with Germany, as merely increasing their own vulnerability to Germany. The British Government understood this well, but, with growing concern at the prospect of German rearmament, they saw little incentive to compromise an already uncertain Western security by the addition of a potential entanglement in Eastern European hostilities. Consequently the more German and

Polish opposition to a multilateral Eastern guarantee scheme became apparent, the more the British welcome for it cooled. Their dilemma was that they liked even less the prospect of a direct bilateral Franco-Soviet alliance. The risk was only too clear. If France, honouring a commitment to Russia, found herself at war with Germany, Britain could be involved in hostilities in relation to an area, Eastern Europe, where, as she perceived it, she had no direct interest and in support of a Soviet Union which seemed substantially less worthy and substantially less capable than Tsarist Russia had been twenty years earlier. The views of Foreign Office officials were divided, but there was certainly much support for the view of Orme Sargent, the Assistant Under-Secretary, who saw a Franco-Soviet alliance as the first step towards the 'horrible prospect' of a return to the pre-war grouping of Powers. It might be inevitable, but, in his view, every effort should be made to prevent it and to this end some alternative form of Eastern pact might be sought – a pact weak enough to be acceptable to Germany and Poland, but adequate to meet Soviet fears. It was the beginning of a desultory debate on which the political-strategic relationship of Britain and the Soviet Union was to turn and on which – in different circumstances and in a different form – the tripartite negotiations of 1939 were to founder.

STRATEGIC ASSESSMENTS IN 1934

It is interesting that at this time, when the Soviet Union was beginning to be seen by Britain as a factor in the international political scene, it was regarded as almost wholly irrelevant in terms of British defence assessments. Only in relation to the obsessive fear of Russian pressure through Afghanistan to India was there any specific consideration of a Soviet threat and it was noted by the Chiefs of Staff[18] that with weakening Soviet influence in Afghanistan, tribal opposition to a Russian invasion would be 'more ardent that previously'. The Chiefs of Staff did in this context note the increase in Russian military strength, although 'it would be a very sweeping assumption to think that the defects have been eliminated'. In parallel with this report, the Defence Requirements Sub-Committee conducted a major review of British needs, in which, apart from a reference to the increase in the strength of the Soviet Air Force, the Soviet Union did not figure as either a positive or negative factor.

EDEN IN MOSCOW

The immediate fruit of the Vansittart–Maisky conversations in the summer of 1934 was a decision that there should be a British ministerial visit to Moscow. Vansittart argued that Russia had been 'offering indications of better behaviour' in relation specifically to Afghanistan and also, more generally, to hostile propaganda. It would, he said, be wrong to overrate the change of heart or to underrate the use to which it might be put. What mattered was to strengthen the Litvinov school of Soviet policy against the Voroshilov school of Soviet–German rapprochment. The Russians wanted a visit. 'On every ground of high and far-sighted policy' the reply should be affirmative. Endorsing Vansittart's recommendation, Eden advised his colleagues of the need to reckon with the 'intensely suspicious nature of the Russian regime' and with the fact that Russia must eventually figure in an overall negotiation, if only because Germany was constantly citing the Russian threat.[19] The possibility of a ministerial visit to Berlin was already being considered. The Prime Minister, Ramsay MacDonald, was keen that the two should be kept distinct. 'It is essential', he minuted,[20] 'that we should improve our contacts with Russia, but in nearly every respect Russia and Germany are fundamentally different propositions to us, and the fitting of Russia into a European scheme of cooperation cannot be done in the same way as Germany.' Nevertheless, the project for a Russian visit was accepted. It was decided that Simon and Eden should jointly visit Berlin and that Eden should continue to Moscow and Warsaw.

Events moved quickly. The publication of the British White Paper on Defence on 4 March, followed by the Parliamentary Debate on 11 March, brought a tantrum by Hitler, followed on 16 March by the announcement that Germany was introducing conscription. Welcoming the forthcoming talks with British ministers, Hitler remarked that any country which allied itself with the 'filthy crew' in Russia was doomed to perdition. In thoroughly unpropitious circumstances and against a background of substantial French anxiety, the British ministerial visit to Berlin nevertheless went ahead and the discussions between Hitler, Neurath and Ribbentrop on the German side and Simon and Eden on the British were in a relatively low key. The Germans were, however, wholly opposed to participation in an Eastern pact which contained provisions for mutual assistance in the event of aggression, and made much of the potential Soviet military threat. Eden noted in his diary that the total result of the meeting was very disappointing and, commenting on Hitler's obsession with Russia, he wrote that he was strongly against letting Germany expand eastwards: 'Apart from its dishonesty, it would be our turn next.'[21] From Berlin, Simon returned home to report to the Cabinet, while Eden took the train to Moscow. On the way, he composed a telegram to London concluding that there was no basis for a general settlement with Germany and that the only course for Britain was to uphold the principles of the League Covenant and consolidate against Germany all those nations which believed in the collective system.[22]

So it was that on 28 March 1935 Mr Eden, still only 37, but already a rising star of the Conservative party and, as Lord Privy Seal with responsibility for League of Nations questions, Simon's junior in the Foreign Office, became the first British minister to visit Russia since the Revolution.[23] His first impression was of weather, streets and people all grey, sad and unending. His reception was, however, warm and he quickly got down to a detailed discussion with Litvinov, in which he gave a very full report of the Berlin talks. Litvinov, who commented that Germany was bent first upon revenge and then upon domination, asked about Eden's conclusions from the talks. For his part, Eden said, those Governments which believed in collective security should hold to it even more strongly – but he did not know the views of the British Cabinet. (Here in fact, was the weakness of his position. He might not know the latest view of the Cabinet but he knew only too well the instincts of many of its members and so did Litvinov.) The discussion of bilateral questions was relatively brief. The British side expressed satisfaction at the working of the commercial agreement and indicated that if extra orders were forthcoming, credit might be possible. Eden made no headway when he remarked that if the two countries were to enter upon an era of friendliness and greater frankness, this could not be reconciled with the continuance of propaganda. Apart from this, he said, there were no real differences between the two Governments. The high point of the visit was a meeting between Eden, accompanied by Chilston and Strang, and Stalin, Molotov, Litvinov and Maisky. It was the first time Stalin had received a Western political leader. Eden commented upon his remarkable knowledge and understanding of international affairs, his unshakeable assurance and control and his implacable ruthlessness. The substance of the discussion was unremarkable, Stalin confirming that the Soviet Union had no desire to interfere in the internal affairs of the British Empire, speaking of the menace of Germany and Japan, urging the need for collective

security and the importance, in that context, of British policy.[24] A
final communiqué on the talks stated 'that there is at present no
conflict of interest between the two Governments on any of the main
issues of international policy . . . that the integrity and prosperity of
each is to the advantage of the other' and recorded the 'primary
importance' of cooperation between the two countries for the 'collective organization of peace and security'. It was an endorsement of
the Litvinov slogan, 'Peace is indivisible', carved in butter among the
caviar at lunch. The spirit of cooperation was to prove scarcely more
durable than the butter. By the summer of that year the Seventh
World Congress of the Comintern was passing a resolution aligning
Britain with the fascist powers: 'Great Britain is striving . . . to
strengthen the anti-Soviet tendencies not only of Germany, but also
of Japan and Poland.'[25]

THE APPEASEMENT YEARS

The facts of British policy during the years of appeasement have
been well recorded and much analysed. It is a period which, even
for those of us who were in our teens at the time, is still not easy to
treat dispassionately, despite the passage of half a century. The
reader will have little trouble in sensing how I viewed British policy
at the time. The years may have mellowed my criticism, but they
have not changed its essence. My purpose here, however, is not to
reopen the old debate, but to describe the handling of a single
element of British policy, the relationship with the Soviet Union.
The volume of directly relevant material is not great. Its very thinness
speaks much for the quality of the relationship.

For the Soviet historian, the analysis is simple: Britain and France,
motivated by fear, greed and hatred of Communism, sought to buy
off the aggressors with every available concession, preferably at the
expense of others, in the hope of avoiding the inevitable intra-
capitalist conflict in the West and turning Germany eastwards. It is
perhaps enough that the charge is made by those whose standard of
international morality was set by Stalin. Yet it must be examined.
The record of these years is indeed one of the search for measures
which might avoid military conflict with Germany. It is, sadly, also
the record of a British Prime Minister, a British Government and a
large part of the British people prepared for long – but not for ever –
to surrender the interests of others in this process. The principles by

which they were guided were, for the most part, not ignoble. The structure of Europe after Versailles contained the seeds of its own disintegration. It may be that the year gained for British rearmament and for the consolidation of British opinion justified even that brief and shameful period during which the search for peace at almost any price left honour to weigh little in the scales of judgment. There was more of emotion than of calculation in the decisions of the British government, and emotion does not lend itself to measurement. How is one to weigh the emotions aroused by the Versailles Treaty, the sympathy with Germany's post-war plight, the instinctive anti-Soviet prejudice of a large sector of society, the passionate desire of those who had experienced the carnage of 1914–18 to spare another generation its repetition? What is relevant for this study is that these and many other emotions combined to produce policies in which the Soviet Union counted for little. But they did not produce an anti-Soviet conspiracy. In the conduct of relations with the Soviet Union the errors – and they were not insignificant – were of omission, not of commission. Ministers and officials, battered from crisis to crisis, did not consider the Soviet Union as a substantial factor in their policy until they were within a few months of the outbreak of war. Cabinet minutes, which in earlier years have entry after entry dealing with Russia, reveal almost nothing. In times of crisis there are often policies too sensitive to be recorded, but the sad fact is that policy towards the Soviet Union, open or concealed, barely existed between the spring of 1935 and the spring of 1939.

Let us now examine the facts. Sparse though they are, they make a coherent picture. The policy, or more accurately the lack of it, is not difficult to chart. Nor is the reasoning – and also the lack of it – difficult to follow. Immediately after the Eden visit to Moscow, the early summer of 1935 saw a significant realignment of the East–West relationship in Europe, with the signature on 2 May of the Franco–Soviet treaty and on 16 May of the Czech–Soviet Treaty. With these treaties, the situation which British policymakers had been hoping to avoid had come to pass. In the Locarno context France had already given a guarantee to Czechoslovakia and now, instead of a loosely-worded Eastern pact, with which the British Government for a brief moment hoped to see Germany associated, there was a direct Franco-Czech-Soviet combination which, to those whose aim was the appeasement of Germany, brought the prospect of hostilities measurably closer. It is worth recalling the essential features of the three treaties. The French guarantee to Czechoslovakia, given in the original Locarno context, was linked with the League Covenant and provided for mutual assistance in the event of an attack resulting from failure of the respective undertakings with Germany. The Franco-Soviet Treaty, also linked to the Covenant, provided for the parties to come to each other's aid against unprovoked aggression by any European state. The Czech–Soviet Treaty was similar, but conditional upon assistance being rendered by France. The British response to the situation created by these interlocking commitments was threefold: to intensify the effort to appease Germany; to oppose any strengthening of the Franco-Soviet Treaty; and to seek to frustrate a German–Soviet rapprochement. We can see the latter element reflected as early as February 1936 in a memorandum by Sir Robert Vansittart, 'Britain, France and Germany'.[26] He saw the risk that 'if he [Hitler] were to beckon the Russian Government . . . they might step forward' and argued that if a German–Soviet alliance were to be avoided, the relationship between Germany and the Western powers must be improved. He would not wish this to take place at the expense of others in Europe, but if, for instance, Britain were prepared to restore the German colonies, then, he argued, it would not make sense to arouse German suspicion by the grant of a loan to Russia. Delay in the ratification of the Franco-Soviet Treaty meant that it was only in September 1936 that the Cabinet considered its implications.[27] The Chiefs of Staff Sub-Committee had recommended that Britain should 'reserve complete freedom to decide for ourselves whether we should intervene in any conflict arising out of German aspirations or French commitments in Eastern Europe'. In line with this view, the Foreign Policy Committee of the Cabinet recorded general agreement 'that at some stage we should make it clear to France that we had no intention of being drawn into any troubles arising out of her Eastern commitments' and the Cabinet accepted the view that British commitments ought not to be increased by reason of the Treaty.

A year after the Eden visit to Moscow, despite a blast of organised Comintern hostility, the bilateral relationship was still in reasonable shape. In January 1936 Litvinov visited London for the funeral of King George V and took the opportunity to have talks with Eden and Baldwin, and in September Major-General Wavell attended Soviet army manoeuvres at Minsk. By then, however, the situation in Western Europe had already deteriorated sharply. On 7 March 1936 the German army's reoccupation of the Rhineland precipitated a major crisis, the effect of which was to concentrate thinking on the

German threat in the West. In justifying this action, the German Government alleged that the Franco-Soviet Treaty constituted a breach of Locarno. To British ministers, not only was the allegation unfounded, but the Soviet Union seemed largely irrelevant to the whole issue. It was only in response to Labour pressure that Austen Chamberlain confirmed that British obligations under the League Covenant applied 'equally, wherever aggression takes place in the Eastern or Western parts of Europe'.[28] To Soviet policy-makers, it seemed more probable that Britain might seek to safeguard its Western security at the expense of Eastern Europe and Litvinov expressed his anxiety to Eden shortly after the German move. In reply, he received an assurance of the British desire for a peaceful settlement for the whole of Europe, not merely its Western half. It was at this time that the old problem of British and Soviet interests in access to and egress from the Black Sea once again brought a clash at the Montreux Conference. A compromise was, however, found. Relations, if not close, were stable and, in the commercial field, they were further improved by agreement on the availability of guarantees by the Export Credits Guarantee Department in respect of exports to the Soviet Union.

THE SPANISH CIVIL WAR

In the light of present-day Soviet influence in Ethiopia, it is interesting to recall that the Soviet Union played no significant part in the crisis over the Italian invasion of Ethiopia in the autumn of 1935, although, within the League of Nations, Litvinov was to receive an early warning of the infirmity of collective security in the face of an armed challenge. With the outbreak of the Spanish Civil War in the summer of 1936 there was, however, direct Soviet involvement. That conflict was to polarise British opinion in relation to Communism and Fascism more sharply than any other event since 1917 and to colour the sympathies of a generation. Since the ending of the Soviet–Polish war, Soviet policy had been considered by successive British Governments very much in terms of trade and propaganda. Now the struggle between Fascism and Bolshevism took the form of an armed struggle in Western Europe. As Anthony Blunt wrote:[29] 'Even for the most ivory-tower intellectual it meant that the time of not taking sides was past'. These were the years in which, on one side of the divide, idealistic British volunteers were fighting with the Government forces in Spain – the time too when Philby in Spain and Blunt, Burgess and Maclean in Britain were being led towards their careers as Soviet agents. On the other side a substantial – and in government circles influential – segment of British opinion, alarmed at the prospect of Communist domination of Spain, deplored Nazi and Fascist methods, but nevertheless wanted to see victory go to the Franco rebels.

It was not easy for the Soviet Union to assess British policy. At first they saw in Eden's policy of non-intervention the possibility of frustrating German and Italian ambitions and there was, at the outset of the Civil War, a brief possibility of British–Soviet collaboration, with the Soviet Union taking an active part in the work of the Non-Intervention Committee, meeting in London under British chairmanship. As the ineffectiveness of the Committee became increasingly apparent, Soviet disillusion mounted and the Soviet Union began, albeit more modestly, its own interventionist policy. In a perceptive despatch from Moscow in October 1936,[30] the Chargé d'Affaires, MacKillop, commented that the Soviet interest in collaborating with Britain and France had at first overcome instinct and led to participation in the work of the Committee, but if there were no results, doctrine and class sympathy would come to the fore. He saw the Soviet hope of British participation in collective security as faint and if the Franco-Soviet Treaty, the cornerstone of Soviet policy, were broken, the Soviet Union would be forced into a 'defensive and anxious isolation' in which its 'specific eccentricities' would be less restrained.

The conclusion of the Anti-Comintern Pact between Germany and Japan in November heightened Soviet concern at the prospect of a threat from East and West and reinforced the logic of Litvinov's search for collective security. British opinion, on the other hand, was coming increasingly to see the Soviet Union as a complication rather than as an asset against the German threat in the West. The trial of Zinoviev and Kamenev in the summer of 1936 heralded the great Stalin purges in which the new Soviet state seemed to be tearing itself apart. They came at the very moment at which the Soviet Union had begun to be accepted on the international scene and at which a closer Soviet–British relationship might have given some substance to collective security. During the next two critical years, a healthy British repugnance at the process of mass judicial murder and a calculation of its effect upon the Soviet armed forces made the Soviet Union seem markedly less attractive as a potential friend and markedly less relevant as a factor in the European military equation.

The Soviet Government could see very clearly that the risk of an appeasement policy pursued at their expense was heightened by their identification with an ideological struggle in Spain. In November 1936 Maisky sought to persuade Eden that Soviet support for the Spanish Government was not for ideological reasons, but because of the need to prevent a German–Italian victory. He recalled the spirit of the Moscow Communiqué of the previous year, but evoked little response from Eden. By the end of the year Vansittart, with Eden's approval, was implementing the spirit of the Cabinet decision of September and warning Reynaud of the danger that any strengthening of the Franco-Soviet Treaty with a military treaty or staff talks might make an agreement with Germany more difficult to achieve. He was not to know that two and a half years later, in the summer of 1939, Soviet irritation and suspicion at the French refusal to undertake these staff talks was to underlie a Soviet refusal to accept political commitments without parallel military commitments and add a substantial complication to the negotiations for a tripartite British–French–Soviet alliance.

Despite the political hesitation, British defence planners at this time saw the Soviet Union as a potential ally rather than an enemy. The purge of the Soviet armed forces was only beginning. A major Review of Imperial Defence produced by the Chiefs of Staff Sub-Committee on 20 February 1937[31] noted that until 1931 Soviet policy had been one of open hostility to the Versailles system and in particular to the British and French Governments, but that subsequently – and especially since 1935 – the attitude towards Britain had improved *pari passu* with the deterioration in relations with Germany and Japan. It was expected that this would continue, with the proviso that, whereas it was contrary to British interests that there should be war anywhere, the Soviet Government would have no objection to a war between the capitalist powers of Europe, so long as the Soviet Union was not involved. The military development of the Soviet Union had progressed to the point at which she possessed the largest army and air force in the world and a submarine force of possibly similar dimensions. For the next few years at least, 'the British Empire and the Soviet Union are likely to have two common potential enemies in Germany and Japan as well as a common desire for peace'. The ultimate Soviet hope of world revolution had not been abandoned and, in the long run, there might be trouble over India, but there were no immediate serious causes of friction and even in relation to Spain it was unlikely that British–Soviet relations would be seriously disturbed. Finally, the report noted that in the event of a German attack on the Low Countries, Britain and France might find themselves fighting with the Soviet Union against Germany and, in the event of war with Japan, Soviet assistance might be of considerable value.

As Chancellor of the Exchequer at this time, Chamberlain was already exercising a substantial influence on foreign policy. The whole thrust of his policy was to minimise the confrontation with Germany. Like many others, he saw Eastern and South-Eastern Europe as an area in which German economic influence might well be dominant, and doubted, as did many in the Foreign Office, both the equity and the viability of the post-war settlement of the German frontier with this region. Despite the belief that frontier revision would sooner or later be inevitable, he was looking for measures by Germany which would 'reassure the Governments of Central and Eastern Europe of Germany's intention to respect their territorial integrity and sovereign independence', including 'an indirect arrangement with regard to the Soviet Union'.[32] The determination of the Foreign Office, under Eden, to avoid being drawn into an anti-Soviet bloc as the price of a better relationship with Germany may be seen in the instructions sent on 15 July 1937 to Sir Nevile Henderson, HM Ambassador in Berlin, for a meeting with Goering:

> The German Government complain that His Majesty's Government continue to cooperate with the Soviet Government in European affairs; whereas Germany would like to see the Soviet Government completely isolated. This . . . raises a fundamental issue on which His Majesty's Government have made their position quite clear and on which they cannot compromise. His Majesty's Government must take the Soviet Government as they find them in the conduct of international affairs, nor refuse cooperation if its offer appears to be genuinely made, simply on account of divergence of political creed.

THE AUSTRIAN AND CZECH CRISES

Immediately after Chamberlain became Prime Minister, in May 1937, the balance of political and strategic assessment began to change and, without any conscious decision, the process of excluding the Soviet Union from participation in the resolution of Europe's growing crisis began to take shape. Within the Soviet Union, Stalin's purge was exacting a toll across the population which was rising into the millions. A leadership which had brought famine and death to the countryside by the forced collectivisation was now devouring its soldiers, its administrators, its managers and its workers. In the armed forces alone, some 30 000 officers were believed to have been removed and many of them executed between 1937 and 1939. Neither in terms of moral authority nor of military power was the Soviet regime in any position to command acceptance as a partner to Britain. In April 1938 Lord Chilston forwarded to the Foreign Secretary[33] an assessment by his Military Attaché, commenting on the disastrous effect of the purge on morale and efficiency. In the Ambassador's view, 'nothing short of an immediate threat to the integrity of Soviet territory would be held by the rulers of this country to justify entry into a war': a German occupation of part of Czechoslovakia would not fall into this category and for the time being, the Soviet Union must be 'counted out of European politics'.

As the European crisis gathered force, with the German Anschluss with Austria in the spring of 1938 followed by the Czech crisis in the summer and autumn, the prospect of war with Germany became clearer, but British rearmament was proceeding slowly and time was needed. The resignation of Eden in February 1938 and his replacement by Halifax left the conduct of British foreign policy very much in the hands of the Prime Minister. The search for peace by the satisfaction of German demands now resulted in the exclusion of almost all other factors. Chamberlain saw no merit in an American suggestion of participation in the search for a European settlement and was well pleased at its abandonment. There was certainly no political will on the part of his government, nor, it seemed, any military justification for the consolidation of relations with the Soviet Union as a partner in thwarting German expansion. There was instead a substantial reinforcement of the fear, already apparent in 1936, that too close a relationship would make even more difficult the appeasement of Germany.

Litvinov had now been struggling for five years to make a reality of the policy of collective security.[34] His belief in it was probably genuine, but he lacked the power base of Politburo membership, his instincts were not those of Stalin and he was not securing any demonstrable success. It was a tribute to his skill that the policy was not abandoned sooner. By 1938, however, the Soviet Union, increasingly irritated at the coolness of Britain and France, was beginning to hint at the alternative of a Soviet–German rapprochement[35] and similar hints were emanating from Berlin. There was no great disposition, at this point, to take such hints very seriously and the British Government, while refraining from being drawn into an anti-Soviet coalition, were equally disinclined to join the Soviet Union in one directed against Germany. In March 1938, immediately after the Austrian Anschluss, the Soviet Government drew attention in a statement by Litvinov to the immediate menace to Czechoslovakia and beyond it to the other states bordering on Germany as well as those further away. They formally proposed to the British and other Governments consideration within or outside the League of collective action against the further development of aggression, a proposal rejected in a formal note by the Foreign Secretary. Halifax, with a courtesy which did little to conceal his instinctive aversion, pointed out that a comprehensive conference could not be arranged, and a conference attended only by some Powers and designed less to secure the settlement of outstanding problems than to organise concerted action against aggression would not necessarily have a favourable effect.[36]

Throughout the critical year of 1938, the Soviet Government can have had few doubts about the trend of British policy. Their Foreign Office agent, Captain J. H. King, was supplying copies of secret telegrams and Maisky's reports of his talks with Halifax, Cadogan, Vansittart, Beaverbrook, Churchill, Lloyd George and others were illustrating the range of British opinion. We may, for instance, note his meetings with Chamberlain's adviser, Horace Wilson, whom Maisky had known in a different capacity during the negotiation of the 1934 Trade Agreement. In a telegram of 11 May[37] Maisky reports Wilson's description of Chamberlain's policy: German expansion into the smaller states of Central and South-Eastern Europe would be less harmful than an early war. It would give time for British rearmament and the resulting mixture of pressures might in ten to fifteen years lead to a more moderate German foreign policy. So far as the Soviet Union was concerned, Wilson continued, Chamberlain was less hostile than Baldwin, but simply did not regard the relationship as important at that time. He was a practical man who recognised the Soviet defence capability, but saw the Soviet Union as an essentially passive factor on the European scene, of doubtful value as a potential ally against Germany. Wilson saw him, therefore, according to Maisky, as being disinclined towards any activity over the 'Russian question'.

Even against this political background, it is remarkable that, throughout the Czech crisis in September 1938, the Soviet Union was almost wholly ignored as a factor in the situation. On 27 August, Halifax had a discussion with Maisky, in which the latter said that, in the event of a German attack, the Soviet Union would 'certainly do her bit', but in the crucial Anglo-French discussions on 18 September there was no consideration of the possible role of the Soviet Union. The Soviet records show[38] that, in formal terms, the Soviet Union had indicated that it would honour its obligations and had offered joint staff talks with France and Czechoslovakia, but by 15 September, Litvinov had concluded that Czechoslovakia would be sacrificed and saw no reason to develop a practical plan for Soviet assistance. The assurance of Soviet support in the event of action by France which was given to Beneš on 20 September must be seen in that light. Subsequently, on 23 September, when it seemed that a settlement with Germany was unlikely, instructions were sent to Butler in Geneva to speak to Litvinov, explain to him the supreme effort being made by the Prime Minister in his talks with Hitler at Bad Godesberg and ask for 'any precise indication of what action the Soviet Government would take in the event of Czechoslovakia being involved in war with Germany and at what point they would be prepared to take it'. Litvinov had, in fact, already stated publicly that if France were to honour its obligation towards Czechoslovakia and fight, the Soviet Government would 'come to the aid of Czechoslovakia', but he must have known that his own Government was in no position to take effective action and had no plan to do so. In any case, he could scarcely expect a productive discussion with Butler. In response to the British enquiry, he therefore refused to amplify his statement, saying merely that Russia would 'take action'. He did, however, suggest that a separate tripartite British, French, Soviet Conference might be held, together perhaps with Romania and any other 'reliable' small power, at which he would be prepared to discuss 'military and air questions'.[39] In his memoirs,[40] Lord Butler condemns the theory that Britain deliberately 'excluded Russia from Europe' and says that his interview with Litvinov 'only confirmed our conclusion that, both on political and military grounds, Russia could not be trusted to wage war in defence of interests that were not bound up with her own security'. (It would indeed have come as a surprise to Stalin that anyone might have supposed otherwise.) Litvinov's report of the meeting with Butler[41] indicates that, in response to Butler's questions, he complained that the British

Government, having ignored the Soviet Union, was now wanting answers without being willing to provide any information about British policy and that the Soviet Union would not, in any case, act in advance of France. Maisky subsequently received a telegram in which the Foreign Ministry spoke of the need to give the impression of taking at face value the British 'eyewash' about 'cooperation' with the Soviet Union, although it was really all a fraud.

As the crisis came to its height, the British Government was concerned that Soviet participation at any conference would be wholly unacceptable to Germany. Consequently, although the Cabinet contemplated the inclusion of the Soviet Union in a tripartite guarantee of the new Czechoslovak frontier[43] there was no question of an invitation to Munich. Munich may not have figured directly in the British–Soviet relationship, but it was critical to the Soviet assessment of British policies and to the setting of the stage for the 1939 negotiations. For Pravda it 'surpassed in shamelessness' anything since 1918. It must have been a powerful factor in that reshaping of Soviet policy which was to culminate in the German–Soviet agreement of the following summer. In London, the exclusion of the Soviet Union from the crucial policy nexus continued to be a guiding principle. By November[44] the Foreign Secretary was reporting that the French were anxious to 'disentangle themselves from the Russian connexion' and recommending avoidance of 'a position in which we might find ourselves asked to take action with France and Russia against Germany and Italy on behalf of a state which we were unable effectively to defend'. In Franco-British discussions in Paris, later in November[45] the Prime Minister remarked that it would be 'much easier for everyone' if the Czechs were to say that they did not want a Russian guarantee. There were at this time rumours of German support for Ukrainian separatist agitation and Chamberlain was able to secure from Bonnet an assurance that France's obligations would be effective only in the event of a direct attack by Germany on Russian territory.

Towards the end of the year, Lord Chilston was replaced as Ambassador in Moscow by Sir William Seeds. Seeds spoke Russian, but his only experience of Russia was as a young man in the years before the Revolution. He spoke with determination to Litvinov of the British Government's 'real desire to know – and give friendly consideration to – the Soviet Government's views of international questions', but he was heard with some scepticism and reported Litvinov as saying on one occasion that Britain would continue to capitulate and the Soviet Union would 'leave us to our own folly'. Butler also gained the impression from Maisky that the Soviet Union would now pursue a 'more isolationist policy'.[46] On 6 March, Seeds wrote a major despatch on the state of the Soviet Union in which he commented that the Government was 'as firmly established as any regime can reasonably be expected to be' and that the army, if not of great value in an offensive war, was loyal and would constitute a serious obstacle to an attacker. Of greater interest than the despatch was an important note appended to it by Fitzroy Maclean, at that time an attaché in the Embassy. 'It must be remembered', he wrote, 'that Soviet policy is purely opportunist . . . were they to consider that their own interests or those of the Soviet Union required it, the rulers of this country would not hesitate to change horses in midstream.' His comments preceded by only a few days the speech to the 18th Party Congress in which Stalin spoke of the failure of Britain and France to pursue a policy of collective security, their encouragement of Germany to turn eastwards and their plan to involve Japan and Germany in a war with the Soviet Union at the end of which the democracies would be able to dictate their own terms. Seeds warned that the 'innocents at home' should heed Stalin's advice that Soviet Russia would 'not be drawn into conflicts by warmongers who are accustomed to have others pull the chestnuts out of the fire.'

THE 1939 NEGOTIATIONS

Throughout the winter of 1938–9, after having decided to abandon the joint guarantee of the frontiers of Czechoslovakia, the British Government gave little more thought to Russia. The only substantial issue which they considered was the need for a visit to Moscow by the Secretary for Overseas Trade, Robert Hudson, in order to make a further effort to settle the problem of the pre-Revolution debts and, more important, to renegotiate – or if necessary denounce – the 1934 Trade Agreement on the ground that the Soviet Union was using its sterling earnings to purchase re-exported raw materials rather than British manufactures. Rumours of possible denunciation reached the Soviet authorities and did little to help the climate of relations.

It was only after the German occupation of the rump of Czechoslovakia on 12 March that the British Government began to consider the desirability of Soviet support in the resistance to further German aggression. A sudden panic arose as a result of an alarmist statement by the Romanian minister in London about the imminent German threat to his country and immediately an enquiry was directed to the Soviet Government as to whether they would actively help Romania in the event of German aggression. Litvinov, in reply, proposed a conference 'to discuss possibilities of common action'. It was essentially the proposal which he had made exactly a year earlier and which the British Government had declined. On this occasion, even before the Soviet reply had arrived, the Government had decided that the risk to Romania had been overstated and that the threat to Poland was of more immediate concern. They therefore proposed instead a joint declaration by the British, French, Soviet and Polish Governments providing for immediate consultation on joint resistance to 'any action which constitutes a threat to the independence of any European state'.[47] The Soviet Government, although preferring a conference, declared themselves ready to accept, provided France and Poland did likewise. By this time, Hudson was in Moscow and was assured by Litvinov that the Soviet Government was prepared to consult with the British and other Governments 'regarding all suitable measures of resistance, whether diplomatic or military or economic'. There was, however, still no enthusiasm from the British side. Poland, as was to be expected, objected to joining with the Soviet Union in any declaration and on 22 March the Cabinet considered the matter. The Foreign Secretary commented that the essential was to secure the support of Poland, but added: 'At the same time, he would take what steps were possible to keep in with Russia.' Suddenly, on 31 March, fearing an imminent German attack on Poland, the British Government undertook to 'give all support in their power . . . in the event of any action which clearly threatened Polish independence and which the Polish Government accordingly considered it vital to resist with their national forces'.

The guarantee to Poland, in form, if not in reality, the proximate cause of the Second World War, was conceived as a deterrent and given in haste, with no prior consideration of the strategy for its implementation if it failed to deter. In giving it, the Prime Minister tried to imply the Soviet Union's indirect association by referring in Parliament to a discussion which Maisky had had with the Foreign Secretary and saying that he had no doubt that the Soviet Government 'fully understood and appreciated' the principles upon which the British Government were acting. Neither Maisky nor his Government welcomed this involvement and Chamberlain's subsequent statement that there were no 'ideological impediments' between Britain and the Soviet Union[48] can have carried no conviction.

The need for an urgent reassessment of the British–Soviet relationship was clear. There were after 31 March 1939 commitments which, in the likely event of a German attack upon Poland and the less immediate threat to Romania or Greece, would result in war between Britain and Germany. There was little practical aid which could be given to these states and, if the guarantees were to be invoked, it was desirable, both in terms of the defence of either country and in terms of the wider British defence interest, that the Soviet Union should be enlisted as an ally. So began the negotiations for a tripartite British–French–Soviet alliance. Those negotiations have led to allegations of bad faith which have persisted throughout the subsequent years: Soviet historians allege that the British Government's main objective was merely to entangle the Soviet Union in hostilities with Germany as a means of diverting the threat to itself; that they never seriously desired an effective alliance with the Soviet Union; that to this end they deliberately spun out the negotiations and left them in the hands of a Foreign Office official rather than a minister; and that they refused to accompany the political negotiations with serious military contingency planning. Against this, the Soviet Government is accused of duplicity in the initiation and conclusion of an agreement with Germany behind the backs of the British and French Governments, an agreement which, by removing the risk of Soviet opposition, cleared the way for the German attack on Poland and the seizure of Polish territory by the Soviet Union itself. Space does not permit a detailed account of the negotiations, but they occupy an important place in the history and mythology of British–Soviet relations and if we are to assess their significance in this context, it is necessary to examine briefly the main stages in their conduct.

Soviet policy in the spring of 1939 had been indicated by Stalin's speech of 10 March in which he effectively indicated the end of the search for collective security with the Western democracies and a retreat into isolation. By the time of the German occupation of Czechoslovakia, no actual change of policy had, however, been implemented and the Soviet response, as we have seen, still echoed the old policy of collective security. On the British side, there was a recognition of the possible value of Soviet support if war should break out, but certainly, as yet, no readiness for an alliance in advance of the event. On 26 March, the Prime Minister wrote to his sister: 'I must confess to the most profound distrust of Russia. I have no belief whatever in her ability to maintain an effective offensive, even if she wanted to. And I distrust her motives, which seem to me to have little connection with our ideas of liberty.'[49] On 5 April he said much the same in Cabinet: he 'had very considerable distrust of Russia and had no confidence that we should obtain active and constant support from that country.' He was supported by Hudson, who remarked that Russia would be of 'little or no assistance except for defensive purposes'. It was easy for ministers to conclude that 'the question of making any arrangement with Russia was obviously one which required a great deal of further consideration'.[50] It was, nevertheless, clearly in the British interest to seek some arrangement under which, if the guarantees to Poland or Romania were invoked and Britain were involved in war with Germany, Soviet assistance would be available. The Polish Government, for their part, having received the British guarantee, had no incentive to abandon their traditional hatred of Russia. The Polish Foreign Minister, Beck, visiting London early in April, had stated bluntly that Poland would keep clear of any British–Soviet conversations and was 'not in a position to accept any agreement which would have the effect, if only indirectly, of linking Poland with the Soviet Union'. From Moscow, Seeds warned of the temptation to the Soviet Union to stand aloof and urged that the Government should prevail on Poland and Romania to accept the idea of some form of Soviet military assistance. At this stage, there was, however, no realistic possibility of this. What Britain was seeking was simply a unilateral Soviet guarantee matching the British guarantees to Poland and Romania. Such an arrangement would imply no new British commitment and, equally, no enhancement to Soviet security.

The negotiating climate had not been improved by the Prime Minister's remark, when announcing the guarantee to Poland, that he believed the Soviet Government understood and appreciated the principles on which the Government were acting. Litvinov made it wholly clear to Seeds that, on the contrary, the British action was not at all appreciated. The British Government, having first proposed a four-power declaration, had dropped the idea, despite Soviet acceptance, and had ignored the Soviet proposal for a six-power conference. The Soviet Government 'had had enough and would henceforward stand apart free of any commitments'.[51] It was an inauspicious start. Nevertheless, when a proposal for matching unilateral guarantees to Poland and Romania was put to the Soviet

Government, it elicited a formal response envisaging a far closer defence relationship than the British Government was at that time prepared to consider. The Soviet Government offered a tripartite British–French–Soviet treaty for a period of five to ten years which would provide for mutual assistance, including military assistance both between the parties themselves and also to the East European states bordering the Soviet Union, from the Baltic to the Black Sea. Simultaneous political and military agreements would be concluded and there would be a commitment, in the event of war, not to conclude a separate peace.

British policy at this point was well indicated by the remark of Lord Halifax to the Romanian Foreign Minister[52] that 'it was desirable not to cold shoulder Russia too much'. There was little effort to conceal the patrician distaste at the prospect of close association with such a regime. More formally,[53] the objectives of British policy were set out in a fine quadruple negative as being:

a) Not to forgo the chance of our receiving help from the Soviet Government.
b) Not to jeopardise the common front by disregarding the susceptibilities of Poland and Romania.
c) Not to forfeit the sympathy of the world at large by giving a handle to Germany's anti-Comintern propaganda.
d) Not to jeopardise the cause of peace by provoking violent action by Germany.

On 26 April, when the Cabinet[54] considered the Soviet proposal for a tripartite pact, the Foreign Secretary suggested that the value of Russia as an ally was by no means as high as seemed to be believed by prominent members of the Labour party. It was generally agreed that the Soviet proposal 'took too little account of the practical difficulties', prominent among which was the Polish objection, and that to go beyond matching unilateral declarations would be to run the risk of 'breaking the common front'. On 3 May[55] the matter was considered again. The Foreign Secretary noted regretfully that Mr Churchill was entirely in favour of the tripartite pact and had been quite unmoved by Lord Halifax's arguments. Halifax maintained, however, that a tripartite pact 'would make war inevitable'. If the Soviet proposal were rejected, 'Russia would sulk' and there was a bare possibility that refusal 'might even throw her into Germany's arms'. It was, however, noted that Canada, South Africa, Portugal and Spain would all cause difficulty and that Cardinal Hinsley had expressed his anxiety in a long letter to the Foreign Secretary. Accordingly, it was decided to maintain the British counter-proposals, in the confidence that Russia would not break off on the spot.

At this point, in Moscow, on 4 May came the first consequence of the Stalin speech. Litvinov who, since his days in Britain during the 1914–18 war, had been intimately connected with Soviet–British affairs, was replaced as Foreign Minister by Molotov. There was at the time and subsequently much speculation about the significance of this move. Was it confirmation that the Soviet Union had abandoned the search for collective security with the Western democracies and had begun to explore, if not yet to adopt, the policy of closer association with Germany? Seeds certainly saw the risk of a policy switch. He had already warned that British policy would merely confirm the Soviet leadership in their belief that Britain was trying to evade association with them.[56] Now, with the sophisticated Jewish influence of Litvinov gone, 'the great men of the Kremlin will be more apt to plunge off into the deep if disappointed or indignant'. The published Soviet documents cannot be regarded as conclusive and, even with the benefit of the captured German documents, it is not easy to come to a definitive judgment. Some assumptions may, however, reasonably, be made. The policy of collective security was very much a Litvinov creation. He could scarcely have pursued it as far as he did without at least the acquiescence of Stalin. We cannot yet know the true facts – although they may soon emerge – but Stalin was probably never convinced, any more than was Chamberlain, that the policy merited a full commitment. By 1939 it had suffered failure after failure, culminating in the sacrifice of Czechoslovakia. The policy and its author were discredited and the argument that the Soviet Union had no option but to act independently to safeguard its own security was powerfully reinforced. A new, harsher, spirit was needed and it must be accompanied by a more direct subordination of foreign policy to the supreme leadership of the Party. There was no good reason to trust either Germany on the one hand or Britain and France on the other. The direct threat to Soviet security came from Germany and, while the apparent infirmity of Britain and France made them less menacing, it equally made them unattractive as allies. There were moreover, enough hints of the search for a new basis of accommodation between Britain and Germany to make the possibility of a new Munich a real one. Soviet policy has always been founded upon a calculation of the harsh realities of power and in that calculation it was Germany which was the dominant factor on the European continent. In such a situation, there was no incentive to compromise Soviet freedom of action by an alliance with Britain and France, unless the terms of that alliance were such as to bring a reinforcement of Soviet security powerful enough to offset the added risk of conflict with Germany as well as the threat from Japan. Moreover, there were signs that Germany would be glad to improve her relationship with the Soviet Union. Thus, in some respects, the considerations influencing Soviet policy were the obverse of those which had led the British Government for the past three years to eschew a closer relationship with the Soviet Union and seek its security in the appeasement of Germany. The documents suggest, however, that at the time of Litvinov's fall, no definite decision had been taken. From the German side, there was mounting pressure for a political deal with the Soviet Union which would remove the threat of a British–French–Soviet alliance. On the Soviet side, there was the beginning of a readiness to consider the switch, but for the time being the Germans were stalled, while Molotov formed his own judgment as to the value of the negotiations with Britain and France.

The British reply, delivered on 6 May, to Molotov's offer of a comprehensive treaty was well calculated to intensify his suspicions. It amounted to little more than a slightly improved variant of the original proposal for a unilateral Soviet declaration and was swiftly and formally rejected, with the comment that it 'cannot serve as a basis for the organisation of a front of resistance'.[57] Nevertheless, in Seeds' view, the Soviet Government were, for the present, 'still prepared to pursue a policy of collaboration, to a degree which may be found embarrassing'.[58] Their essential requirement was for full reciprocity and this meant a formal triple alliance. So the pressure on the British Government began to mount. They had to recognise that, if they were not to forfeit the possibility of Soviet assistance, they would have to pay the price of commitment to a formal alliance, with all this meant in terms of the heightened provocation to Germany, the complication to relations with Poland and Romania, the possible alienation of support elsewhere in the world and the opposition of a large section of British opinion. To add to the pressure, rumours of a possible Soviet–German rapprochement were being revived. In Geneva, Halifax spoke to the French Premier, Daladier, of the British desire to avoid a straight triple alliance and was warned that there could be a sudden change of policy in which the Soviet Union would 'retire into isolation and let Europe destroy itself'.[59] Halifax next spoke to Maisky and received much the same warning. According to Maisky, the Soviet Union could take care of herself and enter into no obligations, in which event she might have to defend herself single-handed, but would preserve liberty of action. Alternatively she could collaborate with others and, at the price of losing freedom of action, gain the chance of preventing war. But to accept the British proposals would mean losing freedom of action without avoiding war.

While Halifax was talking to Maisky in Geneva, Foreign Office officials were putting together a memorandum summing up the dilemma[60] and concluding that, despite all the disadvantages, it might be more dangerous to have the Soviet Union, completely untrammelled and playing off one side against the other than to 'collaborate with a dishonest or an incompetent partner'. It was scarcely a recipe for a whole-hearted attempt to forge an alliance.

In Parliament, meanwhile, pressure was growing. On 19 May, Lloyd George called for an end to 'this political snobbery that only wants to help a proletarian Government provided you do not rub shoulders with it'. Eden advocated a full tripartite alliance and Churchill who, cheerfully oblivious of the political realities of the smaller states of Eastern Europe, had been arguing for the construction of a solid front from the Baltic to the Black Sea, came out firmly in favour of the Soviet offer of a treaty of alliance. It was 'a fair offer, and a better offer . . . than the terms which the Government seek to get for themselves; a more simple, a more direct and a more effective offer. Let it not be put aside and come to nothing'.[61] The logic of the situation could not be escaped. Within the Cabinet, even Hoare had said that he was 'more and more impressed by the serious consequences which would result from a breakdown'[62] and the Chiefs of Staff had come to the view that although the military value of Russia as an ally was 'not nearly as great as was commonly supposed', full alliance was 'a better bargain' than the kind of middle course which the Foreign Office was advocating. On 24 May, the Cabinet faced the issue squarely.[63] There was, said the Foreign Secretary, a clear choice of alternatives. The risk of a Soviet–German rapprochement 'could not be altogether disregarded'. He 'had never disguised his own views on the subject of close association with the Russian Government', but it was not possible to contemplate breakdown. Failure to oppose Hitler with a solid bloc would make war more likely and it was therefore necessary to enter into a direct mutual guarantee with the Soviet Government. Ministers decided that, if there were to be any prospect of securing Soviet support, they would have to pay the price of accepting the principle of the Molotov proposal. The Prime Minister, too, although admitting that he 'viewed anything in the nature of an alliance with Russia with considerable misgiving', agreed that it was 'impossible to stand out against it'.

So it was that the major reversal of British policy took place and on 27 May the British and French Ambassadors put to Molotov a proposal for a triple alliance, linked to the principles of the League of Nations and providing for mutual assistance either in the event of a direct attack, or in the event of a signatory being involved in war as a result of an agreement with or a request for assistance from a third country. It was a move of profound significance, intended to meet the essential Soviet requirement. The Ambassadors could, as Seeds commented, scarcely believe their ears, when Molotov gave a negative response, alleging that references to the principles of the League meant involvement in League procedures, that no concrete agreement on forms of assistance was envisaged and that the Soviet Union wanted effective action, not words. Seeds commented on Molotov as a man with the 'foolish cunning' of a peasant 'totally ignorant of foreign affairs and to whom the idea of negotiation – as distinct from imposing the will of his party leader – is utterly alien'. Nevertheless, having now committed themselves to the principle of an alliance, the British Government, with increasing desperation, sought to meet Soviet objections. A Soviet counter-draft produced on 2 June made explicit the Soviet requirement for the guarantees to the Eastern European states to include the Baltic states of Latvia, Estonia and Finland and to take effect whether or not those states so desired. Here was a major stumbling block. The British Government knew that these states, fearing the Soviet Union at least as much as they feared Germany, were opposed to a Soviet guarantee which, on the basis of an allegation of indirect German aggression, might well serve as the pretext for a pre-emptive Soviet occupation. The Prime Minister commented[64] that it was 'manifestly impossible to impose a guarantee on States which do not desire it'. In a speech of 31 May, Molotov had already indicated the resumption of commercial negotiations with Germany, but the advice from Seeds was that a German–Soviet political agreement, never more than a possibility, was now unlikely, even if the tripartite negotiations were to break down. Nevertheless, the British need for the Soviet alliance was great. In a letter to Henderson in Berlin, Halifax described the negotiations as 'now the most important factor in the situation'.[65] An offer by Eden to go to Moscow himself was rejected by Chamberlain and it was decided that the British and French Ambassadors in Moscow should continue the negotiations with the assistance, on the British side, of William Strang.[66]

Strang arrived in Moscow on 14 June and revised proposals were put to Molotov on the following day. These provided for assistance in the event of one of the three parties being involved in hostilities as a result, *inter alia* of aggression against another European State which it had *in conformity with the wishes of that state* (author's italics) undertaken to assist. Since it was apparent to all that the Soviet Union's neighbours were opposed to receiving her guarantees, this scarcely moved matters forward and was rejected immediately by Molotov. To compound the failure, it was now envisaged on the British side that the Eastern guarantees should be matched by guarantees not only to Belgium and Luxembourg, but also to Switzerland and the Netherlands, the two latter being countries which had refused to recognise the Soviet Government. Molotov therefore proposed that the question of guarantees for the minor states should be dropped altogether and that there should instead be a simple triple alliance. This, of course, would have left the British Government exposed by reason of their existing unilateral guarantee to Poland and Romania, while providing no watertight assurance of Soviet support if that guarantee were invoked.

Puzzled, Halifax wrote to Seeds asking him to find out what Molotov really wanted before any new proposals were put forward: 'You are doubtless as bewildered as I am . . . . We have declared ourselves ready to give him the substance of everything he requires.' Seeds had no need to consult Molotov. He spelt out bluntly the Soviet position as he saw it. The Soviet Union wanted 'assistance or connivance if they found it expedient to intervene in the Baltic States (. . . in conditions which we would not regard as threatening the peace of Europe) on the plea that the Governments and ruling classes as distinct from the rest of the population . . . were about to compound with Germany'. The French Government had from the outset been less ready than the British to stand out for the interests of the Baltic States and the British Government now conceded once more. The guarantee would cover countries which the 'contracting country concerned felt obliged to assist'. The list of countries guaranteed might be unpublished; but if it were published it would contain the Baltic States, Poland, Romania, Turkey, Greece, Belgium, the Netherlands and Switzerland. Again the British proposal was rejected and now the Soviet Union concentrated on two points:

the need for an accepted definition of 'indirect aggression' (i.e. the abandonment by one of the border countries of its neutrality or independence); and the need for simultaneous negotiation and entry into force of a military agreement parallel to the political agreement. Halifax commented in a letter to HM Ambassador in Paris[67] that the Russian business was 'quite infuriating, it blocks everything and frays everybody's nerves'. He considered reverting to the idea of a simple tripartite pact, ignoring the border states, and warning Molotov 'that he will do well not to presume any further on our readiness to yield to the Soviet Government each time they put forward a new demand'. In the end, however, the British Government again decided to concede. The principle of a guarantee covering 'indirect aggression' was accepted on a basis which excluded only 'anything capable of being interpreted as an intention of interfering in another country's internal affairs' and it was agreed that a Franco-British military mission should proceed to Moscow to conduct negotiations for the parallel military agreement. On one point, however, Britain remained firm. They would not concede a Soviet demand that 'indirect aggression' should cover situations in which one of the border countries sacrificed its neutrality or independence even without threat of force. Strang commented in a letter to Sir Orme Sargent,[68] that the negotiations had been a 'humiliating experience. Time after time we have taken up a position and a week later we have abandoned it; and we have had the feeling that Molotov was convinced from the beginning that we should be forced to abandon it.' Strang recognised that the weakness of the British position flowed inevitably from the fact that Britain, committed to Poland and Romania, needed agreement, whereas the Soviet Union had a choice of at least two other policies, isolation or accommodation with Germany. He considered the possibility of breakdown, but still recommended that, on balance, continuation of the 'indeterminate situation' of protracted negotiations would be preferable.

At this point there was a pause. The political negotiations seemed close to conclusion. Surely, the British Government thought, with all else conceded, Molotov could afford to accept a formulation of 'indirect aggression' which did not make blatantly obvious the possibility of direct interference in the border states. It would take a fortnight or so before the military teams could be assembled, briefed and transported to Moscow. Meanwhile, the initiation of the military discussions would itself serve as a warning signal to Germany. So, wrote Halifax,[69] 'Having followed a policy of concession throughout these negotiations and gained nothing by it . . . there is no danger now of an imminent breakdown during the next crucial weeks . . . we feel we can afford to take a somewhat stiffer line.' It is likely that, at this point, the Soviet Government, already engaged in major hostilities with Japan and conscious of the risk of war on two fronts, were approaching their crucial policy decision in favour of collaboration with Germany.[70] On 22 July, the Soviet Commissariat of Foreign Trade had announced that trade and credit negotiations had been reopened with Germany. On the 25th the Soviet Government were told of the British and French readiness to open immediate military conversations and it was proposed that an announcement should be made that 'such a measure of agreement has been reached on the provisions of the political Agreement . . . that they can now proceed without delay to the consequential examination . . . of practical measures'.[71] Molotov objected not merely to the relatively optimistic tone of this announcement, but to any announcement at all: the Soviet Government 'decline to associate themselves with any joint statement'. It is scarcely possible, with the advantage of hindsight, to see this refusal other than as a reflection of the preparation to move to a relationship with Germany. At this point the Soviet Government knew that they could obtain with Britain and France an agreement which covered them against every possibility other than hostilities caused by their own intervention in one of the border states in a situation not provoked by a threat of force by Germany. If they had wished to use the prospect of the alliance as a deterrent to Germany, it was clearly to their advantage to proclaim rather than to obscure the extent of agreement. Moreover, it must have been abundantly apparent that even given maximum good will on both sides, the negotiation of a military agreement covering all the possible situations on the Eastern and Western fronts which might lead to war with Germany would require many months. Thus, the moment of initiation of staff talks was the moment at which the prospect of the alliance, if it was ever to serve as a deterrent to Germany, needed to be deployed. At this point the Soviet Government chose to remain silent.

The remaining difference in relation to 'indirect aggression' was put with perhaps excessive frankness to the House of Commons on 31 July by the Prime Minister, who indicated that the Soviet formula appeared to carry the signification of permitting encroachment upon the independence of other states. Butler then added to Soviet irritation by adding: 'The main question is whether we should encroach on the independence of the Baltic States.' The Government, Butler said, was opposed to this 'and the difficulty of reaching a formula on this point is one of the main reasons why there has been delay in these negotiations'. Accurate though his statement was, it was scarcely calculated to improve the climate for the military talks. Reporting a meeting on 2 August at which Molotov spoke of Butler's 'gross misrepresentation' of the Soviet position, Seeds commented that the negotiations had received a severe set-back. It was in fact to be the last of the negotiating meetings with Molotov.

THE GERMAN–SOVIET NON-AGGRESSION TREATY

In discussions between Schnurre, an official of the German Economics Ministry and Astakhov, the Soviet Chargé d'Affaires, the Germans had since May been hinting at the possibility not merely of trade negotiations, but of a more general understanding. On the latter point they received little encouragement until the beginning of August, when Astakhov said that his latest report to Molotov 'had created great interest'. But, he said, 'nothing concrete' was known of Germany's attitude'.[72] It was a fairly clear invitation to produce more detailed proposals. On 2 August Ribbentrop put to Astakhov a proposal for conclusion of a Soviet–German political protocol. There were, he said, no outstanding issues between the two countries in the whole territory from the Black Sea to the Baltic. On the following day, the German Ambassador in Moscow, Schulenburg, saw Molotov. He reported that Molotov had abandoned his habitual reserve. Schulenburg told him that, so far as Poland was concerned, the German Government 'were prepared to protect all Soviet interests and come to an understanding with the Soviet Government in the matter'. Reporting the discussion, he commented, however, that the old Soviet mistrust remained and that the Soviet Government seemed 'determined to conclude an agreement with Britain and France if they fulfil all Soviet wishes'.[73] On 12 August, the Soviet Government took the next step. Astakhov informed the German Government that the Soviet Government would be willing to open discussions in Moscow on a wide range of questions including the Polish question and the old German–Soviet political agreements.

For a further week, however, the Soviet Government played its hand with some caution, Astakhov stating that the discussions in Moscow must proceed by stages, with the political relationship as the final stage. The German pressure was, however, insistent. After negotiation in Moscow between the German Ambassador, Schulenburg, and Molotov, Tass announced on 22 August that Ribbentrop would visit Moscow for conversations on a Non-Aggression Treaty. On the following day he and Molotov signed the Treaty. Together with it, they signed a secret protocol, the existence of which was, until recently, denied by the Soviet Union, delimiting spheres of interest 'in the event of a territorial and political transformation' of Poland and the Baltic States. 'The question whether the interest of both parties makes the maintenance of an independent Polish State appear desirable and how the frontiers of this State should be drawn' was left for determination 'in the course of further political developments'. With regard to Bessarabia, the Soviet Union secured a free hand.[74] As Stalin, Molotov and Ribbentrop celebrated the signature, Molotov toasted Stalin 'who, – through his speech of March of this year, which had been well understood in Germany – had introduced the reversal in political relations'.[75]

In ignorance of the German–Soviet exchanges, the British and French military missions, having concluded that to cross Germany by train would be 'unnecessarily provocative', that no satisfactory arrangement for air travel was available and that to travel by cruiser would be 'inadvisable', were travelling slowly to Moscow via Leningrad in a small chartered passenger vessel arriving on 13 August. Their brief[76] was to go very slowly until such time as the political agreement was concluded and to try to confine the Military Agreement to the broadest possible terms – 'something on the lines of an agreed statement of policy'.[77] The Soviet negotiators, under Voroshilov, brushed aside the British draft principles on the ground that they were 'too abstract and immaterial'. What was needed, they said, was 'a complete military convention which should fix the number of divisions, artillery, tanks, aircraft and naval squadrons, which each of the three States should contribute'. In practice, however, the Soviet negotiators chose to stand on the issue that no progress could be made until the British and French Governments could secure from Poland and Romania permission for Soviet forces to transit their territory. They refused to address themselves direct to those two Governments on the ground that the Soviet Union had no military agreement with them and that the danger of aggression was most likely to affect Britain, France, Poland and Romania. It was therefore for the two former to make the approaches. It was, of course, well known to all concerned, that Polish and Romanian hostility to the

Soviet Union was so deep rooted that there was no prospect of this agreement being given. Only eighteen years ago the Poles had occupied Kiev and the Soviet army had thrust to the suburbs of Warsaw. Nevertheless, there ensued a week of frenzied exchanges between London, Paris, Warsaw and Bucharest. The main interest was in Poland, but the Polish Government remained obdurate. Finally, on 22 August, the day before Ribbentrop arrived in Moscow, the Head of the French mission informed Voroshilov 'that France's answer to the Soviet question re the right of passage through Polish territory is yes as soon as Poland is at war with Germany'. Voroshilov, however, declared himself unsatisfied and declined any further meeting until the political situation was clearer. In instructing Doumenc to give this assurance, the French Government, more desperate than the British to frustrate the conclusion of a Soviet–German deal, overstated the highly qualified assurances which were all they could obtain from Warsaw. The British Government, doubtful though they were, in an attempt to continue the discussions, authorised Seeds to support the French answer on passage through Polish territory. However, on 25 August, in response to a direct enquiry by Seeds, Molotov stated that the political situation had changed and the talks could not continue. The British and French military missions left immediately and there was no further contact between the British and Soviet Governments before the German forces moved into Poland on 1 September.

Gromyko and Ponomarev claimed[78] that the Soviet Government agreed to the Treaty with Germany 'only after it had finally become apparent that Britain and France were unwilling to cooperate with the USSR in resisting Nazi aggression'. Now, with the re-evaluation of the history of the Stalin years and with a sharp debate about the significance of the 1939 agreements for the Baltic states, the protocol has become an active question for the historians of the Gorbachev era and it may be that we shall have a new interpretation of Soviet policy. The record is, however, clear enough to justify the following conclusions:

a) The British Government was unwilling prior to the spring of 1939 to consider any effective collaboration with the Soviet Union to resist further German expansion. The Stalin purges had heightened British abhorrence of the Soviet system and scepticism as to the capability of the Soviet forces. The Government's objective was to avoid war and it judged that a closer relationship with the Soviet

Union would make war with Germany more, rather than less, likely.

b) The British initiatives in the spring of 1939, the over-hasty guarantees to Greece, Poland and Romania and the proposal for a joint declaration with the Soviet Union, reflected an impulsive reaction to crisis rather than a considered revision of policy. The proposal for a Soviet guarantee to Poland and Romania fell into the same category.

c) Only from the Cabinet meeting on 24 May 1939 did the British Government commit itself to the principle of a tripartite alliance with France and the Soviet Union. From this point onward, although less ready than the French to offer quick concessions, the British Government met, one by one, those Soviet conditions which lay within its own competence, reserving its position only in relation to a Soviet right of interference in Poland, Romania and the Baltic States other than in response to a threat of force by Germany. Having committed itself, it had little bargaining power and was hamstrung by the Polish refusal to accept any matching commitment in regard to the Soviet Union. Mistrustful of Soviet military capability, it sought a deterrent alliance rather than a coordinated strategy.

d) The need to coordinate policy with France did not constrain British initiative. French policy throughout placed greater emphasis upon the need for the tripartite alliance. Consultation with Paris may have added slightly to the response time. The Soviet Government was quicker in its responses, but this is scarcely surprising in view of the fact that the Soviet response was normally a simple negative.

e) The Soviet Government had long proclaimed the policy of 'collective security'. It had stated its intention of honouring its obligation to Czechoslovakia in September 1938, but gave no substantial evidence of this. Stalin's speech of 10 March was intended as an indication of the reorientation of policy. It probably indicated the abandonment of collective security and a determination to revert to an isolationist policy. The replacement of Litvinov by Molotov represented the implementation of that policy.

f) The Soviet Union was deeply mistrustful of British and French policy and wholly indifferent to the rights of small states. Taking a short-term view of its strategic interests, the Soviet Union thought it had little to gain from an alliance with Britain and France. The British guarantees to Poland and Romania came as a surprise and, in the light of Munich, there must have been genuine doubt whether they would be honoured. In any case, if they failed to deter Germany, it was hard to see how they could be implemented. If they were, the consequence would be an inter-imperialist war in which the primary interest of Britain and France would be to protect their own interests. If they waged war actively in the West, a quick German victory seemed unlikely and the balance of forces would move in favour of the Soviet Union, but the Soviet interest would still be best served by non-involvement. To accept the tri-partite alliance would mean that the Soviet Union might face the main burden of the combat with Germany and possibly also full-scale war with Japan. The Soviet Western front with Poland and the Baltic States was vulnerable. Britain and France offered no encouragement to the seizure of territory from these states, whereas Germany did. If Germany dishonoured her Treaty, the Soviet Union would still be in a better position to fight after having advanced her Western frontier.

g) The Soviet Government used the Moscow negotiations as a test of British and French policy. From the outset, their disposition was not to commit themselves, but they decided to establish the maximum which could be obtained from this source while keeping their options in relation to Germany open. Meanwhile, they left it to Germany to make the running if it wished to supplant the British and French. The decision in principle against the Franco-British alliance was probably taken in early August, between the end of the political and the beginning of the military negotiations and the definitive commitment to the German Treaty in the final few days before Ribbentrop's arrival. It is unlikely that any different handling of the political negotiations would have enabled the British and French Governments to secure Soviet cooperation against Germany without a commitment to sacrifice the states on the Soviet Union's western border and even this might not have sufficed. The military negotiations were never serious on either side and were largely irrelevant to the outcome.

So the first British attempt to establish a politico–military alliance with the Soviet Union, bedevilled from the outset by mutual suspicion, failed and in its failing left a legacy of mutual recrimination. The pressure of events was such that, in the days which remained before the outbreak of war, the British Government had little time to reflect on this major reverse. The Foreign Secretary remarked in Cabinet on 22 August[79] that if it was true that a German–Soviet pact had been concluded, the moral effect would be very great, but the pact was 'perhaps not of very great importance in itself'. With that, the British Government, its prejudices confirmed, having included the Soviet Union in its calculations for a brief and unfruitful six months, proceeded once again with some relief to do its best to ignore it.

7 Alliance

NEUTRAL – BUT IN WHOSE FAVOUR?[1]

In judging the policies of the British Government towards the Soviet Union during the period between September 1939 and June 1941, it is necessary constantly to have in mind three underlying factors:

a) The attempt to forge a British–French–Soviet alliance in the summer of 1939 had represented a deep but brief reversal of traditional British policies and instincts. Its failure left British policy-makers with a sense of betrayal and a reinforcement of the ingrained mistrust of the Soviet Union.
b) The trauma of Munich had left a determination to have no complicity with another apparently aggressive power in the East.
c) The sense of standing alone after the fall of France produced a certain elation of the spirit, in which purity of motive could easily prevail over cold calculation of the odds.

Against this background, it is scarcely surprising that, after the declaration of war on Germany, the British Government had little time – and less inclination – for consideration of its relationship with the Soviet Union. The consequences of the German–Soviet secret protocol of August 1939 were soon made apparent as Soviet forces moved into eastern Poland and the formal partition of Poland was effected by a German–Soviet agreement of 29 September. The Cabinet noted with some relief that the British guarantee to Poland, now given treaty form, was applicable only in respect of the German aggression. There was at this stage no desire to engage in hostilities against the Soviet Union, but the old conviction that there was little to choose between Nazi and Communist dictatorship was powerfully reinforced. Churchill subsequently wrote[2] that he did not give way to the general indignation in Cabinet, but instead put forward a paper indicating the possible strategic advantage of the new Soviet frontier with Germany and advocating a 'renewal of relations with Russia'.

In a much-quoted broadcast of 1 October, he spoke of Russian action as 'a riddle wrapped in a mystery inside an enigma'. The key to the riddle was, for him, the historic Russian national interest which ran wholly contrary to German domination of South-eastern Europe and the Balkans and it was with this key that, in the spring of 1941, he tried to loosen the German–Soviet link. In 1939 and 1940 there was, however, no general desire in Britain for a renewal of the British–Soviet relationship and certainly no practical possibility of bringing it about. After the collapse of Poland, with no active pursuit of the war in the West, the interest of British ministers was concentrated very largely on economic measures against Germany, including the need to minimise the leakage of strategic supplies through the Soviet Union.

THE SOVIET–FINNISH WAR

Mutual Assistance Pacts between the Soviet Union and Latvia, Lithuania and Estonia provided the pretext for the subsequent introduction of Soviet forces into these three Baltic States and when, on 30 November 1939, the Soviet forces attacked Finland, the public outcry in Britain was intense. The Cabinet, however, noted that Russian expansion in the Baltic would have no direct adverse effect on British strategic interests and accepted the advice of the Chiefs of Staff against being drawn into war with Russia.[3] The lead in the expulsion of the Soviet Union from the League of Nations was taken by France, but Britain, after first seeking to avoid a vote, joined in voting for expulsion and Maisky noted an 'icy void' around his Embassy. As the war dragged on, the flow of British defence supplies to Finland, although never substantial, was gradually stepped up. It was first recognised that a certain number of specialists would need to accompany them, then the raising of a volunteer force was agreed to and finally a substantial British regular force was prepared for a landing at Narvik with the joint objective of completing the northern blockade of Germany and aiding the Finns against the Soviet Union. It was in connexion with this enterprise that Harold Macmillan, visiting Finland, acquired the white fur hat which attracted so much attention on his visit to Moscow in 1959. A formal proposal of British mediation to bring about a settlement of the Soviet–Finnish war was put forward by Maisky to Butler on 22 February 1940, but the taint of Munich was still strong. Could a British Government, still smarting at the way it had been exploited by Hitler to bring about the dismemberment of Czechoslovakia, now be seen to lend its good offices to Stalin to bring about the dismemberment of Finland? Stafford Cripps visited Moscow privately at Soviet invitation early in 1940, but his report that Molotov seemed anxious to cultivate better relations with Britain was firmly set aside. Indeed, some views expressed in the Foreign Office at this time were, if anything, more belligerently anti-Soviet than those of the Chiefs of Staff. Vansittart minuted about 'Stalin and his psuedo-Communism which it is just as necessary to destroy as Nazism'. Only Butler sounded a warning note that by never meeting the Russians we should tend to increase rather than decrease German–Russian amity.

It was at this point that French pressure was being exerted in favour of an attack upon the oilfields at Baku, on which the Chiefs of Staff advised[4] that the risk of initiating war with Russia would be acceptable only if it led to the early defeat of Germany, but that there was no action against Russia which would achieve this result. In the Foreign Office, Fitzroy Maclean commented that the risks seemed negligible in comparison with the certain advantages and his view was endorsed by Orme Sargent, with only a mild dissent from the Foreign Secretary who noted that the paper was 'rather more decided in favour of action against Russia than I am at present'.[5] With neither the Foreign Secretary nor the Chiefs of Staff showing much enthusiasm, the project did not progress very far.

A NEW EQUILIBRIUM IN EUROPE

Fortunately for the British Government, the Finnish-Soviet war ended in March 1940, before the major volunteer force had embarked. During the brief period between the fiasco of the British attempt to preempt the German occupation of Norway and the German invasion of the Low Countries in May, there was some consideration of the possibility of renewing trade negotiations with the Soviet Union, but it was made clear by Maisky that his Government would not buy an agreement with Britain at the price of discontinuing their economic collaboration with Germany. Nevertheless, after the attack on Holland and Belgium, there was renewed pressure in Britain for the appointment of an Ambassador to Moscow to replace Seeds, who had been withdrawn for consultation at the time of the Soviet attack on Finland. The original plan was that Stafford Cripps should act as a special emissary for the purpose of trade negotiations, but at Soviet insistence he was appointed as Ambassador and embarked upon the task of restoring relations at the most unpropitious moment, arriving in Moscow on 12 June 1940, two days before the fall of Paris.

With Churchill having replaced Chamberlain as Prime Minister, there was now the possibility of a new impulse in British–Soviet relations. Churchill's antipathy to Soviet Communism was at least as great as that of Chamberlain and his record as an active opponent of the Soviet Union went far beyond that of Chamberlain. Nevertheless, in the critical military situation facing the new British Government there was no place for squeamishness. Within Europe, the Soviet Union had the potential either to level the balance or to tilt it so decisively in favour of Germany as to ensure the defeat of Britain. On 25 June Cripps was sent a personal message for delivery from Churchill to Stalin[6] designed to place the re-establishment of contact between the two countries on as firm a base as possible. Churchill referred to the 1939 negotiations and stated bluntly: 'Germany became your friend almost at the same moment as she became our enemy.' Now, he continued, there was the 'prospect of Germany establishing a hegemony over the Continent'. Britain, he said, had two objectives – to save herself and to free the rest of Europe – and was ready 'to discuss fully with the Soviet Government any of the vast problems raised by Germany's present attempt to pursue in Europe the methodical process by successive stages of conquest and absorption'. On the basis of this message, Cripps had a discussion of two and three-quarter hours with Stalin. Churchill thought it 'an interview of a formal and frigid character', but it was not without substance. Stalin questioned whether Germany had the strength to dominate Europe; stated that the Soviet Union had no intention of going further into Romania or the Balkans; hinted that British assistance in the improvement of Soviet–Turkish relations might be welcome and maintained that although the trade agreement with Germany would not be broken, it would not be used against Britain. The most important part of the discussion was, however, that in which Stalin foreshadowed the post-war reconstruction of Europe. The basis of the German–Soviet agreement had, he said, been 'a common desire to get rid of the old equilibrium in Europe which, prior to the war, Great Britain and France had sought to preserve'. 'If the Prime Minister wishes to restore the old equilibrium, he continued, 'we cannot agree with him.'[7] The history of the next forty years was to be very largely the history of the steps by which the

Soviet Union first established and then maintained a new equilibrium based upon its own effective control over Eastern Europe.

THE BALTIC STATES

Stalin was at this time disposed to strengthen the security of the Soviet Union by such action as lay within his own power and certainly not to compromise it by closer association with Britain. Having already occupied Eastern Poland, his first steps towards the reshaping of European frontiers were already in train when Cripps met him. On 15–16 June, under the pretext of thwarting a military conspiracy against the Soviet Union, Soviet forces entered the Baltic States, Latvia, Lithuania and Estonia, and puppet governments were quickly established. On 27 June, faced with a Soviet ultimatum, Romania ceded Bessarabia and in the first week of August the three Baltic States were formally incorporated into the Soviet Union. This action confronted the British Government with the need to decide its policy on recognition. The Cabinet was at first inclined to accept the Soviet action as a military necessity in preparation against a possible German attack, but eventually, influenced in part by American pressure against recognition and in part by the determination of the Foreign Office not to repeat the appeasement of the previous decade, decided to recognize the incorporation *de facto*, and to withhold *de jure* recognition until after the war. Meanwhile the gold deposits of the Baltic states in Britain were held against eventual compensation for seized British property.

Throughout the summer and autumn of 1940, the British Government continued its efforts to deflect Soviet policy away from alignment with Germany. The Soviet Government, for its part, careful to preserve that relationship, informed the German Embassy in Moscow of Churchill's proposal.[8] There is, nevertheless, some evidence to suggest that fear of a British–Soviet rapprochement may have helped to precipitate the German attack on the Soviet Union. On 31 July, when Hitler announced to his generals his decision to attack Russia, he was recorded as saying, 'Russia is the factor on which Britain is relying the most . . . with Russia smashed, Britain's last hope will be shattered'.[9] The elimination of Soviet power was an objective in its own right and the British factor may have been relevant only to the timing. But timing could be critical. In Germany at this time, Operation Sealion, the invasion of Britain, was still being prepared for September. The decision to postpone it was not taken until October, by which time it was clear that there was no hope of obtaining air supremacy over Britain. By the end of July, however, Hitler had probably begun to have doubts about Sealion and preparations for the attack on Russia began shortly after the July conference.

For some months longer, the diplomatic tussle for Soviet support continued to be waged by the British and German Ambassadors in Moscow, with little enthusiasm on the part of their Governments. In October, Cripps followed up Stalin's thinking about the new equilibrium by putting to Vyshinsky a suggestion that those who helped Britain during the war might expect to 'share actively in the task of reconstruction'.[10] British successes in the Battle of Britain were having some effect on Soviet opinion, but no realistic assessment of the balance of power in Europe could have led Stalin to gamble Soviet security on a closer relationship with Britain while the reconstruction of Europe was already proceeding apace under the German armed forces. When Ribbentrop invited Molotov to Berlin, there was little hesitation about acceptance. The proposal put to him by Hitler and Ribbentrop was for a joint German–Soviet liquidation of the 'world-wide estate in bankruptcy' of the British Empire. From both the German and the Soviet accounts of this meeting, it is clear that Molotov was non-committal in his response and insisted upon German confirmation of the 1939 agreement placing Finland in the Soviet sphere. An air raid on Berlin had, on Cripps's recommendation, been timed to coincide with his talks and, as Stalin subsequently recounted to Churchill, it prompted Molotov to enquire of Ribbentrop: 'If England is finished, why are we in this shelter, and whose are these bombs which fall?' It must be doubtful whether a ready Soviet acceptance of the German offer would have served to delay the attack on the Soviet Union until after the defeat of Britain, but non-acceptance must have helped to confirm its timing for the summer of 1941. It took only a little more than a month after the meeting with Molotov before, on 18 December, the German Government took the operational decision to proceed with Operation Barbarossa, the attack on the Soviet Union. To the policy-makers in London, however, Molotov's visit seemed to demonstrate that, faced with the need to choose, the Soviet Union had, as in the summer of 1939, preferred to align herself with Germany, and on 13 November the Chiefs of Staff were instructed to consider possible military action by Britain against the Soviet Union.[11]

THE PREPARATION FOR OPERATION BARBAROSSA

It did not take long before the first intelligence indications of preparations for a German attack on the Soviet Union began to reach London, but British analysts found it hard to decide whether the German Government was bent upon invasion or merely intended to use the threat in order to secure concessions. It still seemed that the Soviet Union would prefer to accommodate Germany rather than fight her. The British Government had, at this time, as indeed later, little to offer by way of inducement and, as June approached, there was still no British–Soviet rapprochement. *De facto* recognition of the incorporation of the Baltic States had been conceded. The withholding of *de jure* recognition was an irritant, but the grant of it would have counted for little. The trade negotiations were given desultory attention, but, as Stalin had already made clear to Cripps, what Britain could offer by way of rubber and non-ferrous metals was not enough to wean the Soviet Union away from its German trade. Indeed, the Soviet Union so misjudged its own national interest that it continued to supply strategic materials necessary for the maintenance of the German war effort right up to June 1941. British influence was used to enable the Soviet Union to improve its relationship with Turkey, but there was little negotiating leverage in this. Soviet reporting of the war showed a distinct bias in favour of Germany and the British assessment – which was probably correct – was that the Soviet Union would not prejudice its relationship with an apparently victorious Germany for the sake of a Britain still struggling to avoid defeat. Cadogan noted in his diary, 'Russia has no fear of us and we have nothing to offer. No use juggling with words and jiggling with drafts'.[12] As seen from Moscow, there were two courses open to Britain: she could seek to improve her own military fortunes by embroiling the Soviet Union in war with Germany and, additionally or alternatively, she could seek a separate peace with Germany and then join Germany in a second war of intervention in the Soviet Union. Either course would divert the thrust of German power eastwards and, given the known anti-Soviet sentiments of the British establishment, either seemed feasible.

Hitler needed to keep the Soviet Union quiet until his own attack had been fully prepared. He was, with good reason, confident of his ability to do this. In his New Year message to Mussolini, he described relations with the Soviet Union as good and commented: 'I do not envisage any Russian initiative against us so long as Stalin is alive and we ourselves are not victims of serious setbacks.' So, having secured the cooperation of Romania and Hungary, he continued his drive south-eastwards with the objective of effecting the subjugation of Greece and Yugoslavia before redeploying his forces for the attack on the Soviet Union. To the British Government there seemed little reason for Germany to attack a benevolently neutral Soviet Union. The principal theatre of land operations was North Africa and German strategy was consistent with preparations to destroy the British position in the Middle East.

In March it had seemed that Yugoslavia would capitulate without fighting, but the revolution in Belgrade made it necessary for three Panzer divisions which were being moved into Poland in readiness for the attack on the Soviet Union to be redeployed in the Balkans. An intelligence report of this move prompted Churchill to try to persuade Stalin that the Soviet Union could best delay a German attack on itself by action to increase German difficulties in the Balkans. On 3 April, he sent Stalin a personal message informing him of both the original move and the redeployment and added, 'Your Excellency will readily appreciate the significance of these facts'.[13] Cripps' handling of the message was, in Churchill's words, 'obstinate and obstructive'. He argued that Churchill's brief and cryptic message might merely detract from the impression made by his own representations, recommended against delivery and on 11 April wrote his own warning letter to Vyshinsky. Only in response to the Prime Minister's insistence did he eventually transmit the original message on 19 April through Vyshinsky. By this time, a day before the German attack on Yugoslavia, the Soviet Government had concluded a Treaty of Friendship with the new Yugoslav Government. Stalin later professed to have no recollection of Churchill's message and it is not unlikely that this was true. It is just possible that, had the message been personally delivered with some ceremony on 3 April, it might have served to open up a direct contact with Stalin, but even then it must be very doubtful whether he would have taken any more notice of it than he did of the warnings from his own sources.[14]

Even before delivering Churchill's message, Cripps sent a further remarkable memorandum to Molotov on 18 April, proposing an immediate improvement of relations. Cripps warned of German plans to obtain Soviet supplies either by humiliating concessions or by occupation, for all of which, he said, a plan existed for that spring.[15] The memorandum, which was curtly rejected by Vyshinsky, could scarcely have had any positive effect, but might have done no harm had it not also referred to the possibility that 'if the war were protracted for a long period there might be a temptation for Great Britain (and especially for certain circles in Great Britain) to come to some arrangement to end the war'. If Soviet suspicions of a British–German understanding needed any further boost it was given by the dramatic flight of Rudolf Hess to Britain on 11 May, with proposals – promptly dismissed in Berlin as a 'hallucination' – for a peace settlement between Britain and Germany. Soviet doctrine[16] is that there was, by this time, no realistic possibility of British and American collusion with Germany, but Churchill recounts how, even three years later, Stalin was still fascinated by the Hess incident and disposed to see it in the context of a plot against the Soviet Union.[17]

While Soviet suspicions were concentrated on the possibility of a British–German deal, the British Government was forced to evaluate an increasing volume of evidence from intercepted German communications, pointing to the assembly of the forces for Barbarossa.[18] As spring moved into summer, it was still possible to account for these moves as a show of force designed to secure Soviet concessions. After all, German policy provided examples enough of securing the spoils of war without the need to wage it and, it could be reasoned, the temptation to pursue such a course with the Soviet Union must be strong.

The tragedy was played out even through the final weeks preceding the invasion. Cripps was so badly out of sympathy with opinion in London that on 2 June he was recalled for consultations, arriving on 11 June. Even before he arrived, the British press was beginning to carry stories of German troop concentrations and by 10 June evidence of the pending invasion had become so strong that women and children were evacuated from the Embassy in Moscow. On 12 June the Joint Intelligence Committee decided that hostilities were highly probable and that the most likely period was the second half of June. This assessment was communicated to the Soviet Ambassador in London by the Foreign Secretary, but was brushed aside as a provocation by the Soviet Government. The only response from Moscow was a Tass communiqué on 14 June, denouncing rumours of an early Soviet–German war as 'nothing but clumsy propaganda by forces interested in an extension of the war'. During the final ten days preceding 21 June, the Chiefs of Staff considered policy in preparation for the German attack. It was estimated that the occupation of the Ukraine and Moscow would take the German forces something between three and six weeks and that thereafter the Soviet Government would disintegrate.[19] In terms of British interests, even a campaign as brief as this would impose a useful delay upon the German plan for the invasion of Britain and allow further time for the strengthening of British defences. As Eden put it: 'We need a breathing space.' It did not, however, provide much justification for substantial aid, even if this had been feasible, and all that was envisaged was the despatch of a Liaison Mission combined with an offer – scarcely likely to be received with enthusiasm in Moscow – of assistance in the destruction of the Caucasian oilfields and the supply of oil in replacement.[20] Fortunately, the importance of strengthening Soviet resistance received rather more recognition in Cabinet and a formal decision to pledge aid was taken in advance of the German attack. On 15 June Churchill informed Roosevelt that 'we shall of course give all encouragement and any help we can spare to the Russians'. He refrained from speaking of an alliance, but Roosevelt's reply indicated a readiness to support any statement 'welcoming Russia as an ally'. To Moscow, nothing further was said. Mutual suspicion, founded on established antipathy and proven experience, had destroyed any possibility of advance planning.

'THE PAST FLASHES AWAY'

The German forces crossed the Soviet borders on the morning of Sunday 22 June 1941 and that evening Churchill made one of his most memorable wartime broadcasts. 'No one', he said, 'has been a more consistent opponent of Communism than I have for the last twenty-five years. I will unsay no word that I have spoken about it. But all this fades away before the spectacle which is now unfolding. The past, with its crimes, its follies, and its tragedies, flashes away.' With emotion he conjured up a picture of the Russian people upon whom a 'cataract of horrors' had been launched and declared, 'Any man or state who fights on against Nazidom will have our aid. . . . It follows therefore that we shall give whatever help we can to Russia and the Russian people.'

It is tempting to date a transformation in British-Soviet relations from this speech. It did indeed inaugurate a period in which the British Government was to be committed to full alliance in war and peace with the power which the British Prime Minister was subsequently to describe on his first visit to Moscow as 'this sullen, sinister Bolshevik State I had once tried so hard to strangle at its birth, and which, until Hitler appeared, I had regarded as the mortal foe of civilised freedom'.[21] The past did not, however, flash away. On the British side, it was not easy for ministers or their civil and military advisers to forget the Molotov–Ribbentrop agreement of August 1939 or to ignore the fact that the Soviet Union had sought its own salvation in a policy of benevolent neutrality towards Germany during the year when Britain was struggling alone for survival. As Churchill reminded Cripps: 'No one wants to recriminate, but it is not our fault that Hitler was able to destroy Poland before turning his forces against France, or to destroy France before turning them against Russia.'[22]

All the mistrust of the Soviet regime which had built up over the years was at its deepest in June 1941 and it undoubtedly coloured the initial British response to the German attack. With the progress of the war, suspicion did indeed gradually give way to respect and sympathy as the scale of the Soviet war effort and the depth of suffering of the Soviet people became apparent, but the day-to-day conduct of relations was rarely free from friction. There were good moments, for instance at the Teheran conference, but there was no point at which it could be said that a genuine mutual understanding had been arrived at. On the Soviet side, Churchill's innate dislike was fully reciprocated by a Soviet leadership basing its policies upon a doctrine of irreconcilable struggle with the forces of capitalism represented by the British Government. There was a measure of respect for the British achievement in continuing the war alone, but the mistrust was never wholly eradicated and, with the approach of victory, the savour of military triumph was to overwhelm all other political factors in a heady blend of Russian nationalism and Soviet doctrine. The bond between Britain and the Soviet Union, in so far as it existed, depended upon the common enemy and dissolved with his defeat.

In following the course of British–Soviet relations during this period, it will, on occasion, be convenient to depart from the chronological narrative in order to separate out the two main strands, the pursuit of the war and the preparation for the peace, intertwined though they were throughout all the intergovernmental exchanges of the period. Within the former, it is appropriate to follow separately the controversy over the opening of a second front in Europe and the problems connected with the delivery of supplies to the Soviet Union.

THE INITIAL RESPONSE

The prospect of alliance with the Soviet Union, had, as we have seen, been contemplated shortly in advance of the German attack and by the time the attack was launched, the basis for Churchill's speech had been established. Practical considerations meant that at this stage little more than token gestures were possible. Britain certainly had no spare supplies. The war material already on order from the United States was all urgently needed and there was little incentive to sacrifice it, with prejudice to the defence of Britain itself, if the effect were merely a slight prolongation of an apparently forlorn Soviet resistance. Memories of the collapse of France were not far below the surface and after the Stalin purges Soviet military capability was regarded as, if anything, even less reliable than that of France in the weeks before surrender. As Churchill summed up the policy: 'In the early days of our alliance there was little we could do, and I tried to fill the void by civilities'.[23] Nevertheless, a Military Mission under General Mason-Macfarlane was established in Moscow, a Soviet mission was received in London and, at the urging of Cripps, who had resumed his post in Moscow, an Anglo-Soviet Declaration was signed on 12 July,[24] in which the two Governments undertook to 'render each other assistance and support of all kinds' and neither to negotiate nor to conclude a separate peace. The Anglo-Soviet agreement was followed by a Polish–Soviet agreement, negotiated with British participation and accompanied by a British reaffirmation of the guarantee to Poland. By the Polish–Soviet agreement of 30 July the Soviet Government recognised 'the Soviet–German treaties of 1939 as to territorial changes in Poland' as having lost their validity and provided for the formation of a Polish army in the Soviet Union, while leaving open the question of Poland's post-war frontiers.

Within a month of the German attack on the Soviet Union, the problem of opening a second front came to the fore. The first direct communication received by Churchill from Stalin came on 19 July,[25] immediately after the signature of the Declaration, and contained a proposal for the establishment of a front in northern France as well as a joint operation in northern Norway, where British naval and air support was sought. In terms of the pursuit of the war, there was little problem about the common objective, the defeat of Nazi Germany. The opportunity for a common strategy had, however, been largely vitiated by the conclusion of the Soviet–German Agreement of August 1939 which made possible a single-front operation by Germany against Britain and France in 1940 and, hence, a single-front operation against the Soviet Union itself in 1941. The opportunity which the Soviet Union had squandered in 1939 could not easily be reconstituted once Germany had effective control of the whole land mass of Western Europe. The logic of a two-front ground operation against Germany was, however, still inescapable and the establishment of the second front in the West was a primary purpose of Allied planning. The insistent Soviet demand for its premature implementation was to dominate bilateral and tripartite exchanges with the Soviet Union on the conduct of the war.

At the time of Stalin's first message, British land forces were still being reformed after the defeats of 1940 and were heavily engaged with the Axis forces in North Africa, while, at sea, the Navy was fully stretched with the task of holding open the lines of communication upon which the country's survival depended. Even had the forces been available, there were virtually no landing craft and only over the Pas de Calais was there the possibility of establishing any effective air cover. There was no way in which, within a period of less than two years, any effective Allied landing could have been made. There was no point in concealing the reality. In his reply of July 20 Churchill was able to offer naval operations in the Arctic and the possible basing of Hurricanes in Murmansk, but in relation to ground operations, he could only say: 'The Chiefs of Staff do not see any way of doing anything on a scale likely to be of the slightest use to you.'[26] It was the beginning of a series of exchanges on this topic which was to last for two years, but before following their course we must turn briefly to the more immediate problem of Allied aid to Russia, namely the provision of supplies.

The first tripartite conference of the war was devoted almost wholly to the supply problem and came about through the joint efforts of Cripps and President Roosevelt's emissary, Harry Hopkins. It was proposed in a message sent on 12 August[27] by Churchill and Roosevelt from their conference at Placentia Bay at which the Atlantic Charter was agreed. It took place at the end of September, at a time when the German offensive was threatening to overwhelm the Soviet armies and when Stalin, in a desperate message to Churchill, had asked once again for the opening of a second front in the West, or, failing that, the despatch of 25 to 30 divisions to the Soviet Union through Iran or Archangel. It might have been possible for British troops to relieve the five Soviet divisions in Persia and thus free them for service on the Russian front, but it would have taken three months to put even two fully armed British divisions into South Russia. Stalin's request was, in Churchill's words 'utter unreality', but its very unreality reinforced the case for a British–Soviet discussion of strategy. In the event, however, although the British delegation was prepared for this, Beaverbrook so handled the conference that it was confined to a discussion of supply arrangements. As Minister of Supply, he led on the British side and Averell Harriman represented the United States. There could scarcely have been two more mutually antipathetic British representatives in one city than Cripps and Beaverbrook. For all Cripps's intelligence, his political vision and his sympathy with the Soviet Union, Beaverbrook's mixture of brute energy and political cunning was better attuned to a negotiation with Stalin and, from this point on, he was to establish himself as an advocate for the Soviet Union within the War Cabinet and in the country at large. Having effectively excluded Cripps from the conduct of the Moscow negotiations, he ended with agreement on a schedule of deliveries running up to June 1942.[28] Subsequent protocols were negotiated on an annual basis.

Concurrently with the conference, the one joint British–Soviet land campaign of the war was successfully accomplished, when, in August–September, after overcoming slight opposition from the Persian Army, British and Soviet forces linked up from north and south to open a supply route through Persia to the Caspian. The operation stemmed primarily from the British concern to safeguard the oil supplies – and indeed the whole Middle East position – against a German thrust southwards through the Caucasus, rather than from a desire to aid the Soviet Union. A formal Treaty of Alliance between the United Kingdom, the Soviet Union and Iran was signed on 29 January 1942 and the route, when opened, carried, over a period of four and a half years, five million tons of supplies to the Soviet Union.

THE ANGLO-SOVIET TREATY

The high-water mark of relations between Britain and the Soviet Union was the signature on 26 May 1942 of the 'Treaty for an Alliance in the War against Hitlerite Germany and her Associates in Europe and Providing Also for Collaboration and Mutual Assistance Thereafter'.[29] Immediately after the Beaverbrook–Harriman mission, the German offensive against Moscow was intensified and, with the partial evacuation of the city, there was concern that the Soviet Union might be forced into a separate peace, leaving the German forces, in a repeat of 1917, free to resume the offensive in the West. There was growing Soviet bitterness at the absence of any British military diversion in the West or the provision of any land forces for the Soviet front. British reluctance to declare war on Finland, Romania and Hungary served as a further irritant. Matters were brought to a head by a message from Stalin to Churchill, dated 8 November 1941, complaining of a 'lack of clarity' in relations and stating bluntly: 'As long as the present situation exists there will be difficulty in establishing mutual confidence.' Churchill had proposed a visit to Moscow by Generals Wavell and Paget, but this was rejected by Stalin unless the visit was 'with a view to concluding agreement on two fundamental questions . . . , a definite understanding on war aims and on plans for the post-war organisation of peace' and an 'agreement on mutual military assistance against Hitler in Europe' as well as the immediate declaration of war on Finland, Romania and Hungary.[30] Stalin's message was received with 'pain and surprise'[31] and this was made clear to Maisky, but gradually, aided by a more moderately phrased second message, the British government accepted that, if the war effort were not to be seriously prejudiced, some positive response had to be given. So war was declared on Finland, Romania and Hungary and Eden was sent to Moscow to take, with the Soviet leadership, 'a broad survey of the war as a whole' as well as the 'post-war organisation of peace'. He made it clear, however, to Cripps, that the Government envisaged a 'gradual and tentative procedure' rather than 'to attempt prematurely to define our collaboration in treaty form'.[32] The hope was that in exchange for a relatively modest offer of additional supplies, it would be possible to secure a joint public declaration on policy for the defeat of Germany.[33]

Eden arrived in Moscow on 15 December 1941 at a moment which was perhaps the turning point of the war. In October, when the German advance guard had penetrated to the suburbs of Moscow, it had seemed that the capital might fall and the Embassies had been evacuated to Kuibyshev. Now the German advance had been stemmed and while Eden was on his way by sea, the Japanese attack on Pearl Harbor had brought the United States into the war. Much had changed since he and Litvinov had discussed the rising threat of Nazi Germany in 1935, but the Soviet position still resembled in many respects that of 1939, with the requirement for matching political and military treaties embodying commitments in respect of the conduct of the war and the future frontiers of the Soviet Union, particularly in relation to the Baltic States, Finland, Poland and Romania. Commitments relating to post-war territorial adjustments were bluntly rejected by Churchill and no text could be agreed during Eden's discussions. Matters had, however, moved a long way since the ill-fated negotiations of the summer of 1939 and now neither Britain nor the Soviet Union could afford an open breach. It was left that Eden would return to London for further discussions with the Cabinet.

Debate within the Cabinet and discussion with the United States lasted from December 1941 until May 1942. Within the Cabinet it was clear that the Polish–Soviet frontier could not be the subject of a formal commitment at this stage. It was, however, accepted that there should be a formal treaty and there was a disposition to find some way of meeting the Soviet requirement in respect of recognition of the 1941 frontiers as well as to acquiesce in a post-war commitment in respect of the integration of the Baltic States into the Soviet Union. Victory was still far off. The Soviet Union was engaged in a desperate struggle and the outcome was far from clear, but if the Allies were to be victorious the Soviet forces would certainly have to re-occupy the area within their 1941 borders. There was no way in which the Soviet Government would then accept that it should conclude peace on a basis which left it with less territory and less security than when Hitler attacked. Opposition to commitments in respect of post-war frontiers was, however, particularly strong in the United States and this carried the day. In the hope, quickly confirmed, of securing an American assurance about the opening of a second front in Europe, the Soviet Government abandoned its insistence on a frontier commitment and the Anglo-Soviet Treaty, in the form eventually negotiated between Eden and Molotov in London, left the territorial question wholly open. In retrospect, it is clear that the Soviet Union must have made the realistic calculation that victory over Hitler would leave the Red Army as a far more effective means of securing the reversal of the 'old equilibrium' and guaranteeing Soviet security than heavily qualified inter-governmental understandings. Military victory had to be the Soviet priority. The Treaty as concluded contained a preambular reference to Soviet adherence to the Atlantic Charter. The body of it was in two parts, the first, valid until the establishment of peace, provided for a formal alliance against

Germany and states associated with her in acts of aggression in Europe (i.e. excluding Japan) and for no armistice or peace treaty except by mutual consent. Part II, valid for twenty years, provided for 'common action to preserve peace and resist aggression in the post-war period', measures to prevent renewed aggression by Germany and collaboration in the organisation of security and economic prosperity in Europe.

THE COORDINATION OF STRATEGY

The course of military operations must fall outside the scope of this study, but it is necessary to address the problem of the extent to which, as allies, the British and Soviet Governments – together with the United States – were able to coordinate the broad strategy for the conduct of the war. We have noted the early exchanges on the opening of a second front and the execution of the joint campaign in Persia. There was, however, in the early stages of the alliance, virtually no joint consideration of strategy. Nor, given the refusal of the Soviet Government to disclose any information about its own military planning, were any profitable exchanges possible through the Military Mission in Moscow. Shortly after the German attack, largely in response to pressure from the Prime Minister, Enigma material, i.e. intercepted German cypher traffic, was passed, with the source camouflaged, to the Soviet authorities, but because of the lack of reciprocity the supply dwindled and finally lapsed in 1944 after Soviet closure of the intercept station at Murmansk. Indeed, the British Government seem to have obtained more information about operations on the Eastern front from the interception of German communications than they did from the Soviet Union itself. A somewhat surprising agreement on collaboration in subversion and propaganda in countries outside the Soviet Union and the Commonwealth seems to have borne equally little fruit.[34] It was the resumption of Soviet pressure for the establishment of a second front in northern France which prompted the first serious consideration of strategy during the Prime Minister's visit to Moscow in August 1942.

The need for a landing in Western Europe was clear enough. The problem was one of timing. In a memorandum of 18 December 1941 Churchill defined the objective of 'liberating conquered Europe by the landing during the summer of 1943 of United States and British armies on their shore' and planning went ahead on this basis. Soviet pressure for early action was, however, intense. After the preliminary discussions on the Anglo-Soviet Treaty in London in March 1942, Molotov continued to Washington. Cordell Hull, with Roosevelt's backing, was determined to avoid the inclusion of any territorial commitment in the British Treaty and believed that the offer of a second front during 1942 'should take the heat off Russia's diplomatic demands upon England'. The President therefore authorised Molotov to inform Stalin that 'we expect the formation of a second front this year'. It was not a firm promise and it did not specify where the second front would be. The communiqué issued at the end of the Washington talks however, included a sentence drafted by Molotov to the effect that 'complete agreement was reached with regard to the urgent task of opening a second front in Europe in 1942'. Returning through London, he secured a British communiqué in the same terms, but it was accompanied by an aide-memoire stating, 'We are making preparations for a landing on the Continent in August or September 1942. . . . It is impossible to say in advance whether the situation will be such as to make this operation feasible when the time comes. We can therefore give no promise in the matter, but provided that it appears sound and sensible we shall not hesistate to put our plans into effect'. The aide-memoire also confirmed that maximum effort would be put into a 'large-scale invasion' in 1943.[35] It was true that consideration was being given to Operation Sledge-hammer, designed to seize the Cherbourg peninsula, but there was no plan at that time, nor could there have been, for the effective establishment of a sustainable second front in France in 1942. There was little cause for the Soviet Union to be misled, since, in addition to the formal aide-memoire, Churchill personally made the reservations clear to Molotov. Nevertheless, it is not improbable that a communiqué designed in part to mislead the Germans into holding an excessively large force in France may also have encouraged the Soviet leadership to cherish unrealistic hopes. Certainly, they lost no opportunity to represent it as a formal commitment.

The final recognition of the need to defer the main landing until 1943 came during British-American discussions in London in July 1942 at which the decision was taken that the principal operation for 1942 should be 'Torch', the joint British-American operation to destroy the German forces in North Africa and pave the way for the opening up of the Mediterranean. This strategic decision coincided unhappily with the decision to suspend the Arctic convoys to Russia during the summer months, a decision to which we shall return later. The Soviet Union had, ever since the Molotov visit, waged an assiduous campaign of publicity and lobbying designed to ensure the early opening of a second front and the confirmation of British reservations brought a peremptory message from Stalin on 23 July stating 'in the most emphatic manner' that the Soviet Government could not acquiesce in the postponement of a second front in Europe until 1943.[36]

CHURCHILL IN MOSCOW

Sir Archibald Clark Kerr, who had succeeded Cripps in the Moscow Embassy, suggested that Molotov might have failed to brief Stalin properly on Churchill's thinking and it was agreed that the Prime Minister should visit Moscow in August in order to put British strategic planning personally to Stalin. This, the first-ever meeting between British and Soviet Heads of Government, should have been a momentous occasion. On the one side was Churchill who hated all the Soviet state stood for and had, as he recollected, tried to strangle it at its birth. On the other was Stalin, the legatee of a long Russian tradition of conspiracy, terror and repression who, two years earlier, would have contentedly warmed his hands over the funeral pyre of that society of which Churchill now stood as the supreme champion. They met in Moscow at a time when the fate of the Soviet forces still hung in the balance. The immediate threat to Moscow had been contained and the front-line was stabilised to the west of the city, but in the south the threat to Stalingrad and the Caucasus was critical. (See Map, p. 28.)

Churchill's task was to secure Stalin's confidence in a revised strategy which brought little immediate and apparent relief to the Soviet Union. He did not expect the meeting to be agreeable and, on the whole, it was not, although both officially and personally he was shown every courtesy and hospitality. After a rough start, Stalin recognised the strategic merit of the North African operation, but in relation to the second front and the suspension of convoys it was not easy to receive without anger his taunts about the broken promises of a country afraid of fighting the Germans. One incidental product of the discussions was agreement on the merit of a joint operation to capture German bases in northern Norway and Finland, an operation which was close to Churchill's heart but not to that of his Service advisers. In his alternation of joviality and brutality, Stalin followed a practice which was to become familiar to all those who had dealings with the Soviet leadership. Churchill met his recriminations firmly, but refrained from reproaches about the 1939 treaty with Germany and the encounter ended with a private meeting of seven hours, culminating in dinner in Stalin's private apartment. The meeting served to establish a certain rapport between the two men, a rapport which was of some value to Stalin in the later wartime conferences.

The strategic discussion took very much the form of a British exposition of British–American planning and a Soviet interrogation. Little insight was gained into Soviet planning. Churchill was left with the impresson that there was an 'even chance' that the Russians would hold, but his military advisers were less certain. The final communiqué spoke optimistically of 'an atmosphere of cordiality and complete sincerity' and 'close friendship and understanding'. What might, at best, have been claimed was the creation of a measure of mutual respect.

FURTHER STRATEGIC DIFFERENCES

If proof of the impossibility of establishing a front in France in 1942 were needed, it was afforded on 17 August, immediately after Churchill left Moscow, when he received the news of the outcome of the raid on Dieppe, involving a total of some 10 000 members of all three forces. Casualties were extremely heavy. Churchill's assessment was that it had been 'a costly but not unfruitful reconnaissance in force' which, by holding German forces in the West, 'did something to take the weight off Russia'.[37] What it did was to make clear the magnitude of the task which would have to be faced when the time came to re-establish a major army in France.

One effect of the Moscow Conference was to make the commitment to open a second front in 1943 proportionately stronger. British and American planning went ahead on this basis. Two other operations designed to afford direct assistance to the Soviet Union were also considered, but neither materialised. First was Operation Jupiter, the plan for an attack on Northern Norway which Churchill had discussed with Stalin but for which he was unable to secure the support of the Chiefs of Staff. Second was a proposal, which both Churchill and Roosevelt found attractive, to establish in the Caucasus an Anglo-American airforce formed early in the New Year of 1943 by the withdrawal of aircraft from the Middle East. The force was envisaged as comprising nine Fighter and five Bomber Squadrons from the Royal Air Force as well as a Heavy Bomber Group and a Transport Group from the US Air Force. It took time to move from the initial concept to a formal plan, but on 21 November 1942 Air Marshall Drummond, together with an American officer, went to Moscow to negotiate the detailed arrangements for an operation which, it was hoped, would be 'a genuine comradeship in arms'. By this time, however, the German army had been surrounded at Stalingrad and the Alamein victory had stemmed the German drive eastwards in Africa. The Soviet Union had already shown a preference for receiving aircraft rather than complete Allied formations and, with competing demands arising in other theatres, this project also faded away with a note by Churchill: 'I do not wish to force upon them what it costs us so much to give.'[38]

The strategic relationship continued to hinge on the establishment of a second front in France and as late as 9 February 1943, Churchill telegraphed to Stalin that the British and American Governments were 'Pushing preparations to the limit of our resources for a cross-Channel operation in August. . . . If the operation is delayed by weather or other reasons, it will be prepared with stronger forces for September'.[39] In reply, Stalin stressed that it was 'extremely important to deliver the blow from the West in the spring or in the early summer and not to postpone it until the second half of the year'. Further exchanges took place in March, with Churchill hinting at the possibility of a strike even before August and Stalin warning 'in the strongest possible manner' against further delay. By May, however, when Churchill and Roosevelt met in Washington, it was clear to both that the major cross-Channel operation could not take place before 1944 and that, meanwhile, the conquest of Italy offered the best prospect of engaging maximum German forces and easing the task of the Soviet armies. On 2 June a message was sent through the US Embassy with news of the postponement and this led to a further Stalin-Churchill-Roosevelt exchange in which Stalin complained that a decision which might have grave consequences for the further course of the war had been taken without Soviet participation.[40] Churchill observed to Maisky that he was 'getting rather tired of being scolded' and doubted the value of further personal correspondence, but eventually an emollient reply was sent, proposing a tripartite meeting at Scapa Flow.

Meanwhile, British and American planning for the final stage of

1. (*above*) The British landing in Vladivostok, 1918. *The Hulton Picture Company*

ВОЛЬШЕВИКИ.

ГЕРМАНІЯ ПОДПИСАЛА МИРЪ СЪ СОЮЗНИКАМИ

ПНУЖДЕННАЯ КЪ ТОМУ СИЛОН ОРУЖІЯ.

ШИТЕ И ВЫ ЗАКЛЮЧИТЬ МИРЪ ИБО ЧАСЪ

ЕЗДІЯ БЛИЗОКЪ.

LATION)

OLSHEVIKI !

VE JUST FORCED GERMANY

N PEACE AT THE POINT OF THE

HASTEN AND SIGN PEACE YOURSELVES

HE POINT OF THE SWORD APPROACHETH YOU !!

2. (*left*) Propaganda leaflet, 1918–19, with the original florid translation. *The Hulton Picture Company*

3. (*above*) Chicherin and Litvinov at Genoa 1922. *The Hulton Picture Company*

It's Your
MONEY
He
Wants

4. (*left*) 1924 election poster warning John Bull not to let his pockets be emptied by Labour's Bolshevik friends. *The Illustrated London News*

THE ARCOS RAID: POLICE SEARCH FOR A MISSING STATE DOCUMENT.

A GENERAL VIEW OF THE RAIDED PREMISES IN MOORGATE, BUILT FOR ARCOS, LTD., AT A COST OF OVER £300,000 : PUBLIC INTEREST IN THE CITY.

THE ENTRANCE OF 49, MOORGATE, SHARED BY ARCOS, LTD., AND THE RUSSIAN TRADE DELEGATION, DURING THE RAID : CITY POLICE ON GUARD AT THE DOOR.

THE HOME SECRETARY, WHO AUTHORISED APPLICATION FOR A SEARCH WARRANT : SIR WILLIAM JOYNSON-HICKS.

THE SOVIET TRADE AGENT IN BRITAIN, WHO CLAIMED DIPLOMATIC IMMUNITY : M. KHINCHUK.

THE SOVIET CHARGÉ D'AFFAIRES, WHO PROTESTED TO THE FOREIGN SECRETARY : M. ROSENGOLZ.

HEAD OF THE SPECIAL BRANCH OF SCOTLAND YARD : MAJOR-GENERAL SIR WYNDHAM CHILDS, WHO VISITED THE ARCOS BUILDING DURING THE RAID.

[DUR]ING THE RAID, WHEN THE STAFF OF ARCOS, LTD., WERE DETAINED FOR A TIME [IN] THE CORRIDORS : MEMBERS OF THE CITY POLICE ON GUARD AT THE ENTRANCE.

AN INSPECTOR OF THE CITY POLICE QUESTIONING CALLERS AT THE OFFICES OF ARCOS, LTD., IN MOORGATE : AN INCIDENT DURING THE RAID.

...y 12 the police raided the offices of Arcos, Ltd., the well-known Russian [compan]y in Moorgate. In a statement to the House of Commons on the 16th, [the Ho]me Secretary (Sir William Joynson-Hicks) said : " The information sent to [me] the Secretary for War satisfied me that a certain official document was, [had] been, improperly in the possession of a person employed in the premises [occupie]d by Arcos at 49, Moorgate. . . . In view of that information, I consulted

Ltd., and the Russian Trade Delegation, and there is free intercommunication. The warrant accordingly authorised search of the premises occupied by Arcos, Ltd., and the Trade Delegation. The document in question was not found, but the police have taken possession of certain papers." When the raid began, the Arcos staff, numbering over 1000, were marshalled in the corridors, but most of the women employees were allowed to leave after about an hour. M. Rosengolz, the

5. Police raid Soviet Commercial Offices in Moorgate, 22 May 1927. *The Illustrated London News*

6. (*above*) Departure of the Soviet Chargé, 1927. *The Hulton Picture Company*

7. (*below*) Eden leaves for Moscow, 1935. *The Hulton Picture Company*

(*above*) Stalin, Molotov and Ribbentrop celebrate signature of Non-aggression treaty, August 1939. *Popperfoto*

(*below*) Stalin, Truman and Churchill at Potsdam, 1945. *Bettmann/The Hulton Picture Company*

10. (*above*) A Russian girl sniper in London, 1942. *The Hulton Picture Company*

11. (*below*) Hurricanes at Murmansk, January 1942. *Imperial War Museum*

RUSSIA'S FIGHT IS OURS!

These posters from Moscow show the determination of our Ally to destroy Hitlerite Germany. But with a large part of their industrial resources already overrun they desperately need our help. Production is the key. Russia's fight is ours and **OUR FIGHT IS RUSSIA'S**

БЕЙ ФАШИСТСКОГО **ГАДА!**

TRANSLATION *Kill the Fascist Reptile!*

БЕСПОЩАДНО РАЗГРОМИМ И УНИЧТОЖИМ ВРАГА!

ДОГОВОР о ненападении между СССР и Германией

TRANSLATION *The enemy will be mercilessly defeated and annihilated*

СМЕРТЬ ФАШИСТСКОЙ ГАДИНЕ!

TRANSLATION *Death to the Fascist Reptile!*

КАЛАЛЕОН ПОТЕРПЕЛ ПОРАЖЕНИЕ. ТО ЖЕ БУДЕТ И С ЗАЗНАВШИМСЯ ГИТЛЕРОМ!

1819

TRANSLATION *Napoleon failed and so will that blackguard Hitler!*

12. A Ministry of Information wartime poster. *Crown Copyright. HMSO/The Public Record Office*

13.   Eden, Bidault and Dulles prepare for the 1954 Berlin Conference. Author second from left at top

14. (*above*) Sir Anthony Eden and the Russian leaders Marshal Bulganin and Mr Khrushchev, signing the official communiqué at the Foreign Office, 26 April 1956. *Popperfoto*

15. (*below*) Soviet forces in Hungary, November 1956. *The Hulton Picture Company*

16.   Macmillan and Selwyn Lloyd with Khrushchev and Gromyko in Moscow, 21 February 1959. *Popperfoto*

7. *(above)* The author presenting credentials in Moscow, March 1978.

Foxtrotsky

The farewell for our ambassador leaving Moscow, Sir Curtis Keeble, had Muscovites gaping as the British 'community' danced in evening dress to a jazz band on board the ss Maxim Gorky. It would have disgruntled Stalin, for whose use the ship was built in 1934. The only pity was the captain did not feel able to chug downstream to salute the Union Flag flying on the British Embassy opposite the Kremlin. The palatial establishment was a constant annoyance to Stalin, who tried for years to evict the British from their embankment site.

"All right! Who told the ambassador that it was fancy dress?"

18. *(left)* Farewell to Moscow.
© *Cartoons International*

19. (*left*) The author and wi[...]
    the Moscow Embassy.

20. (*below*) *On tour in Uz*[...]
    istan.

1. (*above*) While Sir Geoffrey Howe and Mr Eduard Shevardnadze sign a Memorandum of Understanding in Moscow, March 1987, the Prime Minister and the General Secretary continue their discussion. *Novosti/Camera Press*

2. (*below*) The Gorbachevs and Mrs Thatcher at Brize Norton during their stopover for Washington Summit, 7 December 1987. *Popperfoto/Reuters*

23. The polythene plant at Budyennovsk, built by John Brown in the early 1980s and now being upgraded to 300 000 tons a year.
John Brown/Offshore Photography

British Ambassador's Residence
Spasopeskovskaya Square, Moscow

Architect Julian Bicknell with Chris Hay & Steve Chapman
20 Bedford Street London WC2E 9HP Tel 836 5875

Staff flats and offices

Architects Ahrends, Burton and Koralek
Artist Jeremy Peacock

24. and 25.   Architects' impressions of the new British Embassy in Moscow: (*above*) the Ambassador's residence; (*below*) staff flats and offices. *Both drawings are reproduced by courtesy of the Foreign and Commonwealth Office*

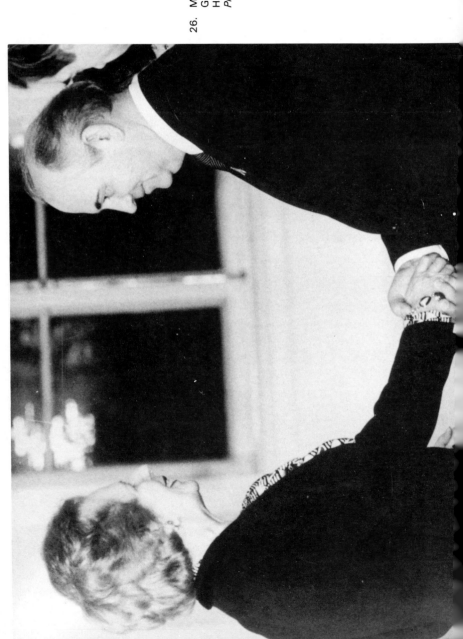

26. Mrs Thatcher and Mikhail Gorbachev in St George's Hall in the Kremlin. *Camera Press/TASS*

the war was moving ahead and came to a culmination at the Quebec Conference in August 1943. At this stage, coordination with the Soviet Union became more urgent, in relation not only to military operations in Europe, North Africa and the Far East, but also to the problems of the peace which would follow. We shall turn separately to the way in which these matters were handled at the three great summit conferences, but first the final stage of the controversy over the date for the second front must be noted. In October 1943, at the tripartite meeting of Foreign Ministers in Moscow prior to the Teheran Conference, Molotov and Stalin pressed Eden to confirm that the deadline of spring 1944 held good. Warned by Churchill against the danger of letting battles be governed by 'lawyers'' agreements made in good faith months before, Eden confirmed that it would be at the 'earliest possible moment'. At Teheran, in November, a date of May 1944 was established for the main cross-Channel operation. The Soviet Union undertook to initiate a large-scale offensive at the same time and, in the event, this materialised on 23 June, a fortnight after the postponed Allied landings. So ended a controversy which had soured the relationship with the Soviet Union for much of the war.

Perhaps the current process of Soviet historical reassessment will extend to this issue. The references to allied cooperation in general during the war have begun to be less grudging, but until a new definitive history rejects the existing interpretation, one must record with regret the repetition by Gromyko and Ponomarev of Maisky's assessment in July 1942 that 'in our most critical hour we are being abandoned to the will of fate by our allies'; and their own language about 'blatant deception of an ally and betrayal of a promise' in the pursuit of 'a policy designed to weaken the USSR to the maximum extent'.[41] With the advantage of hindsight, it is not difficult to envisage the disaster which would have struck an Allied invasion in the summer of 1943, not to speak of 1942. Clark Kerr commented in July 1942[42] that the weakness in the British case lay 'not in our inablity to open this second front but in our having let [Stalin] believe we were going to'. If there is one lesson from these exchanges, it must, sadly, be of the rashness of using an over-optimistic forecast – no matter how carefully hedged around – in an attempt to comfort a mistrustful partner on a critical issue.

THE ARCTIC CONVOYS

We have followed the course of the Soviet recriminations over the date for the invasion of France. It is now necessary to turn to the other main element in the British–Soviet operational relationship during the war years, the provision of supplies, and to take up the account from the point of the Beaverbrook–Harriman mission to Moscow in September 1941. The outcome of that meeting was agreement on a schedule of deliveries running from October 1941 to June 1942. Supplies were to be made available 'at British and United States centres of production', but the only undertaking in respect of their transportation was that Britain and the United States would 'give aid to the transportation to the Soviet Union and help with the delivery'. At this most critical stage of the war in Russia, the German forces were close to the suburbs of Moscow and Leningrad, there were serious doubts as to the ability of the Soviet forces to hold out, and the United States was still neutral. There can at the time have been no serious expectation in London or Washington that the Soviet Union would in fact be able to arrange its own transportation and from the outset the primary responsibility for transportation of British and American supplies by the most direct route around northern Norway to Archangel and Murmansk fell to the British. In the second protocol, covering the period to July 1943, the British and American Governments agreed to 'supply the shipping necessary to lift that part of this programme for which USSR ships cannot be made available'.[43] In giving this undertaking the two Governments can scarcely have envisaged the accusations which would flow from it.

Despite a critical shortage of shipping, the convoys were organised and three-quarters of the merchant ships were British or American. Throughout the winter of 1941–2 the operation was surprisingly successful, only one ship being lost, but in the spring of 1942 German attacks were intensified and out of the 83 ships in the April and May convoys 11 were lost, together with an escorting cruiser. Even at a rate of three convoys in two months, a backlog of supplies was building up and there was pressure on Britain from both the United States and the Soviet Union for an increased shipping effort. The German air and naval forces in northern Norway had, however, been reinforced and, with the approach of summer, the long Arctic day gave maximum opportunity for German aerial and surface reconnaissance and attack. Disaster came with convoy PQ 17 which sailed from Iceland to Archangel on 27 June 1942. The scale of the operation was indicated by the fact that 34 merchant ships carrying 200 000 tons of cargo required a total naval commitment, direct and indirect, for escort, immediate cover and Home Fleet back-up, of 2 battleships, one aircraft carrier, 5 cruisers, 9 destroyers, 2 anti-aircraft ships, 13 submarines and 11 smaller craft. The Home Fleet could not be committed to the passage east from Bear Island and, as a result of a threatened German attack by a heavy naval force, the convoy was ordered to scatter when just to the east of Spitsbergen. The naval escort withdrew westwards, expecting to engage the German surface vessels, but, with the convoy scattered, the German forces could rely on aircraft and U-boats to hunt down the individual vessels. In all, 23 merchant ships were sunk and only 11 eventually reached Russia.

Reluctantly, Churchill accepted the naval advice that there was no realistic possibility that future convoys during the summer months would fare any better and informed Stalin that the next convoy could not be run, but that if suitable arrangements could be devised, the system would be restarted. The response was a sharp and unfriendly message[44] on 23 July in which Stalin spoke in terms of fulfilment of 'contracted obligations'. He did not, however, make much of the issue when he met Churchill in Moscow in August. A further convoy sailed in September with the loss of 12 out of 39 ships to a heavy air attack in which 24 German aircraft were destroyed. A total of 77 warships were, however, employed in this operation and the demand for naval forces to support the North African landings later in the year was such that further convoys had to be suspended until December, when an attack by a German force led by a pocket-battleship, a heavy cruiser and supporting forces was beaten off with the loss of only one merchant ship and one destroyer. In the summer of 1943, the Arctic convoys were again suspended, but before their resumption in the autumn a new controversy arose over the severe restrictions imposed by the Soviet authorities upon the small British group of service personnel stationed in Murmansk. There were problems over the use of radio equipment, over mail deliveries and over the refusal of entry visas for replacements. No one was permitted to land from a British naval or merchant vessel except by a Soviet boat in the presence of a Soviet official and, on top of other minor restrictions, permission to establish a small British medical unit to care for the casualties was refused. After other representations had proved ineffective, Churchill took up the difficulties with Stalin, asking that they might be 'smoothed out in a friendly spirit'.[45] In notifying the planned resumption, he made the point that this was 'no contract or bargain'. This caught Stalin on the raw and in his reply[46] he referred to 'a refusal of the British Government to fulfil the obligations it undertook', stated that it would be 'inadmissible to have the supplies of the Soviet armies depend on the arbitrary judgment of the British side', described the British complaints as inaccurate and made various allegations about the behaviour of the British forces. Churchill found the reply so offensive that he personally gave it back to the Soviet Ambassador. The problems were eventually resolved by Eden in discussion with Stalin and Molotov when he was in Moscow for the Foreign Ministers' Conference in October and, with Soviet expressions of appreciation, the convoys were duly resumed and ran until the end of the war.

By the time hostilities ceased, Britain had supplied over 5000 tanks and 7000 aircraft (including some of Canadian and American origin), while the United States had supplied over 7000 tanks and nearly 15 000 aircraft.[47] (By way of comparison, the operational strength of the German air force at its peak was estimated at about 6000 aircraft.) Deliveries by the Arctic route accounted in fact for the smaller part of the total supplies and it has been argued that a greater concentration upon the Persian route might have produced a better outcome at lower cost in ships and lives. Out of a total of 811 ships in the 40 Arctic convoys, 98 were lost from various causes. In terms of the goods carried, the loss rate of 15 per cent for the period to April 1944 and $7\frac{1}{2}$ per cent for the whole war compared with only 0.7 per cent on the Atlantic convoys.[48]

The bald figures, striking though they are, cannot convey the full significance of this remarkable operation, demonstrating at one and the same time the best and worst aspects of the wartime relationship. The intergovernmental exchanges illustrated only too clearly the classic problems of British–Soviet cooperation and the deep difference of approach. As with the controversy over the opening of the second front, the Soviet Union made it a matter of national pride to regard British help as a contractual obligation and having done so, left the British Government to regret having embodied a goodwill gesture in a formal document. Even at a time when the two countries were allied in a common struggle for survival and the British individuals concerned were suffering in the common cause, the rigidity of Soviet bureaucracy could not be eased, nor could normal considerations of humanity be made to prevail without the personal intervention of the Prime Minister. A seaman might survive for no more than two minutes in the Arctic waters, but such was the suffering of the Soviet armies that the conditions counted for little. In an operation which at the personal level required courage of a singular order and a remarkable devotion to a common cause, trust and confidence were sadly lacking at the governmental level. Perhaps it could not have been otherwise.

PLANNING FOR VICTORY AND PEACE

We have seen how the problems of the Western frontiers of the Soviet Union were raised during the early months of the Alliance and how any commitment in this respect was excluded from the Anglo-Soviet Treaty. A crucial issue was the future of Poland. Neither the politicians nor the public in Britain forgot that it was for Poland that war had been declared and Poland's future remained the subject of British–Soviet discussion throughout most of the war, the tone and tempo of the discussion reflecting both the progress of military operations and the emotional impact of such climactic events as the Katyn massacre and the Warsaw uprising, as well as the death of General Sikorski. On the wider issues of post-war planning, a first abortive attempt to initiate informal talks was made by Clark Kerr in February 1942, but he was rebuffed personally by Stalin, who made it clear that the Soviet Union was not interested in such talks unless they were designed to lead to a binding agreement. Planning went ahead within the Foreign Office, but it was not until the summer of 1943, when Mussolini had fallen, the Soviet forces were advancing and the prospect of victory was beginning to be more real, that a substantial and wide-ranging discussion with the Soviet Government was initiated. Churchill had already made the suggestion of a tripartite meeting at Scapa Flow and the suggestion of such a meeting was raised again in a note sent on 7 August, immediately before the Quebec Conference,[49] explaining that the President and Prime Minister were to meet with the Chiefs of Staff to review future operations in Europe and the Far East, that the Soviet Government would be kept informed, but that the Prime Minister hoped for a meeting of the three Heads of Government. Eventually agreement was reached on the holding of a Conference of Foreign Ministers in Moscow from 19 to 30 October, to be followed by the Conference of Heads of Government in Teheran from 28 November to 1 December.

The meeting of Foreign Ministers was businesslike and productive,

covering not only the pursuit of the war, but the political preparations
for victory. Eden had prepared well and succeeded in covering many
distinct and substantial problems. The primary Soviet interest was,
as we have noted, in the arrangements for the opening of the second
front in 1944. There was discussion of the possibility of bringing
Turkey and Sweden into the war, of Yugoslavaia and of the disposal
of the Italian fleet. A formal Declaration (to which China adhered)
was agreed on the prosecution of the war and the need to establish
a 'general international oganisation . . . for the maintenance of
international peace and security'. There was agreement on the
establishment of the European Advisory Commission, the body of
British, American and Soviet officials which was to draw up the zones
of occupation and the plans for the administration of a defeated
Germany, and also on measures for the re-establishment of democracy
in Italy, the independence of Austria and the punishment of war
criminals. The Soviet Government was not ready for substantive
discussion of the treatment of Germany and blocked two of Eden's
desiderata, a declaration on the disclaiming of 'separate areas of
responsibility' and on the formation of 'associations' of the smaller
countries of Europe. (The Foreign Office obsession with the idea of
establishing federations in Eastern Europe formed one of the more
engaging oddities in British foreign policy from the 1930s onwards.
The theory of a stable buffer between Germany and Russia had
obvious attraction, but it is difficult to see how a federation of small
states would have been capable even of surviving its internal tensions,
let alone resisting determined pressure from East or West.) The
Conference was, however, generally regarded as something of a
personal triumph for Eden. He was well received by Stalin, even
Molotov was in a good mood and it seemed that the Soviet
representatives at last wanted to establish relations on a footing of
permanent friendship. Vyshinsky spoke of it as opening 'a new and
happy chapter'.[50]

The road to military victory, to the post-war political structure of
Europe and to the international framework within which it should
be set was plotted, albeit with varying degrees of clarity and
effectiveness, at the three great tripartite conferences. Teheran in
November 1943, Yalta in February 1945 and Potsdam in July 1945.
For an analysis of the objectives of the participants, the conduct of
the conferences and the consequence of the decisions reached, the
reader must turn to more specialised studies. We examine them here
as a pivotal point in the development of the British–Soviet relationship

and do so from two broad aspects: as establishing the international structure within which the British–Soviet relationship in the post-war world would have to be developed; and as determining certain enduring elements in that relationship, in particular the twin problems of the independence of Poland and the mutual relationship with Germany.

TEHERAN – 'FRIENDS IN FACT, IN SPIRIT AND IN PURPOSE'

The Teheran Conference, following closely on the preparatory meeting of Foreign Ministers in Moscow, ran from 28 November to 1 December 1943 and was the first meeting of the three Heads of Government, Stalin, Roosevelt and Churchill. By this time the German armies had been ejected from Africa and were in retreat along the whole of the front from west of Moscow to the Black Sea. The Soviet Union could plan with some confidence to move within a matter of months into Poland and the Baltic States, while Britain and the United States could at last plan a similar timing for their re-entry in force into France. The primary purpose of the conference was the coordination of these military arrangements and there began to be some sense of common strategic purpose, if not of detailed coordination. It was confirmed that the landings in northern France should take place in May 1944, that they should be accompanied by a landing in southern France and that a Soviet offensive should be timed so as to prevent the transfer of German forces from East to West. On the main strategic issues, there was little division of opinion, but on the possible use of a part of the forces already in the Mediterranean theatre to open up the Aegean, bring Turkey into the war and link up with the southern flank of the Soviet forces, Churchill had to concede in the face of American opposition. It was, however, agreed that action should be taken to try to bring Turkey into the war on the side of the Allies. Despite the marked change in the military prospects of the Allies, the strategic discussion still turned almost wholly on the future deployment of British and American forces. To a certain extent this reflected the greater range of options open to them by comparison with the more concentrated Soviet objective which limited the Soviet commitments to the timing of the Eastern offensive to coincide with the landings in France and a possible declaration of war on Bulgaria.

While the military discussions at Teheran led to formal conclusions, the political did not. There was only very preliminary discussion of the treatment of Germany, but Poland was a more immediate issue. It had been the subject of many bilateral exchanges between Britain and the Soviet Union. Now it was dealt with in formal tripartite conference and, largely at Churchill's instigation, the question of Poland's frontiers was discussed in some detail. Churchill's objective was, he said, a 'strong and independent Poland friendly to Russia'. Britain had given no commitment to the restoration of Poland's 1939 frontier and the outcome at Teheran was a broad measure of agreement on the proposition that the eastern frontier should be based generally upon the Curzon Line, while the western should be that of the Oder. Much was left open, including the southern extension of the Oder Line and the treatment of Lvov, but Churchill certainly committed himself to the general proposition and remarked that he 'was not going to make a great squawk about Lvov'. He made it clear that he had no mandate to take formal decisions, but indicated that he would recommend the outcome to the Poles. So, in effect, was decided the future shape of Poland. (See Map, p. 71.) So far as the re-establishment of relations between Poland and the Soviet Union was concerned, the future controversy was clearly indicated in the Soviet objection to dealings with the London-based Polish Government in exile.[51]

The conference was used as the occasion for the presentation by Churchill to Stalin of the sword of Honour given by King George VI in token of 'the homage of the British people to the steel-hearted citizens of Stalingrad'. The gesture was well received and helped to cement the personal relationship with Stalin which Churchill was beginning to enjoy and which was, without doubt, a key element in the intergovernmental relationship. In his memoirs, he noted: 'It would not have been right at Teheran for the Western democracies to found their plans upon suspicions of the Russian attitude in the hour of triumph.'[52] For each of the leaders, the conference seemed a success. There was, indeed, every reason why it should be. It took place at the point when thoughts could be turned to victory, when the strengthening of Soviet confidence lessened the impulse to recrimination, when the natural coincidence of strategic interest made joint planning a real possibility and when the political problems of the post-war world were still below the horizon. In the failure of Churchill's attempt to secure the use of British and American forces in a northward thrust into the Balkans came the first erosion by the United States of the British dominance in the wartime relationship

with the Soviet Union, but it was an inevitable reflection of the
changing power relationship. There was even a momentary ring of
truth about the joint Declaration of 1 December: 'We came here
with hope and determination. We leave here friends in fact, in spirit
and in purpose'.

It was in the course of 1944, between Teheran and Yalta, that the
victories of the Allied armies in West and East combined with the
work of the Foreign Ministries of the three great powers to form the
first elements of the pattern within which the East–West confrontation
of the post-war world was to be played out. The coordinated military
strategy agreed at Teheran was largely effective. The Allied landings
in France were deferred only from May until early June and the
Soviet offensive in the east followed little more than two weeks later.
By the beginning of February 1945, as the three leaders met again in
Yalta, the Soviet armies had occupied most of Poland and were
poised to enter Germany from the east, while the British and
American forces, having liberated France, were already inside Ger-
many and preparing for the crossing of the Rhine. The halting of the
Soviet offensive outside Warsaw had stirred a major controversy, to
which we shall return, and attempts to coordinate Allied bomb-lines
on the southern sector of the Eastern front had proved unrewarding.
At one critical point, when the German counter-offensive in the
Ardennes had posed a major threat to the Western advance, the
Soviet winter offensive had been brought forward in order to ease
the pressure, but for the most part the operations in East and West
had each progressed according to their individual momentum. It was
this momentum, coupled with the effect of German defence strategy,
rather than detailed inter-Allied coordination, which had brought
them more or less simultaneously to the German frontier.

Planning for the peace went ahead swiftly during 1944 and was
concentrated on two major topics, on the one hand the arrangements
for the occupation and future political structure of Germany, including
the problem of reparations; and on the other the establishment of
some wider international structure to maintain the peace. The
structure of the occupation regime was worked out in the European
Advisory Commission which had been agreed at the Conference of
Foreign Ministers in Moscow, prior to Teheran. The meetings took
place in London and the outcome was largely the work of Strang.
Progress was slow, particularly on the part of the Russians, but it
was the United States which posed the major problems of substance.
The allocation of zones between Britain and the United States and
the eventual provision for a French zone caused difficulty and at one

point the planners were wondering whether they would be able to reach agreement on the terms of a German surrender before the surrender took place. Eventually both the boundaries and the terms of the occupation were agreed, and the Commission's work, ratified by subsequent quadripartite agreement and consolidated by the accumulation of precedents, established the basis for Allied rights in Berlin, for the eventual frontier between the German Democratic Republic and the Federal Republic of Germany and hence for the East–West frontier through Central Europe.

In parallel with the work of the European Advisory Commission, the second main task of political planning was the creation of a comprehensive international organisation. This, like the work of the European Advisory Commission, stemmed from a British initiative at the meeting of Foreign Ministers in Moscow in October 1943, but subsequent work was more American-oriented. Tripartite conversations were carried out in Washington during the first half of 1944 and led, through the Dumbarton Oaks Conference in August–September of that year to the tripartite decisions at Yalta and the eventual establishment of the United Nations at the San Francisco Conference from April to June 1945. The negotiations were directly relevant to the British–Soviet relationship as it was to develop in the post-war years, in that they established the permanent British membership of the Security Council and thus, in a certain measure, the continuation, albeit less directly, of the great power relationship between the two countries which had existed prior to 1939 and had been at its peak in the wartime conferences. Throughout the negotiations leading up to San Francisco, British–Soviet diplomacy played a full part and the Soviet Union made much of the Commonwealth analogy in its bid for independent representation of its constituent republics.

A third, less obvious aspect of the preparatory work of 1944 must be noted. With the approach of victory over Germany, the British Chiefs of Staff began to consider the military problems of the post-war era. Work was put in hand in the Post-Hostilities Planning Committee. It was accepted that the primary object of British policy must be the preservation of a unity of purpose among the three powers. What concerned the Chiefs of Staff was the risk that this might not be achievable. In that event, they saw the only possible future enemy as the Soviet Union and the only route to British security in the formation of some Western European organisation, with which Germany – or part of it – would need to be associated and for which American support would be important.[53] This line of argument was also advanced by Duff Cooper, at that time British representative with de Gaulle, who recommended to Eden in May 1944 that, rather than relying solely on the new World Organisation, Britain would need to seek a system of Western European alliances as a protection against Russian domination of Europe. Western European unity was in line with Foreign Office thinking, but a military alliance against the Soviet Union was not. Pursuit of the Chiefs of Staff line might, in their view, create the very danger it was intended to avoid. Eden regarded the Chiefs of Staff's paper as 'terrible' and Duff Cooper was told that any West European system would need to be based squarely on the Anglo–Soviet alliance: 'A Western group organised as a defensive measure against the possibility of Russia embarking at some future date on a policy of aggression and domination would be a most dangerous experiment which might well precipitate the evils against which it was intended to guard.'[54]

Churchill's own concern at this time was beginning to be directed not so much at the possible organisation of post-war alliances, but rather more at what he described as 'the upsurge of Communist influence which slid on before, as well as followed' the westward movement of the Soviet forces.[55] He was deeply moved by the ordeal of the Polish population in the struggle to liberate Warsaw. In view of the position of Poland in the British–Soviet relationship the facts merit a brief restatement. In the last week of July, the German forces in Poland were hard pressed. The Soviet forces were ten miles from Warsaw and on 29 July Moscow Radio broadcast an appeal from the Polish Communists urging the people of Warsaw to begin 'direct, active struggle in the streets'. Then, faced with a difficult crossing of the Vistula, the Red Army halted at the outskirts of the city for some six weeks, while, with appalling violence the German forces destroyed much of the city and people of Warsaw. After first offering to supply arms themselves to the Polish Home Army in Warsaw, the Soviet Government refused permisson for British or American aircraft to land on Soviet airfields after supply drops (thereby reducing the effectiveness of the operation and adding to the Allied losses) and Stalin informed Churchill that 'the Soviet command must dissociate itself from the Warsaw adventure'.[56] Ministers considered hard whether a further effort could be made to drop supplies, but an accurate drop required a low-level approach across German positions and losses in the first attempts had been high. On 11 September, the War Cabinet endorsed the opinion of the Air Staff that 'a large scale operation to assist the Poles in Warsaw would be militarily unjustifiable'. Shortly afterwards the Soviet forces gave some assistance to the Poles and permitted American landings at Soviet airfields, but by then it was too late.[57] On 25 September Stalin told Clark Kerr that 'all idea of a frontal attack had been given up'.[58] On 2 October the Polish forces surrendered.

It is not easy to assess Soviet policy. The difficulty of the Vistula crossing and the immovability of the Soviet bureaucracy in its dealings with the Western powers were real factors, but it is hard to resist the conclusion that underlying it all was the calculation that, with the destruction of the Polish Home Army in Warsaw, the subsequent control of the country by the Moscow Lublin Committee would be substantially facilitated. In 1944, Polish–Soviet relations had not recovered from the shock of the murder of some 6000 Polish officers and men at Katyn. The fate of the Poles who were deported, many of them to Siberia, when the Soviet Union seized eastern Poland in 1939 is a story deserving fuller treatment than it can be given here. It must suffice to note that among the total, believed to be close to two million, were some 60 000 who, with 30 000 women and children, were allowed to leave the Soviet Union in 1942 and fight with the Allied forces. (Did Stalin perhaps have recollections of the Czechs in Siberia in 1918?) Some 13 000 officers remained unaccounted for, and when the discovery of mass graves at Katyn was announced by Germany in 1943, it was generally accepted in London that the Soviet Union was responsible. At that time, the British Government, concerned primarily with the pursuit of the war and the avoidance of a rift between Poland and the Soviet Union, had not forced the issue and in its short-term impact on British–Soviet relations it was soon overtaken by Churchill's successful visit to Moscow. Against the long history of Polish–Russian conflict, however, and on top of the shock of the Katyn massacre, the emotional effect of the Warsaw tragedy was to bring a new depth of bitterness into Polish–Soviet relations and, in the longer run, to heighten British awareness of the policies and methods of the Soviet leadership in the Stalin era.

With the advance of the Soviet forces into Poland, the problem of the country's political future was urgent. Was control to lie with the Polish Government in exile in London or with the Soviet-sponsored Lublin Committee? The need to resolve this issue was to the fore when Churchill proposed his second bilateral meeting with Stalin in Moscow in October 1944.[59] He was also concerned more generally with the position in Eastern Europe and with the problem of voting in the World Organisation which had not been resolved at Dumbarton

Oaks. At his first meeting with Stalin on 9 October Churchill scribbled out the celebrated list of percentages:

Romania
    Russia 90% Others 10%
Greece
    Great Britain (in accord with USA) 90%
    Russia 10%
Yugoslavia 50–50
Hungary 50–50
Bulgaria
    Russia 75% Others 25%

As Churchill explained the percentages afterwards to his colleagues, they were not intended to define rigid spheres of interest, but were an indication of the relative 'interest and sentiment' of the British and Soviet Governments. So the paper, with Stalin's tick on it, was left with Churchill. There was a full discussion of military planning, in which, for the first time, the Russians gave valuable indications of their further operations against Germany. Political discussions ranged from the future of Germany and Austria, to revision of the Montreux Convention and the entry of the Soviet Union into the war against Japan. On the central issue of the future of Poland, for which delegations from the London and Lublin Poles were present, little progress was made, but at least the principle of a merged administration seemed to be accepted. Churchill was, by the end, left with the feeling that he had got closer to his Soviet ally than ever before. He could scarcely have thought, as he left Moscow, looking forward to the tripartite summit at Yalta, that almost fifteen years were to elapse before a British Prime Minister again visited Moscow.

YALTA – 'THEIR WORD IS THEIR BOND'

The hopes entertained by Churchill in Moscow as regards the future Government of Poland were quickly proved vain. Correspondence, primarily between Roosevelt and Stalin, was acrimonious. Stalin accused the London-based Poles of undertaking 'terroristic actions creating a threat of civil war in the rear of the Red Army' and on 31 December 1944[60] the Lublin Committee was recognised by the Soviet Union as the Government of Poland. It was against this background

EUROPEAN BATTLEFRONTS JANUARY–MAY 1945

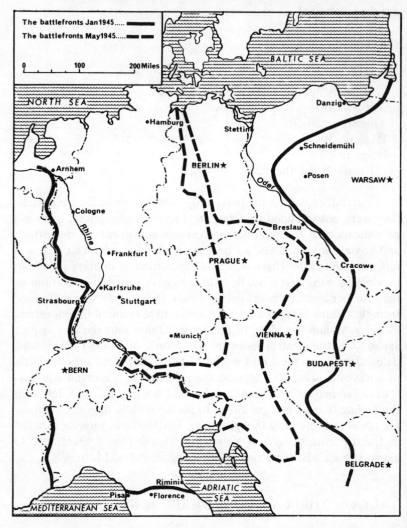

that Churchill went to Yalta to 'talk all these matters over, not only as isolated problems, but in relation to the whole world situation both of the war and the transition to peace'.

The tripartite meeting was preceded by a meeting between Churchill and Roosevelt at Malta. It is perhaps not irrelevant to the subsequent course of relations that the very natural process of close and continuous British–American consultation throughout the war, vital though it was, must to some extent have increased the Soviet Union's feeling of isolation and heightened their already extreme sensitivity. We may also, however, well note the remark by Sir Llewellyn Woodward[61] that, at Malta, 'The President and his entourage continued to assume that, unlike Great Britain, Russia was not an "imperialist" Power'. The temptation to seek an American–Soviet understanding at British expense was not wholly absent during the tripartite discussions.

The Yalta Conference itself ran from 4 to 11 February 1945. Much has been written about its significance in determining the structure of post-war Europe. In reality, however, that structure was already largely determined by the progress of military operations, which, as we have noted earlier, had brought the British, American and Soviet forces, by the time of the Conference to the borders of Germany both in the East and the West. (See Map, p. 192.) In so far as the Soviet military grip on Eastern Europe was in large measure established, it could not realistically be challenged. The fate of Poland was sealed. Militarily, central Europe remained open, but the work of the European Advisory Commission had effectively pre-determined the area of Soviet control in Germany. Considering these facts, the Declaration on Liberated Europe agreed at Yalta,[62] with its commitment to representative interim governments and free elections and its operational clause providing only for consultation, could represent little more than a pious aspiration. The future of Poland played a major part in the proceedings of the Conference and agreement was eventually reached that the existing Provisional Government should be 'reorganised on a broader democratic basis, with the inclusion of democratic leaders from Poland itself and from Poles abroad'. The reorganisation was to be the subject of consultation between Molotov and the British and American Ambassadors in Moscow and, after a new Government had been formed, elections were to be held. The three Governments would then recognise the new Polish Government of National Unity. The eastern frontier of Poland was agreed broadly on the basis of the Curzon Line, but the western boundary was left for decision at the Peace Conference because of the difference of view as to whether it should, in the south, be based on the eastern or western branch of the Neisse River. In verbal terms, the compromise settlement was not unreasonable. In real terms, it did not and could not significantly change the Soviet plan for the establishment in Poland of a subservient satellite regime.

On the wider front, there was satisfaction that it had been possible to reach agreement on the future World Organisation. Churchill felt that Stalin had been helpful over Greece and Stalin accepted his pleas for French participation in the occupation of Germany. There was also agreement in principle on the need for the eventual dismemberment of Germany, but on this and other matters such as reparations it was recognised that further discussion would be necessary.

One of the matters dealt with at Yalta was the repatriation of those citizens of the three powers who had been liberated during the advance from West and East. The British Government was greatly concerned to secure the swift repatriation of British prisoners-of-war from camps in Poland and eastern Germany and had not been disposed, in preliminary negotiation in Moscow, to complicate matters by seeking to distinguish between Soviet prisoners-of-war and deported civilians or to deal separately with those Soviet citizens wearing German uniform. Controversy has subsequently raged over this issue, but at the time it seemed clear to the British Government that, as the Allied armies moved into the debris of Europe, a general return home was the only feasible solution. The administrative difficulties were substantial, but despite some division of opinion in the United States, tripartite agreements on the principles governing the repatriation arrangements was reached with no difficulty at Yalta. It was this repatriation which provided me with my first contact with the Soviet forces. On a British troop-ship, the *Staffordshire*, we picked up the Russians from Liverpool, Marseilles and Naples and took them back to Odessa. They came on board dirty and squalid, mostly in American uniforms, indistinguishable in rank or status. Some had tried to commit suicide. The others were wild with joy at the prospect of returning home. With the help of one young officer from the Soviet Military Mission we changed them from a rabble to a tidy and disciplined body of troops who disembarked in Odessa to the welcome of a military band. We never discovered what they had done. Nor could we be certain of their fate. We could only suspect that it was cruel. But at my humble level, the balance of moral and practical considerations did not seem very different from the way it did to Eden. It was a brief lesson, but it left impressions of the frightening and erratic power of the system represented by that young officer as well as the strange mixture of warmth and brutality in the Russian character. It was already apparent that accommodation to the reality of Soviet power would be the dominant problem for post-war Europe.

I remember feeling uneasy at the prospect. But it made me want to see more of the country and its people.[63]

By the time of Yalta, the United States Government was beginning to be increasingly concerned about the need for Soviet entry into the war against Japan and a bilateral US–Soviet agreement was reached on this point. In relation to the future of Europe, the full impact of Roosevelt's announcement that American troops would not stay in Europe for more than two years after the end of the war was slow to develop, but it cannot have been lost on the Russians. In Britain there was anxiety about the future, and, in presenting the results of Yalta to Parliament[64] Churchill warned of the danger of 'some awful schism' with the Soviet Union. However, he declined 'absolutely to embark on a discussion about Russian good faith'. 'Their word is their bond', he said. He knew of 'no Government which stands to its obligations, even in its own despite, more solidly than the Russian Soviet Government'. So far as the future of Poland was concerned, Churchill's public expression of confidence was not shared by the twenty-five Members of Parliament who, led by a group of Conservatives, voted for an amendment to the motion of confidence on the outcome of the Conference.

'AN IRON CURTAIN IS DRAWN DOWN'

There is a sorry symmetry to the role of Poland in British–Soviet relations at the outbreak of the war and at its end. In the summer of 1939 the Soviet Union had chosen partition of Poland by agreement with Germany in preference to defence of Poland in alliance with Britain and France. As the war was approaching its victorious conclusion in the spring of 1945, it was the fate of Poland which, following the Soviet disregard of the Declaration on Liberated Europe and the installation of pro-Soviet regimes in Hungary and Romania, symbolised the disintegration of the alliance. Within weeks of the end of the Yalta Conference, it became clear to the British Government that the Soviet interpretation of the agreement on Poland was very different from that which might have been expected. Having already precipitated a substantial crisis within his own party by placing his faith in Soviet implementation of the agreement, Churchill was the more determined to ensure it. He saw the fate of Poland as the crucial test of Soviet willingness to cooperate in the wider problems of the post-war settlement. In that test, the central element was the setting up of a representative Polish Government which Britain and the United States could recognise. As he put it to Roosevelt on 13 March: 'Poland has lost her frontier. Is she now to lose her freedom?' Failure, in his view, would represent an utter breakdown of what had been agreed at Yalta.[65]

The arrest and trial of members of the Polish Home Army by the Soviet authorities augured ill and the negotiations between Molotov and the British and American Ambassadors in Moscow on reconstruction of the Lublin Government proved fruitless. The Allied relationship with the Soviet Union was souring quickly. There had been intense Soviet suspicion that the Western powers might conclude a separate peace and sharp exchanges took place over Soviet charges of British and American bad faith in relation to Soviet participation in possible surrender negotiations by the German forces in Italy. There was tension with Yugoslavia over Trieste and the communisation of Eastern Europe was proceeding swiftly. Some thought was given to the possibility that bargaining leverage might be secured if Berlin, Prague and Vienna were to be reached first by British or American forces, but even if this had proved militarily possible – as, in the case of Prague, it almost certainly was – there was no American enthusiasm for it. It was plain that, in practical terms, Britain had little more chance of securing the independence of Poland in 1945 than in 1939. By 29 April Churchill was warning Stalin of a future in which the English-speaking nations and their associates might be drawn up against the Communist states in a quarrel which would 'tear the world to pieces'.[66] Stalin was unmoved. Some progress was made as a result of a visit to Moscow by the American emissary, Harry Hopkins, and a new Polish government, including Polish representatives from London, was eventually recognised by Britain and the United States on 5 June. Mikolajčik placed some reliance on the ability of the Polish people to determine their future through free elections in accordance with the Declaration on Liberated Europe, but the Western powers had effectively recognised a Soviet fait accompli.

The danger of Soviet domination of Europe was heightened in Churchill's mind by the probability that, with the end of the war in Europe at midnight on 8 May, there would be a swift withdrawal of American forces. On 12 May, he telegraphed to Truman[67] that an 'iron curtain' had been drawn across the Soviet front and that it would be open to the Russians to advance to the North Sea and the Atlantic. It was vital, he urged, to come to an understanding with the Soviet Union before the British and American armies were weakened and before the withdrawal of those forces which, when hostilities ended, were in occupation of substantial areas – up to 100 miles in depth – to the east of the agreed border of the Western occupation zones.

In an attempt to secure such an understanding, the last of the great tripartite conferences was arranged at Potsdam. Before it could take place, there was, however, an incident which revealed graphically the change in the relationship with the United States after the death of Roosevelt. Churchill was, to his astonishment, told of an American proposal that Truman, who, since becoming President had not met either Stalin or Churchill, might meet Stalin bilaterally somewhere in Europe prior to a tripartite meeting. This proposal probably stemmed from Truman's natural and sensible desire to make his own private assessment of Stalin, before embarking on the main conference. It may also have reflected an American feeling that the sharp deterioration in relations with the Soviet Union was an essentially European phenomenon in which Churchill, reverting to his longstanding hostility to the Soviet regime, was aggravating the tensions and perhaps prejudicing the attainment of American objectives in relation to the pursuit of the war against Japan and the subsequent organisation of the post-war world. At this point in history, the potential problems of the projection of a new Soviet power onto the international scene were less vivid in the perception of many Americans than the colonial issues represented by British imperial power. The trend of American opinion was well illustrated by a telegram from Lord Halifax, Ambassador in Washington, to Churchill, shortly before the opening of the Conference.[68] Halifax spoke of American unresponsiveness to pleas about the risk of the spread of Communism and of nervousness at his portrayal of the clash of Soviet and Western influence on Europe. He saw the United States as 'half expecting to play, or at any rate to represent themselves as playing, a moderating role between ourselves and the Russians'. An American–Soviet meeting would have represented a staggering reversal of the tradition of prior bilateral British–American consultation. Churchill made it plain that, on this basis, there would be no tripartite meeting. He would not agree to British participation in any meeting except 'as equal partners from its opening'.[69] The proposal was dropped, but it had been a clear reflection of those realities of power which were to complicate the handling of the British–Soviet relationship in the early post-war years.

POTSDAM

The date of 15 July for the opening of the Berlin, or, as it is more commonly known, the Potsdam Conference, was established by correspondence between Truman and Stalin. It fell oddly in relation to the British General Election which was to take place on 5 July, in that the delay in receiving postal votes from the forces overseas meant that the result would not be declared until 26 July. Churchill sought to bring the date forward, hoping that this might make it possible to hold the conference before the withdrawal of British and American forces to the agreed occupation zone border. In this he failed. The United States Government insisted on prior withdrawal to the lines established by the European Advisory Commission and a potential bargaining counter – albeit of very doubtful utility or applicability – was given up.

The British view of the political scene at the time of Potsdam was well illustrated by a Foreign Office memorandum by Sargent, 'Stock-taking after VE Day',[70] an attempt to assess Britain's international position in the post-war years. There had been some evolution of policy since the controversy over the report of the Post-Hostilities Planning Committee. The objective of three-power cooperation was still central to British foreign policy, but it had to be pursued in the context of a divided Europe, in which Britain would need by its diplomacy to compensate for its lack of material power. On the question of Soviet long-term objectives, Sargent was cautious, but realistic. Stalin's obsession with security and his fear of Germany were recognised. It was assumed that he did not want and could not afford another war in Europe and that his objective was the consolidation of Soviet power in Eastern Europe rather than further territorial expansion. In a contest for influence in Europe between Britain and the Soviet Union, Britain would need the support of the United States, but there was a risk that the United States would prefer the 'less arduous role' of mediator and that the two supreme world powers might be content to arrange matters between themselves, a 'misconception' which Britain would need to combat. Britain, he argued, should not be afraid of an independent, anti-totalitarian policy and should be ready to take the lead in challenging Communist penetration in Eastern Europe. It might have to be accepted in Romania and Hungary, but in Finland, Poland, Czechoslovakia, Austria, Yugoslavia and Bulgaria the challenge could be realistic.

The agenda for the Conference reflected the major issues on which the contest would turn: the future of Germany; policy towards Italy; the application of the Declaration on Liberated Europe with particular reference to Poland; and the peace settlement with Germany's former East European satellites. Japan had not yet been defeated and it was only after the conference opened that the news was received of the successful test of the atomic bomb. With Germany defeated, this was, in Churchill's terms, the final opportunity to come to an understanding with the Soviet Union on the future of Europe. On 10 July Eden sent the Prime Minister a note[71] on 'what cards we hold for a general negotiation with the Russians, in the shape of things which the Russians want from us and which it is in our power to give or withhold'. The list covered credits (which would have to be American), German industrial equipment, the Italian fleet, modification of the regime in the Straits, participation in the regime for Tangier and recognition of the Soviet acquisition of the Baltic states. There was little in this list to encourage expectations that the Soviet Union could be persuaded to relax its grip on Central and Eastern Europe. Eden remarked that he found 'the world outlook gloomy and signs of Russian penetration everywhere'.[72]

In its outcome,[73] the Conference did not substantially affect the British perception of the relationship with the Soviet Union. Churchill's own performance was disappointing. Much of his time was taken up with discussion of the Polish question, in particular the Polish–German border. Eden found him under the spell of Stalin, having failed to read his briefs, 'confused and woolly and verbose', while Cadogan said he 'talks the most irrelevant rubbish and risks giving away our case at every point'.[74] He left for Britain on 25 July and, after the Labour victory in the General Election, Clement Attlee returned as Prime Minister, with Bevin as his Foreign Secretary for the final days from 28 July to 1 August.

This was the first occasion since Ramsay MacDonald had appointed the first British Ambassador to Moscow at the end of 1929 that Labour had had the opportunity to conduct relations with the Soviet Union. During the election campaign, they had made a certain amount of play with the argument that left could talk to left. In practice, however, the change made little difference to the outcome of Potsdam. As Deputy Prime Minister, Attlee had been fully associated with the handling of relations during the war and had accompanied Churchill for the first part of the Conference itself. Bevin could draw not only on his Cabinet experience, but on his knowledge of Soviet policy towards British labour during the 1920s and 1930s. Neither had any illusions about the nature of the problems they faced. They had no wish to offer a new challenge to the Soviet Union, but there was little room for constructive initiative on any of the major issues and they were in no mood to concede. Like Churchill, they had to devote most of their time to Poland. The reality had to be accepted that the German territory lying East of the line of the Oder and the Western Neisse had been handed over by the Soviet Union to a Polish Government which the Western powers had already been forced to recognise. Bevin was, however, determined to extract what price he could for the territorial concession by making it part of a larger package and securing concessions from the Poles in respect of the holding of elections. In this he had some success. He succeeded from the outset in making his personality felt, but he could have little confidence in the value of the assurances he received.

With the principles of the occupation regime for Germany already settled, discussion at Potsdam turned largely on economic questions, in part those flowing from the Soviet demand for reparations and in part the problem of feeding the industrial areas of the Western zones, in particular that occupied by the British. Here were visible some of the problems which were eventually to precipitate the economic reform of the Western zones and the Berlin blockade, but that still lay far in the future. In terms of the conduct of British–Soviet relations during the immediate post-war years, the Conference took a key decision by establishing the Council of Foreign Ministers, with its Secretariat in London. By doing so, it had provided a machinery through which, if the will existed, the powers of the wartime alliance might shape the peace and through which the British Government might try to work out its relationship with the Soviet Union. On his return from Potsdam, Attlee reported to his colleagues, paying a warm tribute to Bevin and commenting that 'on the whole we could be very well satisfied' with the outcome.[75]

THE EXPERIENCE OF ALLIANCE

With the Potsdam Conference, the wartime partnership between Britain and the Soviet Union had, in just over four years, run its course. Immediately beset by the internal and external problems of adjustment to the post-war world, Attlee had little time for reflection on the quite remarkable experience which it represented. Now, however, when the alliance is sometimes recalled as an illustration of the possibility of cooperation and as an example for the future, it is appropriate briefly to examine the nature of the wartime relationship.

Governments, no matter by what ideology they are guided or to what external and internal pressures they are subject, are composed of individuals. The alliance was what it was made by the politicians, the diplomats, the bureaucrats, the members of the armed forces – all those individuals in whose hands rested the actual conduct of relations. Singly and collectively, in Britain and in the Soviet Union, it was they who, guided by their instinct, their training, their emotion and their experience would determine whether the alliance would amount to more than a greeting between two vessels whose courses briefly coincided. For all of them, personal experience and historical perception, whether true or false, were a potent factor in shaping their response to the new fact of the alliance. Their comments give a little of the flavour of thinking, for which a recital of facts and dates is no substitute.

The fact that in the summer of 1941 German forces crossed the Soviet border could not, of itself, destroy the Soviet recollection of British participation in the intervention or of their ostracism by the pre-war British Conservative Governments. It could not erase two decades of indoctrination about the irreconcilable struggle between the forces of socialism and capitalism. It could not make the British public forget the Stalin purges. The diplomats, the sailors and the soldiers who had conducted the abortive 1939 negotiations still remembered how they had been left to pack their bags while Stalin, Molotov and Ribbentrop raised their champagne glasses in celebration of a new-found friendship.

It is hard to judge from first-hand evidence the evolution of opinion towards Britain in the Soviet Union between 1941 and 1945. Nor, from a British perspective, is it easy to form a valid assessment of such evidence as is available. From the summer of 1941 to the summer of 1944 the German forces were on Soviet soil and the whole people of the Soviet Union were engaged in a struggle to the death to eject them. In such a situaton, the only thing which mattered – as it mattered to Lloyd George in the different circumstances of 1917 – was the pursuit of the war, and the only relevance of Britain was in the extent to which she could contribute to that end. The quality of the alliance, in Soviet eyes, was measured in these terms. The practices of Russian bureaucracy, with roots deeper than 1917, could not, as we have seen in the problems at Murmansk, easily be changed. At the official level, the records are filled with accounts of the frustration of the Military Mission in Moscow and the difficulty of securing any useful information about the conduct of Soviet operations. Even when, in preparation for the cross-Channel landings, the Mission sought permission to inspect German beach defences constructed at Odessa, this was refused. When the Foreign Secretary was at Yalta, Sir Alexander Cadogan sent him a briefing telegram[76] in which he stated, 'Russian attitude to our mission in Moscow has been throughout deliberately uncooperative and both before and after D-Day there has been no attempt to work on basis of reciprocity. . . . As a matter of policy, very little information about the Red Army is given and practically no worthwhile information on the course of fighting in progress.'

In February 1943, Clark Kerr devoted the whole of a longish talk with Stalin to a plea that he might be allowed some contact with the country in which he was serving as Ambassador. Reporting his remarks to the Foreign Office,[77] he said that he had pointed out the wide contacts which Maisky enjoyed in London, whereas 'after some ten months in this country, I found myself isolated and friendless. Day in and day out, I saw no-one but my staff . . . I was allowed to see nothing.' In April he was able to report 'a consciousness that feeling towards us has been taking a kinder shape', perhaps as a result of some Kremlin edict, but the effect did not seem to have percolated very far. In the Foreign Office archives is a bitter letter[78] dated 20 January 1944 from the Moscow correspondent of the *News Chronicle* complaining, 'We are making no progress here getting nearer to the Russians. . . . 'The position is becoming stickier, contacts are fewer, obstruction is greater. . . . They are an impossible crowd to work with, close, secretive, jesuitical and, unless they can use you, indifferent.' There is a sad little story, familiar enough through the decades, of the lady who was rash enough to give Russian lessons to one of the British in Moscow and was last heard of in the Lubyanka. Yet against this can be set examples of warmth and kindness by individual Russians and instances such as the performance in Baku of a remarkable little play celebrating the heroism of the British and Soviet sailors engaged in the Arctic convoys.

In London, Maisky was constantly pleading for British understanding of the Soviet inferiority complex in dealing with Britain. His countrymen, he said, were inexperienced in the conduct of diplomacy and felt themselves 'country cousins'. Clark Kerr had some sympathy.

He wrote on 10 August 1943:[79] 'I feel indeed that we are still holding these people at an arm's length. We have not yet let them into the club. They are still scrutinised by the hall porter, stared at by the members and made to feel that they do not really belong, whereas we fall over ourselves to make the Americans feel at home. In a word, we consult Washington and we inform Moscow.'

There must have been much substance to the concern of the two Ambassadors. Yet there were instances of solid practical cooperation, not merely in the pursuit of the war but also in the more contentious task of preparing for the peace. In Britain, many of the responsible officials were those who had experience in dealing with the Soviet Union before the war. Among them, one may single out William Strang, who, after his 1939 experience, can have had few illusions. He took the lead in the work of the European Advisory Commission and, although he had cause to complain of Soviet delay, he was cited in the spring of 1944, in a Foreign Office Minute[80] as saying that his Soviet counterparts 'genuinely want to cooperate and in so far as they fail to do so there is little to choose between them and the Americans'. Subsequently, in his memoirs, he wrote of this work: 'Though for eighteen months we relied again and again on unrecorded oral understandings and undertakings, never once, so far as I can recollect, was there ever any serious misunderstanding amongst us or any breach of given word.'[81] When one considers how little experience the diplomats of the two countries had had of joint work, either bilaterally or in the work of the League of Nations, the achievements of the Commission and of those concerned with the preparatory work for the United Nations were the more noteworthy.

The most remarkable feature of alliance diplomacy was undoubtedly the series of summit meetings. By 1941, Stalin had been in power for seventeen years. His only contact with a British Minister had been his meeting with Eden in 1935. Between 1941 and 1945 he was to meet Churchill twice in Moscow and three times at the tripartite summits. It has been convenient to chronicle much of the British–Soviet wartime relationship by reference to the voluminous and often acrimonious correspondence between them. There is a risk, in doing so, of underrating the contribution of others, but the wartime relationship was exceptional. The summit correspondence was no mere set of formal exchanges. Churchill was personally responsible for the drafting of many of his messages. In the other direction, it is hard to judge how far Molotov's pen was responsible, but the result is probably a fair reflection both of the personalities of the two men and of the relationship between their two countries.[82] There can be little doubt that Churchill greatly relished the contact; that he tried by every means to use it for the direct exercise of personal diplomacy on major issues; and that he had some success. Eden, however, clearly had doubts about this method of diplomacy. He observed in his memoirs that the summits 'had their merits, though the orderly despatch of business was not one of them' and remarked of Churchill's handling of them: 'The spoils in the diplomatic game do not necessarily go to the man most eager to debate.' Cadogan noted after Teheran that Eden was 'rather in despair about this hazy conference'.[83] By contrast, Eden greatly admired Stalin's tactics at Yalta: 'He never wasted a word. He never stormed, he was seldom even irritated. Hooded, calm, never raising his voice, he avoided the repeated negatives of Molotov. . . . By more subtle methods he got what he wanted without having seemed so obdurate.'[84]

On other occasions, Stalin deployed the classical alternation of anger and joviality to unsettle his negotiating partners. At the first tense meeting in Moscow in the summer of 1942, when Churchill broke the news of the deferment of the second front, he had to endure a full session of Stalin's bitter reproaches, yet, by the end, he was able to report to his colleagues: 'I feel I have established a personal relationship which will be helpful.'[85] At Teheran, in the autumn of 1943, he noted Stalin's brutality, but also his 'captivating manner when he chooses to use it'. By the spring of 1944, he was thoroughly gloomy about the personal relationship. The mood of Teheran was fading. Cordell Hull had spoken of a possible need for a show-down and Churchill was inclined to agree. He minuted to Eden:[86] 'Although I have tried in every way to put myself in sympathy with these Communist leaders, I cannot feel the slightest trust or confidence in them. Force and facts are their only realities.' He did not want to go back on the effort to establish a friendly relationship, but felt that 'courteous and even effusive personal approaches' had done no good and that a few months of 'moody silence' would be useful. Foreign Office officials were disposed to attribute Soviet behaviour to 'ignorance and clumsiness' rather than 'ill-will or careful calculation'. Eden was less hopeful. He admitted to 'growing apprehension that Russia has vast aims and that these may include the domination of Eastern Europe and even the Mediterranean and the "communisation" of much that remains', but advised: 'On the whole I would be inclined to let matters drift a little longer before considering a show-down with Stalin'. Yet, six months later, at

Churchill's second bilateral meeting in Moscow, there was for the first time a significant supply of military information about Soviet operations against Germany and plans for entry into the war against Japan. Churchill's report spoke of an 'extraordinary atmosphere of goodwill' and 'an atmosphere of friendliness and frankness which is an enormous advance on anything we have known before'.[87] At Yalta, with Roosevelt close to death and Stalin confident of victory, lavish Soviet hospitality contributed to a certain euphoria, which did nothing to further the achievement of British objectives. On balance, whatever the defects of this summitry, it is probable that, without it, the wartime relationship would have been worse, the losses which were sustained through the Soviet control of Eastern Europe would have been no less, and the agreements reached in other areas such as the foundation of the United Nations would have been harder to secure.

Four years of war had shown Britain that where a direct Soviet strategic interest, whether real or perceived, was at stake and where the Soviet Union could, without risk, secure it by force, concession to the spirit of the alliance was not to be expected and verbal understandings were ineffective. The Soviet leaders expected Britain to be equally ruthless in protecting its security interest in Western Europe. Where the issues were in the longer range area of national interest, the normal processes of official diplomacy and the extraordinary processes of summit diplomacy could be effective, but the validity of the result had yet to be tested. The mistrust had been eased only slightly, if at all. The relationship was excessively concentrated at the summit, thin among the diplomats, even thinner among the military. As we shall see, it was, by 1945, possible for Whitehall to appraise Soviet policy with some accuracy. Whether Soviet appreciations were as accurate we cannot say. What is certain is that among the policy-makers on both sides mutual mistrust was still deep and that, on the British side, it was for the first time aggravated by apprehension about Soviet military power. Nevertheless, as the war ended, the popular mood in Britain, largely untempered by the reality of direct contact, was still one of respect for a gallant, if unlovable, ally and readiness to embark on a joint effort to create a safer structure of international society. A policy of open confrontation would have found little support among the electorate in the summer of 1945.[88]

8 Post-War Confrontation

THE BREACH WITH RUSSIA AND THE DIVISION OF GERMANY

Earlier chapters have traced the sequence of events which culminated in the failure of the pre-war Conservative Government to establish an alliance with the Soviet Union against Nazi Germany. Now, after the brief interlude of the wartime alliance, we have to trace the evolving British perception of Soviet policy in the post-war world and the gradual hardening of the response until, ten years after the end of the war, the British–Soviet Treaty of Alliance was formally annulled and Britain and West Germany were allied in defence against the possibility of war with the Soviet Union.

In the summer of 1945 and well into 1946 the British Government still based its policy on the hope of developing a cooperative relationship with the Soviet Union. Later in 1946 and throughout 1947 and 1948 a progressive and almost uninterrupted deterioration in relations marked the descent into that state of political and military confrontation which became known as the Cold War, a term which the Foreign Office reluctantly accepted and proceeded to define as 'a struggle against Stalinist Communism on a world wide scale not involving a world war".[1] The early hopes were replaced by a realisation that for many years to come the best that could be expected was that the confrontation with Soviet power and Soviet ideology could be contained without the danger of war or the erosion of essential British interests. The history of the next forty years was the history of that containment.

The policy of 'containment' has acquired a certain doctrinal significance as a result of its advocacy by George Kennan in 1947. He defined it as meaning that the West should 'confront the Russians with unalterable counter-force at every point where they show signs of encroaching upon the interests of a peaceful and stable world'. There are those who, ignoring the popular mood of 1945, argue that Kennan's policy was over-cautious and that the West, with its monopoly of the nuclear weapon, could have enforced the liberation of Eastern Europe. Others have argued that, by basing their policies upon an exaggerated fear of Soviet expansion, the British and American Governments created the very danger they had then to overcome. It is only too easy to quibble with Kennan. He himself was not completely happy that his article became a doctrinal text, but he summed it up rather well later as, 'Stand up to them, but not aggressively and give the hand of time a chance to work'.[2] That, by and large is what the post-war British Governments did and I believe they were right. The world is not a Marxist world of socialists and imperialists, nor, irrespective of the tensions created by the 'irreconcilable struggle' of Marxism–Leninism, is it naturally peaceful or stable. We may regret that the United States did not more quickly realise the threat posed by the Soviet Union, but even fewer Europeans would have supported a 'roll-back' policy in 1945 than in 1951. Equally, with the East–West border already on the Elbe, no responsible British statesman could have afforded to gamble British security on Soviet goodwill. My purpose in this chapter is not, however, to argue the doctrine of 'containment'.[3] I use the term merely as a factual description of the policies of successive British Governments as they tried to create a structure of international relations which would withstand the pressure of Communist doctrine and Soviet subversion and would provide a credible defence against the Soviet armed forces, while seeking at the same time to reduce the inherent tension by dialogue with the Soviet Union.

The years 1945–50 saw the framework established within which the East–West confrontation was to be played out over the next thirty years. The diplomatic exchanges with the Soviet Union, for all their sterility, were arguably more significant than the great wartime summits.[4] Throughout the first three critical years, while the nations of Western Europe picked themselves up from the rubble, and opinion in the United States first hesitated and then hardened, the British Government, although handicapped by severe economic constraints, was able very largely to set the tone and the substance of policy towards the Soviet Union. When the Labour Government took office, the wartime alliance had all but run its course. Its fruit had been military victory. The Soviet state which Churchill had hoped to break, which Austen Chamberlain had kept 'as distant as possible' and to which Neville Chamberlain had allowed no voice in the fate of Czechoslovakia, had won its right to play a dominant part in the shaping of the post-war world. It had become, in the opinion of Admiral Leahy, President Truman's Chief of Staff, the 'unquestioned all-powerful influence in Europe'. It had done this by harnessing the total human and economic resources of the state to the attainment of military power. It had done it at the price of twenty million lives and the devastation of large areas of the country. Britain, too, emerged victorious, uninvaded, its national self-confidence enhanced by the recollection of the year during which the British Empire had stood alone against German hegemony. Its loss of life had been only a fraction that of the Soviet Union, but the repair of an economy dependent upon external trade, shipping and finance was in some respects a more complex task than that faced by the Soviet Union. The will to play the full part of a great power was still there, but there was a consciousness of limited means, of resources far inferior to those of the United States, of a need to base foreign policy on cooperation rather than dominion. In parallel with the change in the power ratio was the creation of new machinery, within which the British–Soviet relationship had in large measure to be conducted. The Council of Foreign Ministers was established as the body in which the victorious great powers, together with France and China, would prepare the peace treaties and seek to resolve the immediate problems of the transition from war to peace, while the Security Council of the United Nations would provide for their cooperation in handling the tensions of the post-war world. The peacetime provisions of the Treaty of Alliance were clearly going to be tested in very different conditions from those which governed the pre-war relationship.

Many of the features which were to determine the course of British-Soviet relations throughout the next forty years had already been established by the outcome of the conflict in Europe. In Bulgaria, Hungary, Romania and Poland, the Soviet Union had established a form of Government subservient to its own control. British policy had to be based upon recognition that, for better or for worse, Eastern Europe was now an area in which Soviet power would be dominant. In relation to Poland, for whose independence Britain had gone to war, this was a bitter outcome. Of itself, however, it did not constitute a threat to British interests and there was still some room for hope about the way in which that power would be exercised. Elsewhere in Europe, the extent to which the Soviet Union could secure control over Finland, Czechoslovakia, Austria and Yugoslavia remained to be tested, as did Soviet ability to influence the political scene in Greece, Turkey, Italy and France. Possible Soviet ambitions in terms of the extension of power and influence westwards and southwards in Europe, the Middle East and Central Asia, and the wider policies which the Soviet Union would pursue in the newly established United Nations Organisation were all a matter of speculation. It was, however, Germany which had once again to be the key to European security and the central issue in British–Soviet relations. Where, in the new Europe, would the power to control its centre reside and how would that power be exercised? For the four powers, Britain, France, the United States and the Soviet Union, this was the issue which underlay the assumption of quadripartite control in Germany.

For its part, the Soviet Union must also have felt the need to test British and American policy. Would Britain adapt to the reality of the new structure of international power in the post-war world? Would she seek, with American help, to restore the old structure of imperial power, to constrain the Soviet Union within its own boundaries, perhaps to challenge its domination of Eastern Europe? Or would the imperialists, under pressure, move aside in order to accommodate the Soviet Union, not merely as dominant in Eastern Europe, but as exercising that role in relation to global policy which the structure of the Security Council envisaged? So far as Britain was concerned, the conclusion must have been that, given the chance, a British Labour Government would still seek to re-establish Churchill's 'old equilibrium'; but that its resources were limited, it could not be sure of American support and, lacking the firm hand of Churchill, it could well be forced to concede positions of power and influence to the Soviet Union. Now, however, it was the United States which, alone among the great powers to end the war with its economy greatly strengthened, constituted the stronghold of imperialist power. Would she assume the responsibilities of leadership, or would her people, as in 1918, prefer to stand aside from Europe's troubles? To Stalin, it must have seemed that, with so much still open, to hold back would be to risk forfeiting the fruit of military victory; to consolidate the gains already made was essential; and to press beyond them was worth trying.

The Soviet mood at that time was a strange mixture of confidence and uncertainty. Victory had given them every reason for confidence in their ability to defeat any conceivable threat based on conventional military force and to play, in the widest international arena, the role of a great power. With the explosion of the atomic bomb, that confidence in military invulnerability was now tinged with doubt and the doubt was aggravated by each indication of a hardening Western policy. It soon became apparent that Britain and the United States were maintaining their claim to worldwide power and influence, extending even to areas of critical importance to Soviet security such as the entry to the Black Sea, while denying to the Soviet Union any comparable influence, for instance in the Mediterranean and in Japan. The Soviet mood was well sensed by Frank Roberts, who was in charge of the Moscow Embassy for much of this period. He sent a telegram to the Foreign Office on 28 September 1945,[5] in which he reported how Stalin had said to visiting US Congressmen that Britain and the Soviet Union had little to give one another, whereas Soviet–American relations were all important. This was more than mere flattery. There can be little doubt that Stalin was on the one hand genuinely reflecting the Soviet assessment of the reality of post-war power and on the other playing to American suspicion that hard-line British policies might precipitate an unnecessary split. Roberts went on to describe the Soviet mood as 'a dangerous mixture of suspicion with a temporarily uncertain sense of power', a combination which made the leadership the more determined to safeguard its own strategic interests and to 'pocket whatever may be going before the general world situation crystallises'. He saw many 'frankly imperialist aspects of Soviet policy', but thought recent Soviet intransigence more a matter of genuine suspicion and advocated a recognition of the respective British and Soviet spheres of influence. Roberts found a surprising ally in Bertrand Russell who wrote in the *Manchester Guardian* on 2 October, arguing that the history of British policy towards Russia 'is not creditable either to our intelligence or to our virtue'; that present difficulties arose out of Soviet imperialism; that appeasement was wrong; but that the right course was to concede the Soviet Union a free hand in Eastern Europe other than Greece and Turkey in exchange for acknowledgement of the British interest in the Mediterranean. For the present, 'we must trust to expedients, hoping that in time the Russian regime may become more liberal and more cooperative' and build up a Western bloc 'not hostile to Russia, not subservient, not susceptible to political penetration by Communist totalitarianism'. The *Manchester Guardian*'s leader writer was somewhat more emollient when he wrote on 20 December of the Soviet Union, 'anxious for the friendship of the two Great Powers, but more than half anticipating their enmity' and urging the need to 'extend to the Russian ideas and needs the sympathy and respect which we expect for ourselves'.

Having ample advice but little direct evidence of Soviet thinking, the British Government could be guided only by the external manifestations of Soviet policy. It was scarcely to be expected that Soviet diplomacy, in this new and strange set of international relationships moulded by force of arms, would be marked by much subtlety and indeed it was not. Little enlightenment and no comfort were to be derived from the obduracy with which Molotov handled both procedural and substantive questions in the Council of Foreign Ministers. On the ground, where the Soviet Union held power, that power was exercised ruthlessly in the Soviet interest and it could only be assumed that, given the opportunity elsewhere, Soviet policy would be similar. In consequence, British opinion – and in particular Bevin's opinion – steadily hardened throughout the sequence of frustrating meetings in London from 11 September to 2 October 1945, in Moscow from 16 to 26 December 1945, in Paris from 25 April to 16 May and 15 June to 12 July 1946, in New York from 4 November to 12 December 1946, in Moscow again from 10 March to 24 April 1947, and finally in London from 25 November to 15 December 1947.

The first meeting of the Council was the occasion for an immediate trial of strength with Molotov. Eastern Europe might be a lost cause, but President Truman was not disposed to write it off and, although the US Secretary of State, James Byrnes, vacillated, Bevin sought an independent inquiry into the maintenance of democratic liberties in Bulgaria and Romania. Molotov, in return, challenged the status of France as a party to the peace treaties with the Eastern European countries and staked the Soviet Union's own claim to trusteeship over Tripolitania. The meeting ended in procedural disagreement on the question of entitlement to participation in the preparation and conclusion of the peace treaties. In substance it changed little, but as a first test of the peacetime relationship it was depressing. Soviet tactics had squandered much of the wartime stock of public goodwill in Britain and to the British Government it seemed that the Soviet Union was seeking to develop from its established bridgehead in Eastern Europe a wider thrust of power and influence. Bevin did not, however, wish to aggravate the dispute in public. In his report to Parliament on 9 October, he spoke of 'temporary breakdown', but looked forward to the 'present divergencies' being overcome.[6] As Roberts saw it in Moscow, the Soviet Union had been surprised by the force with which the United States had challenged their position in Eastern Europe, sought to exclude them from the Far East and tried to dilute the three-power monopoly of major policy. He spoke of their need to 'consolidate their position in Eastern

Europe before the Anglo-Saxon democratic counter-offensive gathers strength'.[7] It must indeed have appeared to the Soviet Government that Britain and the United States were determined to maintain a global supremacy and deny the Soviet Union its rightful place as a world power.

The next meeting of Foreign Ministers in Moscow in December 1945 was not formally a meeting of the Council. It was held without France and China – the latter did not again participate – and was somewhat more productive in that agreement was reached on various aspects of the peace-making process. In terms of British–Soviet relations, it was noteworthy for a long talk between Bevin and Stalin, in the course of which Bevin suggested a possible extension of the Anglo-Soviet Treaty to fifty years, but also pointed out that there was 'a limit beyond which we could not tolerate continued Soviet infiltration and undermining of our position'.[8] It seemed to Bevin, however, that Byrnes, who had taken the initiative in arranging the meeting, was disposed to curry favour with the Soviet Union at Britain's expense and the mutual irritation was aggravated by the sharp British reaction to the American attempt to use the terms of the UK–US Loan Agreement to break open the Commonwealth trading system.

As Soviet policy developed throughout 1946 and 1947, it appeared to have four major elements which caused concern to the British Government: the consolidation of the Soviet hold on Eastern and central Europe; the strengthening of the position in Germany; southwards pressure against Turkey and Iran; and a virulent publicity campaign against the Western democracies. In Germany, the early frustration of the attempt to coordinate policy on a quadripartite basis in the Allied Control Council owed more to French than to Soviet intransigence. Soviet policy was directed towards the establishment of Communist control over the political process in eastern Germany, with the ambition that, from this base, a 'Popular Front' type of Government could eventually be established throughout Germany. With this political objective and with the economic objective of securing reparations from the Western Zones, it was to Soviet advantage, while exercising total control in its own Zone, to maintain the principle of a united Germany under quadripartite control. The first substantial political move was made early in 1946 with the forced amalgamation of Communists and Social Democrats in the Soviet Zone to form the Socialist Unity Party on a basis which provided for effective Communist control by Walter Ulbricht.

At the same time, Roberts was reporting from Moscow a series of Soviet pronouncements on the theme of the power of the Soviet Union, without whom, from Greece to Iceland, no decision could be taken; the mixture of British weakness and hostility; and on the way in which the Labour Government had 'completely taken over the reactionary policy of the Conservatives'. In March of 1946, he summed up the scene in a series of three important despatches on the basis of Soviet policy and its implications for Britain. They provide a good summary of the British assessment of the Soviet Union in the early post-war years. Painting a 'sombre picture' of pressure in Europe, the Middle East and the Far East, Roberts saw the Soviet Union seeking to profit from the fluid state of Europe and making a desperate effort to seize advanced positions before the reaction set in. He was impressed by the 'tremendous revival of orthodox Marxist ideology, which left the impression that the Soviet peoples were a chosen people, and that they were surrounded by a hostile world, composed largely of reactionary capitalists and their willing tools in the social democratic movement' and wondered 'whether the world is not now faced with a modern equivalent of the religious wars of the sixteenth century'. Ideologically and economically, the Soviet Union was a closed community, governed by a small handful of men cut off from the outside world, men with a Jesuit-like belief in their own ideology, absolute confidence in their system, suspicious and mistrustful, with no regard for human relationships. They might not now proclaim the doctrine of world revolution, but their aim was to make the Soviet Union the most powerful state in the world, to weaken the capitalist and socialist democratic countries and encourage 'liberation' movements among the 'so-called oppressed colonial peoples'. Yet the friendly Russian people, with their 'streak of laziness, indiscipline and inefficiency', were not the German people, the new Soviet threat was not the pre-war German threat, Soviet objectives did not call for a war of aggression 'except possibly for a limited aim' and issues were not likely to be pressed to the point of serious conflict 'except as a result of the miscalculation of forces'. On British policy, he admitted to finding it 'easier to draw the conclusion that none of the methods adopted over the past thirty years should be repeated than to put forward any very positive or inspiring substitute for them'. His prescription was a mixture of the old and new diplomacy, firmness and politeness, closer contacts and normal trade. 'Be strong, look strong, but strength should not be paraded unnecessarily' and there should be no sabre-rattling. He summed it up as the 'distant realism' which had for three centuries been a not unsuccessful basis of relations with the old Russia.[9]

Roberts's despatches were well received. They coincided in most respects with the thinking of Bevin and his officials. Indeed they had to some extent been anticipated by the development of opinion in London, and the Foreign Secretary had them circulated to the Cabinet. The situation was, in some respects, not dissimilar to that of the early years after the First World War, when British opinion had been much exercised by the threat of Soviet propaganda in the Empire and the danger of a Communist Germany. Now, however, the doctrinal challenge was backed by Soviet military power.

Within the Foreign Office there was a general recognition of the need to counter the twin elements of Soviet policy, the direct actions of the Government and the indirect use of Communist propaganda. Bevin had no illusions, but he was still inclined towards patience. It was Churchill who, in his speech at Fulton on 5 March 1946, while Roberts was composing his despatches, put into words the new assessment of Soviet policy which ministers and officials were beginning to accept but not yet publicly to enunciate. The Soviet Union, he said, did not desire war: 'What they desire is the fruits of war and the indefinite expansion of their power and doctrine.' He spoke of the Iron Curtain drawn across Europe and called for a special relationship between Britain and the United States, with close defence cooperation. Russia should be welcomed to 'her rightful place among the leading nations of the world' and was entitled to security against Germany, but Russia admired nothing so much as strength. Unity of the western democracies must be the basis for 'a good understanding on all points with Russia'.[10] In substance, the speech was not remarkable, but Churchill spoke with the authority of his unheeded warnings of the Nazi threat and the tone and timing of the speech were well chosen to catch and develop the trend towards a harder policy on both sides of the Atlantic. In Moscow, it was seen by Stalin as an ultimatum to the non-English speaking nations to accept the rule of Britain and the United States.[11] In April, the new mood was marked within the Foreign Office by the re-formation of the Russia Committee, originally constituted in 1918, in order to examine Soviet policy and propaganda throughout the world. In an interesting sidelight on the way British officials still saw the United States playing a secondary role, the Committee was also to examine the 'degree of support to be looked for from the USA' in dealing with the Soviet threat.

It was, however, in relation to Germany rather than to the Soviet

Union that there was an acute need to formulate British policy. Britain was in desperate financial straits and its Zone of Germany was proving an impossible economic burden. Thus economic and political considerations began to coincide in forcing the British Government to abandon the reality, while maintaining the form, of quadripartite control and to reply to the communisation of the Soviet Zone with an economic and political reorganisation of the Western Zones. Bevin warned his colleagues[12] that the danger of Russia in Europe was 'certainly as great as and possibly even greater than, that of a revived Germany' but he was still anxious that if there were to be a break the Russians should be seen to be responsible for it. So, while the moves were set in train which resulted in the amalgamation of the British and American Zones and the effective abandonment of Potsdam, a further effort was made to improve relations with the Soviet Union.

In December 1945 Bevin had mentioned to Stalin the possible extension of the Anglo-Soviet Treaty and when, in May 1946, Sir Maurice Peterson succeeded Sir Archibald Clark Kerr as Ambassador in Moscow he brought with him, as six years earlier Cripps had brought Churchill's letter, a goodwill letter from Attlee to Stalin proposing replacement of the wartime treaty by a fifty-year treaty of alliance.[13] In presenting the proposal, Peterson raised various British grievances: the Soviet press showed 'deep underlying hostility' to Britain and there appeared to be a 'certain mistrust' of Bevin personally; British trade with countries in the Danube basin was being frustrated; the Soviet delegation at the Paris Peace Conference was blocking progress; could not the Russians, who knew 'nothing at all' about the Arabs, accept that the Middle East was 'our area'? The British approach was scarcely calculated to produce acceptance of a fifty-year treaty and it did not. Stalin replied point by point and remarked that he saw no good in prolonging the treaty if account were taken of the present British attitude towards the Soviet Union. In public, Bevin was still reluctant to accept that the relationship was now set firmly on a downward course. In the Foreign Affairs debate on 4 June 1946 his tone was described by Churchill as 'sombre and patient'. Reviewing the problems of negotiation with the Soviet Union in Europe and worldwide, his theme was the need to create mutual respect and confidence.[14] The Prime Minister, speaking of the 'iron curtain between minds' took a similar, if scarcely flattering line: 'We have to look upon the Russian people to some extent as people who have been born and lived in a dark forest. They do not seem to understand the sunlight, wind and air of the free democracies. It would be a fatal thing to accentuate in any way this line of division between Eastern and Western Europe because we have to try to get across the barriers and get a mutual understanding. At the same time we have equally to try and understand the Russian mind and Russian history and why they take the line they do.'[15]

The second half of 1946 brought some easing of the outstanding problems with the Soviet Union and progress was made on the conclusion of peace treaties with Italy, Finland, Hungary, Romania and Bulgaria. Much to the surprise of the British Government, the Soviet Union also suddenly agreed to the British request that the Dodecanese should be incorporated into Greece without insisting upon satisfaction of its own claim to Tripolitania. The conclusion can only be that, for the Soviet Union, the one absolute essential was control over the territories lying directly between Germany and its own western frontier. Outside this area, and even on its northern flank, in Finland, objectives could be more flexible. By this time, however, the downward trend in relations with Britain was not easily reversible. The Foreign Office had already begun the preparation of a campaign to counter Soviet propaganda and in January 1947 they revised the 1945 'Stocktaking' memorandum. It was noted that the phase of American non-involvement in what had been thought of as an Anglo-Soviet conflict was apparently over and the United States was 'tending to claim leadership of any forces in the world which were willing to stand up to excessive Soviet pretensions'. It was thought unlikely that the Soviet Union would seek war within the next five years, but it was clearly bent on using Soviet power and the 'fifth column' of a world Communist movement completely subservient to Moscow 'to undermine British and American influence in all parts of the world and where possible to supplant it'. After eighteen months experience, three-power cooperation was now dismissed as unreal.[16] While the Foreign Office paper was being written, Field Marshal Montgomery was engaged on a visit to the Soviet Union, after which he observed that Russia was immensely acquisitive, but wanted a long period of peace: 'She will watch very carefully that she does not overstep the mark anywhere by careless diplomacy and thus start another war.' During the visit Stalin spoke of the need for a British–Soviet alliance and spoke of the 1942 Treaty being 'suspended in the air' as a result of the formation of the United Nations, to which Bevin responded with confirmation that in the British view Part II, which dealt with post-war relations, remained in force.[17]

By the beginning of 1947, with Kennan's despatches from Moscow commanding increased attention in Washington and George Marshall replacing the vacillating Byrnes as Secretary of State, American policy was turning increasingly towards a more positive effort to contain Soviet expansion. Nevertheless, it was in large measure the British Government which, through Bevin, determined the next steps in the relationship with the Soviet Union. It did so more from weakness than from strength. The point of decision was policy in relation to Germany and the occasion was the meeting of the Council of Foreign Ministers held in Moscow in March. Bevin's handling of this meeting was conditioned by the realisation that Britain could not afford to sustain its role in relation to Germany unless either the whole country or, failing that, the Western Zones, could be set on the road to economic recovery. If the Soviet Union were to take reparations from current German production, Britain and the United States would be left to 'feed the German cow in the West while it was milked in the East'. The process of recovery had been started by the fusion of the British and American Zones of Occupation. It now needed to be taken further. If progress were to be quadripartite, there would have to be a revision of the Potsdam arrangements and the Soviet Union would have to accept that the taking of further reparations was subordinated to the need for economic recovery. Otherwise the Western zones would have to go ahead on their own.[18] He therefore set out requirements for the future handling of reparations and the restoration of effective four-power control over Germany in terms which were likely to prove unacceptable, content that, in the event of failure, responsibility for the breakdown of quadripartite control would rest with the Soviet Union.[19]

The commitment of the United States to a general policy of resistance to Communism was proclaimed by President Truman on 12 March, just after the opening of the Council. Its immediate cause was the need for the United States to take over from Britain the economic burden of support for Greece. The linking of Turkey with this programme was a direct signal to the Soviet Union in relation to access to the Eastern Mediterranean. When, on 5 June, George Marshall made the offer of American aid which set in train the process of Western European recovery, it was Bevin who took the lead in coordinating the European response. Although the offer was formally open to the Soviet Union and the countries of Eastern Europe, it was scarcely conceivable that, in the climate of 1947, a co-ordinated programme could have been formulated with Soviet participation, and there was little surprise when, on 2 July, Molotov withdrew from the preliminary meeting with Bevin and Bidault. Thus the first formal organisational breach between the two halves of Europe was signalled and a further step was taken towards the division of Germany. Czechoslovakia, having originally indicated acceptance, withdrew. Vyshinsky commented: 'The world is now divided into two camps'.[20]

During these early post-war years, the menace of Soviet military power was a source of unease, rather than a direct and immediate threat to Western Europe. The tightening of the Soviet grip on Eastern Europe had certainly proceeded remorselessly and it was intensified after mid-1947. There was evidence enough that Soviet policy was based firmly on the classic Leninist doctrine of irreconcilable struggle with the capitalist world and incitement to the subversion of the 'old equilibrium'. The creation of the Cominform on 23 September 1947 marked the sharpening of this type of attack and the strength of the French and Italian Communist parties left no room for complacency. Faced with a firm Western position, the Soviet Union had, however, withdrawn its forces from Iran, and in Greece, where British forces were committed, Soviet involvement was marked by a certain caution. On the whole, outside Eastern Europe, the deterioration in relations stemmed rather more from a well-founded fear of what the Soviet Union might do than from what it actually was doing. The need for Britain to take the lead in the formation of some kind of Western European security grouping had been apparent even before the end of the war, but so long as there was any slender hope of cooperation with the Soviet Union the Foreign Office was reluctant to prejudice this. There was consequently still a lingering uncertainty as to whether the objective of a Western European grouping should be to contain a resurgent Germany, or whether Germany should be associated with it in order that it might contain an expansionist Soviet Union. As the hope of cooperation faded, such qualms as there were about the need for Western European unity soon disappeared. The course was set which was to lead to the establishment of the North Atlantic Treaty and the incorporation of Western Germany within it.

Defence against the Soviet Union could not, however, be secured from a Western European base alone. In 1946 British military planning was much occupied with the control of the Middle East, not only as a source of oil and a key element in Imperial communications, but also as a base from which in the event of war a bombing effort could be mounted against the main industrial centres of the Soviet Union. Attlee was unhappy with policies which seemed based upon this contingency. When the Chiefs of Staff pressed for the maintenance of the British position in the Eastern Mediterranean and aid for Greece and Turkey, he argued the case for agreement with the Soviet Union that this area should somehow become a neutral zone and wrote on 1 December to Bevin: 'Of course, it is very difficult to tell how far Russian policy is dictated by expansion and how far by fear of attack by the US and ourselves. Fantastic as this is, it may very well be the real grounds of Russian policy. What we consider merely defence may seem to them preparations for an attack'.[21] Again in January, in a minute to Bevin, he questioned the Chiefs of Staff's proposals for defence of imperial communications against a possible Soviet threat. Their broad conclusion that 'The only possible enemy is Russia' and 'the only bases from which Russia could be attacked are situated in the Near East' was, he said, a strategy of despair. In its place, he urged the need to reach agreement with the Soviet Union on points of friction 'unless we are persuaded that the USSR is irrevocably committed to a policy of world domination and that there is no possibility of her alteration'. He put three questions: 'How far is the ideology committed to the conception of the necessity of world revolution? Is it possible to convince the USSR that we have no offensive intentions? What prospects are there of changes in the Russian mentality?' In the margin an unidentified hand has scribbled the answers 'Completely', 'No' and 'Very few'.[22] Attlee was, at that point, far from being persuaded that cooperation was unattainable, but Bevin persuaded him that there was no merit in leading from weakness. The Treaty of Dunkirk between Britain and France, signed on 4 March 1947, was designed to afford reassurance against a revival of the German threat and it was not until the final unsuccessful meeting of the Council of Foreign Ministers in London in December of that year that military planning began overtly to reflect the breach which had already been signalled in the economic field.

The final episode of 1947 in the field of British–Soviet relations was the signature on 31 December of a new Trade Agreement providing not only for an exchange of goods, but for the settlement terms in respect of credits under the 1941 agreement on civil supplies and the waiver of claims in respect of supplies directly concerned with prosecution of the war. It was a personal success for the young Secretary for Overseas Trade, Harold Wilson, and was to influence his later handling of relations with the Soviet Union as President of the Board of Trade and later as Prime Minister. Any political influence it might have had, was, however, wholly overshadowed by the failure of the December meeting of the Council of Foreign Ministers. To the surprise of none of the participants and probably, although it could not be admitted, to the satisfaction of each, the meeting established that there was no prospect of quadripartite control of Germany working on a basis which would satisfy all their requirements. For the British Government, this marked the point at which the dream of a post-war world built on cooperation among the great powers had finally faded. In a party political broadcast on 3 January 1948, Attlee summed up the threat in terms which were to become a standard description of Soviet policy: 'Soviet Communism pursues a policy of imperialism in a new form – ideological, economic and strategic – which threatens the welfare and the way of life of the other nations of Europe.' Interestingly, however, he was careful not to align Britain wholly with the United States, but rather to speak of it as lying geographically and from the point of view of economic and political theory between the Soviet Union and the United States.[23]

The Soviet leadership could scarcely be surprised by the progressive hardening of British policy, but it must be highly doubtful whether they understood the way in which it had evolved any better than they had understood it in the summer of 1939. For its part, the Soviet Union still felt itself in a minority position, striving to assert its claim to great power status against the opposition of Britain and the United States. Its conduct in the areas which it controlled, deplorable though it was in Western eyes, reflected its minimum security requirement against Germany. There is no reason to suppose that the Soviet intelligence service did not know, through their British agents, of the contingency planning of the British Chiefs of Staff and, prudent though such planning might be, it was scarcely calculated to alleviate their mistrust. The Soviet Union might well consider that it had not pressed its own strategic claims outside Eastern and Central Europe with any great force; that it had eventually agreed to withdraw from Iran; that it had shown restraint in relation to Greece and Turkey and moderation in its dealings with Finland; that since 1945 the diplomatic initiative had lain more with Britain and the United States; and that a temporary consolidation of imperialist forces followed by conflict between them was what a prudent Marxist–Leninist theoretician might have predicted. It was scarcely surprising that the Soviet leadership failed to see the world scene in 1948 as it appeared to the British Government.

Attlee had, as we have seen, clung longer than Bevin to the hope of a post-war world built on cooperation with the Soviet Union. Now he was proclaiming to the British public the threat which Bevin had already seen rather earlier and against which Bevin's policies had been directed ever since 1945. Both Bevin and Attlee had been conditioned by the experience of the 1920s and the 1930s, when the Soviet ideology was a menace, and Bevin, in particular, through his trade union experience, was well aware of Soviet techniques for the manipulation of political power. In many respects, however, the Soviet Union itself had been distant and unknown, its armed forces largely ignored in the European balance. The countries of Eastern and Central Europe, on the other hand, troublesome and turbulent though they were, had formed part of a European family of nations. Now, after 1945, the whole political structure of Europe had been upset. Soviet troops stood some 600 miles westwards of the Soviet Union's 1939 frontier and, at their closest, were a mere 100 miles from the North Sea coast. The main mass of Continental Europe east of the Elbe was under Soviet control and, throughout it, democracy had come to mean 'People's Democracy'. The strength of Communism in France and Italy was uncertain, but alarming. Germany had been destroyed as a political entity. Most of Western Europe was in a pitiable state of economic privation and Britain itself no longer capable of sustaining the financial burdens of a major power. If Soviet hostility had to be accepted as a fact, the 'correlation of forces' against Britain was substantially worse than it had been when Europe was threatened with German domination in 1939. Having seen the Soviet Union demonstrate only too clearly the ruthlessness with which it would control the countries of Eastern Europe and the Soviet zone of Germany, Attlee and Bevin could not afford to gamble on Soviet restraint. Nor did the intransigence of Soviet diplomacy and the tone of Soviet propaganda give them any encouragement to do so. They could see no margin of safety, nor any prospect of security save in close association with the United States. The British Government had no desire for, and could ill afford, a still deeper breach with the Soviet Union, yet the only policies which would offer any prospect of guaranteeing the security and prosperity of Western Europe were certain to produce it. They had to assume that, faced with the opportunity of a Western European power vacuum, the Soviet Union would fill it.

It was in this sense that Attlee, extrapolating from Eastern European experience, could justifiably speak of the threat of Soviet imperialism. Only the small body of Communists and one or two on the left wing of the Labour party were inclined to contradict him. Equally, however, there was no reason to suppose that, if the vacuum were filled by Britain and the United States, the Soviet Union, having already adequately ensured its own security, would be prepared to run the risk of war in order to extend its power further westwards. It was therefore possible to carry forward the process of consolidating Western Europe in reasonable confidence that, although the result would be to deepen and institutionalise the East–West split, the relationship with the Soviet Union which would emerge would, despite increased tension, be inherently more stable and more secure. The basis for British policy in this new situation was set out by Bevin in a series of Cabinet papers[24] which included, *inter alia*, a plan to counter Communist propaganda.

Despite initial French hesitation, the response to the Soviet consolidation of Eastern Europe was developed with remarkable speed in the first half of 1948. With the integration of the French Zone of Germany into the combined British–American Zone, the political and economic structure began to be created which would make possible a revival of the West German economy. In February the Soviet-inspired coup in Czechoslovakia, ten years after Munich, brought a swift justification, if one were needed, of Attlee's assessment. On 17 March the process of forming a Western European security structure was taken a stage further with the negotiation of the Brussels Treaty, in which the Anglo-French alliance was extended to include the Benelux countries, and in British–American discussions later that month the first steps were taken which were to culminate in the North Atlantic Treaty. The Benelux countries were also consulted about the plans for the economic and political restructuring of Western Germany, worked out at a British–French–American Conference in London. To this, the Soviet Union responded with a call, backed by the Eastern European countries, for the formation of a 'provisional, democratic, all-German Government'.

THE BERLIN BLOCKADE

Berlin now became the focal point of the European confrontation, not so much in its own right, but rather as a test of will between the Soviet Union and the Western powers over the future of Germany. The risk that the Soviet Union would act against the Western position in Berlin had been foreseen, but Bevin argued[25] that delay in the Western programme would lead to intensified Soviet pressure, demoralisation of Britain's friends and even the risk of a Russo-German combination. The build-up to the blockade was gradual. The first limited restrictions on Western access to Berlin were enforced in April 1948, but the Western plans went ahead. A new currency was introduced on 18 June into the Western zones and shortly thereafter into West Berlin. After introducing its own currency reform, the Soviet Union precipitated the full crisis on 24 June by severing all rail, road and canal access to Berlin from the West. The challenge to the Western position in Berlin was clear.

The Soviet action raised the immediate issue of response by force. At one extreme of British opinion was Churchill who, in April, had suggested that the time had come 'to tell the Soviets that if they do not retire from Berlin and abandon Eastern Germany, withdrawing to the Polish frontier, we will raze their cities'.[26] In practical terms, however, once the blockade had been established, the only options were to negotiate a settlement under pressure, to break through by land or to organise supply by air. The British and American Commanders in Germany were in agreement that they could not guarantee, with the forces available, to break through by land. Plans existed for the supply of the British garrison by air and, on 25 June the Cabinet overrode the doubts of the Deputy British Military Governor and took the decision to try to supply the civilian population also by air.[27] An attempt to break the blockade by the use of ground forces would have meant the initiation of hostilities by the Western side. Aircraft flying through the designated corridors could be blocked only by direct hostile action from the Soviet side, either by aircraft, surface weapons or barrage balloons. The risk of opposition by air was accepted and the decision was taken that if barrage balloons were used they should be shot down. It was calculated correctly that the Soviet Union would not wish to run the risk of war for the sake of gaining control of West Berlin. The British Government's policy, on the other hand, required that, in the event of miscalculation, this risk would have to be accepted. The joint British–American airlift began on the following day.[28] The British response was, in the early stages, both more determined and swifter than that of the United States and, for this, much of the credit must go to Bevin. His achievement was the more remarkable in that, with British resources stretched to the limit, he was grappling simultaneously with the termination of the Palestine mandate. On 30 June, he put his policy to Parliament, warning that it might be necessary to face a 'grave situation', but that there was no alternative than surrender 'and none of us can accept surrender'.[29] The response was whole-hearted Parliamentary support. At the same time, diplomatic action was instituted with the despatch on 6 July of identical British and American notes to the Soviet Government and, in order to add force to the proclaimed determination to stand firm, the British Government agreed to the stationing in Britain, without prior conditions, of a force of American B29 bombers. These aircraft were known to constitute the American nuclear bombing force and, although those initially stationed in Britain had not been adapted for this role, the gesture must have had its effect.

The diplomatic notes were followed by tripartite discussions in Moscow at which the British representative was Frank Roberts who, after his service in Moscow, had become Private Secretary to Ernest Bevin. A weakness of the Allied position was that the arrangements for access to Berlin stemmed in part from the recommendations of the European Advisory Commission and in part from ad hoc arrangements between the commanders of the occupation forces. The Soviet position was firm: any rights which the Western allies enjoyed in Berlin flowed from the quadripartite arrangements for Germany as a whole and until these were restored there could be no restoration of normal communications with the city. No progress could be made. The British Military Governor in Germany, General Robertson, did not believe that Berlin could be supplied by air through the winter and was 'convinced that in the course of time the Soviets will steal the city from under our noses'. A land convoy was dismissed as impracticable, but the British Government was determined not to concede. Measures were taken to put the armed forced 'into a better position to fight'[30] and Bevin, rejecting the argument that the allocation of extra resources for defence would delay economic recovery, argued that 'unless a firm stand were made now, our position in Europe would be hopeless'.[31]

The failure of the Moscow discussions was reported to Parliament by Bevin on 22 September. He indicated that there had been some British readiness to compromise, in that once the blockade was lifted and four-power control over trade between Berlin and the West restored, the Soviet currency could circulate in Berlin under four-power control. The restoration of normal communications must, however, precede discussion of quadripartite control, and, as Bevin put it, he would not accept that once a line had been drawn 'you wake up to demands, revolutions, stirrings up of your people and upsetting of your institutions and everything else to promote an expansion at a very cheap price without war'.[32] On 29 September the British Government referred the Berlin question to the Security Council. The Soviet Union announced its intention not to participate in the proceedings. The airlift was sustained throughout the winter and, by the spring, the Soviet Union accepted the failure of the blockade. In private discussions between the Soviet and American representatives (the latter acting for the three Western Governments) agreement was reached on a face-saving formula which provided that all restrictions on movement would first be removed and that on 23 May a meeting of the Council of Foreign Ministers would be convened 'to consider questions relating to Germany and problems arising out of the situation in Berlin, including also the question of currency in Berlin'. On 4 April the North Atlantic Treaty had been signed and on the day the Council met, the Federal Republic of Germany was constituted. On 30 May, the Soviet Union responded with the creation of the German Democratic Republic, followed by a series of purges in Eastern Europe and the intensification of Soviet pressure against Yugoslavia. The division of Europe, already created in practice by the outcome of the war and symbolised by the outcome of the Marshall Aid negotiations, had now begun to take its definitive political shape.

The Berlin crisis was the only occasion on which the Soviet Union directly challenged, with the backing of its own armed forces, a position held by the forces of the Western powers. Up to this point, the Soviet threat had been inferred by British ministers from Soviet action in Eastern Europe, Soviet diplomacy and Soviet propaganda. With no precedent to guide them, the British Government had to construct policy *ab initio*. Against a background of initial American hesitancy, there can be little doubt that, had Bevin not been prepared to commit Britain to the airlift, the Western position could not have been sustained. Beyond the immediate consequences, a precedent for further Soviet encroachment on Western positions would have been established, with a greater risk of subsequent miscalculation. As it was, the Soviet Government made the initial miscalculation over Berlin, but from the point that the airlift was initiated, both parties understood one another and there was no escalation. Bevin had assessed the situation correctly in Cabinet on 26 July 1948: 'As regards Berlin, to yield to Soviet pressure there would lead to further withdrawals by the Western allies and in the end to war. On the other hand, if we maintained a firm attitude we might reckon on ten years of peace during which the defences of Western Europe might be consolidated'.[33]

THE BOUNDS ARE SET

The ending of the Berlin blockade reduced the tension, but did nothing to resolve the struggle for power between the Soviet Union and the Western allies. Over the course of the next twenty-five years, the Soviet Union gradually developed the full military potential of a nuclear superpower. Blocked in Western Europe, where the East–West frontier was now secure, it sought to extend its power and influence in the Third World. The character of the British–Soviet relationship evolved significantly. The development of the Communist threat outside Europe introduced a new dimension, in which it was not easy to determine the extent of Soviet involvement or the appropriate nature of the response. The breakdown of the old European-based imperial structures, the creation of new independent states in Asia and Africa and the rise of Communist China brought a substantially more complex pattern of international relationships. At the same time, the escalation of nuclear weaponry by the Soviet Union and the United States led to a new bilateral superpower relationship. Nevertheless, the attempt at quadripartite regulation of major issues continued intermittently until the failure of the Paris summit in 1960. Even then, the absence of a definitive settlement of the German problem left a remnant of the key element in the post-war quadripartite relationship. The role of Germany in British–Soviet relations and the continued quadripartite occupation of Berlin made that remnant of more than formal significance.

Successive British Governments, grappling with the problems of restoring the British economy and adjusting to the radically new post-imperial world, had no thirst for confrontation with the Soviet Union. Yet Soviet power could not now be ignored as it had been in the 1930s. Throughout a succession of crises, stretching through more than thirty years, the extent of Soviet involvement was not always easy to determine. When the Soviet armed forces entered Hungary, Czechoslovakia and Afghanistan, or Soviet missiles were introduced into Cuba, there could be debate about the appropriate response, but little doubt as to the underlying facts. The pattern of involvement – military, political or economic – in other areas was more complex.

The emergence of new states from the old imperial structures offered opportunities for the extension of Soviet power and influence. In Korea, Indo-China, Indonesia, Malaysia, Egypt, Angola, Mozambique, South Yemen and Ethiopia the crises were to erupt as competing factions fought for control. The extent of Soviet involvement in the stimulation or prosecution of revolutionary wars was open to argument, but Soviet theorists maintained the classic doctrine of the struggle against all those who did not accept Soviet socialism and, inconclusive though the evidence might sometimes be, it was difficult for any responsible British statesman to see the combination of Marxist-Leninist doctrine, Russian imperial instincts and Soviet armed force as other than a threat to the whole structure of international society. Throughout these decades the problem of dealing with Soviet Union rarely occupied the first place among the issues claiming the attention of the British Government, but it was continuously present and in so far as ministers saw one predominant opponent and one predominant threat to British security, it was the Soviet Union.

The primary response to this perceived threat lay in the consolidation of Britain's other relationships, military, political and economic, in the Atlantic Alliance, in the Commonwealth and the Third World and in Western Europe. The direct relationship with the Soviet Union remained almost wholly intractable. It was necessary to sustain a strategic defence capability within the Alliance, sufficient to deter the Soviet Union from the direct use of armed force against any essential British interest. Yet it was consistently recognised that armed force could not be used for the ultimate resolution of disputes between nuclear powers. The confrontation with the Soviet Union had therefore to be contained at a level below that which might involve recourse to force and, to this end, the search for a productive dialogue had to constitute a central element in British political strategy. The pattern of the 1950s, 1960s and 1970s was one in which the search for some basis of understanding was repeatedly instituted, broken off and resumed. In this fluctuating relationship there was a basic change of motivation from the pre-war years, when policy had alternated with the alternation of political power between Left and Right in Britain. From 1945 onwards, the ideological alignment of the Labour and Conservative parties was less significant and a certain consensus developed in which the trend of British policy was largely responsive to the changing manifestations of Soviet policy.

GERMANY AND KOREA

In the final years of Stalin's regime, British policy was concentrated almost exclusively on realising the full potential of the alliance which had been created in 1949 and bolstering it with the strength of Western Germany. There was no basis here for agreement with the Soviet Union. The Council of Foreign Ministers met as planned in Paris on 23 May 1949. Of the original post-war members, only Bevin remained. Acheson and Schuman represented the United States and France, while Vyshinsky, whose role as prosecutor in the first Stalin show trials did little to inspire confidence on the part of his Western interlocutors, now spoke for the Soviet Union. Agreement was recorded on the normalisation of relations between the Eastern and Western sectors of Berlin and the respective zones of Germany and on the basis for further work on the Austrian Peace Treaty. In substance, however, the agreement was meaningless, except in so far as it ratified the lifting of the blockade. There was deadlock in the negotiation of the Austrian Peace Treaty and no basis for agreement on a unified Germany. The existing relationship between the two alliances was unchanged and the existing differences were unresolved.

A year later the stakes had been raised. The first Soviet nuclear explosion was detected by Britain and the United States in September 1949 and nuclear deterrence, previously a monopoly of the United States, would from that time on constrain the policies not only of the Soviet Union, but also of the Western powers. The control of nuclear energy, one of the first subjects to engage the attention of the United Nations, became more urgent and the chance of Soviet acceptance of its internationalisation on the basis of anything like the original Baruch plan even more remote. The victory of the Communists in the struggle for the control of China brought a new menace, while the declaration of non-alignment by India seemed to the Soviet Union to deal a major blow to British imperial power. In Britain itself, growing economic difficulties weakened the base on which Bevin had to construct his diplomacy and made reliance upon the United States the more necessary.

At the election in February 1950, policy towards the Soviet Union was no longer a major issue. Churchill called for a new summit meeting, 'a supreme effort to bridge the gulf between the two worlds, so that each can live their life, if not in friendship, at least without the hatreds and manoeuvres of the cold war'. His appeal was, however, dismissed by both the British and Soviet Governments as an election stunt. The outcome of the election, a Labour majority of only six, made it inevitable that there would be a second appeal to the electorate within a fairly short time. In the interim, the Government was increasingly preoccupied with domestic issues. The international scene was tense. Bevin's health was failing. He was still determined to press on with the development of the Atlantic alliance and even less disposed to make concessions to the Soviet Union. The Foreign Office did in fact examine the Churchill proposal,[34] but concluded that there was no likelihood of agreement on the major practical issues and that a summit would enable the Soviet Union either to lull Western opinion into a false sense of security or to brand Western Governments as warmongers. A *Times* leader of 10 April was quoted with approval: 'In a war of ideologies the definition of strict spheres of interest is an anachronism.' In May the Foreign Secretary circulated a paper to the Cabinet in preparation for a meeting of the Atlantic Council in which he considered whether the 'time was ripe for any attempt to reach a settlement by negotiation with the Soviets'. His conclusion was that 'general negotiations are unlikely to succeed until such time as we have built up a situation of strength in the West'. The French and American Governments both felt slightly more need to show at least some readiness for negotiation, though there was pressure within the United States to 'heat up the cold war'. It was not too hard to agree that in any case the time was not ripe. The work of the Russia Committee of the Foreign Office at this time was becoming very much oriented towards the threat in Asia and Africa and to the means by which the West might mount a counter-offensive in the ideological struggle.[35] This trend was reflected in the meeting of British, French and American Foreign Ministers in London on 13 May 1950. Although they were concerned primarily with policy regarding Germany, the communiqué envisaged 'a new joint and Western drive to combat Communist imperialism in both Asia and Africa'.

In their concern about the Soviet threat in Asia, the British Labour Government of 1950 were echoing a theme which had been apparent in Conservative polices in the years following the Revolution, when Curzon had been preoccupied with the need to safeguard British India against the threat of Soviet penetration from the north and in 1927 when concern about Soviet instigation of disorders in China played its part in the events leading up to the breach of relations. With the outbreak of the Korean War on 24 June 1950, the new threat in Asia materialised more quickly and more dramatically than had been expected. The conflict had ominous implications, not only for the position of the Western powers, particularly the United States, in the Far East, but also as a portent for what might be expected elsewhere on the fault lines where the stresses of the Communist and non-Communist worlds were concentrated. It had its origin in the post-war division of Korea between the Soviet occupation zone in the north and that of the United States in the south. The extent to which the North Korean attack had been directly instigated by the Soviet Union was uncertain. It is likely that the Soviet Union believed the United States to be unwilling to fight for the independence of South Korea and saw advantage in a quick campaign by the North Korean forces. Initial Soviet moral and material support was clear. The first stage of the Chinese intervention may also have seemed attractive to the Soviet leadership in so far as it tied down a substantial American force in an inherently profitless campaign. Only when the extension and intensification of the conflict began to pose a significant threat did a recognition of the need for restraint begin to gain the upper hand in Soviet policy.

Although British troops were included in the United Nations forces in South Korea, the military operations and the associated diplomacy were primarily conducted by the United States. The war was, however, of significance to British–Soviet relations in various respects. In particular, hostile action by a Soviet client state in a divided country in Asia was an uncomfortable precedent for similar action in Germany and undoubtedly contributed to the case for a defence contribution from Western Germany. Churchill repeated his call for an attempt to arrive at an understanding with the Soviet Union while the United States still held nuclear superiority, arguing in a major Parliamentary speech, applauded from both sides of the House, that it was in Europe and not in the 'Far East diversion' that the world cause would be decided.[36] Equally significant was the change which the war marked in the respective roles of Britain and the United States in relation to the Soviet Union. The pressure for action now came primarily from the American side, where anti-Communist emotion rose to a new pitch, and the British Government found itself torn between the need to retain American confidence and the fear of escalation. A moment of some tension in the British–American relationship came in December when Attlee, concerned at the risk of all-out war between the United States and China, flew to Washington to dissuade President Truman from using the atomic bomb, a course which the President had in fact already rejected.

The difference of approach between Britain and the United States was heightened by the fact that one aim of Soviet policy was to enable the Communist Government to take the Chinese seat at the United Nations. Britain had already recognised the Communists as the Government of China, although diplomatic relations had not at that time been established. The United States had not recognised it and the Soviet Union had boycotted Security Council meetings in protest against the non-admission of Communist China. Soviet absence had made it possible for Britain and the United States to secure the establishment of the United Nations force in Korea. At the outset of the war, the British Government tried to persuade the Soviet Union to use its influence with China to end hostilities. The Soviet response in July 1950 was to propose discussion in the Security Council in which Communist China should be included. This would have meant that, without any prior guarantee of the withdrawal of North Korean forces, the Soviet Union would secure Chinese participation and restore its own power of veto over subsequent developments. The Cabinet had no hesitation in rejecting the Soviet proposal, but, with the recollection of the outcome of bilateral contacts during the Berlin blockade, it was decided to continue discussions.[37] The Soviet Union was asked to use its influence with North Korea to cease hostilities and withdraw to the 38th parallel, but it was not until a year later, on 23 June 1951, when the United Nations had effectively regained control of the South, that the Soviet Ambassador to the United Nations, Y. Malik, proposed discussions for a ceasefire based on a mutual withdrawal from the 38th parallel. The British Government welcomed the suggestion and did what it could to follow it up, but to such an extent was the diplomatic initiative left in American hands that when Sir Alvary Gascoigne replaced Sir David Kelly in Moscow in November 1951 he was dissuaded from even raising the issue of the armistice negotiations in his initial talks. The only discernible result of bilateral British–Soviet talks in Moscow was to secure the eventual release of the British envoy in Seoul, who had been captured by the North Korean forces. It is not easy to judge the subsequent Soviet role in the final settlement, but on the Western side it was undoubtedly American diplomacy backed by American military power which was crucial. The Soviet Union had, since 1945, been clear that its principal opponent was now the United States. The Korean War powerfully reinforced the trend towards a bilateral superpower relationship, but it was to take another decade before, with the Cuban crisis, the full implications of this trend became apparent.

POLICY ON TRADE WITH THE SOVIET UNION

The Korean War also caused the British Government to reconsider its policy for trade with the Communist countries. In the pre-war years, British exports to the Soviet Union had fluctuated between a low point of £4 million in 1923 and 1933 and high points of £19 million in 1925 and £20 million in 1937, while imports had fluctuated around an average of a little more than £20 million a year. Despite moments of British enthusiasm, the development of a policy of economic autarky by Stalin in the 1930s had meant that the potential of the Soviet market had never been fulfilled. After 1945, British purchases of grain and timber had brought a substantial rise in imports, but by 1948 British exports were a mere £7 million and subsequent growth had been handicapped by the introduction in April 1949 of a ban on the export to Eastern Europe of certain machinery which was of direct military value. By 1950, when the Korean War broke out, Britain was, as it had been in 1935, the Soviet Union's principal Western trading partner, but this position now reflected very largely the devastation of the economies of Western Europe during the war. The Soviet market, at £14 million, accounted for only 0.6 per cent of total British exports. Now, however, the Government was faced with American pressure for a much more comprehensive strategic embargo which would have blocked certain British industrial exports as well as hindering the procurement of coarse grains and timber. Some reduction in British sales of critical items such as machine tools was agreed and the Commercial Section of the British Embassy in Moscow was closed. The gestures were largely symbolic, but the problem was to remain for many years as an irritant both to British–Soviet and to British–American relations. Indeed, it became, as it had been in 1921, a focal point in the doctrinal controversy over the nature of East–West relations.[38] Was the purpose of Western policy, as the United States tended to see it, to do everything possible, short of open warfare, to weaken an irredeemably hostile Soviet Union? Or was it rather, as the British Government saw it, not gratuitously to increase the military capability of the Soviet Union, but at the same time to help both the British economy and the international climate by seeking to develop all that network of commercial and other links which might in time build up a genuine community of interest? By the time of the invasion of Afghanistan in 1979 and the Polish crisis in 1982, the issue was still being debated in very much the same terms, and the respective stance of the British and American Governments had not evolved very far from that of 1950.

THE REARMAMENT OF GERMANY

The general policy of the British Government towards the Soviet Union after the outbreak of the Korean War was set out in a paper prepared by the Foreign Office for the tripartite meeting of Western Foreign Ministers in New York in September 1950.[39] In it lay the essence of the cold war strategy:

> The Soviet Union probably does not wish to become involved in general war in the immediate future. It may, however, engage in further aggression by proxy, either in the guise of Civil War or of attack across frontiers by satellites without involvement of Soviet forces, *even at the risk of provoking general war* (author's italics). It will in any case continue its sustained effort to subvert free peoples and undermine their will to resist aggression.

The Western policy which the Foreign Office recommended was intensification of the military, political and economic defence of the Western European 'keystone', the avoidance of unnecessarily provocative action, attempts to relieve tension on specific questions, exploitation of difficulties between the Soviet Union and its satellites and an 'expanded, intensified and coordinated' Western effort in the 'struggle for men's minds', seeking to 'convince them of the falsity of the Kremlin's championship of peace, nationalism and social reform'. The paper was noteworthy both for its assessment – which many would now consider to have been over-pessimistic – that the Soviet Union might have been ready to run the risk of provoking a general war; and also for the call for a counter-offensive in the ideological struggle which was to lead to the reinforcement of the publicity campaign, both direct and indirect, against Soviet Communism which the Foreign Office had initiated in 1947.

At the outbreak of the Korean War the NATO forces in Europe consisted of some 14 divisions, while the strength of the Soviet army was estimated at 175 divisions. At the September meeting in New York, following a meeting of the Atlantic Council, the need for some German contribution to European defence was accepted and, in recognition of French objections, the concept of a European Army was evolved. There was concern in the Foreign Office and the

Ministry of Defence about the possible Soviet reaction to any such move, but, given the overriding importance of maintaining the American contribution to the defence of Europe, the Prime Minister decided against raising this aspect with President Truman. While work on European defence went forward, so did the exchanges with the Soviet Union on a possible ministerial meeting. In December 1950, Bevin put one of his last papers to the Cabinet.[40] The Soviet Union, seeking to prevent West German rearmament, had proposed a new meeting of the Council of Foreign Ministers to consider carrying out the Potsdam Agreement in relation to the demilitarisation of Germany. Bevin accepted that there was 'considerable feeling in Parliament and the country as a whole' against a completely negative reply. As he saw it, however, the Soviet purpose was merely to play upon French susceptibilities and delay the strengthening of Western defences. The British proposal, put forward at Paris in 1949 and pursued subsequently at official level, was for free all-German elections under international supervision. This had elicited no direct response. The Soviet counter-proposal for the formation of a Council with equal representatives from East and West Germany to prepare for an all-German provisional Government seemed only too clearly designed to maximise the opportunities for Soviet interference by proxy in Western Germany. The only armed forces in Germany at this time, other than the occupation forces of the Four Powers, were the militarised East German police units, and Bevin saw the risk that a demilitarised Germany, with occupation forces withdrawn, could easily become a power vacuum, vulnerable to the Soviet Union. In his lengthy paper Bevin considered all the options for either a limited or a global solution to the relationship with the Soviet Union, seeking some means of reducing tension without sacrificing essential interests. Uncharacteristically, perhaps because of his illness, he left his recommendations open and it was eventually decided that officials of the four powers should meet to see whether it was possible to work out an agenda for a meeting of Foreign Ministers.

Exchanges with the Soviet Union dragged on through the first half of 1951, until in June they were suspended. By the time of Bevin's death in April 1951, British policy was firmly on course. One of the Labour Government's last papers before the General Election in September was a brief for meetings between Bevin's successor, Herbert Morrison, and his American and French colleagues. On their agenda was a 'Survey of progress in the policy of containment of the Soviet Union and its Satellites'.[41] The brief recorded a measure of success in the policy of building up positions of strength and a series of Soviet setbacks. Two potential dangers were seen. There was a risk that the Soviet Union might be driven to a full war economy, or even to preventive war, if the West overlooked or misjudged the Soviet reaction in relation to 'sore spots in their security' such as air bases near the Soviet border. In this respect American impulsiveness was seen as a risk. The second potential danger lay in a failure to be constructive and positive, but it was still thought that the time was not yet ripe for full-scale negotiations. In relation to Germany, Morrison considered it right to press on with the arrangements for German participation in Western defence, in default of which there could be a risk that a disillusioned Western Germany might eventually move into the Soviet camp.[42] The risk of a Soviet preventive war in 1951 was not discounted by Sir David Kelly, Ambassador in Moscow. The Politburo, even Stalin, he argued, might be more human and impressionable than Ministers assumed. They might not feel confident that time was on their side, and 'from the purely military point of view . . . there is quite a case for a preventive war by the Russians (and Chinese) this year'. In reply, the new Foreign Secretary assured him on 4 July that the risk had been 'long and carefully weighed', but the conclusion was that the Soviet leaders were 'realistic enough to appreciate the appalling risk' and would refrain 'unless they were to feel themselves under imminent threat of attack'.[43]

MACLEAN AND BURGESS

We have noted the hardening of British official opinion in relation to the threat of Communist subversion of free institutions. One consequence of the coup in Czechoslovakia had been the announcement by the Government on 15 March 1948 of measures to exclude known Communists from work affecting the security of the state. In the United States the mood of virulent anti-Communism had mounted almost to a state of hysteria as Senator McCarthy began his drive against Communist or quasi-Communist activities in public life. At the height of the Korean War, in May 1951, British opinion suffered a severe shock with the news of the flight of the two Soviet agents, Donald Maclean and Guy Burgess, to the Soviet Union.[44] The two men, part of the group whose Communist sympathies had first been kindled during the Spanish Civil War, had been operating on behalf of the Soviet Union for many years. Burgess, a squalid and disreputable junior official, had been an Assistant Private Secretary to Hector McNeil, Bevin's Minister of State, then a member of the Far Eastern Department of the Foreign Office, working across the corridor from me when I was in the South-East Asia Department, and later, to general surprise, posted to the Washington Embassy. Maclean, the senior of the two, an unstable, tortured character, a potential high-flyer of the Service, had spent most of the post-war years in Washington before becoming Head of the American Department. Between them they had access to many of the key papers on the development of British foreign policy and, in the case of Maclean, on Anglo-American nuclear cooperation. There can be little doubt that, as a result of their activities, the Soviet Union was well briefed on the development of British and American policy throughout the critical stages in the development of the cold war. Soviet nuclear espionage had been well exposed as early as 1945 by the confession of the British scientist, Nunn May, and no doubt his work, together with that of Fuchs, helped to accelerate the Soviet development of nuclear weapons. Combined with Maclean's briefing on strategic thinking, it must have been as gravely prejudical to British and American defence interests as was the work of Philby to British counter-intelligence operations.

In the political field, on the other hand, fascinating though the intelligence must have been to the Soviet leadership, it is doubtful whether it materially affected the course of policy. The key decisions on questions such as the rearmament of Germany had, by their very nature, to be publicly aired, and on other matters which have occasionally troubled Western consciences, such as the organisation of active counter-measures against Communist subversion, the knowledge can have come as no surprise. It may well be that the most significant influence of Burgess and Maclean – and subsequently of Blunt and Philby – lay in the shock to British and American opinion caused by the revelation of the route which led from the Communist sympathies prevalent in certain small but well-placed sectors of British society, through the wartime alliance and homosexual blackmail to active espionage on behalf of the Soviet intelligence service. American opinion was excitable and the scandal did much damage not merely to the British–American nuclear relationship, but more widely to the confidence which, largely as a result of Ernest Bevin, had been developed between the two Governments.

The scandal of the Foreign Office spies led to a substantial tightening of security procedures within British Government Service as well as to an intensification of the drive against the intelligence activities of Soviet officials in London. The strand of intelligence and counter-intelligence work which had been woven into the British–Soviet relationship from its earliest days, emerging above the surface with events such as the British interception of Soviet communications in 1920 and the Arcos raid in 1927, was reinforced and remained a significant element to the present day. Even now, with the primary intelligence effort by East and West deployed through the technology of satellite photography and electronic interception, the old-style individual agent has not gone out of business and the exploitation of personal relationships for dubious intelligence gain plays its part, as it has done over the years, in heightening mistrust and impeding the conduct of normal inter-governmental business.

9 The Khrushchev Years

The Conservative Government under Winston Churchill which took office after the General Election in October 1951 found the British–Soviet relationship at its nadir. It had inherited from Labour a hard-line policy based on a broad British–American unity of purpose in containing the Stalinist threat. There had been some fraying of the unity during the Korean War, but, on the whole, it had held. There could scarcely have been a more marked contrast with pre-war experience than the progress by which the Churchill and Eden Governments sought, while carrying forward Labour's policy of the Western alliance, to establish a sounder basis for relations with the Soviet Union and to restrain the United States from belligerent anti-Communism, only to find themselves, five years later, almost simultaneously threatened with rocket attack from the Soviet Union and bankruptcy by the United States. Within a further year, under Macmillan, Britain and the United States were to be realigned in opposition to a newly perceived Soviet threat of global domination. The scope for developing the British–Soviet relationship in the final years of Stalin and throughout the tumultuous Khrushchev decade was determined in part by the uncertain evolution of the Soviet Union and in part by the realities of a divided Europe set in a post-imperial world. This was the era in which, with the first thermonuclear explosions by the United States, the Soviet Union and the United Kingdom, the threat of nuclear destruction came to play an increasing part both in public perception and in the reality of East–West rivalry. Thus there began a concentration of the relationship with the Soviet Union on the problem of controlling nuclear weapons and the development of a bilateral superpower relationship. First, however, came another stage in the struggle of Britain and the Soviet Union over Germany's place in Europe.

In a Foreign Affairs debate on 19 November 1951, Eden, commenting on the state of relations created by the Korean War, observed: 'There is now virtually no diplomatic contact between East and West either side of the iron curtain. That is something new and entirely to be deplored.' East–West relations were, however, already close to the point at which both sides would recognise the need for change. With Truman's dismissal of MacArthur, the decision had been effectively taken to limit the scope of the Korean War and, although fighting was to continue for a further two years, the military stalemate meant that the focus could begin to move to Germany and Indo-China. For the time being, there was no change in British policy. At the first meeting of Churchill's Cabinet, the main point of concern to Eden, back at the Foreign Office, was the defence of Egypt. On Germany, policy was moving steadily ahead and the need to come to grips with the Soviet Union on the whole complex of issues arising from the integration of Western Germany into Western Europe could not long be evaded. Behind all the manoeuvring, the issue was a simple one. What place was Germany to hold in post-war Europe? The British objective was to press ahead with the integration of Western Germany into Western Europe, without prejudice to the eventual reunification of Germany on the basis of free elections. The Soviet objective was to retain control of East Germany, frustrate the Western plans for West Germany and permit reunification only in the unlikely event of it being on terms which would permit the extension of Soviet control, direct or indirect, over the reunited German state.

On 10 March 1952 a Soviet note was received, proposing a meeting of Foreign Ministers to discuss a German Peace Treaty, with the participation of an all-German Government. Eden saw this as no more than an astute manoeuvre, a specious appeal to the German desire for reunification, without any commitment to the holding of free all-German elections under independent supervision. Throughout the summer of 1952 the exchange of notes continued, with the British Government holding firmly to the view that the correct sequence of events was the holding of elections, the formation of an all-German Government, the negotiation of a peace settlement and the withdrawal of occupation forces. Under the Soviet proposals the order would, in key essentials, have been reversed, and the holding of elections would have followed the negotiation of a peace settlement with a provisional government based on representation from the two halves of Germany.

Between the summer of 1952 and the spring of 1953 the British–Soviet relationship itself remained stagnant, but major changes occurred in the international environment within which it would in future be conducted. On 24 May 1952 the signature of the 'contractual arrangement' with the Federal Republic of Germany represented a major step towards the ending of the occupation regime in the West, save for the Western sectors of Berlin; on 27 May the treaty establishing the European Defence Community was signed and the British and American Governments formally linked it to their NATO commitment by undertaking that any threat to the integrity or unity of the Community would be regarded as a threat to their own security; the birth of the European Coal and Steel Community marked a new stage in the long process of the economic integration of Western Europe; on 4 November the victory of President Eisenhower brought a Republican Administration to the United States, with John Foster Dulles, the advocate of rolling back Communism, as Secretary of State in place of Dean Acheson; and on 5 March 1953 Stalin died.

As the post-Stalin era opened, the French Government was still engaged in its long and eventually fruitless battle to secure ratification of the treaty establishing the European Defence Community. The Korean Armistice Agreement was not concluded until 27 July 1953 and in Indo-China and Malaysia fighting was continuing. Nevertheless, Britain and her allies could embark with some confidence on the task of establishing relations with Stalin's successors. It was to be pursued at a series of Conferences of Foreign Ministers and Heads of Government in Berlin and Geneva during 1954 and 1955 which carried forward the process of determining, in a trial of political and military strength, the frontier of the Communist-dominated area in Europe and Asia.

In the summer of 1953, neither the British nor the American Government had any clear view of the policies which might be expected from the new and largely unknown Soviet leadership. Would expansion or stability be the priority task? The return of Molotov to the Foreign Ministry offered no encouraging prospect, but the impact of Malenkov as Chairman of the Council of Ministers and Khrushchev as Secretary (later First Secretary) of the party remained to be seen. It was, however, clear that a new era was opening and both Eisenhower and Churchill appealed to the new Soviet leadership to make a fresh start. Mr Churchill made a major Parliamentary statement on 11 May in which he proposed 'a conference on the highest level between the leading powers without long delay'. Justifying it, he said:

> We have been encouraged by a series of amicable gestures on the part of the new Soviet Government. . . . These have so far taken the form of leaving off doing things which we have not been doing

to them and it is very difficult to find a specific case in which to match their action. . . . I think it would be a mistake to try and map things out too much in detail and expect that grave and fundamental issues which divide the Communist and non-Communist parts of the world can be settled by a single comprehensive agreement.

He recalled a telegram of 29 April 1945 in which he had warned Stalin not to underrate the divergencies which were even then opening up and had seen 'not much comfort in looking into a future where you and the countries you dominate plus the Communist parties of many other states are all drawn up on one side, and those who rally to the English speaking nations and their associates are on the other'. Now he looked forward to the Russian people taking 'the high place in world affairs which is their due, without feeling unsettled about their own security' and sought to assure the Soviet Union that 'so far as human arrangements can run, the terrible events of the Hitler invasion will never be repeated and that Poland will remain a friendly power and a buffer, though not a puppet state'.[1]

A month later, the first crisis of the post-Stalin era erupted with anti-Soviet demonstrations in East Berlin and in several places in the German Democratic Republic, as the Soviet Zone of Germany had now become. I was at this time serving as Deputy Political Adviser to the British Commandant in West Berlin and recollect driving through East Berlin on the morning of 17 June. The normal life of the city had come to a halt and crowds of demonstrators were roaming the streets. At one point my car was immobilised by an obstruction in the roadway and was freed by the advancing crowd. It seemed discourteous to accelerate away in a cloud of dust and for a few embarrassing moments the rioters had at their head a British Military Government car flying the Union Jack. The crowds had, however, no political organisation. As the Soviet tanks rolled through the city, the demonstrators, save only for a small number of casualties, went home to supper. The Soviet action was relatively restrained, as was the reaction of the British Government. Churchill's primary interest was in the renewal of high-level contact with the Soviet Union. He was in no mood to inflate the issue and it had remarkably little effect on the course of British–Soviet relations. What it did, however, was to reawaken sympathy in West Germany for their countrymen in the East, to exacerbate feelings against the Soviet Union and to make the new Soviet leadership, by now uncomfortably aware of the

precarious nature of their hold on Germany, the more determined
not to prejudice it by rashness in negotiation with the West.

THE FOUR-POWER MEETINGS OF 1954 AND 1955

Churchill's enthusiasm for an unprepared, informal summit was
shared neither by Eden nor by his officials. It was, however, in line
with the mood of the time. The question came to Cabinet at a bad
moment in the summer of 1953, when Eden was out of the country,
incapacitated by a severe operation followed by prolonged convales-
cence, and just after the Prime Minister himself had suffered a stroke.
It was consequently in the absence of both Prime Minister and
Foreign Secretary that, on 6 July, the Cabinet considered the complex
of German–Soviet issues. Much had happened since the last fruitless
meeting of the Foreign Ministers of Britain, France, the United States
and the Soviet Union in 1949. The divergence of British and American
opinion was beginning to reach significant proportions. Lord Salisbury, in charge of the Foreign Office during Eden's illness, put
forward a lengthy paper[2] on policy towards the Soviet Union in the
light of changes since Stalin's death. The nub of it was that, although
long-term Soviet policies had not changed, there were signs of change
in the Soviet Union itself which might even go so far as to modify
the nature of the regime. Such moves as there had been to reduce
international tension might stem partly from a desire to weaken and
divide the West and there might be no readiness for serious discussions, but the possibilities ought to be tested. Salisbury was concerned
at the 'new and dangerous American tendency . . . to interpret the
situation behind the iron curtain as already shaky and to advocate
new, although unspecified, measures to encourage and even promote
the early liberation of the satellite countries'. This was the period in
which the Dulles philosophy of 'rollback' was in the centre of
American thinking. Salisbury's recommendations were to discourage
'dangerous new initiatives' by the United States; to continue existing
policies in relation to Germany, with West German membership of
NATO as a reserve solution if the EDC were to fail; to reject
neutralisation; and to persuade the Americans to keep the door open
for informal high-level four-power talks. The Cabinet also took a
paper by the Prime Minister[3] stressing the importance of the European
Defence Community and the goal of German reunification. He was
confident that Germany would not within the next twenty years join

Russia against the West, saw the only solution in a 'real UNO' and recommended that in the meantime the objective should be early ratification of the EDC, followed by a four-power conference. In a decision reflecting the incapacity of the Prime Minister and the Foreign Secretary, the Cabinet accepted both Salisbury's paper and the Prime Minister's recommendations.

THE BERLIN CONFERENCE OF 1954

There was no chance of early French ratification of the EDC and the American Government were determined that a four-power conference should not delay the process even further by introducing a beguiling but unrealistic search for a means of avoiding the need for European defence. By the autumn, Eden was back at his desk and still firmly opposed to an ill-prepared summit. He wrote later in his diary about Churchill's speech that 'It must be long in history since any one speech did so much damage to its own side',[4] and argued with Churchill for a preparatory meeting of Foreign Ministers such as he had had in Moscow in 1943 to prepare for Teheran. It was eventually agreed that the best course was to satisfy public desire for a meeting as quickly as possible and to propose that it should be held between the four Foreign Ministers in Berlin, the location preferred by the Soviet Union, in January 1954. The Western aim was, as it had been in 1950, to discuss the organisation of free elections and the establishment of an all-German Government as the first steps towards a solution of the German problem. The whole of British and American policy was now based on the integration of Western Germany into the European–Atlantic structure and it was reasonable to hope that a Germany reunited on the basis of free elections would voluntarily choose the path of association with Western Europe on which the Federal Republic had already embarked. The course of Soviet policy in Eastern and Central Europe since 1945 and the experience of the Korean War had removed any temptation British ministers might have had to gamble on the alternative of a neutralised Germany. In notes of 4 August and 15 August 1954, the Soviet Union held to its policy that the formation of a provisional government and the holding of a peace conference should precede the elections; they also proposed that the conference should include China and should consider a wider range of world problems. From their point of view, the gamble of German reunification only made sense – if indeed it made sense at all – on a basis which effectively preserved the existing East-German regime as forming half of the first all-German Government, and formally excluded any defence linkage between a reunified Germany and the Western powers. The Soviet objective was perceived by Eden[5] as being to secure an American withdrawal from Europe and to prevent the resurgence of a strong, united Germany integrated with the West. He was entirely correct. As the official Soviet history put it: 'Every new Soviet proposal was a further obstruction to the remilitarisation of West Germany and its inclusion in aggressive military blocs'.[6] After a year's experience of post-Stalinist Russia, the British Government concluded that there was still no evidence of a fundamental change in Soviet foreign policy.

None of the participants embarked on the Berlin conference with any expectation of success. It was in large measure a public contest in which each side hoped to influence the more malleable sections among the Western Europeans – and in particular the Germans – by a public demonstration of the other's intransigence. Shortly before the conference opened, Mr Churchill invited the Soviet Ambassador to lunch at Chequers, and spoke in terms which, he hoped, would help to disabuse the Soviet Government of hopes of exploiting British–American differences. His assurance that the British Government had no desire to change the situation in the Soviet Union's 'satellites' by war was no more calculated to arouse enthusiasm than was his hope that if it proved necessary to break off at Berlin, this might be merely for a year. It was, perhaps, not surprising that when Eden conveyed the Prime Minister's greetings to Molotov at Berlin, the response was 'in no way cordial',[7] or that later Malik should have launched at Roberts a 'rather venomous attack' on Churchill, who was 'no friend of the Soviet Union and had never been one'.[8]

Mistrust played a major part in British–Soviet relations at this time. Misunderstanding did not. British expectations were proved correct, even in the handling of the administrative arrangements for the Berlin Conference. The four Commandants were given the task of making the arrangements for the Conference. Was Berlin one city or four sectors? Were there two sides or four parties? Should there be one meeting place, two, or four? The finer points of occupation theology were at issue as we laboured through a succession of all-night meetings before eventually agreeing that the ministers should meet for one week in West Berlin, followed by one week in the East and a final week in the West. In a final bizarre moment the Soviet Commandant, having been instructed to propose this eminently sensible compromise, was so startled by our immediate acceptance that he refused to agree to his own proposal without first returning to his headquarters for confirmation from higher authority. Such were the minutiae of the four-power relationship.

The Conference, which began on 25 January 1954, proceeded on predictable lines. The agreed Western proposal was put forward by Eden and was countered by the Molotov proposals for a peace treaty providing for the withdrawal of foreign forces and the constitution of a German national army. The Soviet Union continued to insist upon the establishment of a provisional government of representatives from East and West prior to the holding of elections. Molotov spent much time on public denunciation of the EDC and NATO, hoping, in Eden's view, to promote enough dissension in the Western ranks to bring about an American withdrawal from Europe. Deadlock over Germany continued throughout the conference and was extended to Austria, despite Western acceptance of an earlier Soviet draft peace treaty. The only agreement reached was that a subsequent conference should be held in Geneva, with Chinese participation, to consider the problems of Korea and Indo-China. Reporting back to Cabinet, the Foreign Secretary noted the extreme rigidity of the Soviet position over European problems, a rigidity which he thought stemmed from a sense of weakness.

THE RELAXATION OF STRATEGIC CONTROLS

The Prime Minister, neither surprised nor deterred by the outcome of the Berlin Conference, turned his thoughts, as Lloyd George had done in 1919, to the possible expansion of East–West trade as 'evidence that we were continuing to try to find peaceful means of living side by side with the Soviet Union'. A mission of British businessmen had returned from Moscow in January with the offer of substantial contracts, only to learn that more than half the goods the Russians wanted to buy were subject to strategic export control applied in accordance with arrangements agreed at the Allied Coordinating Committee (COCOM). Ministers were soon locked in dispute with the United States over the need for relaxation of the controls. Political instinct and commercial interest coincided and on 24 March the Prime Minister wrote to President Eisenhower: 'I am anxious to promote an easement of relations with Soviet Russia and to encourage and aid any development of Russian life which leads to a wider enjoyment by the Russian masses of the consumer goods of which you speak.' He spoke of relaxing both the 'grim discipline' of the Russian people and the international tension and remarked that the real peril, the development of the hydrogen bomb was 'nearer and more deadly to us than to you'.[9] In the event, some relaxation of controls was agreed.

THE GENEVA CONFERENCE AND INDO-CHINA

The focus of British-Soviet relations now moved away from Germany. The Geneva Conference of Foreign Ministers which opened on 26 April 1954 was primarily concerned with the problem of Indo-China. Here again, as in Korea, was part of the legacy of 1945 and here again the role of the Soviet Union in the doctrines and policies of a worldwide expansion of Communist power and influence had to be tested in the environment of post-imperial Asian nationalism. Britain was heavily and in the end successfully engaged in defeating Communist insurgency in Malaya. It had no standing in the Indo-China dispute other than that which flowed from membership of the Security Council in relation to international disputes and of the Council of Foreign Ministers in relation to the post-war settlements. The French resistance against the Viet Minh forces in Indo-China was already heavily dependent upon American aid and before the conference opened the French Government had appealed for direct American military intervention. The course of the conference need not concern us in terms of British-Soviet relations. The co-chairmanship of Eden and Molotov served, however, to enhance the British role in the eventual agreement on the effective partition of Vietnam and encouraged the hope that a more fruitful bilateral relationship could lead to a measure of agreement on the broader East–West relationship. It is difficult to judge the accuracy of Eden's diary assessment that Molotov 'clearly thinks that he and I have a special task in this conference to try and facilitate agreement'.[10] Agreement was in fact reached and both Britain and the Soviet Union made a contribution to it. It was reached in terms which gave the Communists half of Vietnam, with undertakings regarding reunion which, in the circumstances of that unhappy country, doubtless left them feeling confident about its eventual forcible reunion under their control. Ten years later, the North Vietnamese attack and the United States' intervention found Britain once again seeking to use the relationship with the Soviet Union to secure a settlement, but by then the attempt was doomed to failure. Of the Geneva Conference, Eden's biographer comments[11] that, churlish and unimpressed though the Americans and part of the British press were, 'others recognised one of the most remarkable diplomatic achievements of the post-war world'. Eden had indeed conducted a skilful piece of diplomacy, but the Geneva agreement was little more than a post marking the first stage on the road to Communist control of Vietnam.

'A MEASURE OF TOLERABLE AGREEMENT'

One other outcome of the Geneva Conference of Foreign Ministers was agreement on the holding of a further conference at the level of Heads of Government, also in Geneva, a year later. Before it occurred, however, Churchill took a remarkable personal initiative in an attempt to arrange a summit conference. There was in mid-1954 a concentrated Soviet campaign on the theme of 'peaceful coexistence' in which British policy was contrasted with the 'so-called policy of strength' of the United States. Churchill himself had, on 30 April, made a speech to the Primrose League in which he spoke of the need to 'establish with Russia such relations as, despite all the irritations, misgivings and disagreements, will convince the Russian people and the Soviet Government that we wish them peace, happiness and ever-growing prosperity . . . and that we wish to see them playing a worthy and glorious role in the leadership of mankind'. In Washington, in June, he had expressed the view that 'we ought to have a try for peaceful coexistence'[12] and Eden, in Parliament, had expressed the more modest ambition of 'a measure of tolerable agreement'.[13] Sir William Hayter in Moscow and the officials in the Foreign Office wrote lengthy minutes to one another – and also to the Prime Minister – on the doctrine of 'peaceful coexistence', or, as it was more cynically but more accurately described in one minute, 'hostile co-existence'.[14] Hayter quoted Dryden:

'Tis all a cheat; yet filled with hope
Men favour the deceit.

Nevertheless, any easing of the tension of armed confrontation was welcome in Britain. The stabilisation might, as Hayter believed, be only superficial and subversion might continue, but if the Soviet Union no longer saw advantage in adventure, this was all to the good. William Strang, now in the House of Lords, thought that a peaceful coexistence which meant merely absence of war was attainable but 'a positive spirit of harmony and concord' was not to be hoped for.[15]

While the debate was continuing, Churchill, sensing the mood, was itching for action. On 4 July, on his way home from Washington, he despatched a personal telegram to Molotov suggesting a meeting with Malenkov as a prelude to a possible wider meeting. Within two days he received a welcoming response. Churchill's action had, however, not been cleared with his Cabinet and it provoked a substantial storm. The Prime Minister had in mind a bilateral meeting which would enable him to explore whether a basis could be created, for instance by a Soviet gesture over the Austrian Peace Treaty, for a three- or four-power meeting with Malenkov.[16] He claimed to be doing no more than following up his speech of 11 May 1953 and also a Parliamentary motion of 5 April 1954 calling for an 'immediate initiative' towards a meeting of Heads of Government. His colleagues doubted both the wisdom and the propriety of his action. In Cabinet, Eden noted the anti-American tone of Soviet statements at the end of the Geneva Conference and, although loyally supporting his master, was clearly unhappy. Lord Salisbury was particularly critical of Churchill's move and his remarks confirmed the way in which British opinion was turning against the Dulles policy and the general anti-Soviet mood in Washington. He held firmly to the relationship with the United States as the cornerstone of British policy and was concerned that bilateral talks with the Soviet Union might encourage the development of independent American policies. The Cabinet minutes, however, report him, *inter alia*, in the following terms: 'Some believed that the greatest threat to world peace came from the Russians. He himself believed that the greater risk was that the United States might decide to bring the East–West issue to a head while they still had overwhelming superiority in atomic weapons and were comparatively immune from atomic attack by Russia.'

Churchill had, in fact, cleared his policy with a somewhat reluctant Eisenhower, but his colleagues were unimpressed and the Cabinet's dilemma was only resolved by the Soviet Union choosing this moment to launch a new initiative to prevent the incorporation of West German forces into the alliance by proposing a conference of all European Governments on the establishment of a system of collective security in Europe.[17] Thankfully, the Cabinet agreed that the proposal for a bilateral summit should be left in abeyance. This was the last major intervention of Churchill in the conduct of a relationship in which he had played a prominent part ever since 1917. Having advocated the crushing of the Bolsheviks, urged the breaking of relations, forged the wartime alliance and set the philosophical basis for the cold war, now, as Harold Macmillan was to put it: 'His last service was to have the vision to realise that the Soviet monolith would itself begin to undergo changes inseparable from growth and the lapse of time'.[18]

A month later, with the refusal of the French National Assembly to ratify the EDC Treaty, the British Government had to turn its mind back from the relationship with the Soviet Union to the reconstruction of the Western alliance. There was little doubt where the priority lay. Without the presence of American forces in Europe and substantial American support for the European defence effort, there would be no effective counter to Soviet force in Europe and the whole carefully-constructed Western system might disintegrate. A European, and above all a German, contribution to European defence was seen as a political necessity in the United States and the only route by which it could now be achieved was German membership of NATO. At the end of 1954, after one defeat and by a narrow majority on the second vote, the French National Assembly ratified the Paris agreements which established the basis for German entry into NATO. Britain independently undertook to maintain forces on the European mainland. As Eden put it in his memoirs: 'Germany was now a sovereign partner in the defence of Europe'.[19] It is not easy today to appreciate fully the significance of this action for the Soviet Union. The union of the greater part of Germany under a right-wing Government in a military alliance with the United States and Canada as well as Britain, France and most of the rest of Western Europe, was the combination which the Soviet leadership had foreseen when they tested Allied policy in Berlin in 1948. Now it had come about and in terms of the 'correlation of forces', it marked the failure of ten years of post-war Soviet diplomacy.

DETENTE AND THE STATUS QUO

The response by the new Soviet leadership to this culminating act of Western policy was summed up by Hayter in the summer and autumn of 1955[20] as being the adoption of a policy of detente and the *status quo*. In other words they wished to reduce the tension in their relationship with the West, but to do so at no cost to their established gains. In Hayter's view, the ultimate Soviet objective of the triumph of Communism was unchanged and there would be determination not to prejudice the position in Eastern Germany, but 'practical, limited, short-term bargaining' might be possible. Before Hayter formed this view, there had, however, already been signs of the erratic course which British–Soviet relations were to follow through much of the Khrushchev period. It was soon to become apparent that although preservation of the status quo might be the Soviet objective in Europe, it certainly had no part in Soviet policy outside Europe. In September 1955 the Soviet decision to supply arms to Egypt brought a fruitless exchange of correspondence between Eden and Bulganin and heralded a sequence of events which was to bring both the end of Eden's premiership and the virtual extinction of the Soviet presence in Egypt. That, however, was for the future.

In the field of bilateral relations, one immediate effect of German membership of NATO was Soviet annulment of the bilateral treaties with Britain and France, an action notified on 20 December 1954 and implemented on 7 May 1955. The treaty was not seen in Britain, as it had been by Stalin, as 'a mere scrap of paper'.[21] The British Government expressed their regret, but were firm that they could not 'allow themselves to be deflected by any threat from their chosen course' and the treaty died quietly.

THE AUSTRIAN STATE TREATY

In the summer of 1954, Churchill had hoped that a Soviet gesture on the Austrian Peace Treaty might open the way for a summit meeting at which wider issues might be resolved. What happened instead was that the entry of West Germany into NATO opened the way to the Austrian State Treaty. The Soviet Government saw the Western objective as being to include Austria in NATO and turn it into an 'Alpine fortress'.[22] In order to ensure that Austria did not go the way of Germany, they hastily decided to gamble on neutralisation and, in three days of negotiation with the Austrians in Moscow, agreed to immediate signature of the Austrian State Treaty and the withdrawal of occupation forces in exchange for a guarantee of permanent Austrian neutrality. In consequence, the Austrian State Treaty was signed by the four powers on 15 May. With its signature, a major potential source of friction was removed and Austria, politically neutral, was free to develop its natural economic and cultural links with Western Europe. Ten years had passed since the time when Britain and her partners had been concerned that Austria, Finland, Czechoslovakia and Yugoslavia might all fall into the group of Eastern European Communist states wholly subservient to the Soviet Union. The 1948 coup had brought Czechoslovakia under Soviet control, but the independence of Finland had been secured and when the new Soviet leadership came to terms with Yugoslav independence of Moscow and signed the Austrian State Treaty, the balance sheet was not bad. The Austrian outcome must raise the question whether the West should not have gambled on the creation of a unified neutralised Germany. The answer must be that the circumstances were wholly different. Germany, for better or for worse, was and is the central element in the European power balance. Austrian-style neutralisation was not a realistic concept for Germany and an Austrian-style settlement was not on offer. The Soviet Union could not have afforded to take in Germany the gamble which it took on the basis of a misunderstanding of Western policy in relation to Austria. There can be little doubt of the benefit which the Treaty brought to Austria and, indeed, to Europe. It was rightly seen in the West as an achievement. There were, no doubt, at the time those in the Soviet Union who regretted it. Seen from a thirty-year perspective, it appears more as a proof that the East–West relationship in Europe is not a zero-sum game, but that there is a genuine possibility of mutual benefit in settlements which remove the points of direct confrontation and recognise the heterogeneity of Europe.

THE GENEVA SUMMIT

On 6 April 1955, Churchill's post-war administration came to an end. Eden succeeded him and Harold Macmillan took over the Foreign Office. With the security of Western Europe now on a more solid base than at any time since 1945, Britain could turn back to the search for a resolution of the underlying problems in East–West relations. As Churchill wryly remarked, Eden's dislike of summits waned swiftly after his move into Downing Street and on 10 May 1955 a tripartite proposal was put to Moscow for a meeting of Heads of Government which would hopefully provide the basis for a subsequent meeting of Foreign Ministers and initiate a long diplomatic process, designed to lead, through specialised meetings at various levels, to the gradual resolution of the complex of East–West problems. The outcome was the Geneva summit from 26 October to 17 November 1955 at which President Eisenhower, M. Faure and Mr Eden met the two Soviet leaders, Marshal Bulganin and Mr Khrushchev, the latter having already ousted Malenkov and established his own supremacy. This was the first meeting at Head of Government level between the Soviet Union and the Western powers, either jointly or individually, since Potsdam and, with the failure of the Paris summit in 1960, it was to prove the only quadripartite meeting at that level. As a meeting, despite its unique character, it is now virtually forgotten. The preparatory Cabinet paper noted that there were as yet 'no signs of any new flexibility in the Russian attitude'[23] and, in the event, the substantive discussion of the German problem opened up no new perspectives. Eden was, however, impressed by the fact that the Soviet Union seemed 'more apprehensive of the resurgence of Germany than of encirclement by the United States' and that its leaders were 'genuinely anxious to secure . . . a friendlier relationship with the Western powers'. Various schemes of 'disengagement' designed to lessen the armed confrontation in Europe were beginning to be developed at this time and the conference also enabled Eden to put forward a package of proposals for European security including a plan for joint inspection of forces in Eastern and Western Europe. In Moscow, Bulganin spoke of the Eden plan as 'likely to have a positive influence', and, although the subsequent meeting of Foreign Ministers from 27 October to 16 November proved wholly fruitless, this phase of summit diplomacy did reduce the degree of misunderstanding and lessened the tensions, including those between the United States and China. The Soviet Union made much of the 'spirit of Geneva' and Eden was able to take the opportunity to issue an invitation to Bulganin and Khrushchev to visit Britain in the following year.

BULGANIN AND KHRUSHCHEV IN BRITAIN

The consolidation of Khrushchev's power was marked by the Twentieth Party Congress in February 1956, at which he made his celebrated denunciation of Stalin and affirmed the policy of peaceful coexistence for the conduct of relations with the Western powers. It did not, however, greatly change the British assessment of Soviet policy. The Labour party was beginning to be restive for an end to the 'cold-war posture', but the Government was waiting for deeds rather than words.[24]

In Moscow, Hayter pondered upon the question whether the Soviet Union was becoming conservative rather than expansionist and concluded that it was too early to say whether the hope 'that this state should cease to be expanding, cease to be genuinely Marxist and in fact cease to be a nuisance to the world as a whole' might be realised. The Soviet Union might seek to lull the free world rather than intimidate it, but a 'genuine agreement to live and let live with an expanding Marxist state' was a contradiction in terms. He saw the Soviet Union continuing by a sort of force of inertia to carry out revolutionary activities which had little relevance to its real interests or desires.[25] Lullabies were, in any case, scarcely Khrushchev's style. The first quarter of 1956 was marked by what Hayter described as a 'high pitch of synthetic cordiality', but the tone changed when, baulked in Europe, Khrushchev and Bulganin made a foray to India and Burma, in the course of which and subsequently both men attacked Britain in such violent terms as almost to cause the Cabinet to withdraw Eden's invitation to visit Britain. Eventually, however, Ministers concluded that a policy of coexistence might better be pursued 'until we were in a position to bring all the neutral powers within the Western orbit',[26] and the visit took place from 18 to 27 April 1956.

This visit by Marshal Bulganin as Chairman of the Soviet Council of Ministers and Mr Khrushchev as leader of the Communist Party of the Soviet Union was the first occasion since the October Revolution on which the country's top leadership had visited a Western country.[27] Lenin had indeed spent much of his exile in the West, and part of it in London, but he did not visit it after 1917. Stalin also never visited Western Europe after the Revolution (unless one counts the Potsdam Conference) and it was to be almost another thirty years before Mikhail Gorbachev set foot in Britain.

There was no expectation on the British side that this visit would lead to any early and substantive results. There were many major international issues which might usefully be discussed between the two countries, but few which were susceptible of bilateral negotiation. It was seen essentially as an opportunity to begin the creation of mutual confidence by establishing a personal link with the new Soviet leadership and in this it had a measure of success. The discussions ranged widely over the problems of Europe, the Middle East, the Far East and disarmament. They were not easy, but they were substantial. The final communiqué dealt with the relaxation of international tension; the problems of the Middle East where British concern was growing quickly and on which Eden felt he had obtained concrete results; disarmament and trade. There was talk of the purchase of up to £1000 million of British goods over five years and agreement was reached on increased technical, scientific, sporting and artistic exchanges. A visit to the Palace for tea with the Queen passed off uneventfully, but a dinner with the Labour party was marked by a sharp quarrel. George Brown, at that time on the Opposition front bench, had a temper as volatile as Khrushchev's and when, as one of the British hosts, he questioned the Soviet leaders about the treatment of Social Democratic politicians in Eastern Europe, the dinner ended in disarray. It was only after the Soviet leaders had returned to Moscow that the news of the death of a British naval frogman, Commander Crabb, revealed the sorry outcome of an unauthorised operation, delicately but transparently veiled as 'trials of certain under-water apparatus', in the vicinity of the naval vessels which had brought them. The incident caused some embarrassment to the British Government, which made a formal expression of regret, but although Pravda spoke of a 'shameful operation' the Soviet Government appeared neither greatly surprised nor seriously concerned.

The public reaction to the visit was mixed. The Government received numerous letters of protest, but on balance any move towards an easier relationship was welcomed. In his memoirs, Eden summed up the visit by saying: 'As a result of ten days spent together in almost constant contact, I felt that I knew these Russians as no volumes of despatches could have revealed them to me.'[28] To his colleagues, he spoke of the candour and realism with which both sides had conducted the discussions[29] and in his diary he noted, 'I do not believe that the Russians have any plans at present for military aggression in the West. On the other hand are we prepared with other weapons to meet the new challenge? This seems to me the major issue of foreign policy.'[30] In a broadcast, he remarked that in the long history of diplomacy, suspicion had done more harm than confidence and spoke of the discussions as 'the beginning of a beginning. . . . It may be – I think it is – true that the immediate danger of war has receded and that is good.'[31]

HUNGARY AND SUEZ

The danger had not receded very far. Immediately after the visit, it was noted that the Soviet Union's exchanges with Britain were at a higher level than with any other country, but the new mood was soon to be sharply disrupted. It was Stalin who had fastened the Soviet grip on Eastern Europe and his denunciation by Khrushchev must have aroused latent aspirations to freedom which threatened to disrupt the Soviet imperial structure. The focal points were Poland and Hungary. With Gomulka as the new leader of the Polish party, the crisis in that country was contained. For a time, it seemed that Hungary, under the moderate Imre Nagy, might establish its own, less repressive brand of socialism, with its subordination to the Soviet Union loosened and its links with the West increased. But the threat that Hungary might breach the Soviet defence *glacis* by withdrawing from the Warsaw Pact was too much. After an early indecisive appearance in Budapest, the Soviet forces launched a mass attack on Sunday 4 November 1956 and in the succeeding days heavy civilian casualties were sustained. The Hungarian resistance was estimated to have cost 20 000 lives. Public opinion in Britain was outraged and the Archbishop of Canterbury castigated Her Majesty's recent guests as 'instruments and slaves of the devil', but the Western Governments were wholly preoccupied with the Suez crisis. The British airborne attack on Port Said took place on 5 November and on the same day Marshal Bulganin wrote to the Prime Minister warning of Britain's vulnerability to rocket attack and expressing 'determination to use force to crush the aggressors'. In Moscow, a carefully organised mob invaded the British Embassy. Although the United Nations General Assembly duly called for the withdrawal of Soviet forces from Hungary, Britain was effectively paralysed and virtually the only direct British response, other than verbal reproaches by the Prime Minister, was the cancellation of a planned visit by the Sadlers Wells ballet and the boycotting of the Soviet celebration of the anniversary of the October Revolution. There was a certain feeling that Dulles' strong language had created in Eastern Europe an expectation of more effective Western support, but Eisenhower was quite clear that nothing could be done by force to help the Hungarians. So, as Britain withdrew from Suez and Eden from Downing Street, Khrushchev proceeded methodically to re-establish control over Hungary.

MACMILLAN AND NUCLEAR ARMS

The remarkable feature of relations during the Khrushchev years was the speed with which they alternated between the promise of coexistence and the threat of war. In 1955 Macmillan, as Foreign Secretary, had been complaining that the accommodating attitude of the Soviet Union at the General Assembly was placing the solidarity of the anti-Soviet front in jeopardy.[32] Now, as Prime Minister after Suez, he was to construct a new relationship with the United States and secure British–American collaboration in nuclear weaponry on the basis of resistance to the Communist threat.[33] At Bermuda, in March 1957, he anticipated Reagan when he told Eisenhower: 'You cannot be neutral in a war between two principles, one of which – Communism – is evil.'[34] Hungary had demonstrated the readiness of the Soviet Union to apply force ruthlessly in order to retain control in a key area of Central Europe. The potential consequences of the use of force between nuclear powers were, however, increasingly alarming British public opinion. This was the time of the Aldermaston peace marches and, apart from the intrinsic need for detente, Macmillan needed to make some gesture to the growing demand for an effort to reach an understanding with the Soviet Union. The Rapacki plan for an atom-free zone in Europe was attracting attention and the whole question of arms control and disarmament was moving towards the central position in East–West relations, which it was to hold intermittently throughout the succeeding years. It is a theme which cannot be comprehensively treated within the confines of this study, but it was of particular significance in the development of the British–Soviet relationship during Macmillan's premiership.

In April 1957, Macmillan received a 10 000-word letter from Bulganin, the theme of which was that it was 'exceptionally important' that 'the present tension in relations between the Soviet Union and Great Britain should be replaced by good friendly relations'. In substance, the letter concentrated on disarmament and, in particular, the prohibition of nuclear testing, an awkward point for Britain, since the first thermonuclear tests were due in the following month. In reply, Macmillan pointed to the need for progress in both conventional and nuclear disarmament as well as in matters such as the removal of jamming from BBC broadcasts and of restrictions on the sale of British books and newspapers.[35] It was to be the beginning of a brief but useful exploitation of the bilateral relationship, in which a British

Prime Minister once again took the lead in the conduct of relations by the Western powers.

The repair of the British–American relationship, begun at Bermuda, was dramatically accelerated by the launch of the first Soviet inter-continental ballistic missile in August 1957 and the first Sputnik earth satellite on 4 October 1957. The new mood of extrovert Soviet self-confidence, symbolised by Khrushchev, was having a remarkable effect on the United States. The suppression of Hungary had demonstrated the imperial ruthlessness of the Soviet regime. The recollection of the Soviet Union's wartime achievements had not faded, and it was beginning to seem that the concentration of power in a single-party state of such size might place at the service of a hostile ideology and an ambitious leadership a formidable combination of economic and military power. The spectre of the Soviet Colossus rises from time to time before Western policy-makers and in Khrushchev's final years it assumed a menacing aspect. At a Cabinet meeting on 21 October[36] the Prime Minister told his colleagues of his acceptance of an invitation by President Eisenhower to visit Washington and consider how the collective strength of the free world might be mobilised against the Soviet threat. In Macmillan's view, the United States Government 'appeared to be convinced that, in order to counter the Soviet threat, of which the earth satellite was the most recent and most spectacular warning, the whole structure of Western collaboration needed to be re-examined'. The result of Macmillan's visit was to repair the breach with the United States and to align the two countries in a recognition that 'no single country, however powerful, could alone withstand the Soviet threat' and that there had to be 'a common policy for countering Soviet encroachment, not only by military preparations, but also by political, economic and propaganda measures'.[37] The formal British–American Declaration of Common Purpose of 25 October spoke significantly of the Soviet Union's 'formidable material accomplishments' and provided for joint measures of security against 'the threat of International Communism' and the 'danger of Communist despotism'. What was significant was not merely that Khrushchev had provoked this response, but that in doing so he had provided the means for healing the Anglo-American breach and that this had happened at a crucial point in the British relationship with the newly forming European Economic Community. The British concentration upon the trans-Atlantic relationship as the central element in the organisation of resistance to the Soviet Union re-emphasised the priorities of British policy, complicating the already difficult problems of participation in the movement towards closer integration of Western Europe and hardening de Gaulle's mind in favour of a veto on the subsequent British application for full membership of the Community.

THE BERLIN CRISIS AND MACMILLAN'S VISIT TO MOSCOW

In reinforcing the defence potential of Britain within NATO and securing the future of the British nuclear deterrent, Macmillan did not lose sight of the parallel need to eliminate the causes of tension. A lengthy process of NATO consultation and correspondence with Khrushchev about a possible summit ensued, but throughout 1958 relations deteriorated, first over the Middle East and then over Quemoy and Matsu, leading Macmillan at one point to cite to Dulles the much-quoted minute of Palmerston in 1853 to the effect that 'the policy and practice of the Russian Government has always been to push forward its encroachments as fast and as far as the apathy and want of firmness of other Governments would allow them to go, but always stop and retire when it was met with decided resistance'. In Moscow, Sir Patrick Reilly had succeeded Sir William Hayter as Ambassador and Macmillan raised with him the possibility of taking up the invitation, originally issued to Eden, to visit Moscow. Shepilov had now briefly replaced Molotov in the Soviet Foreign Ministry. Molotov's removal seemed good news, but with each change, Khrushchev's power was enhanced. Reilly was concerned at his apparent megalomania and commented that, although now waged with different weapons, the Soviet Union's worldwide campaign was still the cold war which it had been called over ten years earlier.

There was indeed a frightening unpredictability to Soviet policy and the crisis erupted when on 10 November Khrushchev demanded the withdrawal of Allied troops from Berlin, following this up with a note stating that the Soviet Union regarded the existing arrangements about Berlin as null and void, but did not intend to change the procedures for military traffic for six months and was prepared to negotiate for a 'demilitarised free city'. He then proposed a peace conference with the two German states, after which the Soviet Union would relinquish its functions in respect of communications between Berlin and West Germany. For the West, the situation was more complex than in 1948. Two German states now existed, despite the fact that only one was recognised. West Berlin itself was no longer a city of wartime ruins surviving at subsistence level. Its economy could not be sustained by an airlift. In any case, there was no direct threat to civil supplies. It was arguable that in the circumstances of 1958 there was no reason why the Soviet Union should maintain the fiction of wartime occupation in order to enable the Western powers to maintain their position in Berlin. The very existence of a prosperous West Berlin constituted a challenge to the drab East German state and the flow of refugees was both an economic handicap and a political embarrassment. If the Soviet Government chose to place responsibility for access to West Berlin in the hands of the German Democratic Republic, the Allies could scarcely blockade themselves by refusing to accept German controls. Nor could they go to war because a German official had replaced a Russian. Yet to recognise the German Democratic Republic was to take a further step back from the reunification of Germany. To abandon West Berlin, the symbol of resistance to Soviet pressure, was unthinkable.

At this point Macmillan took the lead, as Bevin had done ten years earlier, in shaping the Western response. The Soviet Government accepted his proposal for a ten-day visit beginning on 21 February 1959 and so, the first British Prime Minister to visit Moscow since the end of the war, wearing his Finnish fur hat, he returned to the city which he had first visited as a tourist nearly thirty years before. He presented the visit as a reconnaissance rather than a negotiation, but he achieved something more. He found Khrushchev an 'excitable, petulant, occasionally impossible, but not unlovable extrovert', a 'mixture between Peter the Great and Lord Beaverbrook'. Macmillan's reception typified all the volatility of Khrushchev's temperament. His decision to give a visit to the dentist precedence over an out-of-town visit with Macmillan was a thinly disguised snub and throughout the visit Macmillan was subjected to a typical Russian alternation of flattery and brutality, lavish hospitality and calculated discourtesy, charm and anger. Yet, in the end, the visit did good. The final communiqué recorded disagreement on Berlin and Germany, but it was agreed that an urgent settlement was necessary and, in the course of discussion, the six-month ultimatum was effectively dropped. Agreement was also recorded on the need to halt nuclear testing under an effective system of international inspection and control. In the field of bilateral relations Khrushchev offered a non-aggression treaty, but this, in Macmillan's view, should be a multilateral agreement representing the end of the road, not a bilateral agreement at the outset. His counter-offer of a joint declaration was not taken up. On his return, Macmillan reported to the Queen that he had found in Khrushchev 'certain elements of sincerity'. At his initiative the Great Britain–USSR Association was set up in order to foster personal contacts between citizens of the two countries and a new British–Soviet Trade Agreement offered a stimulus to the development of trade. Beneath the surface, the intelligence communities were, as ever, active. Within a few years, the Soviet agents in Britain, the Krögers and Gordon Lonsdale, and the British agent in Moscow, Oleg Penkovsky, with his collaborator, Greville Wynne, were all to be arrested. For the time being, however, Macmillan had a favourable bilateral relationship on the basis of which he could pursue his broader aim of developing the route through a Foreign Ministers' Conference to a meeting of the four Heads of Government.

'WHY SHOULD THE U.K. TRY TO STAY IN THE BIG GAME?'

Two sets of negotiations were opened in Geneva in the first half of 1959, a meeting of the four Foreign Ministers, with the association of German representatives, on the problems of Germany as a whole and Berlin in particular; and a lower-level negotiation on the halting of nuclear testing. Macmillan's hope was that, without too much delay, a basis could be established which would justify the holding of a four-power summit. Adenauer and de Gaulle were both, for their own political reasons, taking a hard tactical line and ready to exploit any sign of British appeasement, while Eisenhower, guided no doubt by Dulles and sensitive to his own political standing, was determined to secure some assurance of positive results before agreeing to a summit. Macmillan, equally determined to maintain the substance of the Western position in Berlin, wanted to encourage any readiness for compromise on Khrushchev's part and put it to Eisenhower that 'we and our allies should do and should be seen to do what ordinary people would think reasonable'.[38] This meant that, in relation to Berlin, there should be no military measures until, at least, a summit conference had been tried. Suddenly, without prior consultation, Eisenhower invited Khrushchev to visit the United States, possibly in connexion with a four-power summit in Canada.

Khrushchev accepted the bilateral visit, leaving the summit open. Macmillan saw his careful diplomacy thrown into confusion and wrote angrily in his diary, 'Everyone will assume that the two Great Powers – Russia and the U.S. – are going to fix up a deal over our heads and behind our backs. . . . People will ask, "Why should the U.K. try to stay in the big game? Why should she be a nuclear power?"'[39]

Macmillan's perception was accurate, but premature. The next stage was to be not the fixing up of a deal, but the precipitation of a rupture. Eisenhower's invitation was exactly the kind of initiative for which British opinion was hoping and Macmillan was given credit for having pursued the policy which brought it about. His policy received a further boost when Khrushchev's visit gave Eisenhower the basis for agreement to the holding of the four-power summit in Paris on 15 May 1960. Meanwhile the 1959 General Election had returned Macmillan to power with an increased majority. The election had turned largely on domestic issues. Public opinion was still considerably exercised about the hazards of a nuclear confrontation with the Soviet Union, but Gaitskell's success in holding the majority of the Labour Party against abandonment of the British nuclear deterrent meant that there was no direct party confrontation on the issue of relations with the Soviet Union. The depth of concern within the Labour Party and in the country at large was, however, such that Macmillan had a clear mandate to pursue, as an 'honest broker' his search for measures to reduce the sources of East–West confrontation. As the Conservative election manifesto put it, both sides had to learn to live together and the 'steady improvement in relations with the Soviet Union' had to be maintained.

THE PARIS SUMMIT OF 1960

The meeting of the Heads of Government of the Soviet Union, the United States, the United Kingdom and France, scheduled to take place in Paris on 15 May, brought the post-war process of four-power summit diplomacy to an end in a quite remarkable diplomatic fiasco. A fortnight before it was due to open, a high-altitude American photographic reconnaissance aircraft, the celebrated U2, was brought down over the Soviet Union and the pilot captured. The United States government, at first uncertain whether the real purpose of the mission was known, issued a series of evasive and contradictory statements which did nothing to ease the tension. Khrushchev's anger was rising with each apparent affront to the majesty of the Soviet Union. He took his delegation to Paris, but on the way there – possibly as a result of a meeting with his colleagues immediately before his departure – decided to harden his stand and, on arrival, demanded an apology in terms which no American President could have accepted. Dismissing Eisenhower's assurances as inadequate, he returned to Moscow, the three Western Heads of Government went their separate ways and the new era of confrontation between the two nuclear superpowers began to take shape.

Macmillan had worked hard to set up the summit. He did all he could to save it and the failure caused him deep distress. The outcome, however, was in the hands of the Soviet Union and the United States. Might it have been different? The President had foreseen the risk and had ruled, when authorising the U2 flight, that it should be the last of the series. After the incident, a quick expression of regret might have permitted the summit to proceed. Alternatively, if Khrushchev had wanted, he could have accepted Eisenhower's assurances in Paris and emerged from the whole affair with his own standing and that of the Soviet Union much enhanced. The ways of Western policy are such that he might indeed have secured a gain in terms of the arms control negotiations. To ask whether the Cuba crisis could have been avoided is to push speculation too far. What is certain is that, had the summit taken place, it would not have changed the reality of the new superpower relationship. Summit or no summit, from 1960 onwards, the British–Soviet relationship was to be conducted in a different context.

THE BERLIN WALL AND CUBA

President Eisenhower's term was now nearly at an end and Khrushchev left the Berlin crisis to simmer through the second half of 1960 before his trial of strength with John Kennedy. The emerging pattern of East–West relations was symbolised by Kennedy's proposal to Khrushchev for a personal exchange of views between the two, without any attempt at negotiations. The meeting, held at Vienna on 3–4 June 1961, seems to have left Khrushchev, now at the height of his power, with the impression that the new young President might usefully be subjected to pressure. The situation in Berlin at this time was never far from flash-point. Over the years since the end of the blockade, half the city had become a show-place for some of the more glossy manifestations of Western culture and the other half for some of the more repressive aspects of the socialist state. Between the two halves, the military personnel of the occupying powers and the civilian population of East and West moved freely and the various intelligence organisations conducted their multifarious operations. The escape route from East Germany into East Berlin, from East Berlin into West Berlin and from there to West Germany was simple. Between 1949 and 1961 more than two and a half million of East Germany's reluctant citizens had left, most of them by this route. Khrushchev's ultimata had increased tension to such a point that in the month of July 1961, the flow reached 30 000. The Soviet Union had three possible courses: to let its East German satellite waste slowly away; to enforce the ultimatum and force the West out of the city; or to block the escape route at the simplest point. The building of the wall, begun on 13 August, was, in one sense, a challenge to Western insistence on the unity of the city. More accurately, it could be seen as a defensive act, taken in near desperation, a humiliating confession, at a time when the Soviet Union was brandishing its new power, of total failure to meet the need of the German people for their basic material and moral sustenance. The lessons of the blockade had been learnt. American and Soviet tanks confronted each other at the centre of Berlin, but no action was taken by the West to prevent the construction of the wall or by the East to obstruct the movement of British, French or American forces.

The building of the Wall eased Khrushchev's immediate problem, but it did not remove Berlin from the international agenda. In December 1961 a further long personal message to Macmillan renewed the demand for the withdrawal of Western forces and suggested that West, but not East Berlin should be made a free city. To this Macmillan responded with a suggestion which, in essence, went a long way to meet the main Soviet preoccupation in Europe:

> Just as we do not seek to upset the existing order in Eastern Europe, though we cannot approve of it, so you for your part should respect the existing positions of the Western Powers. This means that, until such time as we can reach agreement on a permanent solution for Germany, neither side should seek to frustrate the arrangements and the policies which are vital to the other.

Six months had passed since the death of Dulles, the advocate of 'rollback'. Kennedy believed in solving the Berlin problem by negotiation and if Khrushchev really wanted, as Hayter had suggested, detente and the status quo, it was effectively on offer so far as Britain was concerned.

Macmillan's letter to Khrushchev was more than a mere stage in a verbal duel. The Soviet Union had resumed the atmospheric testing of major thermonuclear weapons and the United States was ready to follow suit. Macmillan was reflecting continuing and widespread British concern when, early in 1962, he put to Kennedy a proposal to seek a more general basis for detente, through negotiations with the Soviet Union, initially between the Foreign Ministers, on nuclear testing, non-proliferation, disarmament and European security. Kennedy and Khrushchev accepted the proposal for the initial meeting and, with France holding aloof, the American Secretary of State, Dean Rusk, and his British counterpart, Lord Home, had a meeting with Andrei Gromyko in Geneva, only to find him more rigid than ever in refusing to permit on-site inspection in the Soviet Union. Macmillan wrote in his memoirs: 'The controversy ran tediously on, losing itself like some great river in the sands and never reaching the, sea'.[40]

Concurrently with the problems of nuclear weapons and the tussle over Berlin, British–Soviet relations were directly engaged as a result of a Soviet proposal to the British Government, based on the co-chairmanship of the 1954 Geneva Conference, to convene a multilateral conference on the situation in Laos. The Conference, in which fourteen nations participated, formed a stage in the continuing British involvement with the Soviet Union in the attempt to resolve the hostilities in Indo-China, an involvement which was to continue, and indeed to be intensified, during the period of the Labour Government. The 1961 Conference led to a measure of agreement on the independence, neutrality and territorial integrity of Laos, but the realities of the Vietnam War and the conflicting interests of the superpowers made it largely ineffective. The Soviet Union in these years was riding high on what the 22nd Congress of the Party saw as the 'common interests of world socialism and the world national liberation movement'. Its growing power was placed behind the 'peoples fighting for liberation from imperialist oppression' in a move to 'deflate imperialism's omnipotence'.[41] Here was a line of development, easy enough to perceive in the Soviet Union's objectives from the earliest years, proclaimed during Khrushchev and Bulganin's Indian tour in 1956 and brought to a dominant position in East–West relations through the increase in Soviet power and global ambition at a time when the post-war disintegration of the old imperial structures had reached an advanced stage. It was a trend of Soviet policy which was to persist through the remainder of Khrushchev's years and for the greater part of Brezhnev's tenure of office, until by the late 1970s it was largely responsible for the breakdown of the European-based detente of Helsinki.

While the disarmament negotiations were meandering on, the Cuban missile crisis of October 1962 made the possibility of nuclear war seem something more than a theoretical hazard. The failure of the Paris summit had marked the last stage in the post-war quadripartite relationship. Now, with a direct armed challenge and counter-challenge between the superpowers, the new structure of East–West relations was being tested. The details of the crisis do not belong here. What does belong is an assessment of the British role and of the consequences for future British policy towards the Soviet Union. The United States Government in the post-war years, like the British Government in the 1920s and 1930s, had been exercised by the threat of Communist subversion, but the threat to its own territory had been remote. The military aspect of the fight against Communism could be conducted in Europe and Asia. The development of Soviet rocket technology had created an awareness of potential vulnerability, but it was the emplacement of Soviet missiles in Cuba which made the potential threat seem a real one. As Macmillan observed, it was a far less significant threat than that under which the Europeans had long been living, but that did not lessen its psychological impact. Nor did it count for much, in the American reaction, that the Soviet Union was already open to attack by American land-based missiles in Turkey as well as by air-launched missiles from European bases. What mattered, for the purpose of this analysis, was the simple American perception of a direct Soviet nuclear challenge to the territory of the United States. It was a challenge which was bound to happen at some time. The Cuban revolution, the fiasco of the Bay of Pigs, the mood of confidence in the Soviet Union and the erratic judgment of Nikita Khrushchev meant that it happened in Cuba in the autumn of 1962. Throughout the Cuba crisis there was close, full and personal consultation between Kennedy and Macmillan. The outcome proved the judgment of Kennedy and Macmillan correct and that of Khrushchev wrong. The Soviet missiles were removed from Cuba and, by tacit agreement, the American missiles were subsequently withdrawn from Turkey. The decisions which precipitated the crisis and those which ended it were, however, American and Soviet decisions. Because of its very nature, the crisis had to be resolved directly between the two superpowers and, once they had been so engaged, the structure of East–West relations was changed.

10 Between the Europeans and the Superpowers

BRITAIN'S CHANGING ROLE

Henry Kissinger has spoken of the relationship with the Soviet Union as 'a persistent preoccupation for post-war American foreign policy'.[1] It has also been a preoccupation for British foreign policy, but there is a danger, when teasing out the thread of British–Soviet relations from the whole international fabric in which it is set, of giving the British–Soviet relationship a greater prominence in the calculations of British Governments than it has actually possessed. There is a danger, too, of tracing a misleadingly direct course for the bilateral relationship through the complex texture of a Government's many preoccupations. These qualifications apply with particular force to the period after 1962.

After the relative simplicity of an armed struggle, the post-war international scene presented the British Government with an increasingly complex set of circumstances into which the relationship with the Soviet Union had to be fitted and in terms of which its value had to be judged. From 1962 onwards there was an accentuation of this gradual, qualitative change. The relationship with the Soviet Union was still an issue in its own right for the British Government, but the formulation and implementation of a coherent policy required the integration of the day-to-day bilateral relationship with the approach to the Soviet Union as a European state and a nuclear superpower. The present chapter will trace this process through the 1960s and 1970s. For the greater part of that time the leadership of the Soviet Union was held by Leonid Brezhnev, and although Soviet diplomatic historians of that era have described it as 'characterised by further advances in the world revolutionary process',[2] it has subsequently been seen as a period of progressive stagnation in the development of the Soviet Union itself. It was, for Britain, a period which frequently saw the country's diplomacy tossing uneasily in the intersecting wave patterns of the celebrated three circles – Europe, Atlantic and Commonwealth.

While struggling with the problems of an economy in travail and an imperial structure in the throes of reconstruction, successive British Governments had, as we have seen, from 1945 to 1955 to counter the threat of Soviet expansion in post-war Europe and to enlist the power of the United States in a European cause. At this stage, the task, difficult and unrewarding though it was in terms of relations with the Soviet Union, was relatively clear-cut, since the process of welding together Western Europe was an essential element in British policy in its own right and in relation to both the Soviet Union and the United States. The British concept was, however, one of a Europe organised on a basis compatible with Britain's existing internal policies and external obligations. In pursuing a policy of cooperation rather than integration, the British Governments of the post-war years, still conscious of the victory of 1945, were influenced by a mixture of emotions: belief that Britain could indefinitely ride the troika of Europe, the Commonwealth and the United States; reluctance to merge sovereignty into a federal Europe; doubt as to whether the Europeans themselves would welcome full British participation; and alarm at the incompatibility of the European concept with existing British obligations. The preferred pattern was that of the Organisation for European Economic Cooperation and the Council of Europe rather than through the creation of supranational organisations. In this spirit Britain had cooperated with rather than joined the European Coal and Steel Community and the Atomic Community and had agreed to support, but not to join, the European Defence Community. Prior to 1956 this policy appeared – and indeed was – sustainable. The decision not to join in the first Schuman plan discussions was unfortunate, but the conflict between the European and Atlantic aspects of British policy was still reconcilable.

The significant divergence began with the decision to stand aside from the critical stages in the inception of the European Economic Community in 1955–6. From this point on, the growth in the economic power of Western Europe – and above all of an independent West Germany – began to coincide with the recognition by the Soviet Union and the United States of the nature of the new superpower relationship. The whole pattern of Britain's external relations had to adapt to the new scene and it had to do so at a time when the country was, once again, beset by economic problems. The ability to sustain the global responsibilities of a first-order power had been sapped and Suez had laid bare British vulnerability. As a factor in Soviet policy, Britain's significance was declining and, although the Soviet Union remained a major factor in British defence policy, there was progressively less room for Britain to do much about it.

To the extent that Britain was able to pursue the relationship with the Soviet Union during the period in which the integration of Western Europe was being determined, it was doing so in much closer cooperation with the United States than with France and Germany. This was a trend of greater significance for the future of British–Soviet relations than was, perhaps, realised at the time. It reflected in part the realities of nuclear weaponry and in part the political scene in the countries concerned.

The symbolic realignment of British policy was marked politically by the first formal application in 1961 for membership of the European Economic Community and militarily by the withdrawal from east of Suez. The process was, however, a slow one. Despite all the policy papers of the Foreign Office and the speeches of ministers, it was in reality more a matter of gradual adaptation to evolving circumstances – an adaptation frustrated by the de Gaulle vetoes of 1963 and 1967 – than of a single conscious re-evaluation of the British role. The instinctive reluctance to tie Britain's fate irrevocably to continental Europe, the 'great power' syndrome, the attachment to the Commonwealth link and the technical problems of Commonwealth preference remained for many years powerful factors. Full membership of the Community seemed to many to be a betrayal of the Commonwealth and even if Britain had been ready at an earlier stage to join in the European process, success might well not have resulted.

In relation to the Soviet Union, membership of the European Economic Community would constrain Britain's ability to operate an independent commercial policy, one of the traditional elements in the bilateral relationship. This was not, however, seen as a major issue by Britain and indeed, the question of British relations with the Community was treated in isolation from the British–Soviet relationship. Technically, this was correct, but more deeply, in relation to the British Government's concept of its role in world affairs, there was a linkage. The 1963 veto on British membership of the European Communities cannot be attributed wholly to de Gaulle's reaction to the British–American nuclear defence relationship. The evolutionary process in Britain, in Europe, in China, in the Third

World and in the two superpowers was moving swiftly but asynchronously. Paradoxically, both prior to and immediately after the Cuba crisis and the negotiations with the EEC, there was a period in which the British role in East–West relations was enhanced by the rigidity of Adenauer in respect of the East–West relationship in Europe and the determination of de Gaulle to stand aloof from the negotiations over the Berlin crisis and the test-ban treaty. The post-war quadripartite relationship even gave way briefly to a British–American–Soviet relationship. The power ratio in the early 1960s was, however, very different from that of the war years. For the Soviet Union, British policy was significant not so much in its own right, but rather to the extent that it might influence American policy. This was in no sense a recreation of the wartime tripartite relationship.

Nuclear weaponry was now emerging as the central issue in relations with the Soviet Union. Britain, as a nuclear weapons power, was critically dependent upon the United States, Germany was excluded from the nuclear equation and de Gaulle was bent upon the restoration of the power and self-esteem of France. Before long, however, the natural evolution of the political process brought about a situation in which Germany, and to a lesser extent France, began to set the pace in dealing with the Soviet Union as a European power, while on the worldwide scale the American–Soviet bilateral relationship, dominant in its own right, was enhanced in its effect by the open breach between the Soviet Union and China. The Sino–Soviet clash had its origins in 1957 and by 1963 was both profound and public. For the Soviet Union, it represented the greatest adverse change in the correlation of forces since the October Revolution and was a major factor in the redefinition of the whole pattern of East–West relations. Its effects were, however, slow to be felt in terms of British policy towards the Soviet Union.

In the new situation of the 1960s and 1970s, that policy still turned on a familiar axis. The residual quadripartite responsibility for Berlin and Germany as a whole gave Britain a special position in respect of the stabilisation of the German–Soviet relationship, which was the prerequisite for the movement towards European detente leading to the Helsinki Conference. The co-chairmanship of the Geneva Conference also gave Britain some continuing role in the search for a solution to the war in Indo-China. The strategic nuclear arms negotiations had to be conducted at the superpower level, but Britain was actively involved in other aspects of the arms control process and from the mid-1960s to the mid-1970s British diplomacy remained active in both the European and the global relationship with the Soviet Union. Bilaterally, too, the process leading from Macmillan's visit to Moscow in 1959 to Wilson's in 1975 resulted in the most comprehensive network of agreements and exchanges since the time of Lloyd George and Ramsay MacDonald. Nevertheless, this must still count as a period during which the British role in the conduct of relations with the Soviet Union, although extremely active, was less significant in relation to wider issues than at any time since the war. That it coincided in part with a period of Labour Government in Britain was largely irrelevant. The factors which brought it about had already been determined.

THE NUCLEAR TEST BAN TREATY

Macmillan's final success in dealing with the Soviet Union was the signature on 5 August 1963 of the Nuclear Test Ban Treaty with the Soviet Union and the United States. The negotiations had been taking a weary and inconclusive course for some years, before Khrushchev, provoked perhaps by the deepening rift with China and the knowledge that the first Chinese nuclear explosion could not be far off, wrote to Macmillan and Kennedy offering a concession on inspection procedures which Macmillan was able to seize upon as a spur to reopen negotiations. Macmillan was very aware of the pressure of public opinion on this question and his letters to Kennedy doubtless helped to overcome some of the doubts in Washington, although the President was not prepared to accept, on the basis of the limited Soviet inspection offer, an agreement covering underground as well as atmospheric tests. The final tripartite negotiation was conducted on the British side by Lord Hailsham and Sir Humphrey Trevelyan, who had by then taken over the Moscow Embassy, and Edward Heath as Lord Privy Seal visited Moscow for the signature. The limiting factors were set by the American and Soviet Governments, but the substantive issues were of considerable importance in terms of British defence policy and the successful outcome was an example of the way in which the British–Soviet relationship could be used to good effect.

THE LABOUR GOVERNMENT OF 1964–70

After Macmillan's resignation in October 1963, the Douglas-Home Government had no opportunity for major initiatives before the Labour victory in the 1964 General election. There then began a strange period in which the Prime Minister, Harold Wilson, personally committed to a successful British–Soviet relationship to a greater extent than most of his predecessors, found himself operating in circumstances which made it peculiarly difficult to secure substantive results. Wilson took office a day after the fall of Khrushchev, when Brezhnev took up the post of First Secretary of the Party and Kosygin that of Prime Minister – and coincidentally a day after the explosion of the first Chinese nuclear weapon. Throughout the life of his first Government, from October 1964 to October 1970, the East–West relationship was conditioned by two major factors, the Vietnam War and the rift between the Soviet Union and China, while the British political scene was dominated by a succession of industrial troubles and financial crises.

THE THICKENING OF BILATERAL RELATIONS

Wilson had to deal with a new, but not wholly unfamiliar Soviet leadership. *The Times*, looking back over the tumultuous Khrushchev years, was perhaps generous when, instead of echoing *Pravda*'s denunciation of 'hare-brained' policies, it commented that Khrushchev's 'pursuit of relaxation between the two great camps was his greatest and most substantial work'. It was generally expected that a less personal collective leadership of younger men – Brezhnev was still in his fifties – would wish to continue with the search for a better relationship, but that there would need to be a period of marking time. At the time he took office as First Secretary, Brezhnev was a relatively unknown figure and it was natural that Wilson's principal direct relationship should be with Kosygin, who was initially taking a rather larger role in foreign relations than is customary for the Chairman of the Soviet Council of Ministers, a post which is concerned primarily with internal affairs. As President of the Board of Trade, Wilson had known Kosygin in the early post-war years and did his best to capitalise on the existing relationship. He led a Labour party delegation to Moscow shortly before the 1964 election and on that occasion spoke on Soviet television about Britain dealing with the Soviet Union on behalf of the Western alliance. His advocacy of annual quadripartite summits at the United Nations was a short-lived initiative, but, on a bilateral basis he came close to achieving it, with three further official visits, in February and July of 1966 and January 1968 for meetings with Kosygin and Brezhnev, and a visit to Britain by Kosygin in February 1967 at which Wilson spoke of the relationship as being 'at an all-time high'. Brezhnev did not take up the invitation extended to him, but between the beginning of 1965 and the summer of 1968, there came from the Soviet Union the Foreign Minister, the Minister of Culture, the President of the Academy of Sciences, the Minister of Foreign Trade, the Minister for the Coal Industry, the Chairman of the State Committee for Science and Technology and delegations from the trade unions, the Supreme Soviet and the Communist party. An equivalent flow of British ministers and delegations travelled to Moscow. A Consular Convention was signed, as were agreements on the establishment of a 'hot line' between the Kremlin and Downing Street; on the settlement of certain claims in respect of British property in the Baltic states; on technological cooperation; and on navigation. A joint working group on cooperation in electric power was set up and negotiations were started for a new trade agreement.

This progressive thickening of the texture of bilaterial relations, particularly in the commercial and cultural areas, reflected a process which had been initiated during the Khrushchev years, in particular as a result of the Khrushchev and Bulganin visit to Britain in 1956 and the Macmillan visit to Moscow in 1959. On the British side there was something of the hope which had inspired Lloyd George, that the normal process of international intercourse would wean the Soviet Union away from the contest of power and ideology. The hope was not realised. Soviet propaganda was unremitting in its ideological offensive and, on the British side, the proposal for the conclusion of a bilateral treaty of friendship and cooperation, originally made to Macmillan and renewed when Kosygin visited London, was received with some caution. In a comment which must have caused some surprise in Moscow, *The Times* observed that the case of an imprisoned British lecturer, Gerald Brooke, was a greater barrier to relations than the Vietnam War.

BRITISH–SOVIET TRADE AFTER 1959

By the time the Wilson Government took office, there was already the expectation of increased British–Soviet trade, and Britain was in dire need of its realisation. The commercial department of the British Embassy, closed in 1950, had been reopened when the new trade agreement was signed in 1959. The planned long-term expansion of British–Soviet trade was a major feature of Kosygin's visit and he was enthusiastically received by British industry. There were indeed perceptible results. During the 1960s Britain was one of the Soviet Union's leading capitalist trading partners and in 1967 moved briefly into first place as a supplier. A British consortium set the pace in major contracts with the construction of a polyester fibre plant in the Soviet Union. In total, however, results were unexciting. Exports to the Soviet Union, valued at £53 million in 1962, had doubled in cash terms, but not in real terms, to reach £102 million in 1970. As a proportion of total British exports they failed, however, to regain even the modest 1.7 per cent recorded in 1961. Despite major promotional efforts, including the holding in Moscow of a British Industrial Fair and an exhibition of British scientific equipment, the British share of the Soviet market gradually declined in the late 1960s, in the face of growing competition from other European suppliers as well as from Japan. At this stage American competition was a minor factor. As a purchaser of Soviet products, Britain remained significant, but the total British share of the Soviet Union's turnover with the industrial West, which had been 29 per cent in 1950, remained more or less static around 14 per cent during the 1960s, before declining to the range of 4 to 7.5 per cent in the 1970s and 1980s.

VIETNAM

In all the exchanges between Wilson and Kosygin, the dominant political issue was the Vietnam War. Wilson sought to use the British relationship with the Soviet Union as a means of bringing about a ceasefire between the United States and North Vietnam. The involvement of the British Government, and of the Prime Minister personally, forms a remarkable contrast with British diplomacy in the rather different circumstances of the Korean war, almost twenty years earlier, when Attlee's principal intervention was his hurried, and fortunately unnecessary, visit to Washington to dissuade Truman from the use of nuclear weapons. The Geneva Conference of 1955 provided a *locus standi* for Britain in relation to Vietnam, but Wilson's proposal for the reconvening of the conference was not accepted. The Soviet objective was clear. The conduct of the war by North Vietnam may have been largely independent of Soviet control, but there was a direct Soviet interest, backed by Soviet supplies, in a North Vietnamese victory. It was, however, in the Soviet interest that victory should come about with no more than a controlled escalation of the fighting, in circumstances which permitted the Soviet Union to consolidate its own position in Vietnam and ideally which weakened the United States without providing any opening for China. To the extent that the British Government could help to bring about a reduction in the scale of military operations and leave the resolution of the conflict to be concluded by the mixed political–military offensive in which North Vietnam excelled, the Soviet Union would encourage British mediation. It had, however, no incentive to promote a settlement on terms acceptable to the United States. The route to control of all Vietnam by Hanoi was only too obvious. With a little more luck, the British Government might have succeeded in bringing about a pause for negotiations, but no British mediation would have led the Soviet Union to cease its support for North Vietnam, or the United States to accept in the early stages of direct military intervention the route to a settlement which, in defeat, it had to accept in 1973. During Kosygin's visit to London in February 1967, Wilson made a major attempt to secure Soviet support for a scheme to stabilise the situation and give an opportunity for substantive negotiations, but could not bridge the American–Soviet gap. In March 1968, when President Johnson stopped the bombing of North Vietnam and called upon Britain and the Soviet Union for help in doing 'all they can to move from the unilateral act of de-escalation . . . towards genuine peace in south-east Asia', there was little that Britain could do. Indeed, it is difficult to see any way in which, through the British–Soviet relationship, a substantive settlement could have been achieved. A French attempt at mediation was equally fruitless. The course of events between 1965 and 1973 demonstrated once again the limitation upon the exercise of effective influence by a third country, as well as the opportunities and the constraints in respect of effective action by either of the superpowers in a situation where the other was already militarily committed.

CZECHOSLOVAKIA

One of the more promising passages in the communiqué issued at the conclusion of the Kosygin visit in 1967 dealt with the preparation of a conference on security and cooperation, to be attended, among others, by all the countries of Europe. In one form or another, the Soviet proposal had been around for more than a decade and it was eventually to become the symbol of the detente of the 1970s, but it looked decidedly unpromising on 20 August 1968, when Soviet and East European armed forces entered Czechoslovakia, as Tass put it, 'to help the working people of that country safeguard their revolutionary achievements against encroachments by internal and external enemies of socialism'. Perhaps Dubček's real error was that he had come to power twenty years too soon. Be that as it may, in 1968 the Soviet Union under Brezhnev was in no mood to relinquish the grasp which Stalin had fastened on Czechoslovakia in 1945 and consolidated in 1948. In 1956, when the Soviet forces entered Hungary, the Western world had been politically incapacitated by the Suez crisis. In the summer of 1968, Europe was on holiday, the war in Vietnam was unresolved, President Johnson was close to the end of his term of office and the Wilson Government could already see the omens of its defeat at the polls. Parliament was recalled. It was, in Wilson's words, 'quiet, shocked, determined – and impotent'.[3] Beyond the cancellation of some cultural events and ministerial visits, there was little that the Western powers, either individually or collectively, could do. Wilson spoke of the need to prevent a relapse into the 'frozen immobilism of the cold war',[4] but thought it right that the strength and unanimity of feeling throughout the country should be registered. Since 1938, Czechoslovakia had possessed a particular symbolic significance in British foreign policy. The British reaction, both by the Government and by the public, was strong. The TUC severed contact with Soviet trade unions and even the Communist Party of Great Britain issued a statement criticising the Soviet action. The force of this response was recognised by the Soviet Union. In a formal note, Gromyko complained of the British Government 'complicating and aggravating the relations between our two countries' and *Pravda* spoke of policies 'inspired by the spirit of the cold war'. The Soviet Union subsequently described Britain as 'among the most active proponents of a policy of gradually separating individual socialist countries from the socialist community'.[5]

In the final months of the Wilson Government, the bilateral

relationship with the Soviet Union was beginning to recover from the trauma of 1968, but before Wilson could take up the invitation for yet another visit to Moscow, his Government fell and, for Edward Heath, the priority task was to resume the attempt to secure British membership of the European Community, a task which was successfully concluded on 1 January 1973. In October 1970, Gromyko visited London and the two Governments declared their resolve to intensify contacts and to 'work in all possible ways to develop relations'. Relations with the Soviet Union were, however, brought back to crisis point in 1971 when the British Government expelled 90 Soviet agents and excluded another 15, all of whom had been or were currently engaged in intelligence activity in the Soviet Embassy and related Soviet Government organisations in London. It was an action which Sir Alec Douglas-Home, Foreign Secretary at the time, was later to describe as a necessary spraying of the greenfly.

The occasional exposure and arrest or expulsion of individual intelligence officers is a normal feature of relations with the Soviet Union. Their activities have, over the years, added an extra dimension of aggravation to an uneasy relationship and Soviet retaliation against members of the British community in Moscow has added to the tension. The Wynne–Penkovsky penetration of Soviet intelligence and the Lonsdale–Kroger operation in Britain, each in its way a conventional intelligence operation, had contributed to a certain mutual irritation, but had not substantially affected the inter-Governmental relationship. Action on the 1971 scale was, however, unprecedented. Revealing as it did the extent to which Soviet overseas representation had been exploited for intelligence purposes, it was a significant blow both to the esteem of the Soviet Union and to the effectiveness of its intelligence apparatus. The Soviet reaction was sharp. Seventeen British personnel were either expelled or blacklisted in retaliation and, despite the numerical disproportion, the damage to the work of the Embassy was not easy to repair. The political relationship was correspondingly chilled and it was not until December 1973 that, as Foreign Secretary, Sir Alec Douglas-Home first visited Moscow. This period, from 1968 to 1973, when British–Soviet relations were largely inactive, was one in which the East–West relationship was moving into a distinct new phase of development, as Germany under Brandt and the United States under Nixon set out to reshape the relations with the Soviet Union as a European power and a superpower.

THE GERMAN AGREEMENTS

For a quarter of a century after 1945 the Western part of Germany had been moving gradually from being a non-country, an occupied area where the struggle with the Soviet Union for control of the European heartland was at its sharpest, to becoming a power with the ability to shape, by its own policies, the East–West relationship in Europe. By September 1969, when the Brandt Government took office in the Federal Republic, the 'frozen immobilism' of which Wilson had spoken was already becoming unrealistic in relation to Germany. In some respects, the situation had to remain immobile. The twenty-four-year trial of strength had resulted in the consolidation of Western Europe and the securing of its outermost position in Berlin, while the Soviet Union had demonstrated its will and ability to retain its control over those parts of Central and Eastern Europe which it had held since the end of the war. The unreality of a Western challenge to Soviet armed force in Hungary and Czechoslovakia or a Soviet challenge to the Western position in Berlin had both been demonstrated with equal force. The confrontation of the conventional and nuclear forces of NATO and the Warsaw Pact made disturbance of the status quo too dangerous for either party to contemplate. What was needed was a policy which accepted the existing situation, recognised the unreality of any forcible challenge to it, but provided a new basis for intra-European cooperation across the East–West border.

For its realisation, such a policy required the participation of the Soviet Union, the United States, Britain and France, not only by reason of their residual wartime responsibilities, but as a matter of political reality; of the two German states themselves; and of the other nations of Eastern and Western Europe. The key was, however, in German hands. The first moves towards a rethinking of German–Soviet relations were already being made by the CDU–SPD Grand Coalition in the 1960s. In 1967 NATO itself, with the Harmel Report, had looked towards measures to promote European detente and the balanced reduction of armed forces on the continent. In July 1968 the signature of the Nuclear Non-Proliferation Treaty marked a further stage in the process of East–West negotiation on nuclear arms control which had been initiated five years earlier by the Test Ban Treaty. In retrospect, it is remarkable that the trauma of the Soviet action against Czechoslovakia in 1968 was so quickly overtaken. It is doubtful whether any Government in the Federal Republic could have maintained the old policies throughout the 1970s, but the victory of Brandt's SPD in 1969 provided the necessary spur for realisation of the new German Ostpolitik and, with it, for more extensive change in the East–West relationship in Europe.

The formal elements of the new German policy were the treaties which the Federal Republic signed with the Soviet Union on 12 August 1970, with Poland on 7 December 1970, with the German Democratic Republic on 21 December 1972 and with Czechoslovakia on 11 December 1973. Without foreclosing the possibility of peaceful territorial change, their essence lay in the mutual renunciation of territorial claims by the Federal Republic and the Soviet Union and respect for the territorial integrity of all European nations within their present frontiers. Of themselves, these treaties represented a substantial achievement for Soviet foreign policy, while still permitting the Federal Republic to retain the goal of the peaceful reunification of Germany, enshrined in its constitution. The Soviet Union has, however, always craved legitimacy and the legitimisation of the German Democratic Republic was a major gain. A part of the price to be paid for it was the conclusion on 3 September 1971 of the Quadripartite Agreement on Berlin, by which the Allied position in Berlin was effectively confirmed on the basis that West Berlin remained formally not a part of the Federal Republic. With the conclusion of the Berlin Agreement, the way was cleared for conclusion of the Treaty between the two German states, for the ratification in May 1972 of the German–Soviet Treaty and for the establishment of relations between Britain and the German Democratic Republic.

The establishment of relations enabled me, after a lapse of twenty years, to return to Berlin. The new British Embassy was housed in modest premises on Unter den Linden, across the road from the Viceregal palace of the Soviet Ambassador. The reality of a single Berlin under quadripartite control belonged to the past, but the juridical status of the occupying powers was retained. I was in the anomalous situation of an Ambassador accredited to a state which had its seat of government in a city which we did not recognise as part of its territory. It was a situation which typified the new East–West relationship in Europe – a practical compromise reflecting a balance of political and military power which made possible the pursuit of normal relations, while enabling all concerned to protect the slightly tarnished purity of their political principles.

This reshaping of the central nexus of European relationships was a matter of major and direct concern to Britain. As a nuclear power, Britain was one of the initiators of the Non-Proliferation Treaty; within NATO the British Government was supporting the movement towards detente; and in the negotiation of the Berlin Agreement it had a direct role, in which it was represented by the Ambassador in Bonn, Sir Roger Jackling. The impetus for the detente process in Europe came, however, primarily from the governments of the Federal Republic and the Soviet Union and was given added force by the desire of the United States Government to integrate this aspect of East–West relations into the wider relationship between the superpowers.

STRATEGIC RELATIONS BETWEEN THE SUPERPOWERS

In parallel with the German negotiations, the Nixon–Kissinger diplomacy of the early 1970s set the parameters of a new superpower relationship in a form which was to continue into the Gorbachev era. By this time, the Soviet Union had largely remedied the disparity in strategic nuclear arms of which it had been acutely aware at the time of the Cuban missile crisis, and in November 1969 the US–Soviet negotiations for the first Strategic Arms Limitation Treaty were opened in Helsinki. The negotiation of the first SALT Treaty and the Anti-Ballistic Missile Treaty between the Soviet Union and the United States ran concurrently with the British negotiations for entry into the European Community and were followed in September 1973 by the opening of the Helsinki Conference on Security and Cooperation in Europe. Over a period of five years since the Soviet action against Czechoslovakia the tone and content of relations with the Soviet Union had, it seemed, been transformed. The transformation was part of a wider adjustment of the international balance, reflecting the American decision to withdraw from Vietnam and the need of both the Soviet Union on one hand and the United States on the other to adjust to the new role of China. In such a situation, an easing of the bilateral superpower relationship made sense for both parties. Within this new context, both in terms of strategic relationships and in terms of European policy, the British–Soviet relationship had to be reshaped.

HELSINKI AND DETENTE IN EUROPE

As the EEC negotiations had dominated the foreign policy of the Heath Government, so the renegotiation of the entry arrangements was a major commitment for the Labour Government under Harold Wilson which took office in March 1974 and was confirmed by the second General Election in the autumn of that year. The Helsinki Conference was, however, proceeding with active British participation and in February 1975 the Prime Minister and Foreign Secretary took a major initiative to revive the bilateral British–Soviet relationship. Visiting Moscow in February 1975, Wilson concluded a group of agreements[6] including a long-term programme for the development of economic and industrial cooperation, a ten-year programme for scientific and technological cooperation and an agreement on cooperation in medicine and public health. A separate protocol provided that the Foreign Ministers or their representatives should meet annually for consultations on virtually the whole range of international and bilateral problems and included a specific provision for contacts on any situation which 'in the opinion of the two sides endangers peace, involves a breach of the peace or causes international tension'. The two Governments confirmed their adherence to the principles of peaceful coexistence, which they defined as 'long-term, fruitful and mutually beneficial cooperation between states, irrespective of their political, economic and social systems, on the basis of full equality and mutual respect'. In the hope of expanding British exports, agreement was reached on the availability of substantial British credit. There was also provision for the establishment of an Anglo-Soviet Round Table with representatives of public life, science, culture, commerce, the press and other fields; for parliamentary exchanges and for an exchange of visits between representatives of the armed forces. The package could, with some justice, be described as marking 'a new phase in Anglo-Soviet relations'. It was a phase which in its character and its motivation recalled the relationship which Lloyd George had set out to establish in 1919 and Macmillan to revive in 1959. It was in line, too, with the sentiment of most sectors of British political opinion. The question remained: what would it amount to in practice?

The bilateral agreements of February were followed on 1 August by the conclusion of the Conference on Security and Cooperation in Europe, with the Final Act signed at Helsinki by representatives of the European Governments as well as of the United States and

Canada.[7] The provisions of the Final Act, described by Wilson as the 'start of a new chapter in the history of Europe', dealt with questions of security, of economic cooperation and of respect for personal as well as national rights and freedoms. Establishing principles such as the inviolability of frontiers and the territorial integrity of states, the Helsinki Final Act, while still leaving open the possibility of peaceful change, placed its seal, thirty years after the end of the war, upon the political structure of post-war Europe. The Soviet Union gained a valuable assurance of stability and, in exchange, conceded a legal standing to other signatories in respect of the safeguarding of human rights. In this, the British Government felt that it had made a useful move towards the achievement of a detente in which, in Wilson's words, Europeans could 'marry whom they want, hear and read what they want, travel abroad when and where they want, meet whom they want'.

For a brief period, British–Soviet relations developed in the spirit of Helsinki. The US–Soviet relationship was still active and negotiations for the second Treaty on Strategic Arms Limitation took the central role in East–West relations. Among the European powers, however, despite the Wilson initiative, Britain was seen by the Soviet Union as a less significant bilateral partner than the Federal Republic and less enticing than France, both of which were pursuing an active combination of political and commercial diplomacy. In April 1976 James Callaghan succeeded Wilson as Prime Minister and in the following year David Owen as Foreign Secretary visited Moscow to sign with Gromyko an agreement, similar to ones negotiated with France and the United States, on measures to prevent an accidental outbreak of nuclear war. The first glow of Helsinki began to fade as the authorities suppressed the movement to assert human rights within the Soviet Union. The threat that Portugal might fall under Communist control had caused very considerable concern in Britain and the United States during the period when the Helsinki agreements were under negotiation and both Wilson and Callaghan had warned Brezhnev personally in Moscow and at Helsinki that a Communist takeover would ruin the prospect of a successful outcome to the negotiations. In the event, the Portuguese crisis was satisfactorily resolved, but in the winter of 1975 the Soviet–supported intervention began in Angola and in 1977–8 the use of Cuban forces, backed by a Soviet airlift of military advisers and supplies, in support of the Marxist leaders in Ethiopia raised new fears that detente in Europe might be accompanied by the expansion of Soviet power and influence in the Third World. It was therefore appropriate that when Owen saw Gromyko he should not only raise the issue of respect for human rights, but also call for the extension of detente to Africa, where Britain was hoping that the Soviet Union might support – or at least not actively frustrate – the search for a settlement of the Rhodesian problem.

THE MOSCOW EMBASSY

To permit the freedom of contact envisaged at Helsinki was, of course, to admit the possibility of change in the very nature of society, change brought about by the assertion of individual will rather than through party doctrine or government decree. It was scarcely surprising that this challenge was one which the Soviet state viewed with some distaste and the whole Helsinki process was already running into difficulties when, in the traditional diplomatic uniform, with plumed hat, gold braid and sword, I presented my credentials as HM Ambassador in Moscow to the Vice-President of the Presidium in the spring of 1978. I found the relationship between Britain and the Soviet Union in an uneasy state. Despite the political, commercial, cultural and technological contacts established in 1975, the substance of British–Soviet relations was still thin and the flavour was becoming increasingly sour. We could not expect an easy relationship, but we could expect that, with time, there would come change and it seemed to me, as it had done to so many of my predecessors, that, if that change were to be in the direction of a slightly safer rather than a significantly more dangerous world, we could best contribute to it by seeking to build a more active, broadly-based and productive British–Soviet relationship. This was, indeed the policy which had been established by Mr Callaghan. In fact, after a brief period of relative freedom from major tension, the whole climate of East–West relations was to change abruptly with the entry of Soviet forces into Afghanistan at Christmas 1979. My remaining three years in Moscow were a period in which the bilateral relationship was brought back to a level not markedly better than that which had prevailed during the earlier periods of East–West confrontation, while the Soviet Union itself declined slowly into the economic, political and social stagnation of Brezhnev's final years.

The processes of diplomacy do not, in their essentials change greatly over the years, nor, even now, do some aspects of the Government and life of Soviet Russia. The British Embassy in Moscow is substantially more active now than it was in my time, but some description of its practical operation as I knew it may still be helpful. In 1978, if the ambitions expressed in the 1975 agreements were to be realised, the work of the Embassy needed to develop in parallel in its three main traditional sectors. We had to ensure that the British Government was as well informed as possible on the domestic and foreign policies of the Soviet Union; to promote British exports, institute direct bilateral exchanges in culture, science and technology and support the businessmen, students and others involved in them; and to seek to influence Soviet foreign policy in respect of wider international issues.

The Moscow Embassy still occupied the fine mansion which the British Government had acquired on lease when diplomatic relations were resumed in 1930 and which the Soviet authorities had, since the end of the war, been seeking to repossess. Rebuilt in the 1890s by a wealthy merchant Kharitonenko to the designs of the leading Russian architect Shekhtel and decorated in a strange mixture of French Imperial gilt and German–Flemish baronial woodcarvings, it had been taken over by the state in 1917 and had served variously as a state guest house, a headquarters for the Danish Red Cross and a residence for Litvinov as Commissar for Foreign Affairs. Its grandeur, with a ballroom which would comfortably have housed the whole of my London house, was matched by the view, unsurpassed by any British Embassy in the world, of the gilded cathedral domes rising above the red brick of the Kremlin wall across the narrow Moscow River. It had seen much of the history of British–Soviet relations. Lockhart had been entertained there in the last years of Imperial Russia, H. G. Wells had stayed there in the 1920s, Clare Sheridan had come to make a bust of Lenin, Churchill had entertained Stalin during the war, Khrushchev and his colleagues had celebrated with erratic joviality the revival of relations after the death of Stalin, and through it all, with the classic techniques of eavesdropping, observation, blackmail, subversion and electronic interception, the KGB had wound their tedious way. Superbly suited for the formal, representational function of an Embassy, it was inconvenient as a dwelling for the Ambassador and his family; its three bedrooms provided much grandeur but little scope for the accommodation of visiting ministers; its kitchens were separated by seventy stone stairs from the dining room; and its office accommodation on the ground floor was marked by a sad, overcrowded grubbiness of filing cabinets, tape machines and dirty cups, with Kharitonenko's cornices hidden under plaster board and his carved woodwork giving way to steel doors. For all its inconvenience, all its absurdity, all its tensions, my wife and I recall it with affection. Sadly, its days as a British Embassy are now numbered, but it will be close to the end of the century before a new Embassy is ready for occupation. Until then the old house, its various outbuildings and a separate cramped and shabby block of commercial offices will have to house a British staff of some seventy persons, supported by another seventy or so clerical, domestic and maintenance staff as they conduct the business of Her Majesty's Government in the very different circumstances of the Gorbachev regime.

In any country, the formal, inter-governmental business has necessarily to be conducted with those who hold official positions in one sphere of activity or another and nowhere is this more the rule than in the Soviet Union, where the interlinked machinery of party and state permeates the whole life of the country. The avoidance of foreign contamination combined with the acquisition of foreign technology is a longstanding Russian tradition, only partially modified by Peter the Great and resumed with enthusiasm by successive Soviet Governments. The complaints of British Ambassadors about the difficulty of securing open access to Russian society and to the political leadership antedate 1917. There was some freedom of contact in the Khrushchev years and its reappearance is one of the major benefits of the Gorbachev regime, but in 1978 the traditional inhibitions prevailed.

Despite these inhibitions on wider contacts, the Embassy's working relationship with the Foreign Ministry, the Ministry of Foreign Trade and bodies such as the State Committee for Science and Technology functioned, on the whole, efficiently. We had our frigid moments, as, for instance when I had to complain of the attention paid by the KGB to members of my staff. We clashed over questions of human rights, when any reference to Helsinki was rejected as interference in the internal affairs of the Soviet Union. We found difficulty in distinguishing between deliberate obstruction and the natural cumbersomeness of Soviet bureaucracy, and the harassment of visitors to our cultural section was a distasteful reminder of the reality of Soviet life, but it was possible to feel that some progress was being made. I dealt normally with the Deputy Foreign Minister responsible for our affairs, but when I needed to see Gromyko personally, I was usually able to do so. Our exchanges were courteous and businesslike, but on the whole unrewarding. All his long experience and substantial ability were devoted to the well-rehearsed deployment of sterile policies and it was hard to break through into any genuine interplay of ideas. Brezhnev himself was virtually never encountered by Western Ambassadors except on the occasion of a visit by a foreign Head of State. The deterioration in his condition since I had first encountered him in Berlin some years earlier was marked and such brief exchanges as we had in Moscow were not facilitated by the trouble he seemed to have with his hearing aid. The messages which, on occasion, I had to deliver to him were transmitted either through the Foreign Ministry or through a singularly uncommunicative member of his personal staff. Yet for all his incapacity Brezhnev still seemed able, when necessary, to dominate his colleagues on the Politburo, the body which held the destiny of the Soviet Union in its hands and which we saw as a grey group of ageing men, mounting the Lenin mausoleum on ceremonial occasions, but as individuals – with the exception of Gromyko – scarcely more accessible to foreign diplomats than was the General Secretary himself.

All of us in the Embassy saw it as perhaps our most important task to break through the wall of formality and establish a more open relationship with the individuals who were shaping the Soviet Union, whether in the party, the administration, the economy, the arts, on the land or in the factories and mines. The moments of success – and they did occur – were cherished. In our dealings with the administration, there were issues such as arms control or the law of the sea on which serious and productive British–Soviet discussion was possible. There were on occasion useful exchanges on Middle Eastern problems, which, if they did not bring a solution much nearer, at least brought a measure of mutual understanding. On technical matters, there was a good relationship with several of the Soviet industrial ministries.

The thinness of contact at senior level did not prevent us from understanding the processes by which Soviet policy was formulated and we were able to assess with reasonable accuracy its broad trend. It took no great perceptiveness to recognise the stagnation of those years, the morass of inefficiency in the economy and the widespread yearning for a more decisive leadership. We relied heavily upon careful study of the Soviet press, which, deciphered with the care devoted to an Egyptian hieroglyph, could prove surprisingly informative. The leader writer who said, 'Provided I start with Lenin and end with Brezhnev, I can put what I like in the middle', may have been exaggerating, but the pseudonyms indicating the origin of the more authoritative pieces were identifiable and the grains of truth could be extracted from the mounds of official chaff. What one lacked was a feel for the balance of power and the policy debate within the leadership. Speculation over the hawks and the doves in the Kremlin is a popular pastime. The categorisation may be misleading, but there must have been genuine differences of opinion. We might infer them, but we had no direct evidence. The occupation of Afghanistan caught us by surprise. In retrospect, the portents were there for us to see, but policy decisions of this type are closely guarded in any country and we did not draw the threads together. During the Polish crisis of 1980–1 we could recognise clearly enough the preparations for military intervention and could infer the policy debates which must have led to the long hesitation before the decision to stake all on Jaruzelski. Of Gorbachev's stand in relation to the events of those years we had no inkling.

The lack of contact with the centres of Soviet political power constituted a particular handicap in that part of an Ambassador's duties which is concerned more with the presentation of British policy and the exercise of influence over the process of Soviet policy formation than with the reporting and evaluation of Soviet policy. If this is to be done effectively, one needs to be able to go beyond the formal presentation of policy documents and to inspire in one's interlocutors a degree of confidence in the authority and reliability of one's own judgment, a process which is rendered substantially more difficult when personal contact is restricted. This area of an Ambassador's work is ultimately a test of personal qualities, but it can also be crucially affected by the extent to which his own Government demonstrates its confidence in him. His arguments cannot expect to carry weight with a foreign Government unless it is apparent to them that he carries equal weight with his own. In the British Diplomatic Service, the relationship between career diplomats and ministers has with a few sad exceptions, worked well and I was fortunate in that, appointed by a Labour Government, I enjoyed the full support of their Conservative successors.

As a matter of reciprocity, the access to senior ministers accorded to the Soviet Ambassador in London was held at a level broadly comparable to that which I enjoyed in Moscow, but in other respects his opportunity for access to all sectors of opinion in an open multi-polar society was on a scale which no Western Embassy in Moscow could enjoy. Whether his reporting was correspondingly illuminating, we cannot tell. The telegrams and despatches of Ambassador Maisky in the period leading up to the outbreak of war in 1939 provide a good illustration of the range of reporting possible to an energetic Soviet representative in London. Documents for more recent periods are not available, but any inadequacy in Soviet reporting is more likely to have resulted from the attempt to interpret British policy in Soviet ideological terms than from any lack of access.

In the closed society of Moscow in the Brezhnev years the normal gossip of diplomacy tended to acquire an extra interest. The practice of regular consultation among European Community, NATO and Commonwealth Ambassadors was time-consuming, but it could be useful in the assessment of Soviet policy. There was a longstanding and valuable tradition of close cooperation in Moscow among the Ambassadors of Britain, France, the United States and the Federal Republic. Each was, at one point or another, in a leading position in the day-to-day relationship with the Soviet authorities. Each had a distinctive base for that relationship, yet the extent to which our assessments coincided was remarkable. We also profited from discussion with the small group of Western correspondents in Moscow, most of whom had a good understanding of the country and could more easily maintain contacts of a kind which, given the inhibitions of diplomatic propriety, were sometimes difficult for the Embassy.

If we were to help Britain to understand the Soviet Union, we had to go to those roots of national sentiment which have made the party and state what they are and which will determine what they will become. We had to understand the people of Russia and all the other hundred or more nationalities which make up the Soviet Union, to develop some feeling for their way of life, for the challenges of a land mass almost the size of China, India and the United States put together. This was a field of diplomatic activity as rich and varied as the contacts with the machine were arid and stereotyped. Fortunately the restrictions on travel by diplomats in Moscow did not operate in such a way as to prevent Ambassadors from moving throughout most of the country. Our movements were of course known to the authorities, our hotels were booked by them, our appointments arranged by them. There is no doubt that we saw what they wanted us to see and met those whom they wanted us to meet. So, from the Finnish border to Odessa, from Northern Siberia to Kirghizia, my wife and I duly admired the Potemkin villages, the schools, the housing developments, the crèches, the sports arenas, the restored churches, the museums, the factories, the farms, the mines and the power stations. We met the local leaders, we exchanged toasts to peace, to friendship, to the children and to the fallen. Behind the façade, however, one gradually came to learn the reality. The 'peace industry' as it was described by a Moscow playwright was more efficient than most sectors of Soviet industry, but it was built on the basis of a personal experience or parental experience of war which commanded respect. Russian patriotism was exploited as a basis for Soviet patriotism, but it was real enough in its own right. So too was the recognition that, for all its failings, the socialist state had brought tangible gains. The prefabricated flats were shoddily built and cramped, but for those of middle age or over they represented a dramatic improvement on the squalor which they replaced. The younger generation, more cynical, was harder to satisfy, intolerant of the rigidity of the system, impatient for the consumer society.

The administrative and industrial stagnation of the Brezhnev years, now officially acknowledged, was apparent enough at the time. We now know, as we could then only suspect, the extent to which statistics were falsified. But the practical deficiencies of the planned economy were as apparent to us as to every citizen. It could lead the world in rocket technology, but it could not, as a senior official lamented, make women's tights. There were industrial and mining enterprises in Siberia run on a scale which reminded me of the major ventures of multinational corporations and controlled by men in their forties who had the intelligence and ability to command the same success. Even *Pravda* had, however, to bemoan the fact that, sixty years after the Revolution, the production quota for light domestic metalware was set in tonnage terms, with the result that it paid a factory manager to make nothing but large metal buckets, leaving an unsatisfied demand for everything from saucepans to corkscrews. The press had its reports of corruption and even in the theatre and in works such as Aitmatov's book, *A Day is Longer Than a Century*, the current of criticism could be sensed. There is no need to prolong the description. The more graphic examples which we experienced have been surpassed by the reality now paraded by the apostles of the new era. It was all summed up by the story of Stalin, Khrushchev and Brezhnev, travelling together by train. The train stops. Nothing happens. Stalin: 'Shoot the driver.' Khrushchev: 'Sack the station-master.' Brezhnev: 'Pull down the blinds and pretend we are moving.'

Although it was easy enough to identify the circumstances which made the Gorbachev restructuring essential, it was by no means easy to be sure about the nature of likely change. There were many who were actively promoting a return to Stalinist policies. I still have a lapel badge of Stalin given to me by one self-acknowledged Stalinist official. It was no surprise to be shown, in Georgia, his birthplace preserved as a shrine, but more remarkable to be accosted on a train in Uzbekistan by an elderly woman selling Stalin mementoes and to notice a Stalin sticker on the back window of a Moscow car. It was symptomatic of a mood in which, for many, the recollection of the evil of the Stalin years was outweighed by the desperate desire for a leader who would take the country out of a slough of mal-administration.

The limping Soviet economy offered opportunities to British industry and ample credit was available for British exports, but in some respects we were less well placed than our European competitors. American export figures were swollen by the Soviet contracts for the purchase of grain, but at this time, during the Carter administration, the US–Soviet relationship was in a thoroughly unsatisfactory state and the Soviet leadership, irritated by a President whom they never understood, seemed only too happy to seek any opportunity to damage American interests. France and Germany, on the other hand, both conducting an active diplomacy in Moscow, were being wooed and it seemed that their success in securing major contracts reflected, at least in part, a political assessment. With recollections of 1941, it was surprising to hear my German colleague comment: 'We have good friends here. We always have had.' Recollecting the thinking of Austen Chamberlain, it was easier to agree with the Soviet official who put it differently: 'They take us more seriously.'

THE BREAKDOWN OF DETENTE

After the fall of Nixon and the American withdrawal from Vietnam, the Soviet leadership found themselves in an odd position. They had felt that they understood the Nixon–Kissinger diplomacy. Now, suddenly, the correlation of forces had swung in their favour, but they were uncertain how to handle their opportunity. It was as difficult for them to grapple with President Carter's effort to establish a morally-based American policy as it has been for the West to deal with doctrinally-based Soviet policies. The Carter morality represented a clear and enduring strain in American policy, but it did not make for stability or predictability in relationships with the

Soviet Union, and America's allies could not avoid being caught up in the confused waters of the American–Soviet relationship.

After an initial setback, the Salt II Treaty was signed at the Carter–Brezhnev summit of June 1979, immediately after the Conservative victory in the British General Election. Although, after Lloyd George's first efforts, it had been British Labour Governments which had taken the main steps in the establishment of relations with the Soviet Union, the British–Soviet relationship had not, in later years, swung with changes in the balance of political power in Britain. It was thought in Moscow that there might be a sharper tone to British policy, but there was no expectation of radical change. I was on an official visit to Georgia when Mrs Thatcher moved into Downing Street and, with a nice touch, my Georgian hosts presented me with a plaque of Queen Tamara of the Georgians leading her knights into battle. Neither for Britain nor for the Soviet Union was the other partner in the forefront of attention at this time and the impetus of the 1975 agreements was dwindling. The wider international scene was such that I saw little prospect of genuinely constructive British–Soviet cooperation, but it was still possible to expect a period of reasonable stability in the bilateral relationship.

The Duke of Edinburgh visited Moscow in 1979, as President of the International Equestrian Federation, in connection with the preparations for the 1980 Olympics and, although a new source of friction arose over the possible supply of Harrier aircraft by Britain to China, the Prime Minister was able to have her first, and reasonably substantial, discussion with a member of the Soviet leadership when, on her way to China in the summer of 1979, she stopped briefly at Moscow airport, where she was met by Kosygin, the Chairman of the Council of Ministers. The developing relationship was abruptly changed when, a few months later, the Soviet forces entered Afghanistan. Their action and the Western response to it inaugurated the next swing in the oscillating British–Soviet relationship.

The Soviet action in Afghanistan was different in kind from the earlier use of Soviet forces. Deplorable though the Soviet action in Hungary and Czechoslovakia had been, these countries had been accepted by the Western powers as falling within the imperial ring-fence of the Soviet Union. In Africa, the attempt to extend Soviet influence through military intervention had involved the use of Cuban rather than Soviet forces. Now Soviet forces were directly committed to an operation designed apparently to push forward the imperial frontier in Central Asia. Despite some preliminary indications of

Soviet activity, the operation came as a surprise. Yet, in retrospect, it was not wholly surprising. The Afghan revolution of 1978 had, in Brezhnev's words, created a 'qualitatively new relationship' with the Soviet Union. When the ability of the Afghan Government to hold power came into question, it must have seemed that there was a risk that the gains of 1978 would be lost and that an example might be set for counter-revolution elsewhere. The temptation to implement a combined politico-military operation to ensure the maintenance of a pro-Soviet regime was strong. Carter's foreign policy adviser, Zbigniew Brzezinski, had, a year earlier, drawn attention to the 'arc of crisis' along the shores of the Indian Ocean which was of 'vital importance' to the United States. Nevertheless, the Soviet leadership were doing their best to aggravate the humiliation of President Carter over the American hostages in Teheran – whereby they must incidentally have improved the prospect of a Reagan victory a year later – and doubtless calculated that an operation in Afghanistan could be completed without any risk of a direct military clash with the West. Extrapolating from earlier experience, they could expect that the emotional reaction would soon subside.

The scope for a British response was limited. The world had moved a long way since Lloyd George had secured the 1921 assurances about non-interference in Afghanistan. Aid to the Mujaheddin would, in due course, be possible, and, in its consequences, more effective than seemed likely, but there was no direct action which could be taken to halt the Soviet operation. In the assessment of Soviet policy and in discussion of the handling of the Afghanistan crisis, there was an encouraging measure of collaboration among the major Western European Embassies and with the United States. We all had our separate interests and differing approaches, but we all recognised the need to make the Soviet Union understand that a concept of limited detente which left open the use of military force in support of the extension of Soviet imperial control in the Third World was no basis for the establishment of a sound relationship with either the Western powers or the Third World. So, in parallel with the demonstration of international outrage in the United Nations, the British Government adopted a policy which amounted in effect to the ostracism of the Soviet Union. It was a controversial policy, but I believe it was right. It involved the deliberate severance of contacts which we had been trying, against heavy odds, to develop and which would have to develop again if there were ever to be any genuine understanding between the two countries. It involved gestures such as non-attendance at the great ceremonial occasions of the Soviet calendar. We boycotted the May Day and October Revolution parades. It had its element of farce as when our wives, after much serious deliberation, concluded that they could properly accept the invitation to the International Women's Day reception given by Mrs Brezhnev, but should not stay for the dancing. Most controversial of all was the decision to boycott the Olympic Games, a decision which required my temporary withdrawal from Moscow. Politics should have no place in the Olympics, but for Moscow the games were a major political event and the British competitors could not evade the political implications of their presence or absence. It was scarcely surprising that the pressure for a boycott should have caused considerable dissension among the competitors, for whom the price of absence was a heavy one, and many of the British team decided to participate. In the commercial field, the effects were slight, the principal measure being the American embargo on grain exports. In the field of arms control, the Soviet action was the final blow to any chance of ratification of the Salt II Treaty and, more widely, it contributed to the mood which led to the installation in Western Europe of the intermediate range nuclear weapons constituting the response to the Soviet SS20 missiles.

The political dialogue was not wholly severed. The 1975 Protocol provided for bilateral consultations in a case such as this. I had a number of exchanges with the Foreign Ministry. During the United Kingdom presidency in the European Community, Lord Carrington, as Foreign Secretary, came to present the proposals of the Community members concerning a basis for the withdrawal of Soviet forces from Afghanistan and spent a totally unproductive day of discussions with Gromyko. The Western response to the Soviet action in Afghanistan was a strange rag-bag, part planned, part haphazard, but it was soundly conceived. I believe it had its effect and the vast majorities against the Soviet Union in the United Nations were an important part of that effect. The detente of the 1970s was not illusory. It was a necessary stage in the gradual maturing of the relationship with the Soviet Union, but another cycle in the evolutionary process was necessary.

While the situation in Afghanistan remained in deadlock, the Soviet Union was confronted with the rise of the Solidarity movement in Poland. In Moscow, we watched as, throughout 1980 and 1981, the situation in Poland deteriorated and the tension with the Soviet Union rose. The tone of Soviet official comment grew more strident and it seemed clear that the political and military preparations for

Soviet armed intervention were at an advanced stage. Still, the leadership hesitated and eventually, control was regained, at Soviet insistence, as a result of the installation of Jaruzelski and the imposition of martial law. Had Jaruzelski failed, I think it probable that the Soviet forces would have been used as they had been in Hungary and Czechoslovakia. Glasnost will have to go a long way further before we can be privy to the Politburo discussions of those days, but it is not unreasonable to assume that the international response to the Soviet action in Afghanistan was one factor in strengthening the Soviet desire to avoid the use of its own forces in Poland. It was sad to see the suppression – only temporarily – of Solidarity, but Europe had avoided a military operation which might have proved the most dangerous since 1945.

Again the question of a Western response arose and on this occasion the dissent between the United States and her European allies was significant. With President Reagan in the White House, both the tone and the content of American policy had been sharpened. The rhetoric was that of the 'evil empire', but the room for new practical measures was limited. The strengthening of American weaponry was embarked upon, but, in relation to the Soviet Union, the only intensification of the earlier response which seemed feasible was the extension of the existing strategic controls on exports to the Soviet Union. This, in essence, raised the old issue of the validity of economic sanctions. There was little dispute about the principle of preventing the export of advanced equipment directly connected with the development of Soviet military potential, but the central issue became the supply of foreign equipment for use in connection with the project to bring Siberian natural gas to Western Europe. This project was of interest to British equipment suppliers and of rather greater interest to other European countries, in particular France and Germany, both as equipment suppliers and as gas consumers. The disagreement within the Alliance was vocal and public and such measures as were taken proved insignificant, even as a gesture.

The final episode of my period in Moscow was the need for discussion with the Soviet authorities on the Falklands war. It provided an interesting contrast between the formal and public Soviet denunciation of British colonialism and the practical recognition not only by the Soviet public, but also, I believe, by some Soviet officials, of the justice of the British case. The risk of a potentially serious incident as a result of the presence of Soviet submarines in the South

Atlantic was not negligible and the fact that it did not occur must have owed something to the prudence of Soviet policy.

Nevertheless, by the time I left Moscow in the autumn of 1982, relations with the Soviet Union had been reduced to the barest formality of diplomatic contact, a trickle of trade and a handful of academic exchanges. I commented at the time that the Soviet Union had been forced to recognise that it could not sustain a concept of detente under which it remained free to develop its military superiority in Europe, pursue destabilising policies worldwide and repression within its own sphere, and at the same time maintain a stable strategic relationship with the United States. The essential hostility of the Soviet and Western systems was displayed with full clarity: each had the military capacity to annihilate the other and the political relationship was a sullen stalemate.

Within the Soviet Union, the economy was in a bad way and the system was showing the stress of its imperial burden. The preoccupation of the Soviet leadership would have to be with internal policy, but they would not, I thought, refrain from challenging Western interests if they believed that they could secure profit to themselves without incurring any risk. The inertia of the whole state was symptomatic not only of the leadership, but of the system itself. It was clear that a full cure would need something closer to revolution than to reform and the political and ideological opposition was too strong to permit anything more than an ineffective tinkering. We could see that Brezhnev could not last long. My advice was that when he died his senior colleagues would share the spoils of office between one another, but that within five years we could expect this group to be replaced by men in their fifties. They would inherit a tired ideology, a strained economy, a restless empire, a hostile relationship with the major powers and a massive military power. We were approaching a period of major change of a kind which happens rarely in history and the men who would have to manage it were almost wholly unknown to us. In this situation, the task for the Western powers, as I saw it, was to get to know this new generation of potential leaders and to plan a progression from the necessarily negative policies of the post-Afghanistan period. We had first to achieve a safe management of the confrontation and then to establish a dialogue in which we could offer the prospect of a more constructive relationship, with the emphasis on the community of interest rather than the clash of ideology. In this whole process I saw Britain as well-placed to take the lead. The Prime Minister's standing was high and her words would, I thought, carry weight.

I left Moscow in the early autumn of 1982, shortly before the death of Brezhnev provided the spur for the reassessment of British–Soviet relations. Mikhail Gorbachev was already visible as a contender for power, but, as we had expected, his seniors had to have their turn. Andropov's previous responsibility as head of the KGB was a less than encouraging augury, but he was thought to have the intellectual qualities necessary to analyse the sorry state of both the internal and the external policies of the Soviet Union. His illness and early death, followed by the appointment and equally early death of Chernenko, gave little opportunity to test the possibilities, but it is to the credit of the British Government that, during this virtual interregnum, they were among the first to realise that the strident rhetoric and negative policies of the crisis years, necessary though they had been, would have to make way for yet another attempt to bring the Soviet Union into a less confrontational relationship with the remainder of the international community. Britain could indicate its readiness for such a development and this Margaret Thatcher did in speeches to the Conservative Party Conference on 14 October 1983 and a month later, at the Lord Mayor's Banquet, the forum chosen by Lloyd George for the initiation of his Russian policy in 1919, at which she set out the aim of reaching a 'broad understanding' on the 'common interest in peace and security at a lower level of weapons'. The British Government's policy was supported in the following year by other NATO Governments and the alliance committed itself formally to the pursuit of a more stable relationship through dialogue and cooperation and to the search for a genuine long-term detente.[8] A change of policy could, however, only be made effective if there were also in the Soviet Union a leadership which recognised the need for fundamental change and had the ability to initiate the necessary policies.

11 A New Start

The essentially confrontational relationship between Britain and the Soviet Union throughout most of the period since 1917 reflected the response of a society based on parliamentary democracy and individual rights to the challenge of a collectivist, revolutionary ideology claiming universality and backing that claim with ever-increasing military power. In March 1985, the accession of Mikhail Sergeevich Gorbachev to the General Secretaryship of the Communist Party of the Soviet Union and the initiation by him of a major reform of Soviet domestic and foreign policy made it appropriate to reassess the nature of the challenge and to reformulate the response. People and politics being what they are, there can be no confident predictions. Gorbachev has spoken of a 'raging maelstrom of discussion and events', and attempts at prophecy may be confounded before they can be read. In these two final chapters, we shall, however, review the factors which have produced the seventy-year confrontation of power and ideology; the extent to which they may be changed by the Gorbachev reforms; and the implications for British policy.

THE APRIL REVOLUTION OF MIKHAIL GORBACHEV[1]

A schoolboy during the war, Mikhail Gorbachev had studied law at Moscow University in the early post-war years, joined the Communist Party in 1952, a year before the death of Stalin, and made his career as a party official in the agricultural region of Stavropol in South Russia. He remained in Stavropol, progressing through the local hierarchy, until on appointment as a Party Secretary in 1978, he moved to Moscow. In 1980, with the Soviet Union locked in sterile confrontation with the Western powers, he became a full member of Brezhnev's Politburo. At this point, holding the twin appointments of Party Secretaryship and Politburo membership, he was in the clear line of succession to the leadership. The Leningrad-based Romanov, the only competitor in his own generation, was vulnerable and

297

Gorbachev needed only to avoid disaster while death removed his elders, first Suslov, and then in quick succession the three General Secretaries, Brezhnev, Andropov and Chernenko. A professional, a lawyer by training, his whole career was within the party, his direct responsibility was heavily concentrated on the markedly unsuccessful agricultural sector and he had no background in defence or foreign affairs. To the diplomatic community in Moscow he was known as a man of power in the party, but there had been little opportunity for any Western observers to form a personal impression of his qualities. In a major speech on 22 April 1983, in connection with the anniversary of Lenin's birth, he had spoken of the need for change and had taken up his favourite theme that Marxism–Leninism was not a collection of stale recipes. He had been uncompromising in his analysis both of the ills of Soviet society and of the ideological clash between socialism and imperialism. In many respects he was echoing familiar language. It was reasonable to expect that he would inject a new vigour into the machinery of party and Government. At an ideological conference in 1984 he spoke of the need for openness, *glasnost*, but it was still hard for a Western observer, or indeed a Soviet citizen, to judge with any confidence the extent of the changes which he would introduce.

We now know that in those final years of the old regime Gorbachev and his associates were already planning major reforms. Almost immediately upon his assumption of the General Secretaryship the programme of 'restructuring' was initiated. It was to be, as Gorbachev expressed it, a period of 'revolutionary change' and the decisions of the Central Committee Plenum held in April have been referred to as the April Revolution. At the 27th Party Congress in February 1986 at which they were developed, two primary themes were the introduction of the discipline of a market economy into the socialist framework and the enhancement of the moral authority of the party by processes of internal democratisation. The implications of the latter process for the work of the party were then debated, in conditions of remarkable openness, at the Party Conference which began on 28 June 1988. With these major party gatherings successfully carried through, the doctrinal and organisational base for Gorbachev's reforms had been laid down. Its future course was, however, still uncertain.

The British–Soviet relationship was a matter of interest to Gorbachev even before his assumption of the General Secretaryship. In December 1984, a Delegation of the Supreme Soviet was invited to visit Britain. It was significant that, with his eye clearly set on the leadership, Gorbachev took the advantage of this opportunity for a first substantial discussion with a Western leader. His personal impact was immediate. Here was a man of determination, ability and charm, firm in his defence of socialist principles and Soviet interests, but able and apparently willing to cut through the standard ideological clichés and construct a practical working relationship with the West. On the personal level, it was the start of a relationship with Margaret Thatcher which in its blend of mutual interest, personal respect and ideological antipathy typified the relationship between the two countries. After their first encounter, the Prime Minister observed: 'I like him. We can do business together.'

Two years later, in March 1987, the Prime Minister visited Moscow and bilateral agreements were signed on the familiar topics of scientific and cultural cooperation as well as on the construction of new Embassies in London and Moscow. 'It was', said Mrs Thatcher 'a significant visit at what could be a turning point in history.'[2] The substance of the formal agreements was of less significance than the thirteen hours of frank and private exchanges between the two leaders on the whole contemporary scene, both within and outside the Soviet Union. Divergent though their views were, it was possible to discuss them 'frankly and in a spirit of friendship.' With this visit, not only was the political dialogue resumed, but official and unofficial exchanges of all kinds were revived. Gorbachev stopped briefly in Britain in December for a meeting with the Prime Minister before his visit to the United States and in an interview given to Soviet television in December, the Prime Minister described British–Soviet relations as 'better than at any time since the war'. Tass commented that this was an accurate reflection of the real state of affairs.

The developing British–Soviet dialogue had, as in earlier years, to find its place within the context of the differing evolution of US–Soviet and European–Soviet relations. The dominance of the superpower relationship and, within that relationship, of the balance of nuclear weaponry was inescapable. It was significant that the first substantial product of the four Gorbachev–Reagan meetings between 1985 and 1988, the agreement on the abolition of intermediate range nuclear missiles, had a European focus. Requiring as it did a numerically greater sacrifice by the Soviet Union, this was a substantial gesture. Followed by the final withdrawal of Soviet forces from Afghanistan, by a unilateral reduction of Soviet ground forces and by the initiation of negotiations for the further multilateral reduction of non-nuclear forces in Europe, it reinforced the climate of opinion in which reassessment of some of the underlying assumptions about East–West relations became appropriate. A potential divergence within Western circles began to emerge as a result of Soviet pressure for the abandonment of the NATO plan for the modernisation of short-range nuclear weapons and eventually for the removal of nuclear weapons from Europe. In the new mood, this long-standing Soviet objective acquired a heightened appeal, especially in Germany, and raised major issues in relation to the long-term basis of Western defence policy.

The visit to Britain by General Secretary Gorbachev in April 1989 thus came at a point of transition in the new East–West relationship. Within the Soviet Union the difficulties of effecting fundamental change were becoming all too clear. In the West, the initial welcome to the Gorbachev reforms had been bolstered by the early achievements in foreign policy, but growing confidence was tempered by realisation that removal of the sources of mistrust would be a slow and painstaking task. In the United States, the Bush Administration had yet to define its policies. It was therefore not surprising that in his speech at the Guildhall on 7 April 1989 Gorbachev should refer to the substantial difficulties and disagreements as well as the complexity of putting into practice the points on which agreement had been reached in his talks with Mrs Thatcher. One sentence summed up the achievement of four years of the new policies: 'The range of trust has expanded.' Symbolically that increased trust could be seen in the relationship between the two leaders and in the welcome given to the formal invitation to the Queen to visit the Soviet Union. But how far can we expect trust to extend? Seventy years after Lloyd George, in that same Guildhall, inaugurated the establishment of relations with the new Soviet state, this is the question we have now to address.

THE ROOTS OF SOVIET POLICY

Over the decades, changes of leadership in both countries have brought changes in mutual perception, changes in the evaluation of the national interest and changes in policy.[3] In its essence, however, the relationship has evolved less than the parties themselves. The Soviet Union which Gorbachev inherited was no longer that of Stalin, still less that of Lenin. Margaret Thatcher's Britain is far from that

of Lloyd George. Yet, for all its growth to superpower status, the
Soviet Union of 1985 had, especially during the quarter century since
the fall of Khrushchev, been a static society, its immobilism reflected
in both domestic and foreign policies based on ideological confrontation. In the early 1980s that confrontation was still formulated by
the Soviet Union in the language of 1917 and it still evoked much
the same response in the West.

The change of generations in the Kremlin leadership of 1985 did
not, of itself, necessarily imply a lasting, qualitative change in the
British–Soviet relationship or in the factors which had conditioned
it. The new style of leadership and the apparent readiness for a more
constructive relationship were welcome, but for those who recalled
the brief flowering of relations after the death of Stalin, thirty-two
years earlier, it was not easy to be confident that the new mood
would prove irreversible. The record of cyclical fluctuation throughout
the seventy years had been such that profound change would be
required if the future relationship were to be based more on the
continuing search for areas of mutual interest than on the clash of
political belief and military power.

Any international relationship can and must in its day-to-day
conduct reflect a balancing of national interests. In a wider sense,
however, it reflects the interaction of national political instincts and
the perception by each state of both its own international objectives
and those of its neighbours. It may be argued that interests are more
durable than alliances, but interests are susceptible of identification,
evaluation and, to a certain extent, reconciliation. Political instincts
and perceptions, subjective in origin and ill-defined in character
though they may be, can prove more significant and more intractable.
They are, to a certain extent, open to manipulation, yet the manipul-
ators are themselves conditioned by their own political heritage. The
roots of political instinct lie in the very nature of the states, the
mentality and traditions of their peoples, their historical experience,
their political ideology and their national institutions. The relationship
traced in earlier chapters, for all its fluctuations, has been deep
rooted. That part of Soviet policy which has caused the greatest
concern to the United Kingdom has been motivated less by national
interest than by historical tradition, old habits, hardened mistrust
and great-power psychology, all nurtured in an environment cut off
from the world outside and driven by an ideology which has defined
the major powers of the world as enemies of the Soviet Union.

Underlying the clash of external policy has been a conflict between

British and Soviet systems of values based on different assumptions about some of the ultimate problems of the ordering of human society: the relationship between the individual, the society which sets the framework for his life and the source, be it human or divine, of moral authority over both. There is a complex but significant linkage between domestic and external factors in the formation of foreign policy and the deep divergence between the two societies has made peculiarly intractable the task of establishing a stable and productive relationship between the two states. Against such a background the fragility of the wartime alliance was not surprising.

An assessment of the potential for a more productive relationship must reflect an assessment of the potential for change in the societies and this, in present terms, means an assessment of the Gorbachev reforms. Soviet writers claim that 'the policy of any state is determined in its final analysis by its economic and social system',[4] but a society is not a mere system. It is perhaps natural that a British writer should give at least equal priority to the individuals who create, operate and sustain the system. The interlinking of the Russian mind and the Soviet system underlie many of the difficulties we experience in interpreting and responding to Soviet policy. Where they coincide, they powerfully reinforce one another. Where they conflict, the domination of the system over the individual is not absolute and the resultant stresses are beginning now to shape the process of change.

Has the absolutism of the Soviet system, we must ask, been alien to the instincts of the Russian people, or has it responded to them? How far has the expansionist thrust of Soviet foreign policy been the product of Marxist–Leninist doctrine and how far has it been rooted in Russian imperial instincts? There are no clear or easy answers.[5] What can be said is that the problems of constructing a working relationship with Russia did not have all their origins in the events of 1917. The geopolitical factors conditioning Russian policy were not swept away by the October Revolution. Nor did a new proletarian internationalism suppress the tensions on Russia's exposed frontiers. What the October Revolution did was to embrace within the bonds of an alien ideological system much that was essentially Russian. It produced a political structure which, as its revolutionary impulse faded, inhibited the natural processes of internal evolution and external adaptation. Lenin advocated flexibility, but it was essentially a tactical flexibility. The system itself was rigid in its structure, in its ideological base and in its external attitudes. As one dignitary of the Russian Orthodox Church reminded me: 'Conservatism and dogma are the twin pillars of the Orthodox Church and the Soviet state'. Or, as an Asian colleague more picturesquely put it: 'Communism is a car with one gear – good for getting out of the mud, but slow, noisy, and potentially dangerous on the motorway.'

The Soviet system has traditionally placed a relatively high value upon the common interest of society and a relatively low value upon the right of individual dissent. Yet, if conditioning in Marxist–Leninist ideology has lent the Soviet official mind an inflexibility of political analysis, the natural volatility, the unpredictability and the warmth of the Russian have never been wholly suppressed. In Soviet as in Tsarist days, in secular as in religious life, the Russian has accepted the ordering of his ways by higher authority. He has accepted, too, the ordering of the individual's life within the confines of a close community. But, perhaps because of the very rigidity of the system and the repression of dissent, the manifestation of both individual will and institutional change, when it does occur, is the more violent. Even regardless of the rigidity of the system, there are those features of Russia, the Russians and the other peoples of the Soviet Union which make at the same time for a deep continuity of tradition in policy and an occasional violent unpredictability. All this was in the Gorbachev inheritance.

CHANGE IN THE SOVIET SYSTEM

Given this inheritance, how far can we expect the balance between individual and state to be changed by the Gorbachev reforms? If we examine the language, the increased emphasis on individual rights is unmistakeable. There was much in Gorbachev's Party Conference speech of 28 June 1988 about the 'enrichment of human rights', the need to 'strengthen the guarantees of the social and economic rights of the individual' and to safeguard freedom of conscience. There was also a significant reference to the creation of a 'socialist law-based' state. In his report to the first session of the new Congress of People' Deputies he denounced the 'past political practice which proceeded from the pre-eminence of state interests over people's interests' and called for judicial and legal reform both to protect the individual and to strengthen law and order.[6] Such expressions may be no more than words, but in a doctrinally-based system language is important. Moreover, there are signs of substantive change. It is interesting that Soviet lawyers have already been in Britain to gain experience for the legal reform process in areas such as the application of habeas corpus. Even before 1985, the Soviet Union had already moved a long way from the years of Stalinist terror. References to the rights of the individual must, indeed, be interpreted in the limiting context of the Russian tradition and the socialist state, but there can be little doubt that a further significant evolution is now in train. The Soviet Union may well remain an authoritarian state. It need not remain one which is abhorrent to those who accept a Western concept of the rights of the individual.

Critical to the development of the Gorbachev reforms is the relationship of the leader to the party and that of the party to the citizen. In the whole seventy years of the Soviet state, if we exclude Malenkov's momentary grasp on supreme power, only one of its seven leaders, Khrushchev, has been removed from office by forces other than human mortality. At each stage, whether or not the principle of collective leadership has been proclaimed, the personality of one man – Lenin, Stalin, Khrushchev, Brezhnev, Gorbachev – has stamped itself upon the development of the Soviet Union and its foreign policy. But the lessons of Khrushchev's fall cannot have escaped Gorbachev. The system demonstrated its ability to remove a leader who, despite all the merit of his search for a better ordering of the Soviet economy and a more constructive relationship with the West, failed, by reason largely of his very Russian unpredictability, to hold the respect and support of his own party. The individual power of the leader is great, but it rests upon the power of the party and, with the growing sophistication of the Soviet state, it has become progressively more necessary for power to be deployed within the constraints of the system. The stagnation of the final years of Brezhnev reflected in large measure the decline in the powers of a man aged beyond his seventy-odd years, but they reflected also a tired and ageing structure of party and Government. The death in quick succession of Andropov and Chernenko marked symbolically the death of an era. The April Revolution of Gorbachev was a coincidence of the man and the circumstances reminiscent of the impact of Lenin upon the Russia of 1917. This, I have little doubt, is how Gorbachev, basing his reforms upon the conjunction of popular instinct and party power, sees his place in history.

Having risen to power through the party, Gorbachev knows that it is upon this base that his power rests. In none of his speeches or writings is there any suggestion that greater freedom of expression should be accompanied by an ending of the Communist party's

monopoly of power. Indeed, a constant theme is the need to improve
the strength of the party through improving its relationship with the
people and through measures of internal democracy designed to
eliminate inefficiency and corruption. The objective is a smoother,
more efficient, more responsive machine, one better able to implement the policies of the leadership and meet the needs of the people.
The theory and strategy of domestic and foreign policy are reserved
to the party and, as Gorbachev expressed it at the Party Conference:
'Without the directing work of the party and the implementation of
the political course . . . restructuring will be doomed politically,
ideologically and organisationally'. To the Congress, a year later, he
spoke of the party as the 'initiator and the main engine of restructuring', the 'integrating force' in the renewal of socialism.

The constitutional dilemma which the Soviet Union now faces is
to combine the retention of the essential authority of the single-party
state with the introduction of democratic reform. The 2250 members
of the new Congress of Peoples Deputies serve, in effect, as an
electoral college for the much smaller Supreme Soviet, the primary
representative body of the Soviet system, whose commissions are to
be in almost continuous session and to exercise a significant measure
of control over the governmental process. The first Deputies were
elected in March 1989, partly on a constituency basis and partly as
representatives of the great corporate bodies of the Soviet state, led
of course by the Communist Party itself. The elections produced a
remarkable demonstration of the mood of change and made apparent
the contradictions inherent in the reform process. Officially sponsored
candidates were rejected by massive majorities in favour of the
advocates of more far-reaching reform, led in Moscow by Boris
Yeltsin and in the Baltic States by those seeking greater autonomy
from Moscow. The essence of what may be called the Yeltsin
phenomenon lies not so much in specific policies, which in so far as
they are identifiable are an extreme form of Gorbachev's own policies,
but rather in the demonstrative rejection of the representatives of
the entrenched powers of the system and a determination to press
reform to unspecified extremes. The nationalist challenge, on the
other hand, could, in its more extreme manifestations, be seen as a
threat to the very fabric of the state.

The first session of the new Congress demonstrated both the
readiness of individual Deputies to challenge established authority
and the determination of the Party to ensure that its own hold
on supreme power was not placed in question. The election of

Gorbachev, already General Secretary of the Party, as Chairman of the Supreme Soviet (by a vote of 2123 to 87 with 11 abstentions) confirmed the unity of authority at the highest level, but it was significant that Yeltsin, rejected on the first vote as a member of the Supreme Soviet, was subsequently given a seat by the withdrawal of another Deputy. At the time of writing, the process of political reform is still in its earliest stage. Some of the elements are clear, but their practical effect will have to be tested over a period of years. There is, for instance, a clear intention that the term of office of individual members of the leadership, including the General Secretary, should be limited to two five-year terms, rather than being indefinitely prolonged at their own volition, and that there should be a delimitation of the powers of party and state, in which the role of the elected soviets, from the local level up to the Supreme Soviet, would be much enhanced. Reflecting the intention that the party should concern itself with the broad direction of policy rather than with its detailed implementation, a substantial reduction in the number of officials employed in the party apparatus is already taking place. The procedure for new local elections has yet to be devised, but it is expected that the first secretary of the party committee will normally stand for election to the chairmanship of the local soviet, thus linking, at each level, the party and the administrative machinery. The intention appears to be that all strategic decisions will still be prepared within the central machinery of the Party and that although they should then be the subject of rather more public debate, there should not be that organised development of a heterodox view which is the essence of parliamentary democracy. With the formation of the Moscow Group of Deputies and political turmoil in the Republics, the reform began to outpace its originator. The threat has been contained for the moment, but we must expect a period of instability until a new equilibrium is attained. Now, more than ever, the internal development of the Soviet Union is an open question.

So long as the Soviet Union continues to be a single-party state – and this must still be the preferred assumption – the processes of patronage will help to ensure responsiveness of the party to the leader's policies. The lifelong entrenchment of party functionaries may be broken and the natural tendency to sclerosis of the system diminished, but the new regime will breed its own vested interests. The initial power of a Soviet leader to effect radical change is substantial, but the experience of the early years of reform has shown that the combination of bureaucratic inertia, doctrinal rigidity and vested interest is more potent than, perhaps, Gorbachev himself had thought. It is precisely these very natural phenomena which have now produced the popular pressure for more drastic measures at the same time as the nationalist sentiments in the Baltic States, Azerbaidjan and Armenia, repressed for decades, have erupted with an unexpected violence.

It is tempting to see the outcome as either an acceleration of the pace of reform or a new repression. Either is possible, but neither is certain. The need for economic and political reform becomes ever more apparent. So does the potential reward, but so too does the price. The Chinese experience must prompt caution in prediction. The reform process cuts across many vested interests. If it fails to improve the lot of the Soviet citizen, Gorbachev's own tenure of office could be placed in doubt and there could be pressure for a reversion to the centralised control and political repression of earlier periods. The bankruptcy of those policies has, however, been so convincingly demonstrated that the stakes have now been raised. My own view is that there will be an uneasy balance as the initial enthusiasm fades and the magnitude of the task becomes apparent, but that by the imposition of internal discipline, Gorbachev will hold the system together and will press forward with economic reform while moving more cautiously on the political front. Progress may be less dramatic than in the early years, but if he can succeed in bringing together popular instinct and party power, there must be a real prospect that the changes now taking place will acquire a momentum and, with it, a range and a durability which will justify a major reappraisal of the nature of the Soviet state and, hence, of the place of the Soviet Union in the comity of nations.

THE BASIS OF SOVIET FOREIGN POLICY

It is a cardinal point of Marxist–Leninist theory that the October Revolution placed the conduct of international relations on a new basis. As the official History of Soviet Foreign Policy put it:

'there appeared an entirely new foreign policy', a change in 'the nature of foreign policy, its aims and tasks, the source of its strength and its influence, and its methods'.[7]

The concept of 'restructuring' or *perestroika* is now associated with Mikhail Gorbachev, but Gorbachev himself is careful to base his restructuring on Leninist principles. Prior to 1985 Soviet foreign policy had been based on an earlier concept of *perestroika*. In his book on the restructuring of international relations, published in 1978, Academician N. I. Lebedev followed the well-trodden argument that the influence of the October Revolution was felt in every aspect of the life of mankind and that the struggle between socialism and capitalism conditioned 'not only the foreign policy of states with different social systems, but the development of the whole system of international relations'. He quoted Lenin: 'If we lose sight of this, then we cannot pose the issues correctly in respect of even the furthest corner of the world.'[8] Thus, after 1917, the Soviet Union saw itself as the creator of a new type of foreign policy, new both in its techniques and in its basic assumption that the whole course of international relations was governed by the fact that 'the world outlook and class aims of socialism and capitalism are opposite and irreconcilable'.[9]

A proclamation of irreconcilable conflict did not, of itself, constitute a sufficient basis for the practical conduct of relations. It was clear to the leaders of the Soviet Union, from the earliest days, that if the irreconcilable class struggle in its pure form were also to determine the governmental relationship with Western Europe and the United States, the result might well be mutual disaster. The difficulty of avoiding armed conflict with major powers in certain circumstances was demonstrated in 1918 and 1941. Marxist–Leninist theory required the inevitable revolutionary triumph of socialism, but it was necessary to construct a theory which, by differentiating between the methods employed in pursuit of the long-term class conflict and those employed in the conduct of inter-state relations, would minimise the risk of armed conflict during the intervening period. 'Peace' is a basic principle of Leninist policy, but *pax Sovietica* has had a certain kinship with earlier concepts of imperial peace. Through the application of the doctrine of peaceful coexistence, the Soviet Union secured the flexibility which it needed in pursuing the practical conduct of day-to-day relations with the capitalist states, but it was a doctrine explicitly limited to the conduct of inter-state relations and never regarded as implying an abandonment of the 'revolutionary class struggle' or the 'liberation struggle of the oppressed peoples'. It was compatible with Soviet support for Communist activity wherever this seemed profitable and with the use of force in order to prevent the 'export of counter-revolution'. With the progress to socialism held to be scientifically inevitable, regression from that path could easily

be attributed to exported counter-revolutionary forces and the basis
established for the use of the Soviet army in the German Democratic
Republic, Hungary, Czechoslovakia and Afghanistan.

The progressive refinement of the doctrine of peaceful coexistence
has formed a large part of the theory of Soviet foreign policy. In the
early years it was seen as an essentially transient stage and, in relation
to the capitalist states, the formal distinction between inter-state
relations and revolutionary activity was preserved by the mechanism
of the Comintern. In the post-war years, and notably from the time
of Khrushchev onwards, with less opportunity for revolutionary
activity in Western Europe and the United States and the new hazard
of nuclear war, the time scale lengthened and peaceful coexistence
came to be regarded as a policy of indefinite duration. It was defined
in a Joint United Kingdom–Soviet statement of 17 February 1975[10]
as 'long-term, fruitful and mutually beneficial cooperation between
states, irrespective of their political, economic and social systems, on
the basis of full equality and mutual respect'. The problem for
successive British Governments has been that, whatever the 1975
definition might say, the doctrine of peaceful coexistence, as it was
understood by the Brezhnev Politburo, did not negate the concept
of an irreconcilable struggle between the two systems. Nor did a
policy of peace imply abandonment of the principle that the foreign
policy of the Soviet Union was based upon a combination of political
will and armed force, deployed with the objective of a constant
movement of the 'correlation of forces' in favour of socialism. A
fundamental change in the relationship between the Soviet Union
and the Western democracies required not merely a further step in
the progressive subordination of ideology to national interest in the
application of Soviet foreign policy, but a profound change in the
ideological basis of that policy.

A 'new political thinking' has now been proclaimed as the basis
for a new-style Soviet foreign policy. The task which confronts
Western policy makers is to determine whether seventy years of
doctrine and practice are to be discarded or merely repackaged. It
has been a constant theme of Gorbachev, even prior to his assumption
of the General Secretaryship, that ideology is not a set of stale
recipes. In the international field, the old recipes are being modified.
Many of the ingredients are familiar and the implications are as yet
uncertain, but the policy of peaceful coexistence is clearly undergoing
a substantial development in doctrinal as well as practical terms. In
1986, the international scene was regarded as more explosive than at

any time since the war and 'more difficult and unfavourable than in the first half of the 1980s', but the verbal emphasis was markedly less upon the 'irreconcilable struggle' and more upon interdependence, the unacceptability of armed conflict, the attainment of strategic balance at the lowest possible level, the recognition of the common interests of mankind and the pursuit of the continuing confrontation with capitalism by 'peaceful rivalry'. The Party Programme approved by the Congress omitted the classic definition of peaceful coexistence as 'a specific form of class struggle'. Gorbachev's own book, *Perestroika*,[11] was written primarily for an external readership and in it he heavily reinforced this theme, with the emphasis upon the need for policies of interdependence, a balancing of interests, an assertion that 'we are Europeans' and a rejection of confrontation. At a meeting with foreign party leaders to celebrate the 70th anniversary of the October Revolution he went further. He spoke of the search for 'a programmatic alternative to a society of antagonisms and confrontational tension on the world arena', rejected the doctrine of convergence, but rejected also the doctrine of irreconcilable conflict: 'Now it is no longer possible to view world development merely from the viewpoint of the struggle between two opposing systems'.[12] He brought this theme to a public climax in his speech to the United Nations on 9 December 1988 and Shevardnadze was explicit in his assessment of the foreign policy implications of the 19th Party Conference: 'We are fully justified in refusing to see in it [peaceful coexistence] a special form of the class struggle. . . . The struggle between two opposing systems is no longer a determining tendency of the present era'.[13] In articles and speeches, the process of reformulating Soviet foreign policy is progressing and there is talk of a 'new political *modus vivendi*' with the West.[14] In his call for 'liberation from dogmatic ideas and from conclusions which . . . had ceased to correspond with the realities of our days' and in his insistence upon the need for flexibility in the interpretation of Leninist theory, Gorbachev has proclaimed the need for an ideological base which will coincide more closely with the national interest of a Soviet Union where internal reform is incompatible with external confrontation. The practical implications have yet to be fully tested, but what is happening is far more than a change of style. The socialist state can mean many things and the new-style Gorbachev socialism may well provide the ideological basis for a Soviet state with which we may not agree, but alongside which we can live without a sense of mutual menace, while each pursues its national interest.

IDEOLOGY AND NATIONAL INTERESTS

If policies are to be based more on interest than on ideology, we are brought to the central issue in the day-to-day conduct of relations. Where does the Soviet national interest lie? I recollect an early lesson in foreign policy from Ernest Bevin: 'Think', he said, 'what it is you want. Do you want something from the other man or do you just want to kick him where it hurts?' However deep-rooted the mutual antipathy, it is the management of the fluctuating pattern of national interests, sometimes in conflict and sometimes in harmony, which is the stuff of intergovernmental relations. Neither the British nor the Soviet Government has, however, been able consistently to display the realism of Bevin. Neither has been clear as to its own objectives. One of the problems of the British–Soviet relationships has been that, apart from the clash of ideology and power, the areas at which British and Soviet interests intersect are relatively few. This owes something to the natural self-sufficiency of the Soviet Union, something to the fact that the two states are on either side of the main European land-mass, but something also to the self-imposed doctrinal isolation of the Soviet Union within a separate political and economic system of socialist states. The effect has been unnaturally to enhance the role of conflicting ideologies in the totality of the relationship.

It is, as we have seen, through the doctrine of peaceful coexistence that the Soviet Union has tried to ensure compatibility of interest and ideology, safeguarding the peace and security of its own territory and enjoying the practical benefits of intercourse with the West, while maintaining control over its allies and promoting the spread of Soviet socialism elsewhere in the world. It has been a policy designed – as a foreign policy should be – to promote Soviet interests. It has not, however, been well designed to take account of the interests of others. A Soviet reader may feel surprised that this should be perceived as a defect. In his surprise lies one of the traditional weaknesses of Soviet diplomacy and one of the causes of the breakdown of detente in the 1970s. A nation's own interests may be most durably safeguarded by arrangements which accommodate the interests both of its partners and of those who are not natural partners. In diplomacy as in business there can be profit in 'leaving something for the other man'. Sir William Hayter recalls Stalin expounding to Churchill at Potsdam his concept of the proper basis for Allied policy. Revenge, justice, the interests of the masses, the preservation of peace? None of these. It was, quite simply 'the calculation of forces'.[15]

It is not unreasonable to suppose that, behind all the doctrinal theorising, Soviet policy is still constructed upon the calculation, or as it is more normally expressed, the correlation of forces. It would be surprising and irrational if it were otherwise. The term, however, is one which comprises not only, or even primarily, the classic element of military power. It has embraced all those forces which, in Marxist–Leninist doctrine, will lead to the ultimate triumph of socialism and if Soviet policy is still designed to alter the correlation of forces in this direction it is likely to be inimical both to the present structure of Western society and to British overseas interests. It may also, however, prove inimical to the more specific, more limited and more easily attainable short- and medium-term requirements of the Soviet national interest. The experience of the Brezhnev years provided a classic demonstration of the ability of a Government, in pursuit of an ill-conceived attempt to change the correlation of forces in its favour, to end with an adverse shift in the correlation, combined with damage both to its own interests and to those of others. The hope for the future must be that the present Soviet leadership, while seeking by more sophisticated means to enhance the international authority and protect the national interest of the Soviet Union, will recognise that they can best do so by policies which benefit rather than threaten the interests of the Western powers and, indeed, of the wider international community. A rigorous analysis of the Soviet national interest should lead in this direction.

At some stages in Soviet history there has been little room for doubt as to what the Soviet Government believed the national interest to require in terms of foreign policy: the ending of hostilities with Germany in 1917–18; the establishment and maintenance of Bolshevik power throughout as much as possible of the territory of Imperial Russia; the establishment of the frontier; the securing of international recognition; the construction of the economy; security against Germany and Japan; the defeat of Germany and a total safeguard against any repetition of 1941; the attainment first of military and then of economic parity with the United States. In the pursuit of the war against Germany in the autumn of 1917, British and Soviet interests were directly opposed. In the 1920s and 1930s, when ideological considerations were dominant, there was little underlying conflict of interest. Between 1935 and 1939 the potential coincidence of interest was not perceived by the British Government and between 1939 and

1941 it was not perceived by the Soviet Government. Between 1941
and 1945, it was briefly perceived by both. In the post-war world,
where British interests required a stable international structure, the
actual conflict was at its sharpest. But how far was it a conflict of
interest? How far, in a period when the European-based imperial
structures were in process of dismantlement, did it reflect a Soviet
estimate not of the national interest, but of the changing correlation
of forces in relation to the eventual triumph of socialism? The need
for absolute security against any renewed attack from Germany might
have been held to require the political and military domination of
Eastern and much of Central Europe by the Soviet Union even after
the threat had ceased to be realistic. It is, however, arguable that
the Soviet interest was better served by the Austrian State Treaty
than by the suppression of Hungary and Czechoslovakia; and that
no rational calculation of Soviet interests required the attempted
subjugation of Afghanistan or, indeed, the military support accorded
to many of the Soviet Union's proteges in the Third World. Today,
it is arguable that the reform of Soviet foreign policy reflects a
recognition that the old policies have done nothing to enhance either
the prosperity or the security of the Soviet Union; that internal
reform requires all the resources which the state can muster; that
additional external commitments can be accepted only in so far as
they are clearly required in order to safeguard a vital national interest;
and that existing ones should be re-evaluated in accordance with
their resource cost. In every respect, whether in terms of conserving
domestic resources or of acquiring the benefits of scientific, commercial and technological intercourse with the West, a stable strategic
relationship based upon a stable political relationship is the current
requirement. The need to underpin Soviet security by such a
relationship becomes the more apparent as the progressive disintegration of the political structure of Soviet imperial power renders
correspondingly more hazardous any recourse to force in an attempt
to bolster the defence glacis in Eastern Europe.

THE POWER RATIO

Convenient though it has been to analyse the development of British–
Soviet relations in terms of the two partners, such an analysis has
become increasingly unrealistic, not so much by reason of the increase
in the role of multilateral diplomacy, but more as a result of the

changing international power ratio. In the 1920s and 1930s policy towards the United Kingdom was a major element in Soviet foreign policy. After 1945, it was only rarely that the Soviet Union needed to consider policy towards the United Kingdom other than as an element in policy towards the West. The United Kingdom, on the other hand, needed to formulate a policy directed specifically at relations with the Soviet Union, but could implement such a policy only within the bounds of a wider East–West relationship conditioned increasingly by American policy and formulated, in certain aspects, within the NATO alliance, in others within the European Community.

We have noted how Soviet policy has reflected the concept of a correlation of forces embracing the whole range of factors on which power may be based, from the motive power of ideology, through the structure of society, the political system and the economy, to the ultimate of armed force. In 1917 the long-term damage to British power inflicted by the war was not yet apparent. The infant Soviet state, heir though it might be to the territory and power of imperial Russia, was only just capable of survival. Its revolutionary ambitions stretched far beyond its ability to realise them. Britain, by contrast, with its Empire intact, might lack the economic muscle of the United States, but still briefly commanded an unrivalled combination of world-wide political, economic and military power. To the Soviet Union, New York and London were the twin citadels of capitalism and a defeated Germany the proving ground for the next move to the triumph of socialism. In 1922, Lloyd George could regard Rapallo as the alliance between the two pariahs of international society and the Soviet Union and Germany knew that they were so regarded.

Throughout the 1930s, despite the swift decline in British fortunes, the British attitude towards the Soviet Union was still marked by a conscious sense of military, political, economic and moral superiority and the Soviet leadership was in no position to contest this. It was natural that Britain should hold the initiative in determining the scope of the relationship and inevitable, given the political orientation of the parties, that it should be unproductive. Until the early summer of 1939, in so far as the Soviet Union was of any interest at all to the British Government, it was not as a military power but as a potential market for British goods, a source of subversion of the British worker and a focus of revolution internationally. It was in these terms that relations were conducted.

Except in conditions of active warfare – and sometimes even then – the perception of power may matter more than its reality. The

differing perception of the two sides was well illustrated by the
casualness with which Chamberlain pursued the tripartite negotiations
of 1939, the decision of the Soviet Union to conclude the Molotov–
Ribbentrop agreement and the brusqueness with which Stalin rejected
Churchill's approach in 1940. It was the direct use of military power
which enabled the Soviet Union to secure its post-war grip on Europe,
and throughout the years of the cold war, it was the awareness of
Soviet military power which conditioned the British relationship with
the Soviet Union. The politics of the years from 1945 to 1953 were
essentially an extrapolation from the facts of 1945, with military
power and territorial control setting the parameters. What happened
through the following thirty-five years was that military power
continued to dominate the relationship, despite the fact that it was
becoming increasingly irrelevant as an instrument of relations between
major powers. Again, what mattered was the perception. For perception is the essence of deterrence. The perception mattered equally
to both Britain and the Soviet Union. Khrushchev's own personality
was itself a symbol of the confidence of the Soviet Union in its power
and it was a challenge of power to which, in their various ways,
Churchill, Eden, Macmillan, Eisenhower and Kennedy had to respond. So, while the future international role of the United Kingdom
was being constrained by economic weakness, the military confrontation continued. It was the military balance between the two
superpowers and the projection of Soviet military and political power
into the Third World which determined the major items on the
agenda of East–West negotiation. In this situation, the limited
political effectiveness of the very high level of bilateral activity
between Britain and the Soviet Union during the late 1960s was not
surprising.

By the beginning of the 1980s, the balance was changing. Soviet
political analysts were speaking less of the movement of the correlation of forces in favour of socialism and more of the complexity and
danger of the international system. The drive to project Soviet power
had passed its peak. The attempt to subjugate Afghanistan was like
a wave which obscures for a time the ebbing of the tide, but which,
as it in turn ebbs, reveals yet more starkly the reefs and shoals. Soviet
ideology had lost its force both in Europe and in the Third World.
The economy was drifting slowly into the stagnation of the late
Brezhnev years. Only in the technology of space and in the production
and deployment of the less sophisticated forms of conventional and
nuclear military hardware could the Soviet Union still outstrip the

West. The deterrent power of nuclear arms has been the greatest single factor in the history of international relations since 1945, but by 1985 the one threat which the Soviet Union did not face was the threat of armed attack. For a state whose power was constrained by an outdated ideology, a senile leadership, a disillusioned citizenry, a sclerotic economy and a restless empire, the strategic rocket force, the pride of the Soviet armed forces, was as irrelevant as Khrushchev's shoe – and rather more expensive.

As the Soviet Union declined, so the British Government, with the confidence of determined policies backed by economic success, was coming to the fore again in the formation of Western policy. The domination of the East–West negotiating pattern by the bilateral American–Soviet negotiations on nuclear weaponry indicated the extent to which American policy could still define the nature of the relationship with the Soviet Union, but by the time Gorbachev assumed the leadership, the prospect which was beginning to emerge was one of a more complex power structure. To the extent that Soviet policy accepts that the realities of the international scene will not fit conveniently into the straitjacket of a polarised ideological conflict and to the extent that the nuclear confrontation of the superpowers loses its dominant position in East–West relations the scope for an effective British policy is likely to be enhanced.

Already however, the balance is changing once more. Within NATO, the Bush administration has taken the lead with proposals for the attainment of European parity on conventional arms as the route towards a more open, re-integrated Europe and Germany is beginning to regain its pivotal role, as the Soviet Union shapes a strategy designed to secure the fruits of cooperation and restore its flagging vitality without prejudice to the development of socialism within and outside its borders. In the early stages of restructuring, the problems are mounting faster than the achievements. It is not just a matter of repeating Peter the Great's symbolic edict depriving the boyars of their beards, but of resolving the inherent conflict between socialist planning and a market economy, between democracy and the single party system. Externally, the dissolution of the Soviet empire has begun. But will a new rationalism in foreign policy finally displace the old dreams of power? If the Gorbachev reforms fail, the Soviet Union will remain a superpower only in military terms, but an unstable and dangerous superpower. If they achieve even a moderate degree of success, it may gain stability and with it attain the full stature of a European superpower, posing a more compelling challenge to Europe than at any time since the Revolution. In that event, will not the new correlation of forces bring a reassessment of the Soviet national interest which will once again conflict with British objectives?

Here is the dilemma for the policy-makers. There can be no guarantee of future trends. There are, however, substantial grounds for optimism. The Soviet leadership have seen the failure of a crude attempt to move the correlation of forces in favour of Soviet socialism. If the Gorbachev reforms are to succeed and the Soviet Union is to realise its full economic potential, there will have to be an internal structural change and an interlinking of the Soviet and Western economies, so far-reaching that the community of interest will be more deeply rooted than at any time – including 1941–5 – since 1917. In short, the precondition of Soviet success is a realisation of the community of interest. That realisation will not necessarily prevail in the event of a revival of dogmatic nationalism, but the price of its disruption can be so heavy as to constitute a better guarantee of future relations than any formal treaty. Whatever the fate of the Gorbachev reforms and whichever way the power ratio moves, the final years of the century are likely to test the ability of both the British and Soviet Governments to adapt the conduct of their relationship to the requirements of a more complex environment which neither can control.

THE DEVELOPMENT OF BRITISH POLICY

It has been a constant claim of Soviet diplomacy that the Soviet Union pursues a 'principled' foreign policy and it is true that, despite some remarkable reversals, the existence of an elaborate body of doctrine gave Soviet policy prior to 1985 the appearance of a degree of consistency and predictability – sadly in its less attractive features – which was less obvious in the more pragmatically-based policies of British Governments. Foreign Office planning had its effect, for instance in determining the shape of the post-1945 international structure, but it is not in the nature of British Prime Ministers, their Foreign Secretaries or their Foreign Office staffs to spend over-long on the theoretical concepts underlying British policy. Nor, in a democracy, can Government, whatever its doctrinal disposition, pursue indefinitely policies which fail to take account of the lasting instincts, the changing moods or the developing interests of the individual citizen.

The gravity and intractability of the issues bound up in the British–Soviet relationship have made its conduct a matter of particular personal concern to British Prime Ministers from David Lloyd George to Margaret Thatcher. The historical record shows the very different personal imprint of each as well as the occasional conflict of opinion within the Government and among its advisers. (Against this background it should perhaps be parenthetically recorded that during the difficult period at the beginning of the 1980s, when I was personally concerned, despite some public dispute over the course of British policy, there was broad agreement within Government, both on the need to resist Soviet expansion and on the search for a more constructive relationship. There was little room for doubt about where the British interest lay and single-mindedness in its pursuit must have contributed to the effectiveness of British policy.)

Externally, the complex pattern of other relationships has tended over the years to constrain the British Government's ability to formulate and implement a consistent and effective policy for the conduct of relations with the Soviet Union. We have, for instance, noted at various points the need for British policy to take account of the changes in the policies of the United States. From Woodrow Wilson to George Bush, the accent of American policy has changed with each change in the Presidency and no realistic British policy could ignore this factor. Equally, we have noted how British policy has had to take account of the evolution of European opinion, as evidenced for instance in the key role of Germany in the 1920s and 1930s and again in the 1970s; in the alternating intransigence and weakness of France in the early years; in the declining influence of the Communist parties of Western Europe; and in the development of the formal requirements of a common commercial policy combined with the less formal process of political consultation within the European Community. If, in the 1990s, the strategic nuclear relationship plays a less dominant role in East–West relations, the European element in British policy may be expected to loom larger as a factor in both British–American and British–Soviet relations.

With all these provisos, and despite all the twists and turns, the inconsistencies, contradictions and improvisations which have marked British policy towards the Soviet Union, certain persistent elements both of principle and of practice can emerge. From 1918, when the Cabinet rejected Winston Churchill's proposal for a military campaign to crush Bolshevism, successive British Governments, with only brief exceptions, have been trying to come to terms with the Soviet Union. Their object has been more to prevent damage to British interest than to secure positive benefit, the scope for which has normally been limited and, even when it did exist, has been liable to pass unperceived. The element of ideological conflict has not been lacking on the British side, but the pursuit of an ideological campaign against Soviet communism as a distinct and coordinated element of governmental policy was limited to a relatively brief period in the 1950s. Previously and subsequently it has doubtless been perceived by the Soviet Union in areas where British policy has ranged beyond a narrowly-defined national interest, for instance in the attempt to bring about a closer inter-relationship between the countries of Eastern and Western Europe and to exploit the *locus standi* given by the Helsinki agreement in respect of the recognition of human rights. The full application of this instrument may indeed conflict with internal and external policies which the Soviet Union has pursued, but it does not involve an inherent or necessary conflict of British and Soviet interests.

Faced with a Soviet premise of irreconcilable conflict, and since 1945 by a combination of Soviet political power and Soviet armed forces in the heart of Europe, the primary British requirement has been to maintain the security of the United Kingdom against both armed attack and political subversion. The former has become an improbable contingency. The latter, despite the continuing efforts of the KGB and the International Department of the CPSU, has become a diminishing reality. The experience of Soviet policy has, however, been such that no prudent British Government, whether of the left or the right, could ignore either. The need to safeguard the worldwide spread of British interests, dependent upon the maintenance of peace and stability, has required policies opposed to the extension of Soviet power and Communist ideology, not only within but beyond the European continent: consolidation of the European-Atlantic relationship as the basis of British security; reduction of the level of military confrontation both in Europe and globally; and frustration of Soviet-inspired subversion. The nature of British interests is slow to change, but recent decades have seen major change in the environment within which they have to be pursued. Now there is the prospect that one of the more static features of that environment, the Soviet Union, may change. A relationship which has its origin in differing concepts of society, differing concepts of the conduct of international relations and differing concepts of European security will not easily be transformed in response to a change in one factor, but if the Soviet national interest does now require the development of a wide-ranging community of interest with the West, the implications for British policy and for the conduct of British–Soviet relations could be substantial. In place of the comfortable certainties of an entrenched defence are the challenges of mobility. Before addressing the policy issues bound up with this change in the nature of the British–Soviet relationship, it may be appropriate to consider some special features of the mechanism through which that relationship is conducted.

THE CONDUCT OF RELATIONS

The instruments through which relations with the Soviet Union are conducted reflect the peculiar circumstances created by the mismatch of systems. If we look at the relationship between Britain and the United States, France, Germany, or for that matter any of the nations of Western Europe, North America or much of the non-Communist world, we find a complex web of personal and institutional links covering the whole area of human activity and, for the most part, carried on without even the knowledge, let alone the involvement of governments. Businessmen, bankers, students and swimmers; holidaymakers, scientists, priests and professors; dancers, journalists, poets and musicians – all create the reality of a living relationship, while the politicians, the diplomats, the bureaucrats and the soldiers conduct the limited business of government.

In tracing the course of British–Soviet relations we have necessarily concentrated upon the inter-governmental relationship conducted through the Foreign Office and the Moscow Embassy.[16] Because of the nature of the Soviet system, many non-governmental activities have had to be brought within that framework and within it the fostering of commercial and cultural relations can go some way towards giving the relationship the depth and stability which, as yet, it noticeably lacks. It will, however, be a long task to overcome the artificiality inherent in an officially structured relationship.

The importance of the Soviet Union in British foreign policy and the confrontational nature of the relationship have also given a special character to the meetings of Heads of Government and Foreign Ministers. The tripartite summits of the wartime years were *sui generis* in that they took place in pursuit of a common military objective. Their expiry in the acrimony of the Council of Foreign Ministers indicated the intractability of the underlying political conflict and the experience of the Khrushchev era was symbolised by the failure of the Paris summit. With the end of multilateral summitry with the Soviet Union, save for the ceremonial of Helsinki, the subsequent meetings of Heads of Government have been bilateral, their outcome reflecting the respective power, both national and personal, of the participants. They have essentially been encounters across a political divide rather than within a common system. They have not served to resolve major conflict, but where circumstances favourable to a positive development of relations already existed, as with the Thatcher–Gorbachev meetings, a summit could intensify the trend and provide a spur for action.

Below the level of summitry, the practice of regular British–Soviet political consultation at the level of Ministers of Foreign Affairs or their deputies is enshrined in the 1975 Protocol on Consultations. In bad times this rather infertile instrument served to sustain at least a minimal political dialogue. Now that the political climate is easier, there are regular and useful exchanges at both ministerial and official level on major areas of current international interest such as the handling of Middle East problems and arms control negotiations. The practice of quiet, informal discussion between officials of the two Foreign Ministries may, indeed, be one of the more rewarding features of the bilateral relationship. The maintenance of parliamentary exchanges, a process which provided the opportunity for Gorbachev's first visit to Britain, may also prove productive if the Gorbachev reforms lead to a more substantial role for members of the Supreme Soviet. The reality is, however, that consultations will take place not because there is an agreement to that effect but because the will exists in both countries. They will prosper only in so far as there is a recognition of common interest.

The multilateral international organisations have been of only intermittent relevance to the conduct of British–Soviet relations. The Soviet Union has sought and obtained membership of many of the principal organisations, both technical and general, from the time of the League of Nations onwards. It is in the nature of such bodies that groupings of members should develop for the purpose of pursuing certain interests. Sadly, at the political level, this tendency has been aggravated by the use of the United Nations as an arena for the gladiatorial contest of ideology and power and it has only rarely been possible to develop a genuine community of interest. If there is indeed to be a move away from the concept of 'irreconcilable conflict' as the basis for Soviet foreign policy, this may very appropriately be put to the test in the United Nations. In retrospect, we may see the handling of the Iran–Iraq conflict in that forum as the first sign of a new trend. If that trend is sustained and developed, the position of Britain and the Soviet Union as permanent members of the Security Council will assume an increasing importance in the totality of the intergovernmental relationship. In more technical organisations, the search for common ground has been less inhibited, but the underlying political confrontation has never been wholly absent. Across the whole field, the new Gorbachev style of foreign policy, with a greater openness of presentation and a readiness to substitute reasoned argument for public polemics, has begun to make itself felt and the policy of interdependence has brought an interest in Soviet membership of even those organisations such as the General Agreement on Tariffs and Trade and the International Monetary Fund which are rooted in a commercial and financial structure essentially alien to the Soviet system.

POLITICAL SUBVERSION AND COVERT OPERATIONS

One strand of the relationship which merits separate mention is the conduct, in parallel with the Governmental relationship, of Soviet-controlled political activities addressed directly to overseas individuals and organisations. It was a principle of the Communist Party of the Soviet Union that the seizure of power within Russia was only part of a worldwide revolutionary process, the further stages of which were the responsibility not of the Government but of the party. The 'export of revolution' was officially disavowed and the pursuit of revolutionary activity in Britain itself and in the Empire was conducted notionally on a party basis, largely through the Comintern. The dissociation of party and state was, however, never more than formal and Soviet-inspired subversive activity was a major object of British concern in the 1920s. In later years, the direct threat of Communism in Britain became less significant and, in its place, came the heightened use of the whole structure of Soviet organisations devoted to 'peace' and 'friendship' as well as the attempt to exercise influence through Communists within the trade union movement and elsewhere.[17] It is not easy to draw a clear dividing line between the legitimate use of press, radio and direct contact as a means of informing and influencing the citizens of another country and the subversive exploitation of those who sympathise with a particular point of view. The contrast between open and closed societies aggravates the problem and it is from precisely this difficulty of differentiation that the covert operator draws much of his strength. What is relevant here is that such operations are a recognised element in the conduct of Soviet foreign policy and that they have been a cause of damage to Soviet relations both with the British Government itself and with those organisations upon which the Soviet Union has sought to exercise influence. In the reverse direction, the provision of British finance for anti-Bolshevik groups in Russia was a direct, partly overt and partly covert governmental operation. Its total failure has been chronicled in earlier chapters and it was not pursued after the recognition of the Soviet Government. The subsequent 'human rights' strand of British policy, pursued both on an overtly governmental level and by private British organisations, was doubtless seen by the Soviet authorities as an attempt to influence the development of Soviet society and over the years it was a not insignificant element in the total relationship.

The orthodox intelligence operation, by contrast, raises few problems of definition. We have seen how it has surfaced over the years with the suborning of individuals through ideology, sex and greed and the subsequent arrest, expulsion or defection of a variety of Soviet agents engaged in all the classic operations for the illicit acquisition and transmission of intelligence from Britain. This is an area in which all Governments operate to a varying extent, but in which the long Russian tradition and the particular advantage of a closed system operating into an open one have led to a preponderant weight of Soviet effort. It has not been the fact of Soviet intelligence operations in Britain and against the Embassy in Moscow which has aggravated the normal relationship, but the use of peculiarly disagreeable techniques, the occasional remarkable success as with Maclean, Philby and the atomic spies, and, above all, the sheer scale. The exposure of the occasional agent, whether British or Soviet, may be regarded as a normal feature of international life. The exposure of 105 Soviet agents in 1971 suggested a certain obsessive preoccupation with questionable habits. Subsequent Soviet attempts to re-establish the KGB presence in London have resulted in further expulsions, retaliatory expulsions of British citizens and diplomats from Moscow and a succession of unproductive 'visa war' skirmishes. It was not without justification that, in giving evidence to the House of Commons Foreign Affairs Committee on 1 February 1989, my successor in Moscow, Sir Bryan Cartledge, spoke of the KGB's activities in London as the greatest recurrent problem in the bilateral relationship and it is a sorry commentary on the persistence of this strand in the relationship that, as this book goes to press a further wave of mutual expulsions should be precipitated. Within the Soviet Union, KGB attempts to control and exploit normal contact with Soviet citizens have constituted an added constraint to the development of a sounder relationship at the personal level. Less personal, less squalid and perhaps, for this reason, less disruptive in their impact upon relations have been the technical systems employed by Governments on either side of the East–West divide for surveillance of the operations and interception of the communications of the other. It would no doubt be unrealistic to look for any significant change in the relevance of intelligence activities to the wider British–Soviet relationship, but it is hard to see how the full benefits of an expanded bilateral relationship can be achieved without a corresponding change in Soviet policy concerning the use of the machinery of diplomacy for the purpose of covert intelligence activities.

12 A Policy for the 1990s

TOWARDS A COMMUNITY OF INTEREST

The pattern of seventy years of dealings with the Soviet Union has been inherently antagonistic. There has been a cyclical fluctuation in the degree of tension, but the pattern has never been decisively broken. The terms of the confrontation have been in large measure defined by the Soviet Union, but the Soviet Government and the Governments of the Western democracies have learnt to manage their relationship in such a way as to control the confrontation at a level below that which might involve the risk of hostilities between them. The more extreme prophecies, whether of conflict or of harmony, have been unfulfilled and a certain stability has been attained – the stability of balanced and controlled tension, but stability none the less. Viewed in retrospect against such hazards as the Berlin blockade, the Korean War, the Cuban missile crisis, the succession of Third World conflicts and the swiftly escalating level of nuclear weaponry, it has been no small achievement to establish practical limits within which the essential confrontation has been contained. What of the future? An indefinite continuation of the past pattern is an unappealing prospect. What might take its place?

Any realistic appraisal of the scope for future British policy must start from recognition of the extent to which the tone of the whole East–West relationship is still set by the relationship between the Soviet Union and the United States. Its essentially adversarial character has derived in part from a clash of ideology and in part from a clash of superpower psychology. The borderline between national ambition and national interest is hard to define. Viewed objectively, the national interests of the two superpowers are by no means irreconcilable, but a resolution of the conflict requires changes in the policies and perceptions of the two parties. In the Soviet Union these changes are now in train, and, with a new President in the White House, the American–Soviet relationship is beginning to be redefined. The United States and its Western partners have to make certain assumptions about Soviet policy. What should they be?

325

For a British pragmatist it is easy to underrate the ability of the doctrinally motivated leaders of a single-party state to define long-term objectives and to pursue through all the improvisations of day-to-day politics the strategy necessary for their attainment. Within the Soviet Union the Gorbachev reforms are still in the early stages of realisation. We can see the strategy unfolding. We can see, too, the mixture of doctrinal opposition, vested interest and administrative sloth which stands in the way of its rapid and comprehensive implementation. The check to over-rapid reform in China, the popular discontent and the potentially disastrous loss of standing by a party leadership which could sustain itself only by the use of its army against its own people constitute a warning which will not pass unheeded in Moscow. No Western observer – and probably no Soviet participant – can say with confidence how far and how fast the Soviet reforms will proceed. The new policy is, says Gorbachev, no 'temporary zig-zag'. Yet still, the ultimate objective is not clear. A more efficient state, a state in which there is a greater unity and harmony between party and people, a state which will set the world an example of socialist success – all this, certainly. But beyond this the external objectives are less easy to define. Has the ultimate worldwide triumph of socialism faded beyond recall? Is that unity of socialist doctrine and Soviet power which has guided foreign policy for so many years now a thing of the past? Is a revival of the threat of Soviet hegemony in the Europe of the twenty-first century as unreal as the threat of a new German hegemony?

There are those who believe that the new style of Soviet foreign policy represents no more than a temporary readjustment, necessary in order to allow time for the internal reforms to establish a new and firmer base from which Gorbachev or his successors will develop the traditional policies of Russian expansionism and Communist doctrinal imperialism. I have discussed in the previous chapter the reasons why such a policy might not coincide with the Soviet interest, but there can be no certainty on this point. It can be argued that the correct Western course is to pursue policies designed to aggravate the adverse correlation of forces, thus intensifying those pressures which have already induced the first reforms, until in due course the internal tensions already manifest lead to the final collapse of Soviet socialism. This line of argument has been pursued intermittently ever since 1917 and, although little heard now in Britain or in the other countries of Western Europe, it could recur and it has to be addressed, if only briefly. An embattled leadership, still commanding the vast land-mass and military potential of the Soviet Union, would be likely to respond to external pressure with a mixture of internal repression and xenophobic nationalism, intensifying the most dangerous tensions of the contemporary scene. We may already be witnessing the terminal stage of old-style Soviet socialism, but a policy designed to hasten its demise by external pressure, even if it had any theoretical justification, would run so counter to the political instincts of the Western – and, in particular, the Western European – democracies that it could, quite simply, never be implemented. It is necessary only to recall for a moment the disarray in Europe in 1981, when, in circumstances of heightened tension, the United States sought to impose economic sanctions on the Soviet Union, to recognise the total unreality of a policy of increased pressure at a time when the Soviet Union is moving towards a relaxation of tension. The risk, in fact, is not so much that a policy of pressure might be implemented, but that it might at some future moment of heightened tension – and there will be such moments – carry just enough emotional conviction to lead governments into that fitful confusion of policy which began with Balfour's first War Cabinet memorandum and, in the process, to tear the Western alliance apart.

On the other hand, a Soviet reversion to policies of active hostility towards the Western powers and their worldwide interests cannot yet be definitively excluded as a long-term planning assumption. Such policies would have to be met with a response as firm as that which has been given in the past. They would, doubtless, in the final analysis, operate to the disadvantage of the Soviet Union, but the resulting clash would represent a hazard to peace which no responsible Western Government would willingly provoke. Thus the search for policies which will safeguard essential Western interests and at the same time reduce the risk of conflict may proceed from broadly similar premises, whether undertaken in London or Washington. Western policies will need to be such as will reinforce those interests which the Soviet Union has in common with the West and simultaneously weaken those ideological and historical influences which operate in the direction of Soviet geographical and ideological expansion. In the area of economic, scientific and technological cooperation, the potential for mutual advantage is apparent. This – which we might call the 1921 policy – is valid and as I have argued in an earlier passage, it may draw the Soviet Union into a network of common interests which cannot lightly be discarded. Experience suggests, however, that by itself it is not enough. The crucial requirement is to go beyond it and seek to develop a common security interest, based on recognition that no rational concept of national interest involves a threat by either party to the national security of the other; that there are threats which both may face through the escalation of regional conflicts or the accidents of nuclear weaponry; and that cooperation to reduce such risks is in the mutual interest. Expressed in these terms, the community of interest is self-evident. The ability to make the self-evident principle into the political reality is the test of statesmanship.

THE STRATEGIC RELATIONSHIP

The direct conflict of British and Soviet policy is most sharply defined in the area of defence policy. The greater part of British defence planning is still founded upon the presumption that the Soviet Union is a hostile power. If there were any absolutes in history, this presumption would, on the evidence of seventy years which have seen every variation from formal alliance to undeclared war, be a doubtful candidate for inclusion among them. The presumption of hostility has been based upon four principal elements: the proclaimed and proven ideological conflict; the focusing of that conflict on certain identifiable areas of tension, particularly in Europe; the level and disposition of the Soviet armed forces; and the evidence of the Soviet Government's readiness to use those forces in order to secure its political objectives. Given the difficulty of constructing a strategic defence policy without a presumed enemy and the absence, among the major powers, of a credible alternative candidate, the postulate of Soviet hostility has provided a convenient basis for British defence planning and has doubtless been fully reciprocated in Moscow. There is reason to begin to question some of the elements on which it is based, particularly in so far as the current Soviet military posture may no longer coincide with the national interest of the Soviet Union. In formal terms it is now the policy of the Soviet Government to seek security by a combination of 'reasonable sufficiency' in the armed forces and the political search for a balance of interests. The new doctrine is beginning to be translated into practice. The aim of Western policy must be to create a relationship which at the same time promotes this reorientation of Soviet policy and inhibits reversion. The political reality is, however, that a long and gradual development of mutual confidence will be required before the presumption of latent, if not active, hostility ceases to be a cardinal feature of British and Soviet defence policy. Until this happens a certain schizophrenia will not be eliminated from the relationship. Its control requires that strategic policy should be based on realistic political assessment.

Because the British–Soviet relationship has at various critical stages been defence-oriented, British policy has been formulated to an abnormal extent in the context of military alliances. Such alliances, born of a conjunction of national interest and political circumstance, tend, while they endure, to emphasise the particular polarisation of forces which prevailed at their conception and, in their dissolution, to set up new patterns of tension. It was the breach of the 1914–18 alliance by the withdrawal of Russia which brought the first conflict of British–Soviet interest. It was in that same alliance that the Allied military operations in Russia were conceived in 1917–18. The failed search for a British–French–Soviet alliance in 1939 was followed by the British–Soviet Treaty of Alliance in 1942 and the tripartite wartime alliance with the United States, until the post-war confrontation was formalised in the alliance structures of NATO and the Warsaw Pact. Today it is more necessary than ever for the Western powers to reconcile within NATO their military and political objectives in the conduct of relations with the Soviet Union, while within the Warsaw Pact, the Soviet Union faces the still more complex task of reshaping the relationship with reluctant allies. The alliance structure does not absolve the British Government from the responsibility of national policy formulation. It may well complicate the process, but it may also, as with the endorsement of Margaret Thatcher's policy of reopening the dialogue with the Soviet Union, give national policy a firmer multinational base. Within NATO, the need for adequate defence against armed attack has been consistently balanced by recognition of the need for measures of arms limitation and for constructive dialogue. If the alliance is to remain in harmony with the underlying political realities, that balance must reflect their evolution.

In so far as the British strategic relationship to the Soviet Union is a function of the corresponding United States relationship, the progress of US-Soviet negotiations on the balance of strategic weaponry and the whole thrust of the US-Soviet political relationship must condition British assessments. The agreement on intermediate range nuclear forces has begun to establish a measure of East–West confidence and a certain community of interest is demonstrated by the existing agreements on the avoidance of accidental conflict. The further reduction of strategic weapons will take the process further. The level at which the nuclear balance is struck will not, of itself, greatly affect the British–Soviet strategic relationship or invalidate the case for retention of the minimum credible British deterrent until a point is reached at which the basic strategic assumptions have themselves to be revised. Agreement on the final abolition of chemical weapons may be of particular value as an area where recognition of the common interest of the superpowers can provide a basis for action to the general good of humanity. It is hard to envisage any effective agreement to inhibit the continuing development of more sophisticated military technology. Decisive here will be the conclusions of individual Governments on the correlation between the perceived military threat and the available resources. Frustration of the US Strategic Defence Initiative, will continue to be a Soviet objective and, although in this respect the technology differential means that the interests of the two sides do not coincide, the facts themselves may help to resolve an important area of strategic uncertainty, while simultaneously easing one of the budgetary pressures felt by both parties.

It may be concluded from the foregoing that the key to British strategic assumptions lies less in nuclear arms negotiations than in the political relationship with the Soviet Union and the balance of conventional forces in Europe. The East–West frontier through Central Europe has been – certainly in the British perspective – the focal point of strategic tension and although the Far East looms large in Soviet thinking it is in Europe that the critical tests of mutual intentions will be made. In this process the military and political factors are closely linked. In Moscow, I tried without apparent success to persuade Soviet officials to recognise how the disposition of their forces appears when viewed from the West against the simple ratio of the distance from the Elbe to the North Sea in one direction and to the Urals – if not beyond – in the other. But the burden of history weighs heavily on international relations and the scars of 1941 are still felt. If Western concerns are to be recognised, it is necessary to recognise equally the deep, if today unrealistic, Soviet obsession with the security of the Western frontier. After decades of multilateral negotiation, the attempt to reduce the deployment of conventional forces on either side of the European divide is being resumed. A success here will do much to establish confidence, but it will have to be paralleled by progress in the difficult and continuing process of political adjustment. Here, as a result of the accelerating political evolution of Eastern Europe, is the immediate focal point of Western policy. The Eastern European system has been subject to a triple strain: the imposition of a Soviet-controlled political structure on the inherent national diversity of the area; the inefficiency of the economic system; and the existence of flourishing political and economic systems in the adjacent Western-oriented countries. Now, the strains have become too great to contain, and the political grasp of the Soviet Union on Eastern Europe is under open challenge. The Warsaw Pact organisation is not as yet under threat, but its ideological base has been gravely weakened. Neither in Poland nor in Hungary can the retention of power by Soviet-oriented Communist parties be guaranteed. In the German Democratic Republic popular discontent has reached a level which threatens the viability of this keystone in the Soviet Union's European defence strategy and brings the German–Soviet relationship once more towards the head of the European political agenda. In many of its more critical stages, the British–Soviet relationship has been bound up with the political structure of Central and Eastern Europe. So it is today, as the mould of 1945 begins to break.

It is hard to believe that the old structures can now be restored, but harder still to predict the new ones. The internal strains on the Gorbachev administration are such that its current quiescence in Eastern Europe is understandable and the scale of intervention which would now be necessary makes a repetition of 1956, 1968 or even 1981 seem barely conceivable. If to those strains were added a perceived threat to Soviet security, the whole process of *perestroika* could, however, turn sharply in a more reactionary direction.

The pace of events is set by internal pressures within the Soviet Union on the individual countries of Eastern Europe. The scope for Western policy is limited. Its thrust has hitherto been towards a freer interchange between the two halves of the continent and it must be in the broad European interest that this should continue. It has implications not only for national policy but also for the policies of NATO and the European Community. In its pursuit, the full range of national interest of the Eastern European countries has to be respected and there has to be recognition also of the difficult adjustment with which the Soviet Union is confronted. The pace during the past year has been swift. It is not for the West to seek to accelerate it. Sir Geoffrey Howe said in 1985 that Britain specifically rejected 'efforts to promote fragmentation within and between

Warsaw Pact countries' and that the evolutionary process 'can and should result in greater security and confidence for the Soviet Union as well as its allies'.[1] This can be achieved if the progressive liberalisation of the political systems of Eastern Europe and the strengthening of intra-European links leads to a new political stability and greater economic efficiency. The political reconstruction of a large part of Europe is a delicate process. A closer British–Soviet dialogue can contribute much to the mutual confidence which is the prerequisite for success.

The Soviet withdrawal from Afghanistan has not removed the relevance of extra-European developments to the strategic relationship with the Soviet Union. Much has changed since the simultaneous attempt to exploit Third World conflict and repress internal dissent precipitated the breakdown of detente in the 1970s and since the Iranian Revolution brought a change in the correlation of forces in an area of strategic importance which for a brief moment the Soviet Union sought to exploit and which in the event prejudiced the Soviet interest in stability on its southern border as well as in its central strategic relationship with the United States. In the whole area of regional conflicts, Soviet policy has begun to evolve and will have to be continuously tested. The initial experience, for instance in relation to the Iran–Iraq war and the Angolan conflict, is encouraging. The Soviet withdrawal from Afghanistan met an insistent international demand and eliminated a major source of tension. It was as symbolic as was the American withdrawal from Vietnam. But will a post-Afghanistan detente necessarily be of longer duration than the post-Vietnam detente? The task for the future will be to determine whether, in the continuing areas of conflict, especially but not exclusively in the Middle East, it will prove possible, through direct diplomacy and through the position of Britain and the Soviet Union as permanent members of the Security Council, to begin that search for common solutions which was so briefly envisaged at the time of the Organisation's foundation. There are disputes enough in relation to which the major powers have the choice between seeking mutual accommodation or national advantage. The two are fortunately not mutually exclusive. The search for stability in the Middle East can serve both Soviet and Western interests. If both here and elsewhere, sometimes close to its own borders and sometimes close to those of the United States, the Soviet Union is prepared to demonstrate restraint, it may legitimately expect a response which may not always come easily to Western policy-makers.

COMMERCIAL AND ECONOMIC RELATIONS

From the earliest days, when trade negotiations provided a route to the establishment of relations, the promotion – and, on occasion, the frustration – of trade has played a major part in the inter-governmental relationship and in the work of the official representatives in both capitals. This has in part been a simple reflection of the requirements for dealing with a state-trading country and in part a consequence of the linking of political and economic policy by both Governments. Earlier chapters have traced the succession of British–Soviet agreements on bilateral trade, on economic, scientific and technical cooperation and on the settlement of old debts and the grant of new credits. Their conclusion and abrogation has over the years provided a convenient symbolic demonstration of the state of relations. They have not been without effect, but the vision of vastly increased trade with the Soviet Union which has swum intermittently before the eyes of successive generations of British businessmen has not been realised.[2]

Now, a major thrust of the Gorbachev reform programme is the total restructuring of the economic system of the country, with the aim of introducing the disciplines of a market economy into a socialist system. By giving individual firms greater control over their own production programme and independent access to import and export markets, the Government hopes substantially to increase production, to direct it more effectively towards satisfying consumer demand and to ensure that the foreign exchange potential of the country is maximised. The dismantling of the centralised controls and encouragement of plant enterprise is to be accompanied by the transfer of budgetary resources and industrial capacity from the military to the civil sector and by structural economic reforms which should include a measure of external convertibility for the rouble and a major price reform. The theory is excellent, the country has the basic resources to implement it and the long term implications in terms of trading potential are substantial, but the legacy of seventy years of centralised planning is strong, the accumulated administrative inertia is great and the spirit of industrial enterprise is atrophied. The task is daunting. Much that is basic to Soviet socialism will have to be discarded. To transform a planned socialist economy into a sophisticated market economy would not be easy. To do so by decree is to introduce yet another inherent contradiction and to carry it through without violence to the power or the principles of the Party will probably prove impossible. To set the target too low would, however, have been to embark on yet another inadequate reform similar to those which characterised the Brezhnev years. Each month reveals more clearly the depth of the crisis. The aim had to be no less than a profound transformation of the Soviet economy and Soviet society, but there could be no immediate turnround in the economy. Indeed the first four years have seen a deterioration in the availability of some consumer goods.

In this situation, it is equally unrealistic to expect an immediate transformation of the British–Soviet trading relationship. The Soviet requirement for imported plant and technology is very great, Britain is in a position to supply much of it and there was agreement between the two Governments in 1987 on the need for a 40 per cent increase in trade in both directions. It takes time for intentions to be turned into contracts and contracts into deliveries, but by any standards the immediate result was disappointing. British imports from the Soviet Union were £694 million in 1986, £875 million in 1987 and £732 million in 1988. British exports to the Soviet Union, on the other hand, fell sharply from £539 million in 1986 to £492 million in 1987 and recovered only to £512 million in 1988. (The figure of £512 million British exports to the Soviet Union in 1988 compares badly in real terms with the £449 million in 1980, when relations were near their lowest, or, from a different perspective with sales worth £633 million to the 2.5 million people of Singapore, £1885 million to Switzerland or £9522 million to the Federal Republic of Germany.) In terms of the supply and demand position between the two countries, the 40 per cent target was by no means ambitious. The inter-governmental machinery to support it exists in the Joint Commission and various subordinate specialised working groups, backed by the British–Soviet Chamber of Commerce and the diplomatic and commercial representatives of both countries. There have been three principal obstacles: the effective separation of the Soviet Union from the mainstream of the world economy, the confusion of the early years of reconstruction and the inability of the Soviet Union to finance a substantial increase in hard currency imports. Ample commercial credit is available and the Export Credit Guarantee Department still rate the Soviet Union a good risk, but given a relatively conservative Soviet policy on overseas borrowing, the full trading potential will only be realised as the Soviet economy can generate the resources to back it. On the basis of current policy and current opportunities, it is reasonable to expect achievement of the

40 per cent target within another two or three years, but by that time a cash increase of this order will represent a rather unexciting real increase. Even a modest degree of success with the reform process could provide a significant extra boost, but dramatic progress may not be achieved until the final years of the century.

In this longer perspective, the potential could be very substantial. Remarkable though it seems today, there were times in the 1930s and again in the 1950s when Western leaders saw the Soviet economy as about to pose a real challenge to the West. The challenge did not materialise and it could not have materialised without reform of the system. Nevertheless, Soviet achievements in space technology showed what could be achieved when the full resources of the state were directed under centralised control towards a major national objective. The creation of an economic structure capable of producing a competitive range of industrial exports is a more complex task in that it requires a sensitivity, a responsiveness to foreign demand and a degree of flexibility which have as yet been wholly absent from the Soviet scene, but need not be for ever unattainable. To suppose that a revitalised Soviet economy could eventually have an impact on the world economy comparable to that of Japan may be to push conjecture too far, but short of a Japanese-type industrial explosion, it is not necessarily more unrealistic to envisage the Soviet Union a decade from now as a major exporter of industrial goods than, some decades earlier, it would have been to see South Korea or Taiwan in such a role. In agriculture, the experimental farms run in the Soviet Union by Imperial Chemical Industries have shown the kind of potential which, applied more widely, could avoid the need for the Soviet Union to spend in the next decade the $50 billion which it has spent over the past decade on the import of cereals. Resources of this order, applied to industrial imports and accompanied by structural change, could help to provide the stimulus which the Soviet economy needs.

British direct investment contributed much to the industrial development of pre-revolutionary Russia, but after the brief promise of Lenin's policy on concessions, it was virtually eliminated by 1930. Now, a substantial element in the new Soviet policy is the encouragement of joint ventures with foreign companies. A certain enthusiasm has been rekindled and already a number of British partners have been identified. Joint ventures offer the Soviet Union the possibility of acquiring foreign capital and technology for the development of Soviet industry and the satisfaction of internal demand, combined possibly with new export potential. For the foreign partner, they can offer a mutually advantageous route into the Soviet market, but the Soviet system does not yet make for an easy partnership and it is hard to devise schemes which have a reasonable prospect of generating sufficient hard currency to service a major initial investment. The Soviet shortage of foreign exchange must also for some time constrain the ability of the authorities to guarantee conversion of rouble earnings from projects designed to benefit the Soviet consumer. There is obvious scope for hard-currency generating ventures in some sectors of mineral and timber development or chemical engineering where a world market for the product may be identifiable, or in the servicing of foreign visitors to the Soviet Union but, in general, joint ventures have to be seen in the context of long-term cooperation and, even more than in the case of direct export, their success will be dependent upon the long-term success of the reform programme.

A wider problem in the development of economic and commercial relations is the extent to which the reform process will make possible the integration of the Soviet Union not only within the international trading community, but within the organisational structure of that community. The Soviet Government has already indicated its interest in membership of the triad of post-1945 organisations, the International Bank, the International Monetary Fund and the General Agreement on Tariffs and Trade. Conceived with the objective of supporting free trading and financial exchanges, this organisational structure was inherently inappropriate as a means of regulating the economic relationship with a Soviet state applying the rigid centralised state control of the Stalin and Brezhnev eras to the whole of its economy. It is early yet to determine whether the reform process will open up the financial and commercial structure of the country far enough to make possible a meaningful participation by the Soviet Union in these organisations, or, indeed, in the process of economic consultation among the major powers represented in the Organisation for Economic Cooperation and Development. The strains of forty years of international economic development have told heavily upon the organisations themselves and this is not the place to discuss the options for possible reform of the structure. What must be clear is that, if the Soviet Union is to be effectively integrated into the mainstream of the world economy, an appropriate institutional framework for this will need to be devised.

Within Europe, the Soviet Union has already entered into formal relations with the European Community. The process of European economic integration has demonstrated clearly enough the problems of adaptation, even between broadly similar economies, and a meaningful association of the Soviet Union would raise difficulties of an altogether different order. Nevertheless, if the process of knitting together the countries of Eastern and Western Europe is to be a goal of Western policy, the impact of increased industrial and agricultural trade between its two halves will have to be tackled. The bilateral trade agreements which have been an important part of the structure of governmental relations with the Soviet Union have been formally superseded by the Common Commercial Policy of the Community and it is right to see the creation of a structure for development of the trading relationship between the Community and the Soviet Union as a task which the member Governments should not evade.

One specific barrier to the expansion of trade with the Soviet Union is constituted by the strategic controls on Western exports originally instituted in the early period of the cold war. Their formal purpose is not to hinder the development of the Soviet economy, but it is not easy to define where strategic significance begins and there have been illogicalities in the list. Correctly interpreted and applied, the controls should have only a minimal effect on the development of normal trade and this should be the objective of Western policy. Because the controls reflect the assessment of the armed confrontation between the Soviet Union and the West, the prospect for their progressive dismantling must be judged in the light of the evolution of strategic appreciations. It is more realistic to see their final removal as a product of increased political confidence than as a prerequisite for it.

There are thus major tasks and major opportunities for Britain in the area of economic and commercial relations with the Soviet Union. Despite the necessary caution in relation to the speed with which the economic reforms can produce tangible results, it is important in both political and economic terms, that the British Government, British industrialists, British traders and British bankers should be ready to meet this challenge. There is no need to revert to the Lloyd George policy that trading with the Russians would make them forget their political ideas or to the contrary policy of achieving the same objective by economic coercion. The logic of seeking full economic integration as a major element in the process of eliminating the risk of war in Western Europe was accepted with British membership of the European Community and a price was paid to achieve a political end. Now, the process of drawing the Soviet Union, albeit only loosely, into the mainstream of the world economy presents a comparable challenge. It is a process which can only develop *pari passu* with the process of internal reform. The Soviet Union has consistently maintained a linkage between political and economic policy and now, through its reforms, has the opportunity to secure beneficial change in both respects on a basis which will equally advance Western direct interests. British policy has therefore to be based upon the recognition that the processes of Soviet internal reform and external interdependence can only march together; that it is the internal reform which will set the pace; but that success can bring mutual benefit to both countries and that it will be helped by a clear Western response on the external front. In the shaping of that collective response it will be appropriate for the British Government once again to take a lead.

CULTURAL RELATIONS

The cultural relationship between Britain and the Soviet Union is in part a reflection of the basic difference between the two societies. At the same time, in both countries, the deeper roots of a European cultural heritage and a certain community of interest in the contemporary scene provide a basis for mutually beneficial intercourse. There is enough in common in this area for it to have the potential substantially to reinforce the development of that wider community of political interest to which this book has been primarily directed. As with trade, the involvement of government has made the cultural relationship something of a barometer of the state of political relations and, as with trade, there is the problem of linking a state-controlled system with a sector of British life in which the individual is supreme.

The direct propagation of a British view is a proper and necessary activity for government. The provision of governmental support for cultural activities should be seen as a separate and different function, in which the role of government is to open the door to direct contact in every sector of the cultural life of the two countries and then to stand back, leaving the development of a productive cultural exchange to grow out of the direct interest of individuals. Here lies, in fact, a crucial difference between British and Soviet concepts of cultural diplomacy.

One particularly interesting feature of the Gorbachev reforms is the extent to which it may facilitate a more open concept of the cultural relationship and a more broadly-based exchange, less subject to the attentions of the Soviet security apparatus. Already, Soviet visitors to Britain are beginning to be more genuinely representative of the breadth and variety of the cultural life of the country. The hope must be that, on both sides, as cultural exchanges develop their own natural momentum, the role of government may dwindle and the apparatus of cultural bureaucracy become less relevant. For the present, however, we have to build upon the existing base.

As matters stand today, the whole process of cultural exchange could not be sustained without some measure of governmental support. The extent of this, reflecting the fluctuating political relationship between the two countries has been indicated by the biennial inter-governmental Cultural Agreements, the first of which was concluded after Mr Macmillan's visit to Moscow in 1959. On the British side, official support for cultural exchanges is provided primarily through the agency of the British Council and the Great Britain–USSR Association, with the assistance of the Central Office of Information. The British Academy and the Royal Society operate programmes of exchanges and the Central Bureau for Educational Visits and Exchanges deals with exchanges at secondary school level. In Moscow the Cultural Section of the British Embassy has a particularly active, rewarding and enjoyable task, in lending support to this whole range of activities.

Major manifestations such as British or Soviet weeks, concerts, opera, ballet and theatrical performances, give a necessary demonstrative structure to the cultural relationship and place a special demand upon official funding, but more significant in the long run may be the multifarious, less prominent exchanges, not merely of students and teachers, but, to cite recent examples, lawyers, journalists and television producers, all of whom have enjoyed official support. The problems of finance for cultural events are by no means unique to the Soviet Union, nor is their aggravation by the shortage of hard currency. In the case of British visits to the Soviet Union, local costs are artifically inflated by the exchange rate, and the non-transferability of rouble proceeds is a major handicap to independent, commercially viable operations. In respect of Soviet cultural activities in Britain, the shortage of hard currency means that non-commercial visitors are handicapped, unless they are able to secure governmental support, whereas, paradoxically, major revenue-earning events such as visits by the Bolshoi Ballet can be carried out profitably on a commercial basis.

Within the cultural area, the special role of press and broadcasting must be noted. Any organ may be designed to serve jointly or severally, the promotion of a political creed; the commercial or political interest of a private or governmental proprietor; or the public need for accurate information and objective assessment. The differing concept of the role of the media has formed a part of the underlying difference between the two societies and, despite the welcome signs of a growth of independence in the Soviet media, the differing concepts still prevail. The BBC World Service, government-financed, but fiercely independent in its editorial policy, is estimated to have an audience of some 18 million in the Soviet Union. The jamming of BBC broadcasts has been a recurrent source of tension and its removal in 1987 was one of the benefits of the current change of Soviet policy. In the area of printed material, it is to be hoped that, on a commercial basis, means may be found for a wider distribution of British publications within the Soviet Union.

The primary task of British Government policy in the area of cultural relations must be to create the conditions in which private exchanges can flourish; and the purpose of government finance should be to overcome the artificial constraints. The widespread recognition in the Soviet Union of the need for the use of English as a world language has resulted in a relatively high standard of English language teaching and the language barrier is consequently less of a constraint on cultural exchanges than it might have been. Nevertheless, exchanges which are linguistically one-sided lose something of their quality and one feature of the cultural relationship which it is within the power of the British Government to improve is the funding of Russian and Soviet studies. The British commercial demand for Russian speakers is small and their numbers are declining as a result of cutbacks in funding. Yet if the theme of this book is accepted, an understanding of the Soviet Union is a prerequisite for a major area of foreign and defence policy. It cannot be attained without the maintenance of a sound national base for study of the Russian language and of the history, economics and culture of Russia and the Soviet Union. That base exists in a handful of British universities, but it is being eroded by financial pressure. In harsh terms of national interest, this is a proper subject for Government funding and the sums required are minimal by comparison with the defence funding which stems from national assumptions about Soviet policy.

HUMAN RIGHTS

We have noted how the 'human rights' strand has from the outset been woven into the British–Soviet relationship, and indeed how, even before 1917, it was a major source of British antipathy towards Tsarist Russia. From Curzon's time onwards, successive British Foreign Secretaries and Prime Ministers have raised with their Soviet counterparts cases in this area of relations. It is an area where problems may often arise as a result of differences of judicial practice, but in the case of the Soviet Union they have been of an altogether different order. They have in part reflected an underlying difference in the concept of the state as the master or the servant of its people and in part a long tradition of administrative and judicial brutality. In cases concerning the treatment of British citizens or – to cite one of the more frequent causes of complaint – the refusal of the Soviet authorities to permit the emigration of their Russian-born wives, there was a clear British *locus standi*. More widely, however, the treatment by the Soviet Union of its own citizens has placed a strain upon the relationship. Non-interference in the internal affairs of other countries is a very proper principle, but the claim that the civil, political and religious rights enjoyed by the citizens of certain countries are not a proper matter for concern to other governments has never been wholly valid. The provisions of the Helsinki Final Act recognised the principle of non-interference, but also laid obligations upon all signatories in respect of their own citizens as well as those of other parties. Against this background, the Foreign Affairs Committee of the House of Commons noted in 1986[3] that 'Lack of progress on human rights remains a serious obstacle to public perceptions of the Soviet Union and its reliability and integrity'. The Soviet Union had, in fact, at that time already changed beyond recognition from the terror-ridden police state of the Stalin era, but in proportion as the state itself evolved, so expectations rose. It is reasonable to expect that, under Gorbachev, this process will continue and, indeed, be sharply accelerated. Results are already apparent in terms of the specific cases affecting British citizens, the arrangements for emigration from the Soviet Union and the prisoners of conscience held in Soviet custody. It is right that the British Government should acknowledge what has been achieved and that the Soviet leadership, for their part, should look towards the day when their country can effect a qualitative change in its whole international standing by finally freeing itself from this ancient incubus.

'TOO EARLY TO BE SURE?'

The prosperity and security of Britain and her partners will not
ultimately be found in the search for victory in a worldwide armed
confrontation between the Soviet Union and the Western powers,
but rather in the search for mutual accommodation where interests
conflict and mutual benefit where they coincide. In moving towards
this objective, we are now beginning to see the first fruits of decades
of patience and firmness in the conduct of relations with the Soviet
Union. If we are over-hasty, we may garner only a sour and unripe
crop. If we wait over-long, we may find the fruit will rot on the tree.
The building of a new, stable and productive relationship cannot be
achieved by a single political gesture, a single signature on some new
Helsinki. It needs patient, undramatic work in all those areas, many
of them outside direct governmental responsibility, which have been
identified in the preceding paragraphs. The ministerial, political and
diplomatic machinery to support that work is in good shape. In a
speech on 27 October 1988, which deserved an honourable place in
the long catalogue of British efforts to establish a workable policy
for relations with the Soviet Union, Sir Geoffrey Howe set out
logically and convincingly the case for a recognition of legitimate
Soviet interests, a pragmatic testing of the new foreign policy concepts
and a search for opportunities to work in partnership with the Soviet
Union. He ended by asking: 'Are we entering, really, a new, more
constructive era in East–West relations? It is too early to be sure,
but I earnestly hope we are. Certainly we are witnessing some of the
most important developments of our lifetime. . . . And Britain is
ready – and more than ready – to play her part in turning hope into
reality.' It will probably always be too early to be sure, for, in
diplomacy, to wait for the certainty of success may be to ensure that
it is never attained. At a comparable turning point in relations with
the Soviet Union, Ernest Bevin staked all his own authority and his
country's authority on his conviction of the need to contain Soviet
expansion. If, today, hope is to be turned into reality, Britain and
her allies will need to be inspired in their management of the
relationship with the Soviet Union by a comparable conviction
that they can succeed in making the move from confrontation to
cooperation. There is need for public recognition of the fact that the
creation of a sound relationship with the Soviet Union is an objective
of policy very different in type but equivalent in importance to the
attainment of a secure and integrated Western Europe; that it is a

feasible objective; and that the Gorbachev reforms create the possibility of attaining it.

CODA

Let us not forget where foreign policy has its roots. There is much more than Karl Marx in the political genes of the Communist Party of the Soviet Union, but Marx's observations of the social and economic state of nineteenth-century Britain had their part in that evolutionary process which brought into being the Soviet state with which we have had to grapple through these seven decades. The ability of successive British Governments to discredit the Marxist doctrine as they developed and sustained a structure of society combining social justice with economic efficiency, managed the transition from imperial power and accepted the challenge of an integrated Europe in an interdependent world has done as much to influence the favourable evolution of East–West relations as any of the processes of bilateral and multilateral diplomacy. In both East and West the evolution of society will continue and as Gorbachev's Soviet Union seeks to reformulate its doctrines and adapt its policies to the contemporary scene, it is well that we should ensure that our own system does not, in the search for wealth, lose sight of the purposes for which it is created.

Appendix 1: A Chronology of British–Soviet Relations

This chronology contains the dates of the principal events in the relationship between Britain and the Soviet Union during the period 1917–89, together with a somewhat arbitrary selection of lesser events and the dates of a very few key international events establishing the wider framework within which the bilateral relationship was set. Visits by British and Soviet Heads of Government and Foreign Ministers have been included, but most other ministerial and parliamentary visits have not. Dates of agreements are those of signature and dates of meetings are opening dates unless otherwise specified. For dates of changes of Government see Appendix 2.

1917

15 Mar	Abdication of Tsar Nicholas II
7 Nov	Bolshevik seizure of power (October Revolution. The date according to the calendar at that time in use in Russia was 25 October)
15 Dec	Armistice between Russia and Germany
23 Dec	Anglo-French Convention on 'activity in Southern Russia'

1918

Jan	M. M. Litvinov appointed Soviet representative in London and R. B. Lockhart British representative in Petrograd
7 Jan	HM Ambassador leaves Petrograd
Feb	Petrograd Embassy closed
3 Mar	Treaty of Brest–Litovsk signed
Mar	Final German offensive on Western front
6 Mar	First British landing at Murmansk
5 Apr	British–Japanese landing at Vladivostok
24 May	General Poole 'British Military Representative in Russia' at Murmansk
22 Jul	British economic mission in Moscow
2–3–4 Aug	Major Allied operations begun in Russia
9 Aug	British Consulate-General, Moscow, closed
30 Aug	Assassination attempt on Lenin
31 Aug	Murder of British Naval Attaché, Petrograd
Sep	Litvinov expelled
19 Oct	Lockhart returns to Britain

11 Nov	End of hostilities Britain and Germany
13 Nov	Brest–Litovsk Treaty denounced
23–7 Nov	British forces at Novorossisk, Sebastopol and Odessa

1919

4–6 Mar	British Govt decides to withdraw from Russia
15 Mar	Comintern founded
12 Jun	Declaration of Allied support for Kolchak
4 Jul	State of war with Bolsheviks
8 Nov	Lloyd George speech on peace in Russia
8 Dec	'Curzon Line' proposed for Soviet–Polish frontier

1920

10 Jan	*De facto* recognition of Georgia and Azerbaidjan
6 Feb	Kolchak executed
11 Feb	Anglo-Soviet agreement on exchange of prisoners of war
7 May	Poles capture Kiev
31 May	Soviet negotiators arrive London
9 Jun	Soviet company Arcos established London
1 Aug	Formation of National Communist Party in Britain
Aug	Soviet forces outside Warsaw
10 Sep	Soviet negotiator Kamenev expelled

1921

16 Mar	Anglo-Soviet Trade Agreement

1922

10 Apr	Genoa Conference opens
16 Apr	Treaty of Rapallo

1923

8 May	Curzon ultimatum

1924

21 Jan	Death of Lenin
1 Feb	British *de jure* recognition of Soviet Union. Chargés d'affaires appointed London and Moscow
14 Apr	Anglo-Soviet Conference London
8 Aug	Anglo-Soviet General and Commercial Treaties signed
25 Oct	Zinoviev letter published
21 Nov	Anglo-Soviet Treaties repudiated

1925

6 Apr	Anglo-Soviet trade union conference London. Joint Advisory Council established
12 Oct	Leadership of British Communist Party arrested
16 Oct	Treaty of Locarno

1926
24 Apr   Soviet–German Treaty of Neutrality and Friendship
1 May   General Strike in Britain

1927
12 May   Police raid on London office of Arcos
27 May   Diplomatic relations and trade agreement suspended (Note dated 26 May)

1929
3 Oct   Protocol on re-establishment of relations
Dec   Ambassadors appointed London and Moscow

1930
1 Jan   *Daily Worker* founded
16 Apr   Temporary Anglo-Soviet Trade Agreement
2 Oct   Anglo-Soviet Debts and Claims Committee set up

1932
Feb   Debt talks break down
Sep   Macmillan in Soviet Union
17 Oct   Notice of termination of Trade Agreement
29 Nov   Franco-Soviet Treaty

1933
30 Jan   Hitler Chancellor of Germany
12–18 Apr   Trial of British engineers in Moscow
19–20 Apr   British and Soviet trade embargoes
1 Jul   Embargoes removed

1934
16 Feb   Temporary Anglo-Soviet Trade Agreement
Jul   Vansittart–Maisky discussions
18 Sep   Soviet membership of League of Nations

1935
28 Mar   Eden, Lord Privy Seal, in Moscow
2 May   Franco-Soviet Treaty
16 May   Czech-Soviet Treaty

1936
Jan   Litvinov in London
7 Mar   German reoccupation of Rhineland
19 Jul   Spanish Civil War begins
30 Jul   Anglo-Soviet Export Credit Agreement
25 Nov   Anti-Comintern Pact

1937
17 Jul   Anglo-Soviet Naval Agreement

1938
13 Mar	Austrian Anschluss with Germany
29 Sep	Munich agreement on Czechoslovakia

1939
12 Mar	German occupation of Czechoslovakia
31 Mar	British guarantee to Poland
13 Apr	British guarantee to Romania and Greece
14 Jun	Strang arrives Moscow for tripartite negotiations
22 Jul	Soviet–German trade talks
13 Aug	British military delegation arrives Moscow
23 Aug	Soviet–German Non-aggression Treaty and secret Protocol
25 Aug	Tripartite talks broken off
1 Sep	German attack on Poland
3 Sep	British declaration of war on Germany. Anglo-Soviet Naval Agreement suspended
30 Nov	Soviet attack on Finland

1940
12 Mar	Soviet–Finnish peace treaty
1, 5, 8 Aug	Incorporation of Lithuania, Latvia and Estonia into Soviet Union

1941
22 Jun	German attack on Soviet Union
12 Jul	Anglo-Soviet declaration on mutual assistance
4 Oct	Anglo-Soviet agreement on military supplies
7 Dec	Japanese attack on Pearl Harbor
8 Dec	US and UK at war with Japan
15–18 Dec	Eden in Moscow

1942
29 Jan	Treaty of Alliance USSR, UK, Iran
26 May	Anglo-Soviet Treaty of Alliance
27 Jun	Anglo-Soviet agreement on military supplies
12 Aug	Churchill in Moscow

1943
15 May	Dissolution of Comintern
31 Jan	German surrender at Stalingrad
18–30 Oct	Foreign Ministers' Conference, Moscow
19 Oct	Anglo-Soviet agreement on military supplies
28 Nov–1 Dec	Teheran Conference of Heads of Government

1944
1 Jun	Allied landings in northern France
9–18 Oct	Churchill in Moscow

1945

4–12 Feb	Yalta Conference of Heads of Government
Feb–Mar	British Parliamentary Delegation to USSR
2 Apr–10 May	Mrs Churchill in USSR
8 May	Surrender of Germany
17 Jul–2 Aug	Potsdam Conference of Heads of Government
6 Aug	Atomic bomb on Hiroshima
15 Aug	Surrender of Japan
11 Sep–2 Oct	Council of Foreign Ministers, London
16–26 Dec	Council of Foreign Ministers, Moscow

1946

5 Mar	Churchill's Fulton speech
25 Apr–16 May	Council of Foreign Ministers, Paris
15 Jun–12 Jul	Council of Foreign Ministers, Paris
4 Nov–12 Dec	Council of Foreign Ministers, New York

1947

5 Oct	Foundation of Cominform
10 Mar–24 Apr	Council of Foreign Ministers, Moscow
12 Mar	Truman Doctrine
2 Jul	Soviet withdrawal from Marshall Aid talks
25 Nov–15 Dec	Council of Foreign Ministers, London
27 Dec	Anglo-Soviet Trade and Payments Agreement

1948

25 Feb	Communist coup in Czechoslovakia
17 Mar	Brussels Treaty
24 Jun	Berlin Blockade
Jul–Dec	Talks on long-term trade agreement

1949

4 Apr	North Atlantic Treaty
23 May	Council of Foreign Ministers, Paris

1950

26 Apr	War in Korea

1951

25 May	Defection of Burgess and Maclean

1953

5 Mar	Death of Stalin
11 May	Churchill calls for summit conference
Jun	Cruiser 'Sverdlov' visits for Coronation
17 Jun	Riots in East Germany
27 Jul	Korean Armistice

1954

25 Jan–18 Feb	Foreign Ministers' Conference, Berlin
26 Apr–21 Jul	Foreign Ministers' Conference, Geneva
10 Aug	Attlee and Labour party delegation to Moscow
23 Oct	Paris agreements. German membership of NATO and Western European Union

1955

7 May	USSR annuls Anglo-Soviet Treaty of Alliance
15 May	Austrian State Treaty
18–23 Jul	Heads of Government Conference, Geneva
27 Oct–16 Nov	Foreign Ministers' Conference, Geneva

1956

Feb	XXth CPSU Congress denunciation of Stalin
18 Apr	Dissolution of Cominform
18–27 Apr	Bulganin and Khrushchev visit UK
Oct	Riots in Poland
4 Nov	Soviet forces attack Budapest
5 Nov	Anglo-French attack on Port Said

1957

4 Oct	First Soviet earth satellite

1958

31 Oct	UK–US-Soviet talks on nuclear test ban treaty
10 Nov	Soviet ultimatum on Berlin

1959

21 Feb–3 Mar	Macmillan in Moscow
11 May–30 Jun	Foreign Ministers' meeting on Germany
24 May	Anglo-Soviet Trade Agreement. Great Britain-USSR Association formed
13 Jul–5 Aug	Foreign Ministers' meeting on Germany
1 Dec	Anglo-Soviet Cultural Agreement

1960

3 Jan	UK-US-USSR talks on Nuclear Test Ban open in Geneva
4 Feb	Anglo-Soviet Parliamentary group formed
15 May	Abortive Paris summit

1961

22 Mar	Sentences in British naval secrets case
17 Apr	Bay of Pigs invasion of Cuba
3 May	George Blake sentenced
May–Jul	British and Soviet Trade Fairs in Moscow and London
2–4 Jun	Kennedy and Khrushchev in Vienna
9 Aug	British application for membership of EEC
13 Aug	Berlin Wall
10 Oct	Gromyko in London

1962
15–28 Oct   Cuban missile crisis

1963
23 Jan   Philby defects to USSR from Beirut
7–11 May   Wynne–Penkovsky trial in Moscow
3–8 Aug   Earl of Home in Moscow
5 Aug   Partial Test Ban Treaty

1964
23 Apr   Anglo-Soviet Trade Agreement extended
27 Jul–1 Aug   Butler in Moscow
15 Oct   Chinese nuclear device exploded

1965
16–20 Mar   Gromyko in London
22–3 Jul   Trial of Gerald Brooke in Moscow
29 Nov–4 Dec   Stewart in Moscow
2 Dec   Anglo-Soviet Consular Convention

1966
21–4 Feb   Wilson in Moscow
16–19 Jul   Wilson in Moscow for British industrial fair
22–5 Nov   Brown in Moscow

1967
6–13 Feb   Kosygin in UK
24–6 May   Brown in Moscow
5 Jun   Arab–Israeli War
25 Aug   London–Moscow hot line set up

1968
5 Jan   Anglo-Soviet Agreement on Financial and Property
                     Claims
19 Jan   Anglo-Soviet Agreement on Technological
                     Cooperation
22–4 Jan   Wilson in Moscow
26 Mar   Anglo-Soviet Technology Agreement
3 Apr   Anglo-Soviet Navigation Treaty
22–4 May   Stewart in Moscow
1 Jul   Nuclear Non-Proliferation Treaty
20 Aug   Soviet invasion of Czechoslovakia

1969
3 Jun   Long-term Anglo-Soviet Trade Agreement
22 Jul   Gerald Brooke released in exchange for Krogers

1970
12 Aug   FRG-Soviet Treaty

1971

Jan	Anglo-Soviet Joint Commission set up
3 Sep	Quadripartite Agreement on Berlin
24 Sep	105 Soviet officials expelled from London

1972

22–30 May	Nixon in Moscow. Anti-Ballistic Missile Treaty and SALT I
21 Dec	Basic Treaty between FRG and GDR

1973

1 Jan	British entry into EEC
18–22 May	Brezhnev in Bonn
18–25 Jun	Brezhnev in USA
3–7 Jul	European Security Conference, Helsinki
2–10 Sep	Duke of Edinburgh in Soviet Union
Oct	Negotiations on reduction of forces in Central Europe (MBFR), Vienna
6 Oct	Arab–Israeli War
2–5 Dec	Sir A Douglas-Home in Moscow

1974

6 May	Anglo-Soviet Agreement on Economic, Scientific and Technological Cooperation
27 Jun–3 Jul	Nixon in Moscow
23–4 Nov	Ford in Vladivostok

1975

13–17 Feb	Wilson and Callaghan in Moscow. UK–Soviet Protocol on Consultations. Economic and Commercial Agreements.
30 Apr	Fall of Saigon
1 Aug	CSCE Final Act
Oct	Cuban troops in Angola
24–5 Oct	First meeting Anglo-Soviet Round Table

1976

22–5 Mar	Gromyko in London
28 Mar–1 Jun	Exchange of naval visits

1977

9–11 Oct	Owen in Moscow
10 Oct	Anglo-Soviet Agreement on Prevention of Accidental Nuclear War

1979

Mar	Duke of Edinburgh in Moscow
16–18 Jun	Carter and Brezhnev in Geneva
18 Jun	SALT II Agreement
26 Jun	Mrs Thatcher meets Kosygin in Moscow
27 Dec	Soviet invasion of Afghanistan

1980
Jul   Olympic Games in Moscow

1981
30 Jul   Carrington in Moscow
23–5 Nov   Brezhnev in Bonn
13 Dec   Martial Law in Poland

1982
5 Feb   UK sanctions against Poland and Soviet Union
10 Nov   Death of Brezhnev

1984
9 Feb   Death of Andropov
15–21 Dec   Gorbachev in UK

1985
10 Mar   Death of Chernenko. Thatcher in Moscow
18–21 Nov   Reagan–Gorbachev in Geneva

1986
25 Feb–6 Mar   27th Party Congress CPSU
13–16 Jul   Shevardnadze in London
15 Jul   Anglo-Soviet Agreement on Mutual Waiver of Claims
10–13 Oct   Reagan–Gorbachev in Reykjavik

1987
28 Mar–1 Apr   Thatcher in Soviet Union
7 Dec   Gorbachev stopover in UK
7–10 Dec   Gorbachev in Washington
8 Dec   INF Treaty signed

1988
29 May–2 Jun   Reagan in Moscow
1 Jun   INF Treaty ratified

1989
14–16 Feb   Howe in Moscow
15 Feb   Soviet withdrawal from Afghanistan
6 Mar   CSE talks open
5–7 Apr   Gorbachev in UK

Appendix 2: The British and Soviet Leadership 1917–89

The British–Soviet relationship has been so heavily influenced by the personality of the leaders of the two countries that the reader may find it helpful to see them listed. This Appendix therefore contains the names of British Prime Ministers and Soviet Party Leaders, together with their Foreign Ministers from 1917 to the present day, with the year of their accession to office given in brackets.

UNITED KINGDOM		SOVIET UNION	
Prime Minister	Foreign Secretary	First Secretary or General Secretary	People's Commissar for Foreign Affairs/Foreign Minister
D. Lloyd George (1916)	A. J. Balfour (1916)	V. I. Lenin (1917)	L. Trotsky (1917)
			G. V. Chicherin (1918)
	Earl Curzon (1919)		
A. Bonar Law (1922)			
S. Baldwin (1923)			
J. R. MacDonald (1924)	J. R. MacDonald (1924)	J. V. Stalin (1924)	
S. Baldwin (1924)	A. Chamberlain (1924)		
J. R. MacDonald (1929)	A. Henderson (1929)		M. M. Litvinov (1930)
	Marquess of Reading (1931)		
	Sir J. Simon (1931)		
S. Baldwin (1935)	Sir S. Hoare (1935)		
	A. Eden (1935)		
N. Chamberlain (1937)	Lord Halifax (1938)		V. M. Molotov (1939)
W. S. Churchill (1940)	A. Eden (1940)		

C. Attlee
(1945)

W. S. Churchill
(1951)

A. Eden
(1955)

H. Macmillan
(1957)
Sir A. Douglas-
Home
(1963)
H. Wilson
(1964)

E. Heath
(1970)

H. Wilson
(1974)
J. Callaghan
(1976)

M. Thatcher
(1979)

E. Bevin
(1945)
H. Morrison
(1951)
A. Eden
(1951)

H. Macmillan
(1955)
J. Selwyn Lloyd
(1955)
Earl of Home
(1960)
R. A. Butler
(1963)

P. Gordon-Walker
(1964)
M. Stewart
(1965)
G. Brown
(1966)
M. Stewart
(1968)
Sir A. Douglas-
Home
(1970)
J. Callaghan
(1974)
A. Crosland
(1976)
D. Owen
(1977)
Lord Carrington
(1979)
F. Pym
(1982)
Sir G. Howe
(1983)

J. Major
(1989)
D. Hurd
(1989)

G. M. Malenkov
(1953)
N. S. Khrushchev
(1953)

L. I. Brezhnev
(1964)

Y. Andropov
(1982)

K. Chernenko
(1984)
M. S. Gorbachev
(1985)

A. Y. Vyshinsky
(1949)

V. M. Molotov
(1953)
D. Shepilov
(1956)
A. A. Gromyko
(1957)

E. Shevardnadze
(1985)

Appendix 3: British and Soviet Diplomatic Representatives

BRITISH DIPLOMATIC REPRESENTATIVES IN MOSCOW

After the abdication of the Emperor Nicholas in March 1917, Sir George Buchanan remained in Petrograd until 15 January 1918. After his departure Mr F. Lindley remained as Chargé d'Affaires until 8 March 1918 and Mr R. B. Lockhart conducted informal relations with the Soviet authorities as Consul-General first in Petrograd and then in Moscow between January and October 1918. Mr R. M. (later Sir Robert) Hodgson took up his duties as Official Agent in charge of the British Commercial Mission in Moscow in July 1921 and was appointed Chargé d'Affaires on the establishment of diplomatic relations with the Soviet Union on 1 February 1924. He continued in that appointment until the suspension of relations by the British Government on 27 May 1927.

Relations were resumed in accordance with the Protocol of 3 October 1929 and the United Kingdom was subsequently represented by the following Ambassadors Extraordinary and Plenipotentiary.

HM Representatives are shown with date of appointment, but with subsequent style where appropriate:

7 Dec 1929	Sir Esmond Ovey
24 Oct 1933	Viscount Chilston
19 Jan 1939	Sir William Seeds
12 Jun 1940	Sir Stafford Cripps
4 Feb 1942	Sir Archibald Clark Kerr (later Lord Inverchapel)
14 May 1946	Sir Maurice Peterson
22 Jun 1949	Sir David Kelly
18 Oct 1951	Sir Alvary Gascoigne
1 Oct 1953	Sir William Hayter
19 Feb 1957	Sir Patrick Reilly
13 Oct 1960	Sir Frank Roberts
27 Nov 1962	Sir Humphrey (later Lord) Trevelyan
27 Aug 1965	Sir Duncan Wilson
9 Sep 1971	Sir John Killick
12 Nov 1973	Sir Terence Garvey
9 Jan 1976	Sir Howard Smith

28 Mar 1978   Sir Curtis Keeble
16 Sep 1982   Sir Iain Sutherland
18 Jul 1985   Sir Bryan Cartledge
20 Sep 1988   Sir Rodric Braithwaite

SOVIET DIPLOMATIC REPRESENTATIVES IN LONDON

The Government of the Russian Soviet Federative Socialist Republic (later the Union of Soviet Socialist Republics) was represented in the United Kingdom informally by L. B. Krasin during the period from 15 May 1921 to 23 July 1923. Mr Krasin was succeeded on that date by C. G. Rakovsky and on the establishment of diplomatic relations on 8 February 1924, Mr Rakovsky was appointed Charge d'Affaires, an appointment which he held until 14 November 1925. On 30 October 1925 L. B. Krasin was appointed to London, but did not take up the appointment until 11 October 1926 and, although holding the rank of Ambassador, was received in the capacity of Chargé d'Affaires. During the period between 15 November 1925 and 10 October 1926 and again from 25 November 1926 until the suspension of diplomatic relations by the British Government on 27 May 1927 A. P. Rosengolz acted as Chargé d'Affaires.

Relations were resumed in accordance with the Protocol of 3 October 1929 and the Soviet Union was subsequently represented by the following Ambassadors Extraordinary and Plenipotentiary:

20 Dec 1929   G. Y. Sokolnikov
 8 Nov 1932   I. M. Maisky
15 Oct 1943   F. T. Gusev
23 Jan 1947   G. N. Zarubin
 7 Aug 1952   A. A. Gromyko
28 May 1953   Y. A. Malik
25 Mar 1960   A. A. Soldatov
10 Feb 1966   M. N. Smirnovsky
 5 Jul 1973   N. M. Lunkov
10 Dec 1980   V. I. Popov
11 Jun 1986   L. M. Zamyatin

Notes

The purpose of these notes is primarily to aid those who wish to go back to the original sources of quotations and references. The Governmental documents cited are held in the Public Record Office and in most cases are identified in the notes by standard PRO references. References to Cabinet and War Cabinet minutes are identified by PRO Class numbers, Piece numbers and meeting numbers in the CAB 23 series up to September 1939; the CAB 65 series from 1939 to 1945; and the CAB 128 series thereafter. Cabinet memoranda are similarly identified in the CAB 24, CAB 66 and CAB 129 series, together with the memorandum number. Sir Winston Churchill's papers are identified by numbers in the PREM 3 Class. Foreign Office documents are almost exclusively in the FO 371 Class and in most cases are identified by the Class and Piece number only. In some cases, however, the Foreign Office file number and document number have been added. References to Embassy telegrams are normally shown under the name of the originating post and are from the Ambassador or Chargé d'Affaires unless otherwise noted. Telegrams from the Foreign Office issue on the authority of the Secretary of State. Only a study of the jackets will distinguish those which bear his personal imprint from those sent in his name by officials of varying degrees of seniority.

In those cases where documents are reproduced in the collected volumes of *Documents on British Foreign Policy* (DBFP) I have used references from that volume, rather than from the PRO. For the reader who wishes to refer to the full texts, particularly in respect of the exchanges between the Foreign Secretary and HM Representatives, without the need for reference to the Public Record Office, I commend these volumes. They do not, however, indicate the full process of policy formulation.

Those who are not familiar with the Foreign Office filing system as it operated until a few years ago may find it mystifying and frustrating. It had its merits, but the swift identification and location of documents was not, in my experience, high among them. Each document, on receipt, was placed in its own paper jacket, identified by a green band and the letter G if it was of particular sensitivity, numbered in a single consecutive series and also assigned to a file, before being passed to the most junior officer in the responsible Department. He would write on the jacket his observations and recommendations for action, sign his name and pass it on up the chain. A signature alone would send it on its way into the higher reaches and if necessary to the Secretary of State, but, in this variant of snakes and ladders, an initial would return it to the registry, unseen – except in the case of multiple copy telegrams – by those senior to the initialler. The junior reaches of the service tended to divide between the firm-minded initialler, the prudent

357

signer and the loquacious minuter, setting out at length and on occasion with an apparent authority which did not wholly match his standing in the Office, the course of action required of the British Government. Multiple copies of telegrams were made, of which one only was placed in a jacket. The more important documents were, at the discretion of the Department, printed for the information of the Monarch, of Ministers and in many cases of Commonwealth Governments. The volumes of printed documents are a convenient record, but, unfortunately, few telegrams were printed and from the Second World War onwards the print volumes have not been transferred to the Public Record Office.

The original jackets with their minutes are preserved in the PRO Pieces. They can provide a remarkably valuable indication of the process by which policy was formulated and modified between the most junior reaches of the Office and the Secretary of State. The main files of which the jackets formed part were often very generalised. Several subjects would be contained within one file and one topic could span several files. Related jackets on individual topics were tied in bundles until action was complete. The bundles were then split up and the jackets returned to one or more main files in the numerical sequence in which they had been entered. It is in this dispersed form that the jackets appear in the main files at the PRO. It was a system which, well operated, could make for the efficient conduct of business, by bringing together only directly relevant papers, but it tended to frustrate the discovery of relevant documents after a lapse of one year, let alone thirty or more. I gratefully acknowledge the work of earlier researchers and the help of the PRO staff in tracing the sequence of events, but I am only too conscious of the gaps which remain in the record of these seventy years of diplomacy. The reader will not, I hope, seek total consistency in the naming of those who feature in it. I have in general, used the names by which British statesman were known during the period when they were most closely concerned with British–Soviet relations.

In this study of British policy, I have made only limited use of the Soviet documents. The reader's attention is, however, drawn to the bibliography annexed to *Soviet Foreign Policy*, eds A. Gromyko and B. Ponomarev (Moscow: Nauka, 1980); (to which should be added the two volumes of documents on Soviet–British relations 1941–5 published in Moscow in 1983) to J. Degras (ed.) *Soviet Documents on Foreign Policy 1917–1941*, 3 vols (Oxford University Press, RIIA, 1951–3); and to V. A. Ryzhikov, *Soviet–English Relations* (Moscow: Mezhdunarodnye Otnosheniia, 1987). The official volumes of Soviet diplomatic documents, where referred to in the text are noted as DSFP. The German Documents published by HMSO are referred to as DGFP and the United States diplomatic documents as FRUS.

The field of Soviet studies is wide and the range of other works indirectly relevant to the British–Soviet relationship even wider. I have not therefore, attempted a bibliography, but have indicated in the notes, where appropriate, a very few specialised works examining the conduct of relations during certain periods. For a general view of British–Soviet relations, F. S. Northedge and A. Wells, *Britain and Soviet Communism* (Macmillan, 1982) can be recommended, particularly in respect of economic and cultural relations, W. P. and Z. K. Coates, *A History of Anglo–Soviet Relations* (London:

Lawrence and Wishart, 1943–1958) contains some useful information on the early years, but is heavily coloured by the authors' political views.

Introduction: Britain and Imperial Russia

In this chapter, the Gregorian calendar, in general use in Western Europe in 1917, has been adopted. In Russia, at that time, the Julian calendar, earlier by thirteen days, was still in use. Consequently the revolution in the spring of 1917 has been referred to as the March Revolution and the date of November 7 is used for the October Revolution, which, under the old calendar, occurred on October 25.

1. Sir George Buchanan, *My Mission to Russia* (London: Cassell, 1923) vol. I, p. 89.
2. Telegram, Petrograd to Foreign Office no. 1771 of 8 November 1917.
3. Quoted in *Novoe Vremya* (Petrograd despatch of 3 February 1912).
4. Sir Donald Mackenzie Wallace, *Russia*, 2 vols (London: Cassell, 1877; 2nd ed. 1912).
5. Buchanan, *My Mission*, vol. I, p. 91.
6. *Novoe Vremya* (see n. 3).
7. Buchanan, *My Mission*, vol. I, p. 138.
8. *My Mission*, vol. I, p. 139.
9. Lecture by G. Paish, Royal Statistical Society, December 1910, quoted by B. Ischchanian, *Die auslaendischen Elemente in der russischen Volkswirtschaft* (Berlin, 1913).
10. Ibid.
11. I. Maisky, *Journey into the Past* (London: Hutchinson, 1962).
12. PQ answered by Chancellor of the Exchequer, 19 April 1921, quoted on FO 371/9363 (N3530/2407/38). An attempt to convert this and other figures into 1989 equivalents cannot be very meaningful, but as a proportion of budget revenue a figure of £30 000 million would give an indication of the order of magnitude of the British wartime loans in today's terms.
13. Buchanan, *My Mission*, vol. II, p. 28.
14. Ibid., p. 49.
15. D. Lloyd George, *War Memoirs* (London: Odhams, 1933–6) vol. II, p. 1892.
16. Buchanan, *My Mission*, vol. II, pp. 92–100.
17. CAB 23/2 W.C. 100.
18. H. Nicolson, *King George the Fifth* (London: Constable, 1952).
19. CAB 23/2 W.C. 139.
20. CAB 23/2 W.C. 144.
21. Meriel Buchanan, *Petrograd, the City of Trouble* 1914–1918 (London, 1918).

1 Response to Revolution

1. CAB 23/4 W.C. 269.
2. D. Lloyd George, *War Memoirs*, vol. II, p. 1544.

3. Quoted by D. Lloyd George, *War Memoirs*, vol. II, p. 1610. Lloyd
   George says that Haig had underestimated the effect, but later in Cabinet
   he remarked at one point that he was 'unable to understand the rather
   alarmist tone' about the transfer of German forces from the East.
4. CAB 23/4 W.C. 286.
5. Articles by H. N. Brailsford and M. S. Farbman in *The Herald*, 17
   November 1917 and 5 January 1918.
6. Lloyd George, *War Memoirs*, vol. II, p. 1643.
7. CAB 24/35 Memorandum GT 2932 and CAB 23/4 W.C. 295.
8. CAB 23/4 W.C. 289.
9. Telegram, FO to Petrograd, 3 December 1917, quoted in R. H. Ullman,
   Anglo–Soviet Relations 1917–1921 (Princeton University Press, 1961)
   vol. I, p. 46.
10. The text of the Convention is at DBFP Series I, vol. III, pp. 369–70.
11. CAB 23/4 W.C. 306
12. R. H. Bruce Lockhart, *Memoirs of a British Agent* (London: Putnam,
    1932) p. 1.
13. Ibid., p. 206.
14. Ibid., p. 204.
15. CAB 23/4 W.C. 308.
16. CAB 23/4 W.C. 290.

2 Intervention

1. The steps by which the British Government was led into the policy of
   intervention and then extricated itself are described and analysed in
   great detail in Richard Ullman's masterly work *Anglo-Soviet Relations
   1917–1921*. In the present chapter, which is based largely on the War
   Cabinet minutes, space does not permit more than an analysis of the
   main thrust of events. Although the official documents in the Public
   Record Office had not been opened at the time Ullman was writing his
   first volume, they do not significantly change the assessment which he
   formed, and for those who wish to study in detail this important period
   of diplomatic history his book must be regarded as the definitive work.
   Among the various works dealing with the intervention and the civil war
   a lively account of the operations conducted by the British forces in
   Russia is contained in *The Day We Almost Bombed Moscow* by
   Christopher Dobson and John Miller (London: Hodder and Stoughton,
   1986).
2. Buchanan, *My Mission*, vol. II, p. 247.
3. This letter from Captain Garstin, who joined Lockhart's staff, is on FO
   371/3318. Garstin was later transferred to General Poole's forces in
   Archangel, where he won the MC and was killed in August 1918.
4. FO 371/3283 (Petrograd telegram 179 of 20 January 1918).
5. FO Telegram to Petrograd, no. 129.
6. FO Telegram to Petrograd, no. 287.
7. Lockhart, *Memoirs*, p. 230.
8. CAB 23/5 W.C. 341.
9. CAB 23/5 W.C. 353.

10. Quoted from Hoffmann's memoirs by J. W. Wheeler–Bennett, *Brest-Litovsk: The Forgotten Peace* (London: Macmillan, 1938) p. 244.
11. 29 HL Debs 9 April 1918 Col. 618.
12. Lloyd George, *War Memoirs*, vol. II, p. 1889.
13. Wheeler-Bennett, *Brest–Litovsk*, p. 227.
14. Despatch of 16 March by A. J. Balfour quoted in Lloyd George, *War Memoirs*, vol. II, p. 1898.
15. CAB 24/46 Memorandum GT 4046. See also FO 371/3285.
16. FO 371/3285/58693.
17. FO 371/3285/64890 FO Telegram 65 to Moscow (Lockhart) 13 April 1918.
18. CAB 23/6 WC 410. CAB 24/51 Memorandum GT 4519.
19. See, for instance, memorandum by General Knox with covering note by CIGS CAB 24/47 GT 4156.
20. CAB 23/7 WC 446.
21. FO 371/3285/58026.
22. CAB 23/6 WC 413.
23. FO 371/3286 Telegram 210 from Moscow to Foreign Office.
24. FO 371/3286 FO Telegram 191 to Moscow.
25. FO 371/3289.
26. FO Telegram 82 to New York dated 20 June 1918.
27. CAB 24/54 Memorandum GT 4812. Lindley is referred to as HM Principal Representative in Russia. There must be some doubt as to the extent to which his functions went beyond that of political advice to the northern group of forces.
28. CAB 23/6 WC 432.
29. Lloyd George, *War Memoirs*, vol. II, p. 1871.
30. FO 371/3287.
31. Moscow Telegram 347 of 5 August 1918.
32. A. Gromyko and B. Ponomarev (eds) *Soviet Foreign Policy* (Moscow, 1980) vol. 1, p. 75 *et seq*. This work is referred to at various points. With a re-evaluation of Soviet history in train, it should not be regarded as an authoritative source of current doctrine. It has, however, not yet been replaced and still represents a convenient summary of the conventional Soviet view as it was expressed in the late 1970s. V. A. Ryzhikov, *Soviet–English Relations* (Moscow, 1982) contains a carefully researched exposition of the conventional Soviet view, but the pattern which it presents corresponds poorly to the complex evolution of British policy.
33. Gromyko and Ponomarev, *Soviet Foreign Policy*, vol. I, p. 82.
34. See, for instance, R. N. B. Lockhart, *Ace of Spies* (London: Hodder and Stoughton, 1967) on Sidney Reilly; Sir Paul Dukes, *The Story of ST25* (London: Cassell, 1938), and G. Hill, *Go Spy the Land* (London: Cassell, 1932). For the description of Cromie's work see telegram dated 6 September 1918 from Lindley in Archangel to Balfour in *Collection of Reports on Russia No 1 1919* (HMSO).
35. CAB 23/7 WC 469.
36. FO 371/3337/185499.
37. Article by D. Young in *The Herald*, 14 September 1918.
38. CAB 24/63 Memorandum GT 5648.
39. CAB 23/8 WC 481.

40. These figures are taken from a map in W. S. Churchill, *The World Crisis: 'The Aftermath'* (London: Thornton Butterworth, 1929), with some necessary amendment such as the exclusion of the forces in the Caucasus, which arrived shortly after the end of the war with Germany.
41. FO 371/3319/143998 Telegram from Lindley in Archangel.
42. CAB 23/8 WC 489.
43. CAB 23/8 WC 502.
44. Winston S. Churchill, *The World Crisis*, p. 169.
45. D. Lloyd George, *The Truth About the Peace Treaties* (London: Gollancz, 1938) p. 316.
46. CAB 23/42 Imperial War Cabinet, 31 December 1918.
47. Lloyd George, *The Truth* . . . , p. 367.
48. *Soviet Documents* vol. I (Moscow, 1957) p. 549, quoted by Ullman, *Anglo-Soviet Relations.* . . , vol. II, p. 87.
49. CAB 23/42 Imperial War Cabinet, 23 December 1918.
50. CAB 23/9 WC 531.
51. Lloyd George, *The Truth.* . . , p. 370, and Churchill, *World Crisis.* . . , p. 173.
52. CAB 23/9 WC 541.
53. Interdepartmental Conference on Eastern Affairs and CAB 25/9 WC 542.
54. 114 HC Deb, 16 April 1919 Col. 2939–2943.
55. Lloyd George, *The Truth.* . . , p. 568.
56. Churchill, *The World Crisis.* . . , p. 183.
57. CAB 23/15 WC 588A.
58. DBFP Minutes of Supreme Allied Council, 25 July 1919, p. 202, Appendix D.
59. FO 371/4096/110398/11/57.
60. CAB 24/96 CP 469.
61. DBFP, Series I, vol. I, Meeting of Heads of Delegations, 20 August 1919.
62. 116 HC Deb, 29 May 1919 Col. 1522.
63. FO 371/3961/145297/91/38.
64. Lloyd George, *The Truth.* . . , p. 370.
65. *The Times*, 12 April 1919.
66. Cab 24/89 Memorandum GT 8207.
67. DBFP, series I, vol. I, Minutes Heads of Delegations, 15 September 1919.

3   Facing the Facts

1. It has been convenient to refer, up to this point, to the Bolshevik and anti-Bolshevik forces in Russia, since it was largely in these terms that policy was discussed in London during the period of the intervention. The Soviet Government was not recognised *de facto* by Britain until March 1921. The change in terminology was gradual, but with the ending of the intervention and the opening of negotiations for a trade agreement the British Government were in practice dealing with the Soviet Government and, making a somewhat arbitrary choice, I have from the beginning of this chapter referred to the Soviet Government as such.

2. *The Times*, 10 November 1919.
3. For those who wish to follow these negotiations in detail there is a very full account and analysis in Richard H. Ullman, *The Anglo-Soviet Accord* (Princeton University Press, 1972). *Britain and the Bolshevik Revolution* by Stephen White (London: Macmillan, 1979) deals with the conduct of relations from 1917 to 1924 especially from the point of view of the influence of the Labour and financial and industrial interests on the British side.
4. Labour Party Report of the Nineteenth Annual Conference (London, 1919) p. 156 (see S. R. Graubard, *British Labour and the Russian Revolution* (Harvard University Press, 1956) pp. 73–4).
5. CAB 23/11 WC 599.
6. K. Jefferey (ed.), *The Military Correspondence of Field Marshal Sir Henry Wilson 1918–1922* (London: Bodley Head for Army Records Society, 1985).
7. DBFP, series I, vol. III, no. 342.
8. Ibid., vol. II, pp. 867–70.
9. Ibid., vol. III, no. 664.
10. DBFP, series I, vol VII, no. 24.
11. In April 1919 the Government published a *Collection of Reports on Bolshevism in Russia* (HMSO Cmd. 8 of 1919) with descriptions of the early stages of the terror. For Rev. North's views see *The Times*, 24 May 1920. For the memorial to the Prime Minister see *The Times* of 23 February 1920 and for the comment by the CIGS see Jeffery, *Military Correspondence. . .* , Doc. 84.
12. For Churchill's speech at Sunderland on 3 January 1920 see *Manchester Guardian*, 5 January 1920. For his Cabinet Memorandum of 17 January 1920 see file 18/OJ/2 on CAB 21/177.
13. Cmd. 587: Agreement Between His Majesty's Government and the Soviet Government of Russia for the Exchange of Prisoners, 1920.
14. FO 371/195172/1089/38.
15. CAB 24/106 CP 1350. Also DBFP, vol. XII, no. 708.
16. *The Times*, 28 May 1920.
17. 131 HC Deb, 14 July 1920, Col 2369–71 has text.
18. 131 HC Deb, 14 July 1920, Col 2371–4.
19. Sir C. E. Calwell, *Field Marshal Sir Henry Wilson* (London: Cassell, 1927) vol. II, p. 255.
20. 132 HC Deb, 21 July 1920, Col 485.
21. DBFP, series I, vol. VIII, no. 79.
22. For a description of the interception of these telegrams see *The Anglo-Soviet Accord*, R. H. Ullman, vol. III, ch. 7.
23. 133 HC Deb, 10 August 1920, Col. 272.
24. International Labour Office, *The Congress of the Labour and Socialist International*, Geneva, 31 July–5 August 1920 (Geneva, 1920) cited by Graubard, *British Labour*.
25. *The Times* of 19 August 1920 contains the texts of this exchange of messages.
26. CAB 23/22 C 49 (20).
27. Telegram, Lenin to Kamenev, cited by Ullman, *Anglo-Soviet Accord*, p. 296.

28. CAB 23/22 p. 237, Conclusions of Ministerial Conference, 2 September 1920.
29. CAB 23/22 C 61 (20).
30. CAB 24/114 Memorandum CP 2099 of 14 November 1920.
31. CAB 23/23 C 64 (20).
32. Cmd. 1207; *Trade Agreement between His Britannic Majesty's Government and the Government of the Russian Socialist Federal Soviet Republic.*
33. 164 HC Deb, 15 May 1923, Col 282.
34. 139 HC Deb, 22 March 1921, Cols 2511–12.
35. *The Times*, 17 March 1921.

4 Working Relations

1. 139 HC Deb, 22 March 1921, Col. 2506.
2. DBFP, series I, vol. XX, no. 389, N9386/9924/4/38.
3. DBFP, series I, vol. XX, no. 414.
4. Documents on FO 371/6916 contain the report of a Foreign Office examination of the evidence and a detailed note from the Secret Intelligence Service of the means by which an agent had secured documents from the Berlin Office. It was known to the SIS that Berlin was a centre for the circulation of forged Soviet documents, but the circumstances in which this evidence was obtained satisfied them of its accuracy.
5. DBFP, series I, vol. XX, no. 424, Report by Hodgson citing an article by Radek.
6. DBFP, series I, vol. XIX, no. 1.
7. *The Times*, 13 April 1922.
8. DBFP, series I, vol. XIX, no. 6.
9. A very full study of the Conference is contained in *The Genoa Conference*, by Carole Fink (University of North Carolina Press, 1984).
10. DBFP, series I, vol. XX no. 438.
11. Gromyko and Ponomarev, *Soviet Foreign Policy*, p. 165.
12. 154 HC Deb, 25 May 1922, Cols 1449–1468.
13. FO 371/9363 N2524/2524/38.
14. CAB 23/46 C30 (23).
15. DBFP series I, vol. XXV, no. 222, N1670/10/38.
16. 176 HC Deb, 7 August 1924, Col. 3183.
17. Crowe to MacDonald, 26 October 1924, on FO 371/10478 N7838/G.
18. See *inter alia* L. Chester, *The Zinoviev Letter* (London: André Deutsch, 1967) and *Report of Investigation by British Delegation in Russia for the TUC General Council* (London, 1925). In *Ace of Spies*, Lockhart suggests that Sidney Reilly was responsible.

5 Relations Broken and Resumed

1. CAB 23/48 C 49 (24) and CAB 23/49 C 59, C 60 (24).
2. 179 HC Deb, 15 December 1924, Cols 673–679.
3. FO 371/11015/N1314/102/38.

4. DBFP, series I, vol. XXV, p. 677, N3432/102/38.
5. CAB 23/50 C 36 (25). Chicherin's comment is on FO 371/11786 N387/387/38.
6. J. Degras (ed.) *Soviet Documents on Foreign Policy, 1917–1941* (Oxford University Press for RIIA, 1952–3) vol. II, p. 1.
7. Ibid., p. 39.
8. FO 371/11786 N2241/387/38.
9. The development of British–Soviet relations between 1924 and 1926 is described in G. Gorodetsky, *The Precarious Truce* (Cambridge University Press, 1977) and this covers the trade union aspect in particular detail.
10. CAB 23/53 C 40 (26).
11. DBFP, series I, vol. XXV, no. 323, N4187/114/38.
12. CAB 24/180 Memorandum CP 250.
13. 197 HC Deb, 25 June 1926, Col. 776.
14. Cmd. 2862 of 1926.
15. *The Times*, 13 July 1926.
16. CAB 23/54 C 12(27) and CAB 24/184 Memoranda CP 25 (27) and 27 (27).
17. DBFP, series 1A, vol. III, no. 3.
18. DBFP, series 1A, vol. III, no. 21.
19. 203 HC Deb, 3 March 1927, Cols 610–626.
20. CAB 23/55 C 33 (27).
21. 206 HC Deb, 26 May 1927, Col. 2217. Cmd. 2874 of 1927; *Documents Illustrating the Hostile Activities of The Soviet Government and the Third International against Great Britain.*
22. *Manchester Guardian*, 25 July 1927, quoted by W. P. and Z. K. Coates, *A History of Anglo-Soviet Relations* (London: Lawrence and Wishart, 1943) vol. 1.
23. DBFP, series 1A, vol. III, Report from Mr Preston in Leningrad on conditions immediately prior to his departure.
24. DBFP, series II, vol. VII, no. 1.
25. Degras, *Soviet Documents. . .* , vol. II, p. 236.
26. *The Times*, 4 September 1928.
27. Low cartoon reproduced in R. K. Middlemas and A. J. L. Barnes, *Baldwin* (London: Weidenfeld and Nicolson, 1969) p. 525.
28. Note on Anglo-Soviet Relations (1929–1931) reproduced as Appendix 1 to DBFP, series II, vol. VII.
29. DBFP, series II, vol. VII, no. 24. For Sir E. Ovey's impressions on arrival, see FO 371/14052.
30. DBFP, series II, vol. VII, no. 135.
31. 269 HC Deb, 20 October 1932, Col. 449.
32. W. Strang, *Home and Abroad* (London: Deutsch, 1956).
33. The diplomatic exchanges are reproduced at length in DBFP, series II, vol. VII, and will not be individually annotated.
34. 275 HC Deb, 15 March 1933, Col. 1945.
35. 276 HC Deb, 20 March 1933, Col. 19.
36. DBFP, series II, vol. VII, no. 529.
37. DBFP, series II, vol. VII, no. 500.

6 The Approach to War

1. Harold Macmillan, *Winds of Change*, 5 vols (London: Macmillan, 1966–72), vol. 1.
2. Middlemas and Barnes, *Baldwin*, p. 1038.
3. Meeting at 10 Downing Street, 28–9 July 1936, quoted in ibid., p. 947.
4. Strang, *Home and Abroad*.
5. DBFP, series II, vol. VII, no. 487.
6. Ibid., no. 396.
7. I. M. Maisky, *Who Helped Hitler?* (London: Hutchinson, 1964) p. 44.
8. R. G. Vansittart, *The Mist Procession* (London: Hutchinson, 1958).
9. DBFP, series II, vol. VII, no. 545. (For Sir P. Loraine's remark, see no. 575.)
10. DBFP, series II, vol. VII, no. 582.
11. 292 HC Deb, 13 July 1934, Col. 697 *et seq.*
12. Maisky, *Who Helped Hitler?*
13. DBFP, series II, vol. VII, no. 608.
14. Ibid., no. 570.
15. Ibid., vol. XII, no. 121.
16. Ibid., no. 199.
17. Ibid., no. 484.
18. CAB 24/247 Memorandum COS 326 Committee of Imperial Defence February 1934.
19. CAB 24/253 Memorandum CP 41 (35).
20. DBFP, series II, vol. XII, no. 515.
21. A. Eden, *Facing the Dictators* (London: Cassell, 1962) vol. II, p. 141.
22. DBFP, series II, vol. VII, no. 656.
23. Eden, *Facing the Dictators*, p. 144 *et seq.*
24. DBFP, series II, vol. XII, nos 669, 670, 673.
25. Quoted by Gromyko and Ponomarev, *Soviet Foreign Policy*, vol. I, p. 283.
26. DBFP, series II, vol. XV, Appendix IV.
27. CAB 23/85 C 56 (36).
28. 310 HC Deb, 26 March 1926, Col. 1541.
29. A. Blunt, *Picasso's Guernica* (Oxford University Press, 1969) quoted by A. Boyle, *The Climate of Treason* (London: Hutchinson, 1979). This is one of those phases in the British–Soviet relationship which merit a more detailed examination, particularly in the light of the Spanish archives, than is feasible within the compass of this chapter. Its relevance to my theme lies in the contemporary perception of those involved and the consequences which flowed therefrom.
30. DBFP, series II, vol. XVII, no. 311.
31. Ibid., vol. XVIII, Appendix I.
32. Ibid., no. 366. Memorandum by N. Chamberlain, 2 April 1937.
33. DBFP, series III, vol. I, no. 148.
34. See J. Haslam, *The Soviet Union and the Struggle for Collective Security in Europe 1933–39* (London: Macmillan, 1984).
35. See for instance letter from Viscount Chilston of 24 January 1938. DBFP, Series II, vol. XIX, no. 467.

36. DBFP, series III, vol. I, nos 90 and 116.
37. Soviet Foreign Policy Documents (DSFP), vol. XXI, no. 172.
38. DSFP, series II, vol. XXI, nos 348–9.
39. DBFP Series III, vol. II, nos 1043, 1071.
40. Lord Butler, *The Art of the Possible* (London: Hamish Hamilton, 1971).
41. DSFP, series II, vol. XXI, no. 270.
42. Ibid., no. 406.
43. CAB 23/95 C 41 (38). For the Pravda reference see Ryzhikov, *Soviet English Relations*, p. 66.
44. CAB 23/96 C 57 (38).
45. DBFP, series III, vol. III, no. 325.
46. Ibid., vol. IV, nos 24, 103, 121.
47. Ibid., vol. IV, no. 446.
48. 345 HC Deb, 31 March 1939, Cols 2415–6.
49. Sir K. G. Feiling, *Neville Chamberlain* (London: Macmillan, 1970) p. 403.
50. CAB 23/98 C 18 (39).
51. DBFP, series III, vol. IV, no. 597.
52. Ibid., vol. V, no. 279.
53. Ibid., no. 304.
54. CAB 23/99 C 24 (39).
55. CAB 23/99 C 26 (39).
56. DBFP, series III, vol. V, no. 282.
57. Ibid., nos 520, 530.
58. Ibid., no. 509.
59. Ibid., no. 576.
60. Ibid., no. 589.
61. 347 HC Deb, 19 May 1939, Cols 1809–62.
62. CAB 23/99 C 27 (39).
63. CAB 23/99 C 30 (39).
64. 348 HC Deb, 7 June 1939, Cols 400–402.
65. DBFP, series III, vol. VI, no. 55.
66. Strang describes the course of the negotiations in some detail in *Home and Abroad*.
67. DBFP, series III, vol. VI, no. 272.
68. Ibid., no. 376.
69. Ibid., no. 474.
70. A useful analysis of the German–Soviet negotiations is contained in G. H. Weinberg, *Germany and the Soviet Union 1939–41* (Leiden: E. J. Brill, 1954).
71. DBFP, series III, vol. VI, no. 453.
72. Documents on German Foreign Policy (DGFP), series D, vol. VI, no. 761.
73. DGFP, series D, vol. VI, no. 766.
74. Ibid., vol. VII, nos. 229–30.
75. Ibid., no. 213.
76. DBFP, series III, vol. VI, Appendix V.
77. The full records of the military talks are at Appendix II of DBFP, series III, vol. VII.

78. Gromyko and Ponomarev, *Soviet Foreign Policy*, vol. I, p. 376. Ryzhikov (see note 32 to Chapter 2) disposes of the negotiations with Britain and France as the failing of an attempt to entrap the Soviet Union in a one-to-one war with Germany. For a later view, see article by Kovalev and Rzheshevsky in *Pravda*, 1 September 1988 and also an article in the Lithuanian journal, *Tiesa*, of 20 December 1988 which reprints a letter from the FRG Foreign Ministry on the authenticity of the microfilm copy of the German original which had been destroyed. It was announced in the Congress of Peoples' Deputies on 2 June 1989, after Gorbachev had indicated that the Baltic region was 'seething' on these issues, that a commission would be set up to look into the 1939 Treaty and the Chairman A. N. Yakovlev stated (*Pravda*, 18 August 1989) that the existence of the protocol was not in doubt.
79. CAB 23/101 C 41 (39).

7 Alliance

1. The course of British–Soviet diplomatic exchanges during the war is set out in Sir Llewellyn Woodward, *British Foreign Policy in the Second World War* (London: HMSO, 1970) and the military aspect of the relationship may be followed in the official History of the Second World War (7 vols, London: HMSO, 1956–76) as well as in various specialised works. Churchill's *History of the Second World War* sets out the principal top-level governmental exchanges which constituted the essence of the British–Soviet relationship during the war years.
   The British official documents for the period between the declaration of war on Germany in September 1939 and the German attack on the Soviet Union in June 1941 are also dealt with in G. Gorodetsky, *Stafford Cripps' Mission to Moscow 1940–42* (Cambridge University Press, 1984). A Soviet view of the wartime relationship may be found in I. Maisky, *Memoirs of a Soviet Ambassador* (London: Hutchinson, 1967). The Soviet official documents include Stalin's correspondence with Churchill, Attlee, Roosevelt and Truman (2 vols, Moscow, 1976); two further volumes of wartime documents (Moscow, 1983); and records of the wartime conferences (6 vols, Moscow, 1978–80).
2. W. S. Churchill, *History of the Second World War* (London: Cassell, 1950) vol. 1, p. 360.
3. CAB 65/2 W.M. 101 (39).
4. COS (40) 252.
5. For this minuting see FO 371/24845 and FO 371/24846/N2779/40/384.
6. FO 371/24844 N5808/30/38.
7. FO 371/24844 N5937/30/38.
8. W. Warlimont, *Im Hauptquartier der deutschen Wehrmacht 1939–45* (Frankfurt: Bernard and Graebe, 1962).
9. Weinberg, *Germany and the Soviet Union*, p. 116.
10. FO 371/24845 N 6875 N7047/30/38.
11. CAB 65/10 288 C (40) 3.
12. Cadogan diaries, p. 362, quoted in Gorodetsky, *Stafford Cripps' Mission*.
13. PREM 3 403/7 T18.

14. Gorodetsky analyses the incident in some detail, but confuses the picture in one minor respect by failing to understand that Eden's follow-up telegram expressing 'hope' that Cripps would deliver the message constituted, in Foreign office language, an instruction to do so.
15. FO 371/29465 N1658 N1667 and N1828/30/38.
16. Gromyko and Ponomarev, *Soviet Foreign Policy*, vol. 1, p. 410.
17. Churchill, *The Second World War*, vol. III, p. 58.
18. See F. H. Hinsley, *British Intelligence in the Second World War* (London: HMSO, 1981).
19. JIC (41) 234.
20. CAB 79/12 COS(41)218.
21. Churchill, *The Second World War*, vol. IV, p. 388.
22. Telegram to Cripps, 5 September 1941, quoted in ibid., vol. III, p. 365.
23. Ibid., p. 312.
24. Cmd. 6304.
25. PREM 3 403/3 T 417.
26. PREM 3 403/3 T 418.
27. Churchill, *The Second World War*, vol. III, p. 354.
28. WP(41)238 on PREM 3 393/1.
29. Cmd. 6376.
30. PREM 3 403/3 T 802.
31. CAB 65/24 WM (41) 111.
32. PREM 3 395/6.
33. CAB 66/20 Memorandum WP (41) 288 Revise.
34. Hinsley, *British Intelligence . . .*, pp. 58–67.
35. The references to the Washington discussions are based on FRUS, 1942, vol. III, pp. 566–83. For the British aide-memoire see PREM 3 333/8.
36. PREM 3 403/405 T 1031/2.
37. Churchill, *The Second World War*, vol. IV, p. 415.
38. Michael Howard, *Grand Strategy* (London: HMSO, 1972) vol. IV, pp. 34–40.
39. PREM 3 333/3 T 125/2.
40. PREM 3 333/5 T 792/3.
41. Gromyko and Ponomarev, *Soviet Foreign Policy*, vol. I, p. 432.
42. PREM 3 333 T 922/3.
43. PREM 3 393/9.
44. PREM 3 393/3 T 1031/2.
45. PREM 3 393/10 T1464/3 N5746/4013/38.
46. PREM 3 393/10 T1625/3.
47. 421 HC Deb, 16 Apr 1946, Col. 2513–2519.
48. Figures taken from B. B. Schofield, *The Russian Convoys* (London: Batsford, 1964) and HC Deb (see note 47).
49. PREM 3 402 Tel 1049 to Moscow.
50. FO 371/ 6957 N 6353 and 7386/66/38.
51. PREM 3 402 CP (44) 8 and Churchill, *The Second World War*, vol. V, pp. 309–12.
52. Ibid., p. 318.
53. FO 371/40741 U/6254, 7618, 6793, 7841. See V. Rothwell, *Britain and the Cold War* (London: Cape, 1982).
54. FO 371/ 40702, WP (44) 409, U6594/180/70.

55. Churchill, *The Second World War*, vol. VI, p. 180.
56. PREM 3 352 (C 11228/1077/55).
57. CAB 66/47 WM (44) 122, 123.
58. PREM 3 396/5.
59. For the record of the conference see FO 800/414.
60. This date taken from Woodward, *British Foreign Policy*, vol. V, p. 262, differs from that of 5 January given by Churchill.
61. Woodward, *British Foreign Policy*, vol. V, p. 264.
62. For the text of the Declaration see FO 800/416/140.
63. The existing works on this episode should not be relied on. There is, however, an analysis of one of the more controversial issues in the *Interim report on an enquiry into the repatriation of surrendered enemy personnel to the Soviet Union and Yugoslavia from Austria in May 1945 and the alleged 'Klagenfurt conspiracy'*, Anthony Cowgill 1988.
64. 408 HC Deb, 27 February 1945, Col. 1284.
65. Churchill to Roosevelt 13 and 27 March 1945. Churchill, *The Second World War*, vol. VI, p. 349.
66. Ibid., p. 397.
67. Ibid., p. 458.
68. Washington telegram of 7 July 1945 quoted by Woodward, *British Foreign Policy*.
69. Memorandum given to US Ambassador, dated 27 May 1945, quoted in Churchill, *The Second World War*, vol. VI, p. 461.
70. FO 371/50912/5471.
71. Woodward, *British Foreign Policy*, vol. V, p. 353, gives a reference PM/45/322 FO 800/416/63/37 which does not appear to be correct.
72. FO 371/50866 PM/45/324 U6125/3628/70.
73. For the full record of the conference see FO 371/50867 U6197.
74. Eden and Cadogan diaries quoted by Robert Rhodes James in *Anthony Eden* (London: Weidenfeld and Nicolson, 1986).
75. CAB 128/1 CM 18(45).
76. FO 800/415 FO Telegram, 4 February 1945.
77. FO 371/36954.
78. FO 371/43304.
79. FO 371/3695/5158.
80. FO 371/43304.
81. Strang, *Home and Abroad*.
82. The PREM 3 Series of files in the Public Record Office contains Churchill's papers. Cab 120/858 and 120/859 contain the messages exchanged between Churchill and Stalin from November 1942 onwards.
83. D. Dilks, *The Diaries of Sir Alexander Cadogan 1939–45* (London: Cassell, 1971) p. 586.
84. R. A. Eden, *The Reckoning* (London: Cassell, 1960) p. 514.
85. Churchill, *The Second World War*, vol. V, p. 408.
86. FO 371/43304.
87. CAB 120/158.
88. On the mood in Britain see A. Calder, *The People's War: Britain 1939–45* (London: Cape, 1969) and W. James, *The Russia Complex: the British Labour Party and the Soviet Union* (Manchester U.P., 1977).

8   Post-War Confrontation

1. FO 371/86761 Russia Committee minute, 7 February 1950.
2. See 'The Sources of Soviet Conduct' in *American Diplomacy 1900–1950* (University of Chicago, 1951) pp. 107, 121, and also G. F. Kennan, *Memoirs 1925–50* (Boston: Little, Brown, 1967).
3. Among the many works of this topic, one may note, in addition to Kennan's own works, studies such as Adam B. Ulam, *The Rivals* (New York: Viking Press, 1971).
4. The course of British policy during the critical years from 1945 to 1951 has been analysed in detail in Lord Bullock's authoritative work, *Ernest Bevin: Foreign Secretary 1945–51* (London: Heinemann, 1983).
5. FO 371/47856.
6. 414 HC Deb, 9 October 1945, Col. 40.
7. FO 371/47883.
8. FO 371/56763/4065; CAB 133/82; FO 800/507/SU/45/7.
9. FO 371/56763/4065 and 4157.
10. *The Times*, 6 March 1946.
11. *Pravda*, 13 March 1946.
12. CAB 129/9 CP (46) 186.
13. Quoted by Rothwell, *Britain and the Cold War, 1941–47*, p. 264.
14. 423 HC Deb, 24 June 1946, Col. 1850.
15. 423 HC Deb, 5 June 1946, Col. 2038.
16. FO 371/66546/76. In this context, see also Raymond Smith, 'A climate of opinion: British officials and the development of British Soviet Policy 1945–7', *International Affairs*, vol. 64, no. 4, Autumn 1988.
17. FO 371/66279 and 66370/7458.
18. See *inter alia* PREM 9/702 and related documents quoted by Anne Deighton in *International Affairs*, vol. 63, no. 3, p. 460.
19. CAB 129/9 CP (46) 186.
20. FO 371/66467/1038.
21. FO 800/475, ME/64/22 quoted by R. Smith and J. Zametica in *International Affairs*, vol. 61, no. 2 (Spring 1985).
22. FO 800/476 ME 47/1.
23. *The Times*, 5 January 1948.
24. CAB 129/23 CP (48) 5,6,7,8.
25. CAB 129/27 CP (48) 134.
26. FRUS 1948, vol. II, pp. 895–6.
27. CAB 128/13 CM 43 (48).
28. See also G. F. Kennan, *Memoirs* and record of British–US Chiefs of Staff meeting 30 June in W. Condit, *The History of the Joint Chiefs of Staff*, Vol. II: *1947–49*, pp. 136–7, quoted in Avi Shlaim, 'Britain, the Berlin Blockade and the Cold War', *International Affairs*, vol. 60, no. 1 (1983–4).
29. 452 HC Deb, 30 June 1948, Col. 2233.
30. CAB 128/13 CM 57 (48).
31. CAB 128/13 CM 61 (48).
32. 456 HC Deb, 22 September 1948, Col. 911.
33. CAB 128/13 CM 54 (48).

34. FO 371/86766 Minute by Rae and paper by Harrison dated 11 April.
35. FO 371/86761.
36. 481 HC Deb, 30 November 1950, Col. 1336.
37. CAB 128/18 CM 47 (50).
38. CAB 128/18 CM 60 (50).
39. FO 371/86766.
40. CAB 129/43 CP (50) 294.
41. CAB 129/47 CP (51) 239.
43. FO 371/94850 NS 1073/10G.
44. On Burgess and Maclean see Cmd 9577 of 1955. On the wider field, the many revealing works include Andrew Boyle, *The Climate of Treason*, and Chapman Pincher, *Their Trade is Treachery* (London: Sidgwick and Jackson, 1981). A survey of covert Soviet operations in Britain appears in P. Shipley, *Hostile Action* (London: Pinter, 1989).

9 The Khrushchev Years

1. 515 HC Deb, 11 May 1953, Col. 897.
2. CAB 129/61 C (53) 187.
3. CAB 129/61 C (53) 194.
4. Eden diary 27 September 1953, quoted by Robert Rhodes James in *Anthony Eden*.
5. R. A. Eden, *The Reckoning*, pp. 58–9.
6. Gromyko and Ponomarev, *Soviet Foreign Policy*, vol. II, p. 174.
7. FO 371/111690 Letter Roberts 29 January 1954.
8. FO 371/111691.
9. CAB 129/67 C (54) 136.
10. Eden, *The Reckoning*.
11. Rhodes James, *Anthony Eden*, p. 382.
12. FO 371/111706 NS 1073/35.
13. 529 HC Deb, 23 June 1954, Col. 548.
14. FO 371/111691.
15. 189 HL Deb, 28 July 1954, Cols 233–240.
16. CAB 128/27 CC (54) 48, 52 and FO Telegram 873 to Moscow.
17. Soviet note of 24 July 1954 and CAB 128/27 CC (54) 53.
18. Macmillan, *Tides of Fortune* (London: Macmillan, 1969) p. 559.
19. Eden, *The Reckoning*, p. 171.
20. FO 371/116652, NS 1021/38 and FO 371/116654 NS 1021/69.
21. Stalin to Zilliacus, 14 October 1947, FO 371/111670 NS 1051/31G 'Short History of the Anglo-Soviet Treaty'. For the formal annulment of the Treaty see Cmd. 9385 of 1955.
22. Gromyko and Ponomarev, *Soviet Foreign Policy*, vol. II, p. 206.
23. CAB 128/29 CM 23 (55).
24. 549 HC Deb, 27 February 1956, Cols 837–963.
25. FO 371/122770 NS 1015/6.
26. CAB 128/29 CM 45 (55).
27. White Paper SU no. 1 1956.
28. Eden, *The Reckoning*, p. 361.

29. CAB 128/30 CM 31 (56).
30. Eden, *Full Circle* (London: Cassell, 1960–5) p. 363.
31. For a full record of the visit see FO 371/122836 NS 1052/656G.
32. CAB 128/29 CM 34 (55).
33. The Foreign Office and Cabinet archives for the years after 1957 were, at the time of writing, still closed and the account of the diplomatic exchanges during the period 1958–1963 therefore draws heavily on Macmillan's memoirs to supplement the published documents.
34. Macmillan, *Riding the Storm* (London: Macmillan, 1971) p. 252.
35. See Cmd. 380 of 1957 and 423 of 1958 for this exchange and later correspondence with the Soviet Union on summit talks.
36. CAB 128/31 CC 74 (57).
37. CAB 128/31 CC 74, 76 (57).
38. Macmillan, *Pointing the Way* (London: Macmillan, 1972) p. 73.
39. Diary entry 26 July 1959 quoted in Macmillan, *Pointing the Way*, p. 80.
40. Macmillan, *At the End of the Day* (London: Macmillan, 1973) p. 178.
41. *The Road to Communism* (Moscow, 1962) p. 497, quoted by Gromyko and Ponomarev, *Soviet Foreign Policy*, vol. II, p. 262.

10 Between the Europeans and the Superpowers

1. H. Kissinger, *The White House Years* (London: Weidenfeld and Nicolson, 1979).
2. Gromyko and Ponomarev, *Soviet Foreign Policy*, vol. II, p. 245.
3. H. Wilson, *The Labour Government, 1964–1970* (London: Weidenfeld and Nicolson, 1971).
4. Hansard, 26 August 1968, Col. 1283.
5. Gromyko and Ponomarev, *Soviet Foreign Policy*, vol. II, p. 426.
6. Cmd. 5924 of 1975.
7. For a discussion of the complex issues involved in the use of economic instruments in the context of East–West relations see P. Hanson, *Western Economic Statecraft in East–West Relations* (London: Routledge for RIIA, 1988).
8. NATO Council Statement of 31 May 1984.

11 A New Start

1. Two recent biographies of Gorbachev are *Gorbachev* by Christian Schmidt-Hauer (London: Tauris, 1986) and *Gorbachev* by Zhores Medvedev (Oxford: Blackwell, 1986).
2. 113 HC Deb, 2 April 1987, Cols 1223–1237.
3. The leadership changes in the two countries are set out in Appendix 2.
4. Gromyko and Ponomarev, *Soviet Foreign Policy*, vol. I, p. 9.
5. The literature is vast. I have touched on some aspects in an article, 'The roots of Soviet foreign policy', in *International Affairs*, vol. 60 (London, 1984). To the reader who is interested in understanding the Russian mind, I commend R. Hingley, *The Russian Mind* (London: Bodley Head, 1977) and T. Szamuely, *The Russian Tradition* (London: Secker

and Warburg, 1974). There is an excellent short study of the historical roots of Soviet foreign policy in Hugh Seton Watson's chapter in *The Soviet State* (London: Gower, 1985).

6. The texts of Gorbachev's speeches to the Party Conference in 1988 and the Congress in 1989 have been taken from BBC Summary of World Broadcasts, 30 June 1988 and 1 June 1989, reporting Soviet television 28 June 1988 and 30 May 1989 respectively.
7. Gromyko and Ponomarev, *Soviet Foreign Policy*, vol. I, p. 9.
8. N. I. Lebedev, *Great October* (Moscow: Nauka, 1978) pp. 3, 12.
9. L. I. Brezhnev, *Following Lenin's Course* (Moscow: Progress, 1975) pp. 94–5.
10. Cmnd. 5924 of 1975.
11. M. S. Gorbachev, *Perestroika* (London: Collins, 1987).
12. Text taken from BBC Summary of World Broadcasts, 5 November 1987, reporting Soviet television 4 November 1987.
13. Tass, 25 July 1988.
14. See for instance an article of 21 May 1988 in *Literaturnaya Gazeta* by V. Dashichev extolling the policy of Chicherin, Litvinov and Krasin and denouncing the 'hegemonism and great-power mentality' of Stalin as well as the 'miscalculations and incompetence' of Brezhnev which brought the renewed tension of the late 1970s and early 1980s. Dashichev argues that quantitative negotiations on armaments are not enough. What is needed is a 'fundamental reorganisation of Soviet–Western relations' and the creation of a new 'political modus vivendi'. The triumph of socialism remains the objective, but 'the Soviet Union can and must influence world social progress exclusively via its economic, political, scientific and cultural successes'.
15. Sir W. Hayter, *A Double Life* (London: Hamish Hamilton, 1974).
16. See Appendix 3 for chronological list of British Representatives in Moscow and Soviet Representatives in London.
17. The activities of the various Soviet-sponsored 'front' organisations are well described in C. Rose, *Campaigns against Western Defence* (London: Macmillan, 1985).

12 A Policy for the 1990s

1. Speech by Sir Geoffrey Howe to Netherlands Institute of International Affairs at The Hague, 17 June 1985.
2. For a convenient summary of the British–Soviet trading relationship see Memorandum by M. C. Kaser in House of Commons Foreign Affairs Committee report, session 1985–86 HC 28–1 (London: HMSO, 1986).
3. Ibid., p. 46.

Index

Note: Individuals are referred to by the style most commonly used at the time referred to, with a brief indication, where appropriate, of subsequent style.

NORWAY

FINLAN

POLAND

RSFSR

ESTONIA

LATVIA

LITHUANIA

Leningrad

OSLOVAKIA

•Minsk
BYELORUSSIA

•Kiev

Yaro

ANIA

MOLDAVIA

UKRAINE

MOSCOW★

•Yalta

Volg

Don

RKEY

Batumi

GEORGIA

•Tbilisi

ARMENIA

AZERBAIJAN

•Baku

TURKME

•Ashkhab

er
national frontiers
Union Republics
rian Railway

600
MILES

IRAN

AFGH

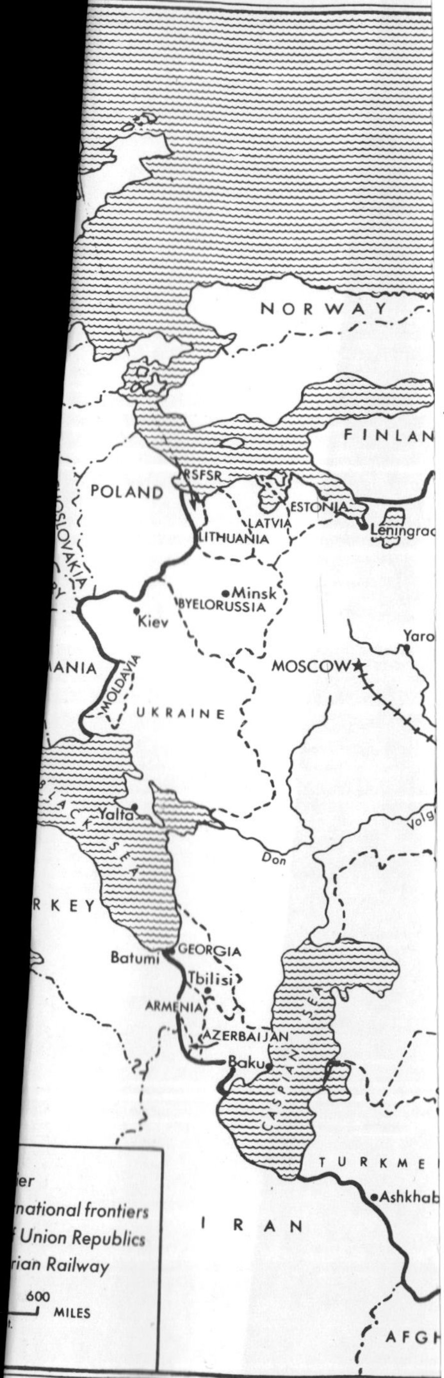

THE SOVIET UNION AN
(Showing locations

CZECH

HUNGA

RO

TU

USSR fron
Other Inte
Frontiers
Trans-Sibe

0   200   400
Scale at 55°